THE ORIGINS OF RESPONSIBILITY

STUDIES IN CONTINENTAL THOUGHT

John Sallis, editor

CONSULTING EDITORS

The Origins of Responsibility

FRANÇOIS RAFFOUL

Indiana University Press

Bloomington & Indianapolis

This book is a publication of

Indiana University Press
601 North Morton Street
Bloomington, Indiana 47404-3797 USA

www.iupress.indiana.edu

Telephone orders   800-842-6796
Fax orders   812-855-7931
Orders by e-mail   iuporder@indiana.edu

♾The paper used in this publication
meets the minimum requirements of
the American National Standard for Information Sciences—Permanence of
Paper for Printed Library Materials,
ANSI Z39.48-1992.

Manufactured in the United States of
America

Library of Congress Cataloging-in-
Publication Data

Raffoul, François, date
    The origins of responsibility /
François Raffoul.
        p. cm. — (Studies in Continental
thought)
    Includes bibliographical references
and index.
    ISBN 978-0-253-35438-9 (cloth : alk.
paper) — ISBN 978-0-253-22173-5
(pbk. : alk. paper) 1. Responsibility.
2. Continental philosophy. I. Title.
    BJ1451.R34 2010
    170—dc22
                                        2009040027

1 2 3 4 5 15 14 13 12 11 10

PARA MERI

CONTENTS

ACKNOWLEDGMENTS

I would like to thank those individuals who have been instrumental in the completion and publication of this work. At Indiana University Press, I am first thankful to John Sallis, general editor of Studies in Continental Thought, for welcoming me in his prestigious series. I am grateful as well to Dee Mortensen and Laura MacLeod for their professionalism and kindness during the production of the book, and to David L. Dusenbury for his expert reading of the manuscript.

At Louisiana State University, I would like to first thank the LSU board of regents for granting me the Regents Awards to Louisiana Artists and Scholars (ATLAS), which allowed me to take a year-long sabbatical and write a first draft of the book. I also would like to thank my colleagues, in particular Gregory Schufreider, for the many and always intellectually exciting discussions we have had over the years, to Jon Cogburn for reading several chapters critically, to Mary Sirridge, Husain Sarkar, Ed Henderson, Jeffrey Roland, and in religious studies, to Delbert Burkett and Stuart Irvine, for their scholarly companionship. My warm thanks also go to the staff, Jen O'Connor and Margaret Toups, for their cheerful and always helpful presence.

I am thankful to James Ryan and Andrea Conque Johnson for their help in reading passages from the book and for their insightful comments, and to Michèle and Costa, in whose beautiful house on the island of Kea in Greece I drafted the first outline of the work. My thanks also go to Charlie Johnson and David Murray, for their friendship, and to Luis Daniel Venegas from the Maragato, for his hospitality.

ABBREVIATIONS

A   Jacques Derrida, *Aporias,* trans. Thomas Dutoit (Stanford, Calif.: Stanford University Press, 1993)

AC   Friedrich Nietzsche, *Twilight of the Idols and The Anti-Christ,* ed. R. J. Hollingdale, trans. Michael Tanner (New York: Penguin, 1990)

AE   Emmanuel Levinas, *Autrement qu'être ou au-delà de l'essence* (Dordrecht: Kluwer Academic, 1996)

BGE   Friedrich Nietzsche, *Beyond Good and Evil,* trans. Walter Kaufmann (New York: Vintage, 1989)

BN   Jean-Paul Sartre, *Being and Nothingness: A Phenomenological Essay on Ontology,* trans. Hazel E. Barnes (New York: Washington Square Press, 1992)

BSP   Jean-Luc Nancy, *Being Singular Plural,* trans. Robert Richardson and Anne O'Byrne (Stanford, Calif.: Stanford University Press, 2000)

BW   Martin Heidegger, *Basic Writings,* rev. and exp. edition, ed. David Farrell Krell (San Francisco: HarperSanFrancisco, 1993)

CP   Martin Heidegger, *Contributions to Philosophy (From Enowning),* trans. Parvis Emad and Kenneth Maly (Bloomington and Indianapolis: Indiana University Press, 1999)

CPR   Immanuel Kant, *The Critique of Pure Reason,* trans. Paul Guyer and Allen W. Wood (Cambridge: Cambridge University Press, 1998)

CPrR Immanuel Kant, *The Critique of Practical Reason,* 3d edition, trans. Lewis White Beck (New York: MacMillan, 1993)

DE Jacques Derrida, with Gad Soussana and Alexis Nouss, *Dire l'événement, est-ce possible?* (Paris: L'Harmattan, 2001)

E Immanuel Kant, "What is Enlightenment?" in *Selections,* ed. Lewis White Beck (Englewood Cliffs, N.J.: Prentice Hall, 1988)

EE Emmanuel Levinas, *Totalité et Infini; Essai sur l'extériorité* (Paris: Le Livre de Poche, 1994)

EH Friedrich Nietzsche, *On the Genealogy of Morals and Ecce Homo,* trans. Walter Kaufmann (New York: Vintage, 1967)

EHF Martin Heidegger, *The Essence of Human Freedom,* trans. Ted Sadler (London: Continuum, 2002)

EI Emmanuel Levinas, *Ethics and Infinity* (Pittsburgh: Duquesne University Press, 1985)

EN Emmanuel Levinas, *Entre Nous,* trans. Michael B. Smith and Barbara Harshav (New York: Columbia University Press, 1998)

FL Jacques Derrida, "Force of Law: The 'Mystical Foundation of Authority,'" in *Deconstruction and the Possibility of Justice,* ed. D. G. Carlson, D. Cornell, and M. Rosenfeld (New York: Routledge, 1992)

FMM Immanuel Kant, *Foundations of the Metaphysics of Morals,* in *Selections,* ed. Lewis White Beck (Englewood Cliffs, N.J.: Prentice Hall, 1988)

FS Martin Heidegger, *Four Seminars,* trans. Andrew Mitchell and François Raffoul (Bloomington and Indianapolis: Indiana University Press, 2003)

GA Martin Heidegger, *Gesamtausgabe* (Frankfurt am Main: Vittorio Klostermann, 1978–)

GD Jacques Derrida, *The Gift of Death,* trans. David Wills (Chicago and London: University of Chicago Press, 1996)

GDT Emmanuel Levinas, *God, Death, and Time* (Stanford, Calif.: Stanford University Press, 2000)

GM Friedrich Nietzsche, *On the Genealogy of Morals and Ecce Homo,* trans. Walter Kaufmann (New York: Vintage, 1967)

GS Friedrich Nietzsche, *The Gay Science,* trans. Walter Kaufmann (New York: Vintage, 1974)

HE Jean-Paul Sartre, "The Humanism of Existentialism," in *Essays in Existentialism* (New York: Citadel Press, 1995)

HF Françoise Dastur, "The Reception and Nonreception of Heidegger in France," in *French Interpretations of Heidegger,* ed. David Pettigrew and François Raffoul (Albany: SUNY Press, 2008)

HH Friedrich Nietzsche, *Human, All Too Human: A Book for Free Spirits,* ed. Richard Schacht, trans. R. J. Hollingdale (New York: Cambridge University Press, 1996)

HPP *Heidegger and Practical Philosophy,* ed. François Raffoul and David Pettigrew (Albany: SUNY Press, 2002)

HQA Françoise Dastur, *Heidegger et la question anthropologique* (Louvain: Editions Peeters, 2003)

HS Martin Heidegger, "Phenomenological Interpretations in Connection with Aristotle: An Indication of the Hermeneutical Situation," in *Supplements,* ed. John Van Buren (Albany: SUNY Press, 2002)

IC Jean-Luc Nancy, *The Inoperative Community,* ed. Peter Connor (Minneapolis: University of Minnesota Press, 1991)

IM Martin Heidegger, *Introduction to Metaphysics,* trans. Gregory Fried and Richard Polt (New Haven, Conn.: Yale University Press, 2000)

IR Hans Jonas, *The Imperative of Responsibility: In Search of an Ethics for the Technological Age* (Chicago: University of Chicago Press, 1985)

OA Paul Ricoeur, *Oneself as Another,* trans. Kathleen Blamey (Chicago: University of Chicago Press, 1995)

OE Emmanuel Levinas, *On Escape,* trans. Bettina Bergo (Stanford, Calif.: Stanford University Press, 2003)

P Jacques Derrida, "Passions," in *On the Name,* ed. Thomas Dutoit (Stanford, Calif.: Stanford University Press, 1995)

PF Giorgio Agamben, "The Passion of Facticity," in *Rethinking Facticity,* ed. François Raffoul and Eric Sean Nelson (Albany: SUNY Press, 2008)

PIA Martin Heidegger, *Phenomenological Interpretations of Aristotle: Initiation into Phenomenological Research,* trans. Richard

Rojcewicz (Bloomington and Indianapolis: Indiana University Press, 2001)

PM Jacques Derrida, *Papier Machine* (Paris: Galilée, 2001)

PTT Jacques Derrida, "Autoimmunity: Real and Symbolic Suicides" and "Deconstructing Terrorism," in Giovanna Borradori, *Philosophy in a Time of Terror: Dialogues with Jürgen Habermas and Jacques Derrida* (Chicago: University of Chicago Press, 2003)

RB Emmanuel Levinas, *Is It Righteous to Be?* ed. Jill Robbins (Stanford, Calif.: Stanford University Press, 2001)

RE Jean-Luc Nancy, "Responding to Existence," in *Studies in Practical Philosophy* 1, no. 1 (Spring 1999)

SZ Martin Heidegger, *Sein und Zeit* (Tübingen: Max Niemeyer Verlag, 1953)

T Emmanuel Levinas, *Le Temps et l'autre* (Paris: Presses Universitaires de France, 1983)

TI Friedrich Nietzsche, *The Twilight of the Idols,* trans. Richard Polt (Indianapolis and Cambridge: Hackett, 1997)

TL Friedrich Nietzsche, *On Truth and Lies in a Nonmoral Sense,* trans. Daniel Brazeale (Atlantic Highlands, N.J.: Humanities Press, 1979)

TS Jacques Derrida and Maurizio Ferraris, *A Taste for the Secret,* ed. G. Donis and D. Webb (Malden, Mass.: Polity Press, 2001)

V Jacques Derrida, *Voyous* (Paris: Galilée, 2003)

VP John Sallis, *The Verge of Philosophy* (Chicago: University of Chicago Press, 2008)

WCT Martin Heidegger, *What is Called Thinking?* trans. J. Glenn Gray (New York: Harper & Row, 1968)

WP Friedrich Nietzsche, *The Will to Power,* trans. Walter Kaufmann and R. J. Hollingdale (New York: Vintage / Random House, 1968)

ZS Martin Heidegger, *The Zollikon Seminars,* trans. Franz Mayr and Richard Askay (Evanston, Ill.: Northwestern University Press, 2001)

THE ORIGINS OF RESPONSIBILITY

INTRODUCTION

The Origins of Responsibility

The Problem of Responsibility

The ambition of the present work is to reengage the question of responsibility as it is elaborated in post-Nietzschean continental thought, and to explore its post-metaphysical, phenomenological and ontological senses, away from its traditional metaphysical interpretation as the accountability of a free autonomous subject. Returning through a historical genealogy to "the origins of responsibility," following the "long history of the origins of responsibility" of which Nietzsche speaks in the second essay of his *Genealogy of Morals*,[1] I will attempt to reveal the emergence of post-metaphysical senses of responsibility in the works of such continental thinkers as Nietzsche, Sartre, Levinas, Heidegger, and Derrida. The guiding hypothesis of this work is two-fold: First, I will suggest that ethics has not only been a constant concern of recent continental thought but has in fact been problematized anew; ethics is approached less as a normative body of moral rules and even less as an applied discipline, and more in terms of a philosophical reflection on the meaning of ethics as such, on the ethicality of ethics. Second, I will suggest that responsibility itself has been rethought in such a context in a novel and original way, that is, away from an ideology of subjectivity, free will, and power.

This project might seem paradoxical in several respects. Nietzsche's critique of morality, despite his own clarifications, has often been described as a nihilistic enterprise of destruction of values leading to the impossibility of ethics. It is as if questioning ethics amounted to an attack against it,

1

an assumption mocked by Merleau-Ponty when he wrote, "From the simple fact that I make of morality a problem, you conclude that I deny it."[2] Consequently, continental philosophies of ethics, which are in their very basis post-Nietzschean, have also been accused of moral relativism and nihilism. It is often alleged that post-Nietzschean continental thought has little to offer in terms of an ethical theory, or worse, that it actually develops the an-ethical posture that is supposedly exemplified in the works of Heidegger, the deconstructive work of Jacques Derrida, or more generally in post-structuralist and deconstructive thought. More precisely, such authors are often reproached for not offering the basis for a responsible engagement in the world, and their work is said to border on or lead to nihilistic irresponsibility. I will argue instead that the notion of responsibility is central to their work, but that it is entirely reconceptualized from the tradition of the history of philosophy.

A clarification may be helpful at the outset of this work, concerning so-called continental philosophy's relation to ethics: Ethical concerns and problematics are never simply absent from philosophical works, however implicit or unthematized they may be. For instance, Derrida has stressed that ethical questions have always been present in his writings, even when they were not *explicitly* raised. There is an ethics of deconstruction as such, before anything is said explicitly with regard to ethics. Derrida did admit that, in his early works, these ethical problematics were not thematized and were only addressed in an "oblique" way. He also recognized—this is the key point—that his more explicit works on ethics (whether on justice, law and right, responsibility, moral decision, forgiveness, the gift, the secret, hospitality, etc.) do not constitute a system of moral norms, a normative ethics in the established sense of the term. In fact, one may ask whether it is the role of philosophy to prescribe norms of ethics, to establish a "morality," to posit norms or values. Jean-Luc Nancy, for instance, considers that "no philosophy either provides or is by itself a 'morality' in this sense. Philosophy is not charged with prescribing norms or values."[3] Rather, the task of philosophy is to question the ethicality of ethics, to engage a philosophical reflection on the meaning of ethics, on what puts us "in the position of having to choose norms or values" (Nancy, in HPP, 66). Philosophy does not indicate a choice, but articulates the situation of being "in the position of making a choice."

A philosophical inquiry would then not so much propose a moral system as inquire into the meaning of ethics, the ethicality of ethics. In an interview given a few months before his death to the daily communist newspaper *Humanité,* Derrida readily conceded that "if by ethics one understands a system of rules, of moral norms, then no, I do not propose an ethics."[4] At issue, rather, is problematizing the ethicality of ethics. For instance, with Sartre, the ethical is not a body of norms but instead a characteristic of existence. Ethics arises out of his phenomenological ontology because, even though ontology is unable to formulate ethical imperatives, it nonetheless allows us to glimpse into the existential situation of ethics. Existence for Sartre is identified with responsibility itself, from the outset a responsibility for existence. To that extent, there is an intrinsic ethicality of existence in Sartre's phenomenological ontology. This strongly suggests that if ontology cannot provide a morality or an ethics *per se,* it nevertheless articulates what one may call here the ethicality of ethics, the very possibility of ethics. When Heidegger was asked in his "Letter on Humanism" why he did not write an ethics to supplement his fundamental ontology, he replied famously that the thinking of being was an originary ethics. The first gesture by Heidegger is thus to no longer separate ethics from ontology, as if they constituted separate, independent spheres. Thought from the question of the meaning of being, ethics cannot be approached except in terms of the event of being. In a sense, for Heidegger, ethics is ontology itself. There is no need to "add" an ethics as an applied discipline to an ontology which would then have been presupposed as unethical. I will pursue this problematizing of the ethical in the works of Sartre, Heidegger, Levinas, and Derrida, and note that responsibility constitutes the cornerstone of such ethics.

As I suggested, the motif of responsibility is central to these thinkers' rethinking of ethics and the ethical, but it is reconceptualized from the ground up in the wake of Nietzsche's genealogical deconstruction of morality and accountability. Deconstruction, one should note at the outset, needs to be taken in its positive sense, following Derrida who defined deconstruction as an affirmative gesture, an originary yes and saying yes—as an *opening* of new possibilities, as the very reopening of the open.[5] One can already ascertain that Nietzsche's genealogy is not the simple dismissal of ethics as such, but is rather an attack on a certain way of understanding ethics. Nietzsche targeted what he termed "life-denying" philosophies, which he saw in Christianity and of course in Platonism, both of which posit a world beyond this world in a projection of ideals which are contrary to life. In *The Will to Power,* in the section titled "Critique of Morality" (§254), Nietzsche explains that "The inquiry into the origin of our evaluations and tables of the good is absolutely no way identical with a critique of them, as is often believed." Further, he clarifies that such inquiry is not a critique but seeks instead to evaluate the value of morality *for life.* "What are our evaluations and moral tables worth? What is the outcome of their rule? For whom? In relation to what?—Answer: for life."[6] By a critique of morality, it is a matter for Nietzsche of reengaging our tradition and its concepts, an attempt at reevaluating its values, that is, evaluating the *value* of its values. By "critique," then, Nietzsche means not a negative enterprise, not an attack on morality as such, but rather an inquiry into the history of the origins of morality. It is thus imperative to distinguish here between a *positive* examination of the origin of morality (Nietzsche's genealogy) and an attack on morality. What is thus at issue is the positing of the ethical values of 'good' and 'evil' as *transcendent* values which lie beyond this world, a movement that indicates an implicit rejection and hatred for *this* life in *this* world (as betrayed by the presence of guilt and shame as cornerstones of such moralities). Hence the sense of Nietzsche's genealogy of morals as a return to its actual basis in life itself, so as to reveal the material, historical, 'human, all-too-human' origins of ethics and values, as opposed to some ideal provenance. Through his dismantling of the tradition of responsibility (as we will see, essentially a critique of the identification of responsibility with accountability), Nietzsche actually calls for a reevaluation of our ways of evaluating, namely for a life-affirming ethics which is signaled in his philosophy by the 'overman' and 'joyful wisdom.' His deconstructive genealogy of responsibility and its fundamental concepts (causality, agency, will, subjectivity) opens the way for a re-elaboration of the senses of responsibility, and will allow for its phenomenological origins to be revealed.

Nietzsche's critique of morality opens the way for a new engagement with the concept of responsibility, henceforth freed from its association with a metaphysics of will and subjectivity. Thus, for example, Sartre posits human existence as absolute responsibility based on the withdrawal of essence, and situates the origin of ethics and responsibility in the disappearance of a theological foundation for values. Human existence is identified with an absolute responsibility for itself based on the surge and self-invention of a groundless freedom. Heidegger rethinks being-responsible in terms of our answering the call of being, and rethinks the ethical by way of a critique of the metaphysical tradition of ethics and a meditation on human beings' sojourn on the earth as *ethos*. He understands Dasein as an ethical notion and our relation to being as one of responsible engagement. Levinas defines the self as a responsibility for the other human, and breaks with Kantian universalism by situating ethics in the encounter with the singular other. Levinas further defines the self as a responsibility for the other human, devotion to the other in his or her vulnerability or mortality. Derrida understands deconstruction as responsiveness that engages—aporetically—in a responsible decision. Responsibility itself is defined as an experience of the impossible. We see the notion of responsibility articulated in terms of phenomenological responsiveness, rather than in terms of the autonomy of the subject. It is clear that in such a context, responsibility itself will be entirely rethought in a novel and original way, away from an ideology of subjectivity, will, and power. Whether explicitly or implicitly, these continental thinkers allow for a rethinking of ethical responsibility as they take issue with traditional models of it, that is, with the model of accountability.

Indeed, the concept of responsibility has traditionally been associated, if not identified, with accountability, under the authority of a philosophy of free will and causality which itself rests upon a subject-based metaphysics. Responsibility is conceived in terms of causality as ground of the act or of the event. For instance, Hegel writes that

> An event, or a situation which has arisen, is a *concrete* external actuality which accordingly has an indeterminable number of attendant circumstances. Every individual moment which is shown to have a *condition, ground* or *cause* of some such circumstance and has thereby contributed *its share* to it, may be regarded as being *wholly,* or at least *partly, responsible* for it.[7]

Accordingly, one is accountable as a subject who is the cause of his or her actions through the freedom of the will.[8] Accountability, as a concept, thus assumes the position of a subject-cause, an agent or an author who can be displayed as a *subjectum* for its actions. Such, for instance, is Kant's definition of accountability or imputability (*Imputabilität*) in the Third Antinomy of the *Critique of Pure Reason*,[9] which he situates in the "transcendental freedom" of the subject, who is capable of absolutely and spontaneously beginning a new series of causes. Identified with the concept of accountability, responsibility thus designates the capacity of an agent to be the cause and ground of its acts. The unceasing calls for responsibility in contemporary culture are always calls to such agency, to the position of a subject-cause. And this insistence as such deserves scrutiny. One might ask at the outset: What concept of responsibility does it seek to reinforce? What lack does it aim at supplementing? What shortcoming is it trying to compensate? What irresponsibility is it trying to suppress, exclude or negate? From what danger does it aim at protecting it? These questions already take us to the heart of the matter. And thus the concept of a 'subject-cause' (along with its unavoidable accompaniment, a system of control and punishment), this 'ready-made,' guiding metaphysical interpretation of the concept of responsibility—namely, *accountability* as indication of the power of a masterful and willful subject—is left to rule exhaustively over the hermeneutic domain of responsibility.

Ironically, this predominant 'ideology of responsibility' is often accompanied by a singular neglect of genuine reflection on the senses of responsibility, on what it means to *be* responsible. Responsibility is simply assumed to mean the accountability of the free agent. An ironic situation to be sure, if it is quite irresponsible not to know what responsibility means while one is calling for it! In Derrida's words, "not knowing, having neither a sufficient knowledge or consciousness of what being responsible *means*, is of itself a lack of responsibility. In order to be responsible it is necessary to respond to or answer to what being responsible means."[10] The issue, as Derrida makes clear, is to reengage a philosophical questioning on ethics, that is, to problematize the ethicality of ethics itself, its very possibility, without presupposing its senses, for instance, through the scheme of application. To understand ethics as an applied discipline forecloses the possibility of raising the indispensable prior question of the ethicality of ethics. The notion of application indeed assumes a ground for ethical precepts. But it may be the case that ethical judgment—as Heidegger, Sartre, Levinas or Derrida would show—takes place in an ungrounded way, indeed, becomes only possible from such groundlessness: For Heidegger, being happens without a ground and the call of conscience has no author and no foundation; for Sartre, responsibility arises out of the groundlessness of existence, and ethics has no '*a priori* Good' to rely upon; for Levinas, ethics arises out of a concern for an infinite other, and not from a rational basis; and for Derrida, responsible decision takes place as a leap and absolute risk beyond knowledge, in an abyssal experience of the undecidable.[11] Applied ethics is thus the name of an ethics whose meaning is not reflected upon and which is inappropriately understood in terms of the theory-praxis, model-application schemas. At stake is a philosophical reflection on the meaning of responsibility, so often covered-over by a problematic of accountability.

In *Beyond Good and Evil*, Nietzsche already took issue with a so-called "science of morals" in which there is always something lacking—"strange as it may sound: the problem of morality itself; what was lacking was any suspicion that there was something problematic there."[12] In §345 of *The Gay Science* (book 5), under the title "Morality as a Problem," Nietzsche also suggests quite plainly that it is a matter of *problematizing* morality and its value, that is, of *questioning* it, as opposed to taking it for granted and leaving it unquestioned. For even

> if a morality has grown out of an error, the realization of this fact would not as much as touch the problem of its value. Thus nobody up to now has examined the *value* of that most famous of all medicines which is called morality; and the first step would be—for once to *question* it. Well then, precisely this is our task.[13]

This task can be taken as the urgency of a questioning on ethicality as such. Insisting on the necessity and urgency of raising anew the question of the ethical, of making it problematic, indeed aporetic, Derrida thus writes:

> All this, therefore, still remains open, suspended, undecided, question-able even beyond the question, indeed, to make use of another figure, absolutely aporetic. What is the ethicality of ethics? The morality of morality? What is responsibility? What is the 'What is?' in this case? Etc. These questions are always urgent.[14]

The first question needs to bear on the identification of responsibility with accountability in the traditional philosophical interpretation of responsibility.

Is the concept, indeed the experience of responsibility—this question will be the guiding one of this work—exhausted by the sense of accountability? Should responsibility be conceived exclusively in terms of the causality of the will? On the basis of the voluntary, or conscious intention? As the subjectivity or ground of the act? Should responsibility be identified with the position of a power, of a sovereign agency? Can responsibility be enframed exclusively within a philosophy of account-ability, in the context of a metaphysics of subjectivity and free will? In fact, it may well be the case that in such an enframing, the phenomeno-logical and ontological sources of what is called "responsibility" have remained obscure and been neglected. It will thus be a matter of disso-ciating the concept of responsibility from its metaphysical interpreta-tion, and to free it from the dominance of the motifs of subjectivity and power so as to retrieve its phenomenological provenance.

Four motifs govern the traditional interpretation of responsibility, what we could call the four "fundamental concepts" of the traditional account of responsibility:

1. *The belief that the human being is an agent or a subject,* i.e., the reli-ance on subjectivity (with *subjectum* in its logical or grammatical sense of foundation) as ground of imputation. A critique of such a subject, whether Nietzschean in inspiration, phenomenological or deconstruc-tive, will radically transform our understanding of what it means to be responsible. For instance, the phenomenological destruction of subjec-tivity leads us to re-conceive responsibility as no longer based on an I-subject, but arising out of a new definition of the self: Heidegger's sense of self is one of having to respond, authentically, to the call of conscience, later rethought as the call of *Ereignis*. Responsibility, as the authentic response of the self to that call, then becomes for Heidegger the most originary sense of being human. How far we find ourselves from the subject of metaphysics and its free will! A reconsideration of responsibil-ity away from the dominance of the motif of the subject will nonetheless never go without a reconsideration of what it means to be human.

2. *The notion that the subject is a voluntary agent*—i.e., the reliance on the voluntary and so-called 'free will'—following either Aristotle, for whom responsibility is identified with voluntariness, or Kant, for whom transcendental freedom is a capacity to begin absolutely. A phenomeno-logical challenge to the notion of free will—whether Nietzschean (free will is a fiction), Heideggerian ('free will' does not capture the essence of free-dom, of what it means to *be free*), or Levinasian in inspiration (responsibil-ity takes place before the freedom of the self, pre-assigned passively to the

other)—would radically transform our understanding of responsibility. It would in any case reveal responsibility, not as the position of the power of the subject, but as a relation to and assumption of a certain passivity—that of our finitude as mortal beings, and of our exposure to the inappropriable alterity that calls us.

3. *The reliance on causality,* with responsibility being defined as the cause of the act. To be the "cause of" and to be "responsible for" are conflated, as they are etymologically connected: The Greek word for cause is *aitia* or *aition,* and the responsible agent is designated as the *aitios.* However, this in itself is problematic: Does the category of "cause" apply to the human being's relation to itself and others? Does it apply to the eventfulness of the event? Is an event, as event, "caused"? Is it caused by a "will"? Does the very eventfulness of the event not precisely point to a certain excess with respect to the enframing of causality? Can an event worthy of its name even be conditioned by a causality? Or should one not assume, as Jean-Luc Marion invites us to do, the excess of the event with respect to causality? Marion speaks of "the character and the dignity of an event— that is, an event or a phenomenon that is unforeseeable (on the basis of the past), not exhaustively comprehensible (on the basis of the present), not reproducible (on the basis of the future), in short, absolute, unique, happening. We will therefore call it a *pure event.*"[15] Finally, does causality capture the original sense of responsibility as responsiveness?

4. *The assumption that the responsible being is a rational subject,* that the basis for ethical responsibility is rational agency and subjectivity. As Nietzsche stated, traditional moral philosophers "wanted to supply a *rational foundation* for morality. . . . Morality itself, however, was accepted as 'given.' . . . What was lacking was any suspicion that there was something problematic here" (BGE, 98). What would happen to the concept of responsibility if it were dissociated from the predominance of reason, of giving reasons (principle of sufficient reason) or providing an account of oneself (a dissociation which is undertaken by Levinas, but also by Heidegger and Derrida)? Should responsibility be placed under the authority of the principle of sufficient reason? Under the request or demand for a ground or justification (accountability), which is characteristic of metaphysical thought? Derrida understands responsibility as response to the event of the other, an event that is always unpredictable, incalculable, and thereby always breaks the demand for sufficient reason, always

exceeds the enframing of the principle of sufficient reason. "The coming of the other, the arriving of the arriving one (*l'arrivée de l'arrivant*), is (what) *who arrives* as an unpredictable event," he explains, an event that can only challenge the demand for reasons, the principle of sufficient reason "insofar as it is limited to a 'rendering of reasons' ('*reddere rationem,*' '*logon didonai*')." Responsibility is not to comply with the demands of such reason-rendering, but instead "not to deny or ignore this incalculable and unpredictable coming of the other."[16]

These four categories have framed the philosophy of responsibility in our tradition. It will be Nietzsche's contribution to expose them as "fictions"—constructions or interpretations, not realities—fictions of the substantial I, of the freedom of the will, of the permanence of the self, of the causal nature of my will, etc. All of these beliefs eventually appear *as* beliefs, thereby opening the void of their lack of ground and calling for thought to invest such spaces.

Once a certain subjectivist bias or assumption has been abandoned, a conceptual work on the very sense of *being* responsible, on what it means to *be responsible,* becomes both possible and necessary. A genealogy of the concept of responsibility will uncover its phenomenological and ontological origins. It will also reveal a rich polysemy of the term, making clear that the prevailing sense of responsibility as the accountability of the subject, within a metaphysics of will and subjectivity, is but *one* sense of the term—and perhaps not even the most primordial one. In fact, a simple, schematic, and preliminary survey of various linguistic expressions points to the plural scope of responsibility, opening onto various problematics, questions, and domains, some of which it is the ambition of this work to explore.

1. One speaks of "being responsible for one's actions," an expression which mobilizes the sense of accountability as authorship over one's actions and over oneself ("being responsible for oneself"). One then speaks of a responsibility for oneself, as we will see with Kant, indicating a subjectivist or egological enclosure of responsibility, within a horizon of selfhood that can culminate in the goal of an absolute responsibility for oneself, in which one should be able to account for oneself integrally and without remainder. Here the expression speaks of the autonomy of the subject—of self-legislation and self-ownership. It also designates re-

sponsibility as an act of appropriation, as taking over a domain, or establishing control over one's actions, a model one finds in Aristotle. It thus belongs to a semantics of power and appropriation, as it is about owning one's actions and owning oneself, about establishing an area of mastery and control. To be responsible in this context means being in a position of power. As one says in French, *les responsables* (literally, "the responsible ones") designate the ones who are "in charge," those who have the power to decide—"the deciders." Responsibility in this sense has to do with the way in which a self is able to appropriate itself entirely in an ideal of sovereign self-responsibility and transparency.

2. One also speaks of "being responsible for the *consequences* of one's actions," an important addition, for in the first instance (in being responsible for one's actions), the stress is essentially on the dimension of the *past*, as one is asked to answer for his or her *past* deeds, whereas to say that one is responsible for the *consequences* of one's actions implies that one is looking toward the *future* of the act, and that there can be a responsibility to the future and not only toward the past. In this sense, responsibility is being accountable *for the future*, for what has not yet happened! This is the very emphasis placed by Hans Jonas in his famed work, *The Imperative of Responsibility: In Search of an Ethics for the Technological Age,*[17] where the author argues that responsibility ought to be directed toward the future—what he calls a "future-oriented ethics" (IR, 12–17) or an "ethics of the future" (IR, 25–31)—in the sense of preserving future generations in the face of human destructiveness. The Kantian formulations of ethics are said to need to include a future humanity (indeed, the very future of humanity!), as well as nature itself. It would be a matter in this future-oriented ethics to "seek not only the human good but also the good of things extrahuman, that is, to extend the recognition of 'ends in themselves' beyond the sphere of man and make the human good include the care of them" (IR, 8). The categorical imperative should be recast so as to include future humanity. As parents are responsible for their children (and for Jonas, the relation parent-child is *the* archetype of responsibility),[18] human beings would be responsible for nature and for the future of humanity.

Yet there are different ways of conceiving of a responsibility toward the future, for it could be taken either as a way to *calculate* the effects of one's actions in the future and thus within the horizon of calculability

and control,[19] *or* it could be taken on the contrary as a responsible opening toward what remains incalculable in what is yet to come. Derrida
will speak of a responsibility to the future, to the arriving of the *arrivant,*
"a future that cannot be anticipated; anticipated but unpredictable; *apprehended,* but, and this is why there is a future, apprehended precisely
as unforeseeable, unpredictable; approached *as* unapproachable" (GD,
54). There would thus be a responsibility toward what has not yet happened, or to what is still coming. In Jonas's work, this implies a relation
of caring toward the vulnerable ones. Such responsibility for the future
is, for Jonas, based on a fear for the vulnerability of the earth. Jonas
clarifies that he is not speaking of a "duty arising *from* procreation" but
of a "duty *to* such procreation" (IR, 40). That duty for future mankind—
which "charges us, in the first place, with ensuring that there *be* a future
mankind" (IR, 40)—is based on the fragility of life. Human existence,
Jonas writes, "has the precarious, vulnerable, and revocable character,
the peculiar mode of transience, of all *life,* which makes it alone a proper
object of 'caring'" (IR, 98). Another sense of responsibility is here introduced, based on care, and no longer authorship: When Jonas speaks of
an attitude of protection toward nature, a responsible concern for its
vulnerability or frailty, responsibility is taken in terms of respect, care.
We are responsible for what is in our care, not first as imputable subjects,
but as care-takers. Care or concern, or respect, belong to semantic sets
that are distinct, if not foreign, to accountability and its problematics of
subjectivity and authorship. We will also see how in Levinas, "not doing
violence to the other" will constitute the very meaning of ethics and
responsibility. Vulnerability now appears as the new ground of responsibility, in the *call* not to do harm to the vulnerable ones.

 3. This last sense leads us to give thought to a certain excess with respect
to the subjective enclosure of the concept of responsibility. For, in contrast
with responsibility for one's own actions and its consequences, and thus by
extension for oneself, another expression does not speak of a responsibility
for self, but instead of a "responsibility for the other." In such a context, it is
clear that one can no longer maintain that the accountability of the subject
constitutes the main sense of responsibility, for one is longer speaking about
one's own actions and one's relationship to them. Responsibility is no longer
about what I have done, but about another for whom I care and am concerned with, another toward whom I have obligations. As Levinas puts it,

"Usually, one is responsible for what one does oneself. I say, in *Otherwise than Being or Beyond Essence,* that responsibility is initially *a for the other.*"[20] This is ultimately what Levinas will call "persecution": I have done nothing and yet I am responsible for the other, excessively and obsessively. Levinas also severs the traditional relation between responsibility and the self, and overcomes the egological enclosure of responsibility, in that it is no longer assigned to the interests of the ego. I am now responsible for what is foreign to me, for "what does not even matter to me" (EI, 95). What can be the ground of such an obligation? Certainly not my own self as subject and author: Its measure is no longer the self-ownership of a subject, the return onto itself of the self, but a pre-originary openness to an other, and the claim made upon me by this other. The emphasis is displaced from the self toward the other, and the subject is overturned as subject*ed* to the other. Thus, the ground of this obligation, if it is not the self, will have to be located *in the other itself,* and in a certain vulnerability to which I will return. This is of course the great divide that Levinas retraced and radicalized, between a responsibility for self and a responsibility for the other, leading to an ethics of otherness apart from all egology or egological thinking.

4. This raises the question of the scope or the measure of responsibility, as visible in the questions: To whom or to what are we responsible? For which other am I responsible? For whom or for what? Indeed, to answer, like Levinas, that the other is the one I am responsible for is only the beginning of the question. We know the Levinasian quandary discussed in its aporetic structure by Derrida in *The Gift of Death: Tout autre est tout autre,* "*every* other is *wholly* other." I am therefore obligated to all others insofar as I am obligated to each and every other. How to discriminate between others if I am each time obligated to a singular other and thus bound in this singular responsibility to sacrifice all other others? For this expression, *tout autre est tout autre,* is a way of "linking alterity to singularity" and "signifies that every other is singular, that everyone is a singularity" (GD, 87). Are these others only human, as Levinas claimed by reading the other in the face, which, as *visage,* is exclusively human? And how can one speak of determinable measure when a certain aporia, or sacrifice, seems to impossibilize the ethical experience? As I respond to one singular other, I sacrifice all the *other* others, and I can only respond ethically by sacrificing or betraying ethics: "I can respond only to the one (or to the One), that is, to the other,

by sacrificing the other to that one . . . and I cannot justify this sacrifice" (GD, 70). This sacrificial space implies that as a consequence "the concepts of responsibility, of decision, or of duty, are condemned a priori to paradox, scandal, and aporia" (GD, 68). The question of responsibility is thus opened from this aporia onto its own undecidability.

This question is addressed frontally by Sartre, leading to a hyperbolic inflation of responsibility in his thought of existence: My responsibility, Sartre claims, is boundless, extends to "all men" and everything concerns me. However, this hyperbolic inflation of responsibility proves to be nothing but the hyperbolic inflation of subjectivity since for Sartre everything that happens happens to me, and what happens *to* me happens *through* me. I am responsible for everything and for all as I project an image to be embraced by all. I am responsible for "all men" in the sense that "I carry the weight of the world" (*je porte le poids du monde*), that is, I embrace the whole world in my will. To that extent, Sartre does not perturb the traditional definition of responsibility as authorship but reinforces and extends it hyperbolically. He writes: "We are taking the word 'responsibility' in its ordinary sense as 'consciousness (of) being the incontestable *author* of an event or of an object.'"[21] For Levinas as well, I am responsible for everyone, but in the opposite sense of Sartre, because for Levinas I am responsible as expropriated and hostage of the other's infinite demand. However, as I will argue, like Sartre, and despite his radical reversal of egological responsibility, Levinas does not perturb the traditional demarcations, which he simply reverses.

One can take this question "To whom or to what are we responsible?" in a different direction, questioning the very division between human and non-human that has structured the history of responsibility, or questioning its egological enclosure: For whom or for what one is responsible? Human beings, animals, things, nature, the world, the cosmos or universe—everything? In the words of Jean-Luc Nancy, "For what are we responsible? . . . responsible for being, for God, for the law, for death, for birth, for existence, ours and that of all beings"?[22] What is the scope or the range, the limits and measures of responsibility? Isn't it always taken in an excessive movement that leads to an exceeding of the very anthropocentric enclosure of the concept of responsibility, thus disturbing the demarcation between what would be a human and a non-human sphere? This disruption would open onto what Nancy calls the singular plurality of being, in which the relation to an other is no longer governed by the human signified, or the human as transcendental signified. Nancy explains in *Being Singular Plural* that in being-with it is the matter of a communication between singularities, where no privilege to human Dasein can be granted. "We would not be 'humans' if there not 'dogs' and 'stones,'" Nancy writes (BSP, 18), indicating that existence is not the property of Dasein. Responsibility exceeds the anthropocentric closure, and is to be situated in the between of singularities:

> If one can put it like this, there is no other meaning than the meaning of circulation. But this circulation goes in all directions at once, in all the directions of all the space-times opened by presence to presence: all things, all beings, all entities, everything past and future, alive, dead, inanimate, stones, plants, nails, gods—and "human," that is, those who expose sharing and circulation as such by saying "we."[23]

The human being does not constitute the center of creation, Nancy insists. Instead, creation (that is, the way the world emerges and exists, *ex nihilo,* for Nancy) "transgresses [*traverse*] humanity," so that "in humanity, or rather right at [*à même*] humanity, existence is exposed and exposing" (BSP, 17). To that extent, there is no human sphere with its accompanying anthropocentric self-responsibility. As Nancy formulates it, the thought of the singular plurality of being would lead us to state the following with respect to the world: It is not a human world, but a world of the co-exposure of the human and the non-human. I would not be "human," he explains, if I did not "have this exteriority 'in me,' in the form of the quasi-minerality of bone" (BSP, 18). Humanity is neither the origin, nor the center, nor the end of the world:

> It is not so much the world of humanity as it is the world of the non-human to which humanity is exposed and which humanity, in turn, exposes. One could try to formulate it in the following way: *humanity is the exposing of the world; it is neither the end nor the ground of the world; the world is the exposure of humanity; it is neither the environment nor the representation of humanity.* (BSP, 18)

As one can see, the expression "responsibility for the other" can explode the self-centered sense of responsibility in many directions, each putting into question our basic beliefs in the structure of being and its composition as well as in our conception of what it means to be human.

5. One speaks of responsibility in the sense of "carrying a weight," of "shouldering" a burden. Ordinary language does speak of the connection between responsibility and weight, of responsibility as the carrying of a weight, and one also notes the etymological connection with the German *Schuld, schuldig,* as guilt. However, what exactly *weighs* in the weight? Heidegger speaks of the human being as a being who is burdened or heavy with a weight, in a situation of care and concern, in contrast to the lightness or carelessness of irresponsible or inauthentic being. (For Heidegger inauthenticity is defined by the avoidance of responsibility, i.e., the refusal to carry a certain weight.) Heidegger evokes the fundamentally "burdensome character of Dasein, even while it alleviates the burden."[24] So-called "moods of elation," which do alleviate the burden, are said to be possible only on the basis of this burdensome character of Dasein's being. The being of the "there," Heidegger writes, "become[s] manifest as a burden [*Last*]" (SZ, 134). Heidegger defines Dasein as "care," as concern: Being is at issue for Dasein, it is a task of being, and is a weight I have to carry and be "responsible for." Responsibility as the carrying of the weight of existence is the originary phenomenon, and irresponsibility—making things easy—is derivative. Ultimately, the weight designates the facticity of existence, a facticity to which we are assigned and have to carry as our very finitude.

In Levinas's thought, the motif of weight marks the ethical situation of the finite subject as assigned (hostage!) to the other, the assigning of a finite subject to the infinite demand of the other: What weighs in this case is the dissymmetry or incommensurability between the finite I and the infinite Other. The other's demand is greater than my capacities to respond, as a finite I—and yet this is how I must respond. This appears in the motif of hospitality as welcome of the other: The welcome of the other is the finite welcome of an infinite. The subject welcomes or receives the other *beyond its own finite capacities of welcoming.* The call of the other is thus "too much" to bear and weighs on the finite subject, an excess which cannot be an argument against ethical responsibility: That I cannot materially do justice to the other does not imply that I am not obligated to him or her; there is no relationship between my capacities as a finite subject and the ethical responsibility that is mine. In fact, as Levinas says, *dissymmetry is the law of responsibility,* as it represents a responsibility for an other that necessarily exceeds my finite capabilities. Such an excess for the subject is the origin of responsibility, and its weight. Furthermore, Levinas stresses that ethical responsibility is not chosen, is not the result of my decision or initiative, but is assigned to me "before freedom," by the other facing me, putting me in a situation of being obligated. The weight of responsibility is thus threefold: It is the weight of a dissymmetry between the infinite other and the finite subject; it is the weight of the *passivity* of an ethical obligation before freedom and choice; and finally, it is the weight of otherness itself. The otherness of the other weighs on me precisely insofar as the other remains other, never appropriable by me—exterior to me, yet calling me to responsibility.

This weightiness, which seems to exceed all limits or measure (and it is in fact this very boundlessness that weighs), can nonetheless take at least two forms. It can take the form, as in Levinas, of the finite self becoming hostage to the infinite other. In this case, as we have seen, the weight is the weight of otherness. But it can also take the Sartrean form, in which I carry the weight of the world on my shoulders because I embrace the whole world *within my will.* I am responsible for everything and for all men, says Sartre. And Levinas also writes that I am responsible, and *more* than all the others—but for opposite reasons. For Sartre, it signifies the absolutizing of the willful subject taking over the whole world and being responsible "for all men" insofar as I am the "author" of the meaning of the world. For Levinas, it means the subjection of the finite subject to an infinite other. Because the subject is ex-posed to an alterity, the very possibility of appropriation is put into question. Weight would thus be the "resistance" of what remains inappropriable for the subject. In either absolutizing the subject (Sartre) or radically emptying and subjecting the subject (Levinas), in both cases responsibility is infinite and overwhelming, and the subject carries the whole weight of the world on its shoulders. The "weight" of responsibility can thus have the following senses: It can designate the absolute authorship of the free subject (Sartre), the dissymmetry of an infinite obligation of the other for a finite subject (Levinas), or the weight of finitude for Dasein (Heidegger).

7. Such resituating of responsibility opens the thematics of answerability and responsiveness, responsibility as "responding to" or answering a call. Derrida considers that any sense of responsibility must be rooted in the experience of responding, and belong to the domain of responsiveness.[25] Responsibility is first and foremost a response, as its etymological origins, which are traceable to the Latin *respondere,* betray. Derrida distinguishes three types of responsiveness: There is "to answer for" (*répondre*

de), "to respond to" (*répondre à*), and "to answer before" (*répondre devant*). Derrida gives a priority to the "responding to," as it mobilizes the inscription of an other to whom or to which I respond. One reads in *The Politics of Friendship*:

> One *answers for,* for self or for something (for someone, for an action, a thought, a discourse), *before,* before an other (a community of others, an institution, a court, a law). And always one *answers for* (for self or for its intention, its action or discourse), *before,* by first responding *to:* this last modality thus appears to be more originary, more fundamental and hence unconditional.[26]

The phenomenological senses of responsibility might be closer to a problematic of answerability than one of accountability, which is too dependent on a metaphysics of subjectivity.[27] Responsibility first needs to be taken as a kind of response, as being assigned to a call. One thinks here, for instance, of Heidegger's call of conscience in *Being and Time,* and later of the call or address of being to which one has to correspond, Heidegger going so far in *The Zollikon Seminars* as to claim: "To be answerable to the claim of presencing is the greatest claim of humanity: ethics is this claim."[28] The motif of the call is also central to Levinas's definition of responsibility—the call of the other person, the other human, out of his or her vulnerability and mortality. One can also evoke here Jean-Luc Marion's problematic of the saturated phenomenon, and the call that this excess places on the called one that I am (*l'interloqué*). For Marion, in fact, the senses of responsibility as accountability of the subject, as well as the Levinasian sense of responding to the other's face, presuppose the original sense of responsibility as response to the call *as such.* "Responsibility can now be redefined," Marion writes, in *Being Given.*

> Nobody will deny that responsibility, understood as the property of a juridical "subject" having to respond for his acts and an ethical "subject" having to respond to what the face of the Other demands (to envisage him [*de l'envisager*] as such), can be deduced from the most general figure of the response to a call by a gifted [*un adonné*].

And the result of this is that the call "always arises from a paradox (saturated phenomenon)."[29]

Responsibility is thus a response and is not, as Kant claimed, based on a spontaneous initiating. The subject is the recipient of the call, and not a transcendental subject; we are respondents, not absolute initiators. For Kant, to be responsible means to be able to begin something absolutely. However, as called, the subject can never begin anything but can only respond. The I always comes after, always comes "late," and its responsibility is that very delay in the form of the registering of and responding to the call. This is where one notes the crucial importance of the conception of the human being which is at the basis of a conception of responsibility: Kant thinks the human being as rational subject, origin ("transcendental freedom"), and foundation. His concept of responsibility will bear these features. Heidegger thinks the human, no longer as a subject, but as Dasein, that is, as a "thrown" existence (to be taken on responsibly). Similarly, with Levinas the subject is understood as assigned to a call, as passivity: The subject is hostage to the other. Responsibility in this sense is not a matter of choice or inclination, but arises out of a demand placed on the "subject," a demand that takes the form of a duty, of an ethical obligation, a call I cannot not answer. That demand needs to be answered: *Having* to respond, to answer (duty, obligation), implies that one cannot *not* answer. In fact, not responding is already a kind of response. And this is exactly how Heidegger would define inauthenticity—it is a not-responding (to the call of conscience) that nonetheless is a kind of response; "responding in the form of not-responding" means, *being inauthentic.* I will later investigate the various interpretations of such calling, and the different philosophical problematics opened through them.

This survey of the polysemic range of the term 'responsibility' reveals that the accountability of the subject is but *one* sense of the term, and perhaps not even the most primordial: Having to respond to a call, exposure to the vulnerability of the other (or to the other *as* vulnerability), openness to the event of being as my own "to be," having to take upon oneself the weight of responsibility (whether that weight is finitude, otherness, or an essenceless existence)—all of these senses point to the experience of and exposure to an inappropriable. The prevalent metaphysical interpretation of responsibility as the accountability of the subject indeed proves to be too narrow, ultimately resting upon an un-phenomenological account of what it means to be human, and is thus subject to a phenomenological genealogy and deconstruction. Here as elsewhere, deconstruction will be synonymous with the opening of new possibilities. I will attempt to reconstruct a history of the decisive moments in the development of the concept of responsibility so as to retrieve its phenomenological origins, thus profoundly transforming the concept of responsibility.

The History of Responsibility

No concept is a-temporal or a-historical. Nietzsche challenges this characteristic of philosophers to approach philosophical problems in an a-historical or de-historicized way, and in particular those so-called historians of morality who lack "historical spirit." Nietzsche claims that "the thinking of all of them is *by nature* unhistorical" (GM, 25). Such would be the "common failing" of philosophers—they do not take account of the historicity of their object, and think of man as an "*aeterna veritas.*" Nietzsche accounts for this a-historicity in reference to what he calls the fetishism of language, i.e., our belief in grammar, and in §11 of book 1 of *Human, All Too Human,* he explains that "man has for long ages believed in the concept and names of things as in *aeternae veritates,*" and that "he really thought that in language he possessed knowledge of the world."[30] Lack of historical sense is therefore "the family failing of all philosophers" (HH, 13); this is what is "idiosyncratic" about them: "their lack of a sense of history, their hatred for the very notion of becoming" (TI, 18). They produce nothing but "conceptual mummies." Challenging the same a-historical approach to the question of responsibility, Derrida states that it "is often thought, on the basis of an analysis of the very concepts of responsibility, freedom, or decision, that to be responsible, free, or capable of deciding cannot be something that is acquired, something conditioned or conditional" (GD, 5). However, as Nietzsche writes, "everything has become: there are *no eternal facts,* just as there are no absolute truths. Consequently, what is needed from now on is *historical philosophizing,* and with it the virtue of modesty" (HH, 13).[31] Responsibility would need to be resituated in its proper historicity. An authentic philosophizing on responsibility would engage the history of the concept of responsibility, would seek to ask with Derrida: "What would responsibility be if it were motivated, conditioned, made possible by a history?" (GD, 5).

The first task of this enterprise will consist in undertaking a deconstructive genealogy of the concept of responsibility and, in such an investigation into the history of the concept of responsibility,[32] to show how responsibility has been *constructed* in such a way as to be progressively identified with accountability under the authority of a philosophy of will and subjectivity. Exposing this construction is already undertaking its deconstruction. In fact, responsibility, the concept of accountability, might already be, in and of itself, in a state of self-deconstruction, according to the "general law of construction" identified by Jean-Luc Nancy, who writes that a conceptual construction, "like any construction, according to the general law of constructions, exposes itself, constitutively and in itself, to its deconstruction."[33] This self-deconstruction of responsibility allows us to understand how the position of an accountable subject never goes without an unavoidable double-bind: Such a subject will be both in a position of mastery *and* as the possible seat of accusation and punishment. The more it will establish its position of power as subject, i.e., the more it will posit its agency, then the more it will propose itself as the potential recipient of an accusation or a persecution and thus undermine itself. In short, the more it will assert its power then the more the "responsible subject" will also undermine itself and deepen the abyss beneath it. The position of the power of the subject of imputation undermines itself in the very moment of its position, which also helps understand how Levinas is able to reverse the subject from the nominative of the tradition to the accusative of the hostage of the other, how the "subject" becomes "the subjected."[34] In a sense, the responsible subject is always undermining itself, always deconstructing itself. *Responsibility deconstructs itself.* This is also why, no doubt, one is never responsible *enough*: Responsibility actually engenders irresponsibility from within itself, it *produces* irresponsibility, all the while reengaging in efforts to suppress it. As we will see with Aristotle, responsibility is a domain that must be purified of irresponsibility and secured in its position of dominance, an effort which is doomed to fail, as irresponsibility will always be an integral and irreducible part of a fuller concept of responsibility.

One may instead imagine a reflection on irresponsibility in which such a neat difference between responsibility and irresponsibility (between the voluntary and the involuntary, to use Aristotle's terms) would not hold, thereby putting into question the identification of responsibility with voluntariness. In fact, one may discern the irreducible presence of a certain irresponsibility at the heart of responsible engagement: Each time, though in different ways in Nietzsche, Heidegger, Sartre, Levinas or Derrida, one notes that responsibility seems to be rooted in an originary experience of irresponsibility, with responsibility *arising out of it*. Nietzsche speaks of the radical unaccountability of all things, negating responsibility and proclaiming the radical innocence of life and becoming. There is no intention, no design, no author, no cause, no responsibility, no agent: Life eventuates in a tragic and innocent play, without a goal, not directed by a divine will. It is thus irresponsibility (as the unaccountability of all things) that is affirmed by Nietzsche! And yet, it is out of this very innocence and unaccountability of all things that a certain responsibility arises, as the affirmation of that very groundlessness and the recognition of a self-overcoming and self-creating humanity. One becomes responsible for a Godless existence, engaged in the creation of an existence that unfolds out of an absence of essence. In Heidegger's work, being happens without reason (the rose has no why, it grows because it grows, states *The Principle of Reason*), and there is no author of being. In *Being and Time*, Heidegger writes that the call of conscience has no author. Yet one has to respond to this authorless call and be responsible for one's thrown existence. The "irresponsibility" of thrownness is taken over by a responsibility for existence. For Sartre, even though he claims that we are responsible for everything and for all men, it is also the case that we have not chosen to be responsible, that we are not free to be free. We are "condemned to be free," and in such condemnation, one should hear both the irresponsibility of our facticity *and* the unavoidability of our responsibility. One should almost speak here of the irresponsibility *of* responsibility. There is an irreducible irresponsibility at the origin of responsibility, so that we could be said to be irresponsibly responsible. Levinas speaks of an infinite and hyperbolic responsibility to the other. But his ethics of responsibility takes place "before freedom," is not chosen, is beyond reason, excessive, and located onto an infinite Other. Responsibility for the other takes place against the background of a radical passivity, a passivity that the tradition, in its emphasis on the active, responsible subject, has equated to an absence of responsibility. (We will see how Aristotle defines the involuntary through the notion of force, where the subject, or patient, is passive and thus irresponsible.) Derrida, for his part, reveals the aporetic and the impossible at the heart of any ethical decision, responsibility being traced back to such irresponsible or a-responsible foundations. Derrida seeks to return to the an-ethical origins of ethics. Hence, Aristotle's separation of the voluntary (responsibility) from the involuntary (irresponsibility) will have to be questioned further. Irresponsibility may not be the opposite or negation of responsibility, may not be external to it, but is perhaps an integral part of the phenomenon of responsibility. Otherwise, why would Aristotle take such pains in trying to distinguish and separate them—and with such difficulties, which border on the aporetic (the so-called examples of "mixed actions")? Does this very effort not betray and reveal an undecidable co-belonging between responsibility and irresponsibility?

The twofold aspect mentioned above of the prevailing metaphysical sense of responsibility—establishment of a power *and* accusation of a subject, supposition of a subject *and* undermining of the subject—in other words, the intimate connection between power and persecution, will appear clearly, not only in Levinas's work (where responsibility is actually defined as persecution), but also in any genealogy of the concept of responsibility. As Nietzsche has shown decisively, at the root of responsibility as accountability we find the need to posit an agent-cause, that is, someone who can be held accountable and punished. A post-metaphysical sense of responsibility will certainly have to be distinguished from a problematics of punishment, just as it will also have to be differentiated from accountability. Whatever the origins of such an obsessional need for accountability—its relation to pain, hurt, *ressentiment,* and sadism (in short, its pathological nature)—we can already state that undertaking such a genealogy of responsibility would allow other possible significations to emerge, which are not dependent on the logic of power, subjection, accountability, and punishment. Existence as essenceless—having to take responsibility from such an absence of ground and invent ethics itself (Sartre), having to respond to a call in an openness to the event of being as my own (Heidegger), exposure to the vulnerability of the other *as* vulnerability (Levinas), undergoing in decision the aporia of the undecidable (Derrida), or having to take upon oneself responsibility as a weight, whether this is the weight of finitude or the weight of inappropriable alterity—all of these senses of responsibility are concealed in the tradition of subjectivity and will, and remain to be explored. Responsibility becomes less about the establishment of a sphere of control and power, less about the establishment of a sovereign subject, and more about exposure to an event that does not come from us and yet calls us. The purpose of this book is to explore these senses so as to rethink the concept of responsibility from the ground up.

To this extent, the present inquiry will therefore resolutely situate itself *outside* of the classical problematics of the opposition between free will and determinism. This opposition, which has enframed traditional accounts of responsibility and continues to structure a large number of discussions on responsibility, will prove inadequate to an exploration of the phenomenological senses of responsibility. An ontological interpretation of responsibility (a questioning of the *being* of responsibility) will necessarily undercut this classic free will/determinism debate, for several essential reasons: Responsibility in its most original sense may not take place within the modern Cartesian opposition between nature (determinism) and freedom (free will), but more originally—whether in the very givenness of existence, in being-in-the-world, or in the Levinasian face-to-face; responsibility may not be tantamount to accountability; causality may not apply to the human being's relation to the world, itself, and others; free will may not exhaust the meaning of freedom; intention may not convey our relation to events; subjectivity may be only one aspect of what it means to be human, and not the most primordial one. Ultimately, the free will/determinism opposition remains an *ontical* distinction, which can only be an obstacle for an ontological analysis of responsibility. All of these dogmas need to be questioned on the way toward a renewed concept of responsibility: Any philosophical reflection worthy of the name needs to question the assumptions of its discourse, and therefore needs to question the identification of responsibility with imputation or accountability. For instance, any juridical, legal or penal definition of responsibility rests upon and presupposes imputability. But imputability, or accountability, itself rests upon and presupposes a certain conception of the human being, a subject-based philosophy of responsibility. A philosophical enterprise would thus need to distinguish responsibility—whose etymological roots, as we have seen, from the Latin *respondere,* mobilize the domain of answerability or responsiveness—from the accountability of a subject, that is, from a metaphysics of the free autonomous subject. What does *to be responsible* mean, if it is no longer referred to the subject? This question still requires a historical genealogy: One of the key tasks of the present work will be to dissociate the senses of responsibility from its enframing in a metaphysics of subjectivity, power, and will.

I will attempt to reconstruct a—by no means exhaustive—history of the decisive moments in the development of the concept of responsibility so as to retrieve what I have called, following an expression of Nietzsche's in the *Genealogy of Morals*, the "origins of responsibility." I begin by addressing how the concept of responsibility has traditionally been constructed in terms of accountability—that is, in terms of will, causality, freedom or free will, authorship, and subjectivity—focusing primarily on two decisive moments in that history, namely Aristotle's discussion of the voluntary and responsible decision in book III of the *Nicomachean Ethics*, and Kant's theory of transcendental freedom as ground of imputability in the *Critique of Pure Reason*, as well as his writings on autonomy. I then consider other ways to think responsibility, once the above-mentioned categories are put into question or challenged with and after Nietzsche's genealogy of responsibility. What would responsibility mean if it is not thought as the consequence of free will? If responsibility no longer designates the capacity of a subject to "own" its thoughts and acts? If the category of causality is no longer operative, or is at least problematized?

In the first two chapters, I reconstitute the construction of accountability and agency in Aristotle and Kant. In chapter 1, I explore Aristotle's definition of responsibility in terms of the voluntary and rational decision as developed in book III of the *Nicomachean Ethics*, and how he attempts to circumscribe responsibility in terms of what is "within our power" or "up to us." One finds in Aristotle's account of responsibility (under the authority of the "voluntary") the basic construction of this notion of rational agency as the bedrock of what will become the dominant sense of responsibility in the Western tradition. More than an account, it is in fact a performative constitution of the sense of responsibility as power of the rational agent over its actions. Responsibility is identified with voluntariness, which is itself deployed as a rational decision where it is a matter of delineating what is within our power. Aristotle structures his reflection on responsibility through a reliance on the concepts of the voluntary (*hekōn, hekousion*) and the involuntary (*akōn, akousion*). These concepts are further determined in terms of decision (*prohairesis*) and deliberation (*bouleusis*). One fundamental assumption indeed governs these analyses, namely that responsibility pertains to the voluntary: Aristotle assumes *the identification of responsibility with the voluntary*. The whole thrust of the argument consists in *isolating* the space of what is *up to us*, that is, in distinguishing (separating) the voluntary from the involuntary. Aristotle seeks to identify and differentiate the voluntary from the non- or in-voluntary, in order to prevent any confusion or overlap between the two, securing a sphere that will then be said to be pure of any contamination from its other. As we have stressed, in this book of the *Nicomachean Ethics,* the analyses are not merely descriptive; rather, they clearly have a performative character as they seek to construct, establish, and secure the space of the voluntary and of responsibility, that is, of agency. What matters to Aristotle is to secure what he repeatedly refers to as what is "within our power" or "up to us" (*eph' hēmin*), or what is "in us" (*en hēmin*). Such a guiding principle is of course the construction of the notion of willful agency, what is *up to us,* as Aristotle stresses by stating that the human being "is a principle, begetting actions as he begets children" (1113b 18–20), recalling what was stated in 1112b 33–34, namely that "a human being would seem to be a principle of action." The agent is then characterized by Aristotle as principle (*arkhē*) of the act, then metaphorically as begetter, and then further by way of a political sense of mastery and control, as in the passage where Aristotle writes that "we are in control (*kurioi*) of actions from the beginning to the end" (1114b 31) or that the responsible agent is "master" (*kurios*) of his effects. Aristotle also describes the domain of what is *up to us* as being the proprietor of one's domain. Responsibility becomes understood in terms of both voluntariness and reason (through the notions of decision and deliberation), and as the indication of our power over our actions.

In chapter 2, I follow Kant's discussion of freedom and causality in the Third Antinomy of the first *Critique,* in order to show how Kant identifies responsibility with imputability and bases the latter on transcendental freedom. Imputability is possible on the basis of transcendental freedom, which, as *causa sui,* has the power of beginning absolutely a new series of causes in the world. Kant situates responsibility within the sphere of the subjectivity of the subject, determines it *as imputation* and further determines such responsibility as *self-responsibility,* which for him is the essence of personhood as such. Responsibility is indeed the differentiating feature between persons and things, the defining characteristic of personhood. In contrast to things, Kant asserts, a person is a subject that is capable of imputation. In his *Doctrine of Right,* Kant explains that a person is "a subject whose actions can be *imputed* to him," whereas a "thing is that to which nothing can be imputed."[35] This capacity to be a subject as ground of imputation is owed to the faculty of freedom, taken as "transcendental freedom," which also determines the possibility of moral responsibility. Freedom makes possible such responsibility and Kant's philosophical reflection on responsibility takes place within the horizon of the freedom of the subject, further specifying what Aristotle had metaphorically designated as the "paternity" of the act. Responsibility is understood in terms of the foundation provided by the free subject as acting. Increasingly, responsibility is defined in terms of the establishment of a ground, or a *subjectum*. It is indeed the subject as *subjectum*, the spontaneous I, which is the causal foundation and absolute beginning (transcendental freedom), and which Kant would designate as the locus and basis of responsibility (under the name of *imputation*). Responsibility is understood in terms of the *subjectum* that lies at the basis of the act. It also involves the empowerment of the subject, as the notion of self-determination or autonomy implies. This sense of freedom as the ground of imputability further opens the space of personhood and autonomy. I follow more positive accounts of freedom and responsibility as autonomy in several texts by Kant on practical philosophy, including his definition of enlightenment as self-responsibility in his essay "What is Enlightenment?" I attempt to show that Kant defines "enlightenment" as the freeing from tutelage, immaturity or irresponsibility (*Unmündigkeit*, both immaturity and dependence, not being of age), which he defines as "man's inability to make use of his understanding *without direction from another*."[36] The ideal of responsibility as self-responsibility thus implies a break with heteronomy, the projecting of a horizon of self-appropriation which is constitutive of the traditional account of responsibility.

In chapter 3, I question such a tradition by following Nietzsche's genealogy of responsibility and deconstruction of accountability. With respect to Aristotle and Kant, we have noted the "performative" character of their "accounts" of responsibility. In particular, in Aristotle's case, we will have seen how he performatively *constituted* responsibility as a sphere of control over events, by emphasizing the voluntary in one's actions, and how he attempted to secure such a sphere through a careful and strict demarcation of the voluntary from the involuntary. With respect to Kant, we analyze how a problematic notion of "transcendental" freedom—one which is literally not of this world!—was made the foundation of responsibility understood as imputation of a subject, and further characterized as autonomous self-responsibility, that is, within the egological horizon that is reductive of alterity (designated as "heteronomy"). Nietzsche exposes the groundlessness of these representations by stressing how the traditional concept of responsibility rests on the constructs—indeed, the *fictions*—of agency, causality, free will, intentionality, and subjectivity, and how these constructs indeed are not of this world! I begin by situating this critique of the traditional accounts of responsibility in terms of what Nietzsche calls the fictitious nature of concepts. For his critique of responsibility is before all else a critique of the *conceptuality* of responsibility—of responsibility as a concept—and even a critique of conceptuality as such. Nietzsche exposes the entirely conventional nature of language and conceptuality; our concepts are metaphors, arbitrary designations, and there is therefore no natural connection whatsoever with sense: *There will not be, there cannot be, a "natural" concept of responsibility.* Responsibility has been constructed, in a history. This leads to the necessity of what Nietzsche calls a historical philosophizing with respect to the concept of responsibility. Nietzsche's genealogy deconstructs the four fundamental concepts at the basis of the traditional account of responsibility—subjectivity, will, causality, and intentional agency. It is important to note here the scope of Nietzsche's deconstruction of these four "idols" of the metaphysics of responsibility: It is not a matter of stating that these concepts are false, but rather of exposing their fictitious nature. Nietzsche reveals that causality, subjectivity, will, and agency are constructs, the motives for which need to be brought out. Nietzsche's destructive genealogy of metaphysical idols means as much for him the exposure of their fictive nature as an attack on the values they subtend and carry. In the end, responsibility is traced back by Nietzsche to a "making-responsible," a making-guilty that is motivated in a certain perspective with respect to life. I follow each of these critiques by showing how they open up, not only new possibilities for life in its self-interpretation, but new possibilities for rethinking responsibility. In particular, I suggest that Nietzsche's genealogy opens the way for a rethinking of the ontological and phenomenological origins of responsibility, once its metaphysical enclosure has been deconstructed. For instance, when Nietzsche proclaims the "unaccountability of all things" or the "innocence of becoming," away from the metaphysical drive to posit a foundation and a subject-cause, one is led to a groundlessness that will become the phenomenological site where responsibility—in an entirely new sense—will paradoxically arise. This is the focus of the following chapters.

In chapter 4, I investigate how a new sense of responsibility emerges from Nietzsche's proclamation of the death of God, from the groundlessness opened by the withdrawal of theological principles. One sees in the existentialism of Jean-Paul Sartre the exposure of ontological and phenomenological origins of responsibility, once existence has been freed from its metaphysical enframing in essence. I attempt to highlight these phenomenological and ontological origins of responsibility as Sartre thematizes them—existence prior to, indeed, without essence; original freedom and original choice as opposed to "free will"; responsibility as identified with existence itself; the role of the nothing in his concept of responsibility; the invention of the law and of ethics in decision; the absolutizing of responsibility and the overcoming of facticity; the problematics of authenticity and bad faith—in short, *original or ontological responsibility*—while also marking its hermeneutic limits, due to Sartre's continued dependency on the Cartesian tradition and the tradition of responsibility as authorship. We will note what I have called a "paradoxical paroxysm" of such authorship, brought to a hyperbolic extreme but already pointing to its self-deconstruction. As Sartre states, existentialism explicitly places itself within the horizon of Nietzsche's genealogy, and particularly understands itself as a consequence of what Nietzsche called the death of God. He thus explains in "The Humanism of Existentialism" that by existentialism, "we mean only that God does not exist and that we have to face all the consequences of this."[37] The death of God has an immediate ethical impact: It is out of the groundlessness of existence that one is thrown into a responsibility that is infinitized to the extent of this absence of ground. This is why freedom is boundless and absolute for Sartre—as ungrounded, it is boundless. Paradoxically, the withdrawal of essence in Nietzsche, taken up by Sartre in the expression "existence precedes essence," becomes the new site of responsibility. Responsibility constitutes the core of existentialist ethics, as the very possibility of ethics—the absolute responsibility of an essenceless existence for itself—is the consequence of the death of God. To that extent, responsibility for Sartre is an originary praxis that is justified by itself alone. There is a performativity of ethical valuation wherein ethics, far from any sense of applying a rule, becomes the matter of a making or an invention (the rule itself needs to be invented). The death of God implies the disappearance of an *a priori* table of values, such that ethics and responsibility are a matter of invention for Sartre, and never of the application of rules. This accounts for the crucial analogy Sartre draws between responsibility, ethics, and the work of art. Ethics itself, that is, the ethical as such, arises out of this lack of an *a priori* morality. It is from this lack of *a priori* norms that ethical responsibility is engaged and emerges in the first place.

I note what in Sartre's existentialism could be called a hyperbolic inflation of responsibility, which is characterized as "universal," "overwhelming," "boundless" or "infinite," indeed "absolute." Responsibility is universalized by Sartre as including "all humans." I "carry the weight of the world on my shoulders," as each of my projects becomes an example for all to follow. It is excessive and overwhelming in this first sense. Responsibility is also infinite because there are no longer any bounds to restrict it. Responsibility as it were expresses the groundlessness of existence. Because there is no essence, I am placed in the position of being responsible for existence, that is, for this lack of essence. To be responsible hence means to be responsible out of and for the lack that subtends responsibility. Responsibility is also absolutized in Sartre's existentialism, following his conception of freedom as absolute, that is, absolutely freed from any deterministic principle. I show how this reference to the absolute is also a thinly veiled reference to Descartes's philosophy, and attests to a certain undeconstructed Cartesianism in Sartre's philosophy of responsibility. Responsibility becomes absolutized in a reduction of facticity, Sartre going so far as to claim that facticity—that is, the very order of the not-chosen, such as birth—is a matter for my responsibility, and is also in a sense chosen. I interpret this hyperbolic inflation of responsibility, which encounters no limits in its movement of appropriation, as paradoxically based on "nothing": Responsibility becomes absolute insofar as it expresses the nothing of existence.

Further, I consider Sartre's peculiar and ambiguous position in the history we are following: While engaging a post-metaphysical thought of responsibility—responsibility as essenceless and groundless existence, thrownness into freedom, originary praxis as invention of the law and ethics—one also notes the maintaining, indeed the paroxysmal culmination, of modern subjectivist metaphysics, the predominance of subjectivity and will. Sartre occupies a peculiar—indeed paradoxical—position in this history of responsibility we are following, a sort of turning-point where he brings the modern tradition of willful subjectivity to a paroxysm while at the same time opening new possibilities, both prefigured and announced, if not fully exploited. Sartre thus develops an ontological analysis of responsibility, based on original freedom and a post-theological analysis of existence, and yet still retains a very classical definition of responsibility, centered on the notion of will and *authorship*. Sartre, although developing this phenomenology of responsibility from a thought of existence as essenceless, falls back on a subjectivist, and ultimately Cartesian, philosophy. To that extent, Sartre continues the tradition of agency, subjectivity, and will that has enclosed the concept of responsibility in our tradition. It becomes necessary, in order to develop such a post-metaphysical philosophy of responsibility, to overcome the very horizon of egology (it will take a veritable overturning of subjectivity to reopen responsibility as an experience of otherness), an overcoming which is the focus of the next chapter.

In chapter 5, I investigate and follow such an overcoming of egology in the retrieval of the origins of responsibility in Levinas's great reversal of the tradition of responsibility—from intentionality to passivity, from the ego to the other, from freedom to subjection, from the spontaneous will to the accusation and persecution of the self. Ultimately for Levinas, the decisive movement is the reversal of the concept of responsibility from a responsibility-for-self to a responsibility-for-the-other, as Jacques Derrida recognized in *The Gift of Death*:

> Levinas wants to remind us that responsibility is not at first responsibility of myself for myself, that the sameness of myself is derived from the other, as if it were second to the other, coming to itself as responsible and mortal from the position of my responsibility before the other, for the other's death and in the face of it. (GD, 46)

Therein lies the revolution in the thought of responsibility: Far from assigning responsibility to the actions of an agent, on the basis of the freedom of the subject, following the entire tradition, Levinas breaks with such a horizon—indeed, breaks with the very concept of horizon— and reconceptualizes responsibility as a being "for-the-other." This "for-the-other" would constitute the primary sense of responsibility, and I argue that this new thinking of responsibility is accompanied by, indeed strictly follows, an overturning (or expropriation) of the agent, from its masterful position as subject toward its assignation to the call of the other, the other for whom it is now responsible. Responsibility is no longer situated within the sphere of the ego, but arises out of the alterity of the other. This extraordinary revolution in thought follows a movement of overturning of the egological tradition, and in that sense, Levinas's thought could be described as taking the exact opposite position as Sartre's philosophy of responsibility. The expropriation of the subject is the basis for this overturning of the concept of responsibility, an expropriation that I first trace in Levinas's definition of the subject as "pre-originary openness" to the other.

With Levinas, responsibility is situated in the relationship to the other human, face to face, and not in relation to some abstract category, be it reason or universality. As I mentioned above, Levinas defines the self as a responsibility for the other human, and breaks with Kantian universalism by situating ethics in the encounter with the singular other, defining the self as a responsibility for the other human, devotion to the other in his or her vulnerability or mortality. As he explains, "To respect is to bow down not before the law, but before a being who commands a work from me."[38] Levinas describes the ethical experience of primordial responsibility as the face to face with the other, in which I am faced with the destitute and vulnerable nature of the other. The origin of ethical responsibility (but also of violence, as Levinas concedes, revealing an irreducible paradox at the heart of ethics) thus lies in the vulnerability of the other. *The face is before anything else how the human faces injury and death.* Faced with such vulnerability (ultimately the mortality or irremediable exposure to death of the other), I am called to care for the other and to attend to the other as other. The mortality of the other thus calls me to responsibility. Ethics understood in this way represents what is truly human in human beings, a new humanism (which Levinas calls "humanism of the other human") that breaks with ego-centered philosophies and opens onto the infinite character of the alterity of the other to whom I am responsible.

Levinas's account of responsibility breaks decisively with the concept of accountability of the subject. Responsibility is for the other, that is, not a responsibility ensuing from my deed, not even for what matters to me, but for the other, precisely in mattering to me *as* other, in the experience of the face. This responsibility for the other is non-reciprocal, dissymmetrical (all concerns for reciprocity, contracts, and agreements with others, are seen by Levinas examples of egoistic thinking), infinite, and non-chosen; it is the experience of a being-"hostage" to the other. This represents for Levinas a responsibility in the accusative—a guilt without faults, an indebtedness without loans, a responsibility as "persecution," "obsession," and "substitution."

I interpret Levinas's thought as an attempt to overcome and reverse the tradition of will and intentionality, while remaining prisoner of it by virtue of simply reversing it. Indeed, reversing a tradition is not the same as freeing oneself from it, and Levinas's revolution owes perhaps more that it would like to admit to the egological tradition that it seeks to reverse, *precisely insofar as it determines itself as its reversal.* Paul Ricoeur in this regard argues that the very vocabulary of Levinas's philosophy—in its hyperbole and excess, in its very desire for rupture, in its exasperation as it were—still attests to the egological tradition secretly determining its itinerary. Levinas targets in particular the modern Cartesian tradition in philosophy, from Descartes to Husserl, that is, the primacy of egology and the predominance of the will. Levinas exceeds the egological enclosure of the concept of responsibility, exceeds the free subject responsible for its actions. Egological responsibility finds itself inverted in Levinas's emphasis on the primacy of the other over the ego. The I is inverted from a nominative position to the passivity of the accusative (already the accusation or persecution of the subject as hostage). Thus "de-posed," the subject is overturned into the subjected. It appears quite clearly, in fact Levinas admits it often, that the definitions of the subject as a "welcome of the other," as "host," then as "hostage" have been forged through a peculiar reversal of the intentional, willful subjectivity of the modern tradition in philosophy. Responsibility for the other, Levinas often writes, goes "against the grain" (*à rebours*) of intentionality and the will. Among the numerous instances of such a reversal, we can mention the following: The subject is not a for-itself, but a for-the-other; the subject is not a freedom, but a passivity; the subject does not posit or constitute the meaning of the other, but is "affected" by the other; the subject does not structure intentionally the meaning of its world, but is exceeded by the other who affects it; the I is not a nominative, but an accusative; the subject does not initiate, but can only respond; the subject does not thematize, but is exposed to the transcendence of the infinite; the host does not receive, but is received in his or her own home, which then becomes a land of asylum, a place of transit; and finally, the subject is precisely not an active subject, a spontaneity, but is subject*ed*, as a hostage, to the other. As one can see, all the "features" of the Levinasian concept of the subject represent the symmetrical reversal of its traditional sense.

Ultimately this situation—which accounts for the radicality as well as the limits of Levinas's thinking—reveals, paradoxically, the Cartesian-Husserlian heritage of Levinas's thought of responsibility. Beginning with the I, he then proceeds to attempt to exceed it toward its outside, toward the exteriority of the other. However, we should note, the other can be considered to be an exteriority only in relation to the interiority of the subject. Rather than begin from the ego, in order to then attempt to leave it by appealing to the only concept that remains— namely, that of exteriority—it should be a question of beginning from a site that is outside of consciousness, outside of Cartesianism! It might be necessary, in order to access the phenomenological origins of responsibility, to begin outside of egology *or* its reversal. This will be the task of the following two chapters, which are devoted to Heidegger and an ontological interpretation of responsibility.

Chapters 6 and 7 explore an ontological understanding of responsibility by focusing on Heidegger's work. First, I situate Heidegger's relation to ethics, by delineating how ethics is approached in terms of being and its event. Second, I attempt to flesh out what "to be responsible" means, in such a renewed context—answerability to the call of conscience, responding and corresponding to the event of being, facticity of responsibility, assumption of finitude, assignation to an irreducible otherness, exposure to an inappropriable, correspondence and belonging to the call of *Ereignis*. Heidegger's thought of ethics needs to be approached, from the outset, in terms of what he himself called in the "Letter on Humanism," an "originary ethics" (*ursprüngliche Ethik*).[39] The first significant aspect of such an expression is that it seeks to capture our relationship to being itself, for it is the thinking of being that is defined as an originary ethics. This already indicates that Heidegger's understanding of ethics and responsibility will develop in terms of being itself, and thus no longer in the tradition of subjectivity, will, and agency. The adjective "originary" is also indicative that it will not be an issue of ethics as an applied discipline, nor even of a normative ethics that could then be applied, but of an originary phenomenon. I reconstitute this originary dimension by stressing how Dasein needs to be understood as an archi-ethical notion; by engaging the ethical outside of a problematic of application or use, and instead as a relation to the "useless"; by situating the ethical outside of subjectivity and freedom outside of the will; finally by approaching ethics in terms of an ethicality of being itself. Ultimately for Heidegger, as he himself states in the "Letter on Humanism," the thinking of being is an "originary ethics" because being is not some substantial ground but an event that calls for a responsible engagement and praxis.

I then engage Heidegger's retrieval of the ontological origins of responsibility. It has not been sufficiently recognized that Heidegger's thinking of being entails an important thought of responsibility, and this misrecognition is probably due to some assumptions regarding his relation to ethics, and to a prevalent misunderstanding of his deconstruction of that tradition. I argue that Heidegger's thought provides key features which allow for a rethinking of what being-responsible as such could mean, an ontological sense that is overlooked in the thought of accountability. Heidegger situates the question of responsibility outside of a problematic of the ego (including its mere reversal, as in Levinas), as arising out of the very openness of being where the human being dwells as Dasein. As we know, the notion of Dasein breaks decisively with the tradition of subjectivity. Ethical responsibility will thus have to find another origin than that of the free autonomous subject. For responsibility does not disappear in the deconstruction of the *subjectum,* since Heidegger consistently insists that Dasein is to be thought in terms of responsibility: (1) The very concept of Dasein means, to be a responsibility of being. This "archi-ethical" dimension of the concept of Dasein appears early in *Being and Time,* when Heidegger states that Dasein is distinctive in the sense that it does not simply occur among beings, but is concerned about its own being. Dasein designates that entity for whom being is at issue. Being is given in such a way that I have to take it over and be responsible for it. This determination of Dasein from the outset determines it as an originary responsibility. (2) Responsibility is thus not conceived as imputability of the free subject, but is instead approached in terms of a response to an event that is also a call; this call is thematized in *Being and Time* as the call of conscience, and in later writings as the call of being and *Ereignis.* Responsibility is not based on subjectness but constitutes the self as the called one. Each time, Dasein is called to itself. This is why the call is also that which I have to answer. Therein lies the hidden source and resource of responsibility: To be responsible means, before anything else, to respond (*respondere*). Having to be oneself, such is the originary responsibility of Dasein. I follow this original obligation in the call of conscience by emphasizing that it reveals a negativity or "being-guilty" that points to the finitude and facticity of responsibility, and ultimately is an exposure to an inappropriable. (3) After *Being and Time*, Dasein will be referred to by Heidegger more and more as the "called one" (*der Gerufene*), one having to answer for the very openness and givenness of being and be its "guardian." To be responsible here means to have been struck, always already, by this event. Responsibility refers to that event by which being "enowns" humans. It represents human beings' very belonging to being as well as their essence as humans.

However, that belongingness to being, to *Ereignis,* happens from a certain expropriative motion, which Heidegger calls *Enteignis.* One notes the presence of such expropriation in all the characterizations of Heidegger's responsibility, of our being-responsible: In the "ruinance" of factical life in the early writings and lecture courses; in the *Uneigentlichkeit* of existence in *Being and Time* and the being-guilty of conscience; in the thrownness felt in moods and the weight of a responsibility assigned to an inappropriable; in withdrawal as origin of the call (what calls to responsibility is a withdrawal), and in the *Enteignis* within *Ereignis* of the later writings—each time and throughout, one finds that responsibility in Heidegger is described as the exposure to and experience of an inappropriable. And furthermore, this inappropriable is not opposed to appropriation, but "plays" in it and lets it be, in a motion named by Derrida, in one word, "ex-appropriation." The "impossible" of expropriation (inappropriable) becomes the possibility of appropriation (responsibility); and it thus becomes necessary to frontally engage such aporias of the origins of responsibility.

In chapter 8, I engage these aporetic origins of responsibility, focusing on Derrida's thought of responsibility as an experience of the impossible. I explore his claim that responsibility can only be the experience and undergoing of an aporia—an experience of the impossible. Derrida problematizes the question of the site and possibility of ethical responsibility in terms of what he calls "aporetic ethics." When speaking of ethics, Derrida does not mean a system of rules, of moral norms, and to that extent he readily concedes that he does not propose an ethics. What interests him in ethics is instead "the aporias of ethics, its limits": Not to point to the simple impossibility of ethics, but on the contrary to reveal aporia as the possibility of ethics—what he calls the an-ethical origins of ethics. Derrida indeed sees the locus of the ethical in a certain experience of the aporia, of the impossible, to the extent that for him the impossible is not the mere stopping at a sheer end leading to a sterile incapacity, but constitutes a limit through which something is made possible.

I reconstitute the main features of such aporetic ethics—the aporia of the law, the undecidable, decision without or beyond knowledge, responsibility as an unconditional (and thus impossible) hospitality. (1) The first aporia marks the excess of ethics in relation to any norm or rule, indeed in relation to duty. It is in fact characteristic of the law, according to Derrida, that it is radically without ground, in the last analysis without foundation or justification. The law itself is without law; there is no law of the law. Ethical responsibility thus cannot consist in applying a rule. Thus it must be a question of moving beyond the very language of duty, precisely out of faithfulness to the ethical command, a command that paradoxically always occurs beyond the rule. Ethics would here be a duty beyond duty. (2) The aporia of the rule leads the ethical decision to the undecidable. For Derrida, there is no decision and no responsibility without the confrontation with the aporia of undecidability. That is to say, with the impossible. A decision must decide without rules to follow, to apply, to conform to, and this is why it is each time (the singularity of an each time) a decision as an event, an event that Derrida calls "impossible" because taking place outside of any possibilizing program. Just as with Sartre, ethical responsibility is thus a matter of *invention*, and not the application of a rule. The undecidable is the horizon of ethical responsibility: A decision made does not suppress the undecidable, because the aporia is the condition of decision. (3) A not-knowing is thus a condition of ethical decision, marking another appearance of the impossible. For there to be a decision, I must not know what to do. The moment of responsible decision, the ethical moment, is independent from knowledge. A leap in the incalculable is necessary and it is a matter of deciding without knowing, as it were without seeing (*voir*) or foreseeing (*prévoir*), and thus from a certain invisible or unforeseeable, without being able to calculate all the consequences of the decision. Ethical decision becomes possible by entering, as Derrida says, into "the night of the unintelligible." (4) Finally, ethics for Derrida is an ethics of the other, assigned to the heteronomy of the other (and not the autonomy of the subject). Derrida stresses the heteronomy of decision. I can never say: I made a decision. Derrida speaks rather of a decision "of the other," of a passive decision. Following Levinas, who precisely "always puts freedom after responsibility,"[40] Derrida seeks to imagine an alterity of decision, *a decision that would be of the other*, and will go so far as to speaks of a decision "of the other in me, an other greater and older than I am."[41] Ultimately for Derrida, the thought of the im-possible, of the aporetic, is inseparable from a thinking of the event, of what happens and arrives. In what was to be his last appearance on French television, in June 2004, answering the interviewer's question, "What is deconstruction?" Derrida replied: "Deconstruction, for me, means what happens; that is to say, the impossible." Responsibility, as an experience of the impossible of such arrival, is here approached in terms of the welcome of this event—of the event in its futural arrival.

ONE

Aristotle: Responsibility as Voluntariness

Situating the Voluntary

The prevailing and traditional concept of responsibility designates the capacity of a subject to be the *author* and the *cause* of its actions. An action is said to depend on the agent in the position of *subjectum*, of "subject-cause." Now the notions of authorship, of agency, indeed of subjectivity, are anything but natural; rather, they are the result of a certain *construction* (what Nietzsche would call a "fiction" or a "lie"), which can be traced historically in a specific genealogy. One finds in Aristotle's account of responsibility, under the authority of the "voluntary," the basic construction of this notion of rational agency as the bedrock of what will become the dominant sense of responsibility in the Western tradition. It has often been emphasized that Aristotle does not propose a unified concept of "the will" in his ethics, such as one finds in modern philosophy, for example in Descartes or in Kant. However, as we will see, he does structure his reflection on responsibility through a reliance on the concepts of the voluntary (*hekōn, hekousion*) and the involuntary (*akōn, akousion*). These concepts are further determined in terms of decision (*prohairesis*) and deliberation (*bouleusis*) that will establish rational agency as the basis for responsibility. What matters to Aristotle is to secure what he repeatedly refers to as what is "within our power" or "up to us" (*eph' hēmin*),[1] on the basis of agency as that which is the principle (*arkhē*) of the act, designated by Aristotle as that which is "in us" (*en hēmin*). Aristotle's account of responsibility thus lies in the establishment of agency as causal efficiency.[2] His task in book III of the *Nicomachean Ethics*[3] is to establish such a power, something like an area of mastery, of what would be *up to us* or dependent upon us. One should thus stress from the outset that his analyses are not merely descriptive, but clearly have a performative scope[4] as they seek to construct, establish, and secure the space of the voluntary and of responsibility. Voluntariness and agency, causality, rationality, and understanding will all be mobilized in this definition.

One fundamental assumption indeed governs these analyses, namely that responsibility pertains to the voluntary. Aristotle assumes *the identification of responsibility with the voluntary*. One is considered responsible if one is acting voluntarily (as well as rationally) and one is considered irresponsible if it can be established that the person was not the voluntary cause of their act, or did not understand the particulars of that act. A significant aspect is the method followed: The whole thrust of the argument consists in *isolating* the space of what is *up to us,* that is, in distinguishing and separating the voluntary from the involuntary. Aristotle seeks to identify and differentiate the voluntary from the non- or in-voluntary, thus preventing any confusion or overlap between the two. A sphere will be constituted (the voluntary) by distinguishing it from its opposite (the involuntary), and this sphere will then be said to be pure of any contamination from its other (under the decisive assumption that one finds remarkably stated in the *Eudemian Ethics:* "it is impossible for the same man to do the same thing voluntarily and involuntarily at the same time in respect of the same" aspect of the situation).[5] This is why Aristotle insists that it is a matter for him of completing the task of distinguishing the voluntary and the involuntary, thereby allowing for a definition of responsibility, or rather, of imputability.[6] The paradox of such an enterprise is that access to the voluntary, to a definition of the voluntary, occurs through an analysis of what constitutes an involuntary act, and that in this process one often gets stuck, as it were, in undecidable or mixed cases between the voluntary and involuntary. Aristotle will then have to decide, in order for there to be any responsibility, that in each instance a mixed act is in the final analysis *not* mixed, but is in fact voluntary. Another key example of such decisions is his distinction between acting *by* ignorance (*di'agnoian*) and acting *in* ignorance (*agnoon*). This distinction will also allow Aristotle to reduce an apparently involuntary act into a voluntary act, and at the very least to make a distinction within mixed acts between voluntary and involuntary elements.

Responsibility (hence identified with the voluntary) is thus distinguished from irresponsibility (henceforth identified with the involuntary), and clearly given priority in the *Nicomachean Ethics,* as Aristotle seeks to establish responsibility as a sphere of control. However, as I indicated above, one may question such delimitations, and question the identification of responsibility with voluntariness as well as the strict separation between voluntariness and involuntariness, between responsibility and irresponsibility. Being-responsible could be traced back to irresponsible or a-responsible foundations, and a certain undecidability between responsibility and irresponsibility may be discerned. Otherwise, why would Aristotle take such pains in trying to distinguish and separate them? Doesn't this very effort betray and reveal an undecidability between responsibility and irresponsibility?

In addition to his work of separation, isolation, or purification, Aristotle thus grants a privilege to the voluntary, confirming the performative character of his analysis that we noted above. In several key moments in the analysis, instances of the involuntary are reduced to the voluntary: The drunk may be irresponsible during his actions, but he *chose* to drink. One may act *in* ignorance (as he was drunk), but not *by* or *through* ignorance (as he chose to drink). Some actions seem to be mixed, almost undecidably voluntary and involuntary, as for instance in the case of "actions done because of fear of greater evils" (1110a 5), since in this case I do something *both* voluntarily and involuntarily. Yet Aristotle still concludes that, although these sorts of actions may be mixed, nonetheless, in the final analysis, because they are "choiceworthy" (*hairetos*), "they are more like voluntary actions" (1110a 13–14). Whenever Aristotle raises the possibility—for him, the threat—of the involuntary, his analysis always leans on the side of the voluntary. The bar is always raised higher for an act to finally qualify as involuntary. Such an act would have to have a cause *completely external* to the agent (hence the patient) and to which "the agent contributes *nothing*" (1110b 2–3; my emphasis). The goal is clearly to delineate the contours, apart from both necessity and fortune, of an area that would be under one's control, of what would be *up to us.* It is in that context that responsibility is defined and its senses determined. It is also not insignificant that Aristotle begins his treatise on responsibility with the general problematic of blame-assigning and punishment. From the very inception of the history of the concept of responsibility, the association between responsibility and punishment has been established, a fact which did not escape Nietzsche in his genealogical deconstruction of responsibility.

Two key motifs govern Aristotle's analysis of responsibility in book III of the *Nicomachean Ethics,* namely the principle of *agency,* which Aristotle determines as that principle which lies "within us," and the ground provided by *rationality,* that is to say, the intelligibility of the act. The human being is defined as a rational agent, acting voluntarily, and thereby as being responsible as the cause of his or her act.[7] The Aristotelian account of responsibility delineates a space of mastery over the event. This is Aristotle's question: What can be within our power? What is *up to us*? Returning to Aristotle's analysis of responsibility and voluntary action in book III of the *Nicomachean Ethics,* one can distinguish two main parts in the text: There is first a discussion of the voluntary and involuntary, leading to a definition of these terms (1109b–1111b); and what follows is a definition of responsible decision (1111b–1114b). As we observed, Aristotle circumscribes his analysis of responsibility under the aegis of the voluntary. Aristotle states that we are responsible when we do what we do in a voluntary way, and that we are irresponsible when we do what we do in an involuntary way. Thus everything in this discussion of responsibility hinges on a definition of the voluntary. It is thus important to dwell on it at the outset of our work. This will require the concept of agency: There is no possibility of voluntariness if *I* do not will my actions—an agent is required. Responsibility is what is up to *us*.

Aristotle begins by indicating that virtues pertain to the voluntary—in book I of the *Nicomachean Ethics,* he posited that *eudaimonia* is not a result of fortune but is instead up to us (1099b 25–28)—and that a study of ethics must engage in a discussion of the voluntary and involuntary. Further, the voluntary is important to define in terms of the blame or praise that a person can receive. The voluntary indeed circumscribes the sphere of the agent insofar as it can be liable to an accusation in the broad sense of the term, i.e., receiving blame or praise. A discussion of the voluntary would thus also matter to the legislator, for the sake of assigning punishments or rewards, as well as for the educator, for the sake of the application of "corrective treatments." The discussion of responsibility is thus, from the outset, situated within a problematic of punishment which is itself made possible by the ascribing of an act to an accountable agent—namely, when the act "lies in the agent's power to perform" (1135a 23). This is why, when Aristotle situates responsibility within a discussion of punishment (1113b 15–1114a 31), the question followed is: Under what conditions can punishment be applied? The answer is—a determination that will prove determinative for our entire tradition—when the agent has acted voluntarily, and with knowledge of the particulars. Aristotle then proceeds, beginning by an analysis of what constitutes an involuntary act, as it were preparing a definition of the voluntary through a prior analysis of the involuntary. Assuredly this is done in order to contrast the two, as if to approach responsibility from what it is not; it remains significant that the access to the problematic of responsibility takes place by way of a passage through the involuntary, that is, through a form of irresponsibility. Aristotle provides two criteria for an involuntary act: Such acts happen either by force, or through ignorance.

FORCE

What does it mean for something to occur "by force" (*biai*)? Aristotle defines it as such: "What is forced has an *external principle,* the sort of principle in which the agent, or [rather] the victim [*ho paschōn,* the one affected], *contributes nothing*" (1110a 2–3; my emphasis). Thus "by force" means that which occurs outside one's agency, when "for instance, a wind or people who have him in their control were to carry him off" (1110a 3–4).[8] The involuntary would then imply the eclipse of agency ("external principle") along with its will or intention ("contributes nothing"), already indicating that responsibility will be understood both in terms of agency and voluntariness. Agency (as willful and cognizant) will be the principle of responsibility.

With respect to being forced, Aristotle raises the following question: What of those acts which I am "forced" to do for fear of a worse outcome, for instance, when I am threatened or blackmailed, as by a tyrant who would hold my family hostage? Am I not acting, then, involuntarily, since I am being forced? Aristotle seems to hesitate here: "These cases raise a dispute about whether they are voluntary or involuntary" (1110a 7–8). He then provides another example, when for instance someone throws cargo overboard a ship during a storm. No one would voluntarily throw away precious property—and hence this act is involuntary in that respect, "for no one willingly throws cargo overboard, without qualification" (1110a 10–11)—but in order to save one's life, one would be insane not to. Thus the act is voluntary when it was done, as "anyone with any sense throws it overboard to save himself and the others" (1110a 11–12). In this case as well, the act could appear as mixed. However, Aristotle's answer is clear: Although these acts can be called "mixed" (acting under duress), they are ultimately voluntary, *because they involve a choice*. Even though in normal conditions such acts would not be willed, "at the time they are done they are choiceworthy (*hairetos*)" (1110a 13). They may be involuntary "in their own right" (1110a 12), but they have been chosen and, most importantly, "their principle is in the agent" (1110a 17). Therefore these "are more like voluntary actions" (1110b 13–14).

Thus, to act voluntarily means that the principle of the action is *within* the agent: "in such actions he has within him (*en autô*) the principle of moving the limbs that are the instruments [of the action]; but if the principle of the actions is in him, it is also up to him to do them or not to do them" (1110a 17–18). The agent is determined as the principle (*arkhē*) of the action, and the action depends upon the agent as resting within that agent itself (*autō*). The opposition thus passes between what is internal to the agent and what is radically and completely outside or external to that agent. "What sorts of things, then, should we say are forced? Perhaps we should say that something is forced without qualification whenever its cause is external and the agent contributes nothing" (1110b).

One notes here Aristotle's "all or nothing" position, its maximalist strategy: An act is done either through an outside force (an external cause in which the agent, or rather the victim, contributes *nothing*) or it is done voluntarily. When some actions appear as mixed they ultimately are not, but are in fact voluntary. For an act to qualify as involuntary, it would have to come about entirely by external force, where the force implies a radical absence of the willful agent. The force is when the agent contributes *nothing*, when the event comes from without, entirely from the outside. Aristotle thus dismisses the idea that one would be forced by the pleasure that one would feel in an action, as if "pleasant things and fine things force us, on the ground that they are outside us and compel us" (1110b 10–11). This is an absurd proposition, for it would imply that everything must be forced, "since everyone in every action aims at something fine or pleasant" (1110b

11–13). It is absurd to "ascribe responsibility to external causes" (1110b 14–15), and not to oneself as "easily snared by such things" (1110b 15). The voluntary comes entirely from *within* the agent. Agency is here practically identified with the voluntary, in the sense that the seat of the voluntary is agency as principle of the act. Either the cause lies within (voluntary), or it lies without (and the act is involuntary). What belongs to force—and thereby qualifies as involuntary or irresponsible—is that action where the principle or cause of which lies outside the agent. "What is forced, then, would seem to be what has its principle outside the person forced, who contributes nothing" (1110b 1–3). Understood in contrast to agency, force would draw the contours of what will qualify as a responsible act, as that which lies *within* the agent: The agent, as an inner principle of action (efficient cause), comes to the fore as the principle of responsibility, the notion of force ensuring the strict distinction between the inside and the outside, between agency and lack thereof, between the voluntary and the involuntary.

IGNORANCE

Aristotle adds to this first condition, when the principle of the act is within the agent, another one: An act is considered to be involuntary if it is done in ignorance (*agnoon*). Or rather, *by* ignorance (*di'agnoian*), as Aristotle makes a key distinction between acting *in* ignorance and acting *by* ignorance, which will have the result of reinforcing the voluntary, and *increasing our agency*. The distinction allows Aristotle to increase the sphere of the voluntary and relativize instances of involuntariness insofar as they can be traced to an earlier voluntary act, as in the example of inebriation, for instance: A drunk may act in ignorance since his judgment is severely impaired. Yet for Aristotle, he chose to drink, and thus he may be acting in ignorance but he is not acting *by* ignorance. The cause of the action is not ignorance, but drunkenness or anger. The fact that his judgment is impaired and that he is mistaken in his thinking and actions does not render his action involuntary. The agent is acting *in ignorance* (he is drunk) while acting *by virtue* of his character. Thus, "action caused by ignorance would seem to be different from action done in ignorance" (1110b 25–26). A state of irresponsibility, here, refers back to a prior and more determinative state of responsibility: The relinquishing of responsibility is somehow performed—and thus annulled—by the agent. It is as if one decided to no longer decide, decided to give up the power of decision. Is one still responsible when one decides to give up one's responsibility? Aristotle seems to think so, and will insist that the voluntary prevails through such an act.

One can see here how Aristotle seeks to establish an area of responsibility for human beings, which he understands as an area under our control and as distinct from chance or fortune, and from a strict determinism of nature, which would lead to fatalism. Hence the emphasis on practical knowledge or *phronēsis*—on knowing the particular circumstances of the act—amounts to an attempt to circumscribe the situation and the context of the act. Aristotle states that an agent is irresponsible if he is ignorant of "the particulars which the action consists in and is concerned with" (1111a 1–2), that an agent "acts involuntarily if he is ignorant of one these particulars" (1111a 2–3). These particulars are "who is doing it, what he is doing, about what or to what he is doing it; sometimes also what he is doing it with—with that instrument, for example; for what result, for example, safety; in what way, for example, gently or hard" (1111a 4–7). Thus, ignorance of these constitutes involuntariness: "Since an agent may be ignorant of any of these particular constituents of his action, someone who was ignorant of one of these seems to have acted unwillingly" (1111a 17–19). The four causes are mobilized here (formal, efficient, final, and material), while Aristotle singles out the efficient cause: "Now certainly someone could not be ignorant of all of these unless he were mad. Nor clearly, could he be ignorant of who is doing it, since he could hardly be ignorant of himself" (1111a 8–10). A few lines below, he takes up the formal and final causes (involuntariness as ignorance of *what* one is doing, and the *result* of what one is doing): "Since an agent may be ignorant of any of these particular constituents of his action, someone who was ignorant of one of these seems to have acted unwillingly, especially if he was ignorant of the most important; these seem to be what is doing, and the result for which he does it" (1111a 17–18). These particulars, as it were, structure the act and its context, its situation. Knowing, understanding these particulars provides a control over that situation, therein structured causally. The voluntary—the understanding of the particulars and the principle of the act located in the agent—contributes to the constitution of responsibility as willful rational decision: "Since involuntary action is either forced or caused by ignorance, voluntary action seems to be what has its principle (*arkhē*) in the agent himself, knowing the particulars that constitute the action" (1111a 22–24).

At the same time, this horizon of intelligibility cannot saturate the field of action, for otherwise there would no longer be a possibility of *choice*. For there to be a choice, one must decide within a certain *indeterminacy* and ultimately it is the practical virtue of *phronēsis* that will be determinative.[9] This is why the discussion continues by focusing on the theme of decision. "Now that we have defined the voluntary and the involuntary, the next task is to discuss decision" (1111b).

Decision, the Possible, and the Impossible

However, the voluntary has been defined mostly in negative terms, as acting without being forced, and the principle of action as being within us remains insufficiently determined. Furthermore, for Aristotle, the voluntary cannot suffice in and of itself to define responsibility, since he observes that both children and animals also "share in voluntary action" (1111b 8–9). Some rational agency—some sense, some rational deliberation—must also be present in responsible action. As Aristotle states in book VI of the *Nicomachean Ethics*, "good deliberation requires reason" (1142b 15), and he also claimed in the *Eudemian Ethics* that "the voluntary consists in action accompanied by thought of some kind" (1224a). Rational agency must therefore be included in the analysis of responsibility, and voluntary action must involve a rational decision (*prohairesis,* literally "a choosing before"), which is itself prepared by a deliberation (*bouleusis,* a calculation of the necessary means to reach a desired end). Aristotle writes that "perhaps what is decided is what has been previously deliberated" (1112a 16–17). The voluntary is not necessarily rational and deliberative, whereas "decision involves reason and thought" (1112a 17). This is why Aristotle clarifies that "now that we have defined the voluntary and the involuntary, the next task is to discuss decision; for decision seems to be most proper to virtue" (1111b 5–6).[10] Aristotle then proceeds to distinguish decision from appetite and spirit, and the criterion used is that of *rationality,* "For decision is not shared with nonrational animals" (1111b 13–14). Decision is not tantamount to appetite, nor is it a momentary impulse; decision is also not a wish (*boulēsis*).

For Aristotle, a wish is about ends, and these do not need to be attainable; I can wish for the unattainable, for the impossible—such as immortality, for instance. I can also wish for possible things, whether these depend on agency or not. Decision, in contrast, is not about ends but about means—not about the impossible, but about what is possible. Aristotle insists that, "we do not decide on impossible things—anyone claiming to decide on them would seem a fool; but we do wish for impossible things" (1111b 21–22).[11] Aristotle thus distinguishes decision from wish in terms of the distinction between the possible and the impossible. Why? *Because it increases our agency.* If we pursue things we can attain, our agency is possibilized, whereas that agency in turn would be diminished it if we pursued impossible ends. The possible as a domain of efficiency increases our agency, while the impossible cancels it. Further on (1112b 25), returning to the question of the possible and the impossible, Aristotle thus emphasizes that when we encounter an "impossible step," such as when we need money but are unable to raise some, "we desist." This is why Aristotle continues by claiming that what we decide on has nothing in common with wishing for some results, and that "what we decide on is never anything of that sort, but what we think would come about *through our own agency*" (1111b 25–27; my emphasis). Decision thus concerns an area of efficiency, an area where we can "make a difference"; in a word, it concerns an area that is *within our power and up to us,* Aristotle adding significantly that "in general the things we decide on would seem to be things that are up to us" (1111b 30–31). Distinguishing wish from decision, the possible from the impossible, will serve to secure such an area of power and control. The impossible is thus excluded from the area of decision and its possibility. Decision pertains to the possible only: "if the action appears possible, we undertake it." How does Aristotle define the possible? *In terms of the power of our agency:* "What is possible is what we could achieve through our agency" (1112b 27–28). Furthermore, "through our agency" means—from a principle of action that is within us, i.e., the voluntary. This is almost tautological or circular:

a) We deliberate about the possible
b) The possible is what we can do.
c) We deliberate about what we can do.

The power of the voluntary agent is simply posited as the possibility of its efficiency, a pure, performative self-positing of the "I can."

Aristotle further distinguishes decision from opinion or belief. Beliefs are indifferent, since "belief seems to be about everything, no less about things that are eternal and things that are impossible [for us] than about things that are up to us" (1112a 32–34), whereas decision is about what matters to us, and in decision what matters is what I decide on. Whereas beliefs are about things that can be either true or false, here it is a matter of practical ethics, where the issue is not about truth and error, but about right and wrong, good and bad. This gap between the theoretical and the practical explains why "Decision is praised more for deciding on what is right, whereas belief is praised for believing rightly" (1112a 6–7). It also accounts for the fact that those who make the best decisions do not always seem to be the same as those with the best beliefs. Decision is thus neither simply the voluntary (although it includes it), nor wish, belief, spirit, or appetite. "Then what, or what sort of thing, is decision, since it is none of the things mentioned?" (1112a 4–5). Since decision involves reason, it might require some type of prior deliberation as opposed to some spur of the moment impulse or appetite (see 1111b 9–10). Aristotle then pursues his analysis on the theme of deliberation (*bouleusis*), which will concern the scope of responsible decision *per se*.

The Scope of Responsibility

Aristotle begins this analysis of the scope of deliberation by asking, what do we deliberate about? "Do we deliberate about everything, and is everything open to deliberation? Or is there no deliberation about some things?" (1112a 19–20). Beginning—indeed centering—his discussion with such a question betrays that his underlying concern in the question of decision is the following: What is within our power, what is the sphere of our agency? The fundamental question, here as elsewhere, remains: What is *up to us*? What is the proper sphere of human agency? Further, it is clear that Aristotle is not content with simply describing a phenomenon, but is actually establishing such a sphere, securing it by distinguishing it from those domains wherein precisely we have no agency—nature, necessity, and fortune. After recalling from the outset that deliberation involves reason and sense, and thus belongs to a rational agent—"By 'open to deliberation,' presumably, we should mean that someone with some sense, not some fool or madman, might deliberate about it" (1112a 20–22)—Aristotle undertakes to delineate the proper scope or sphere of deliberation, typically beginning with what one does *not* deliberate about, before proceeding to more positive determinations.

First, we do not deliberate about the "eternal," the permanent, or mathematical truths. One does not deliberate about the eternal order of things, or the "incommensurability of the sides and the diagonal" (1112a 22–23). Nor do we deliberate about change, or more precisely that kind of change that follows an order of necessity—things which, although in movement, "always come about the same way" (1112a 24–25). One does not deliberate about natural determinism (things that move "by nature"), or about the laws of nature (causal necessity) as "it is impossible to deliberate about what exists by necessity" (1139a 36). Whether they follow from necessity or by nature, the motion of stars and planets is not *up to us:* They are outside our reach, outside human affairs.[12]

Other natural events which happen, *not* through the causal necessity (invariability) of nature, but "in different ways at different times" (1112a 26–27), are also not up to us: Aristotle gives the example of droughts and rains. Similarly, things that happen from fortune—the finding of a treasure, for instance—are not *up to us,* and we therefore do not deliberate about such things. Why? The answer could not be clearer: "For none of these results could be achieved through our agency" (1112a 30). Nature does not depend on our agency, and fortune is foreign to our will. We thus deliberate neither about things that follow natural determinism nor about things that happen by chance, *because they do not involve our agency.*

What then does belong to us, to our agency? Aristotle's answer is: "We deliberate about what is up to us, that is to say, about the actions we can do" (1112a 31–32). One notes again the tautological aspect of this formulation. This can be recognized as the sheer self-positing of a power, tautological because it only refers to itself, a sort of self-affection or self-position of one's power and capacity: We can do what we can do, we can because we can! One also notes how the sphere of deliberation is identified with the sphere of our control, of our power. Responsibility, the sphere of our responsibility, is identical to the sphere of our power. We recall how Aristotle had distinguished the possible from the impossible, and made the possible the area of our agency and power. Aristotle states that this area of human capacity to act is the only area left besides nature and fortune. Besides the order of the universe, besides nature and necessity, besides fortune, there is also human agency, another kind of causality "left [besides the previous cases]. For causes seem to include nature, necessity, and fortune, but besides them mind and everything [operating] through human agency" (1112a 32–34). Human agency is a causal principle, an efficient causality; *prohairesis* is understood by Aristotle as the efficient, and not the final cause of action (1139a 31–33). Things can thus happen in three ways—through nature, through fortune, and through us. Only this last realm will be the province of responsibility. Aristotle nevertheless clarifies that human beings do not deliberate about *all* human affairs, but only about "the actions that they themselves can do" (1112a 33–34). Every group has its own province of action. The focus is efficiency of action, what we can affect: "No Spartan," he argues, "deliberates about how the Scythians might have the best political system" (1112a 28–30).[13] What is strictly *up to us* is the measure of the discussion of responsibility. However, even though we cannot intervene in the affairs of all human beings, Aristotle specifies that it is always possible, "when we distrust our own ability to discern [the right answer]," to "enlist partners in deliberation on large issues" (1112b 10–12), thereby allowing for an extension of our responsibility to a broader context.

Furthermore, one does not deliberate about exact sciences, or a body of knowledge or rules, such as the rules of language (grammar or syntax), but only about how to apply rules and laws to particulars. This occurs in the case of medicine for instance, where it is a matter, not only of a knowledge of rules and laws, but also of a *judgment* regarding which case falls (or does not fall) under which rule. Here, two aspects are in play. First that "we deliberate about what results through our agency" (1112b 3–4), but also that a certain *indeterminacy* in the area of decision is present, as Aristotle clearly states that "what is deliberated about is not yet determined" (1142b 14). Indeed, Aristotle specifies that what results through our agency happens "in different ways on different occasions" (1112b 4). It is as if the *less* exact the field of application, the more relevant and appropriate deliberation becomes. This is why we deliberate about navigation more than about gymnastics: "to the extent that it is less exactly worked out" (1112b 6–7). Indeterminacy appears here as the condition for responsible deliberation and decision. Aristotle thus also claims that we deliberate more about beliefs than about sciences—though he has just asserted that decision is not about belief (1112a 6–7)!—because "we are more in doubt about them" (1112b 7–8). Decision is always situational, attuned to the particulars, and located in the sphere of the inexact and the undetermined. We intervene through our agency, and on a particular situation and its *kairos*. At the beginning of book II of the *Nicomachean Ethics,* Aristotle stressed that virtuous actions "should accord with the subject matter; and questions about actions and expediency, like questions about health, have no fixed answers" (1104a 2–4). Instead, "the agents themselves must consider in each case what the opportune action is, as doctors and navigators do" (1104a 9–10). The space and condition of deliberation is thus inexactitude, and in a sense, the less exact or more doubtful, the more room there is for judging: "We deliberate about navigation more than about gymnastics, *to the extent that it is less exactly worked out,* and similarly with other [crafts]" (1112b; my emphasis). Another condition of decision lies in the fact that the end or result of the act is not given *a priori* and remains unclear, as "deliberation concerns what is usually [one way rather than another], where the outcome is unclear and the right way to act is undefined" (1112b 9–11).

What is *up to us* is thus not only defined by the voluntary, by the circumscription of the area of the possible; what is *up to us* is also, and paradoxically, what pertains to an area that is marked by uncertainty and indefiniteness, an area that escapes theoretical knowledge in order to present itself to a practical judgment. *In decision, the right way to act is not given, not known, undefined.* Responsible decision takes place independently from knowledge, in an act of freedom.[14] This is why, as we just saw, for Aristotle, the human domain is that of indeterminacy, open to a *phronēsis.* Interestingly, Aristotle grounds collective deliberation on this very indeterminacy: It is out of this *lack* of a given right course of action that others are needed, since "we enlist partners in deliberation on large issues when we distrust our own ability to discern [the right answer]" (1112b 11–12). Neither natural necessity (no need to deliberate there), nor chance or fortune (no room for a voluntary action there as a causal action), but indeterminacy or unpredictability *insofar as it allows for a willful intervention in our part* calls for deliberation with others.

The paradox reads as follows: It is to the extent that the outcome is not yet given and is unpredictable, and thus is in a sense *not* up to us, that it becomes *up to us* to decide. It is to the extent of its very unpredictability or incalculability that I can attempt a mastery of what I decide on. The situation is clearly aporetic: How can I master the unpredictable? It is impossible, and yet this is what decision must decide on, what Aristotle considers to be "up to us." This very indeterminacy is what makes action and decision possible. This is why Aristotle concludes this line of analysis by recalling that one does not deliberate about ends (objects of wish), as we recall, but rather about the *means* to attain such ends or *how to decide* without rules that one could mechanically follow. If it "appears that any of several [possible] means will reach it, we examine which of them will reach it most easily and most finely" (1112b 17–18). This examination is a kind of inquiry, but not the same as a theoretical inquiry, such as that which is found in mathematics: ("apparently, all deliberation is inquiry, though not all inquiry—in mathematics for instance—is deliberation" (1112b 22–24). It is instead a deliberation led by the practical judgment of a *phronēsis*. Responsibility here names the determination of the *how* of the act, based on the voluntary principle of an agent and situated in an area of indeterminacy and incalculability.

One can identify all the elements constitutive of a responsible decision: First, the act must be voluntary, according to Aristotle's account of it. Second, the principle of action is the agent, the human being: "As we have said, then, a human being would seem to be a principle of action" (1112b 33–34), for "each of us stops inquiring how to act as soon as he traces the principle to himself, and within himself to the guiding part; for this is the part that decides" (1112b 6–8). Third, deliberation is about the possible and the determination of the possible: "Deliberation is about the actions we can do." Fourth, deliberation is about the means to attain ends, and not about the ends themselves; ("we deliberate about things that promote an end, not about the end" (1113a 1–2). It is to that extent that deliberation limits itself to the possible—by focusing on the *means* to attain some end. Fifth, deliberation is in a sense decision itself, or the preparation of decision, for "what we deliberate about is the same as what we decide to do, except that by the time we decide to do it, it is definite; for what we decide to do is what we have judged [to be right] as a result of deliberation" (1113a 3–5). In the end, what we decide upon is the actions ("among those [which are] up to us") that we are capable of deliberating about. Ultimately, responsibility will be identified with power, as we decide upon actions that are *up to us,* insofar as we are the principles of such acts.

Responsibility as Power

At this stage, Aristotle is able to present a fuller account of responsible action, of responsibility. Let us try to identify and reconstruct its conceptual apparatus and its guiding principle. Such a guiding principle is of course the notion of voluntary agency, what is *up to us,* as Aristotle stresses once more, by stating that the human being "is a principle, begetting actions as he begets children" (1113b 18–20), recalling what was posited earlier (1112b 33–34), namely that "a human being would seem to be a principle of action." Begetting actions as we beget children—a metaphor of parenthood which, as we have seen, was taken up explicitly by Hans Jonas in his account of responsibility in *The Imperative of Responsibility.* As we saw in the introduction, for Jonas we are responsible for the future, that is, for the future world of our *children.* The parent-child relation is the archetype of all responsibility of humans toward other humans, toward the world, and toward the future of the earth. However, a major contrast appears here, since the responsibility for the future in Jonas is based on a fear for the vulnerability of the earth, whereas Aristotle evokes paternity in terms of origination and power. Jonas clarifies that he is not speaking of a "duty arising *from* procreation" (accountability based on authorship) but of a "duty *to* such procreation" (IR, 40). That duty for future mankind, which "charges us, in the first place, with ensuring that there *be* a future mankind" (IR, 40), is based on the fragility of life. Human existence, Jonas writes, "has the precarious, vulnerable, and revocable character, the peculiar mode of transience, of all *life,* which makes it alone a proper object of 'caring'" (IR, 98). Responsibility is based on a fear for the vulnerable, and not on the power of an author, which is the horizon of Aristotle's account.

Aristotle attempts to extend the scope of responsibility as power: We are not only responsible for our actions, we are also responsible for our character and for our states, which are also *up to us.* It can be said that one is essentially responsible for being a good or a bad person (and not only for one's actions), and Aristotle stresses that "if doing, and likewise not doing, fine or shameful actions is *up to us,* and if, as we saw, [doing or not doing them] is [what it is] to be a good or bad person, being decent or base is *up to us*" (1113b 11–14). Further, and most importantly, it can be said that one is responsible for oneself, as a person, and for the end he or she chooses. Each person, Aristotle states, "is in some way responsible (*aitios*) for his own state [of character], he is also himself in some way responsible for how [the end] appears" (1114b 2–3). In this sense, responsibility is not only about "fathering" one's actions, but also about *father-*

ing oneself, and therefore a self-responsibility. This self-responsibility becomes the basis for responsible acting and the standard for responsibility itself. This sense announces what will become in the modern tradition an ideal of self-governance and self-ownership, which we will examine more closely with Kant.

This concept of responsibility—the act has its cause and principle in us, and is *up to us* and voluntary—becomes the ground for the idea of imputability, ascription of an act to an agent, who can then be subject to punishment or reward, and thus held accountable. The act can be imputed back to the agent only if the agent has acted in a voluntary way, that is, neither forced nor by ignorance. Legislators, Aristotle writes, "impose corrective treatments and penalties on anyone who does vicious actions, unless his action is forced or is caused by ignorance that he is not responsible for; and they will honor anyone who does fine actions" (1113b 24–26). Punishment and reward are said to make little sense except in order to "encourage" or "restrain," and only willful agents can be encouraged or restrained: "No one encourages us to do anything that is not up to us and voluntary" (1113b 28), writes Aristotle, consecrating the primacy he grants to the voluntary.

Being Responsible for Irresponsibility

Aristotle seems to attempt to further increase the province of our responsibility, as he then advances the notion that one is in a sense responsible for one's irresponsibility, which would be a deficient mode (but a mode nonetheless) of responsibility. This can be seen in his distinction between acting in ignorance and acting by or though ignorance. He begins by noting that legislators do punish persons who act in ignorance, that "they impose corrective treatments for the ignorance itself" (1113b 30–31). Is that in any way a departure from his own account of responsibility as voluntary, neither forced nor done by ignorance? This is not the case, and for two reasons. First, we recall that he made a distinction between acting in ignorance and acting by ignorance. Second, and precisely relying on that very distinction, he claims that the agent seems to be in fact "responsible for the ignorance" (1113b 31). One is thus responsible for one's irresponsibility. Why? Because, he argues, it is *up to us* not to be ignorant: "they impose [corrective treatments] in other cases likewise for any other ignorance that seems to be caused by the agent's inattention; they assume it is up to him not to be ignorant" (1114a 1–3).

One may be in ignorance of some law—however, "he is required to know," and this knowledge is not difficult to obtain. Furthermore the drunk, Aristotle continues, is punished twice, for he is doubly guilty: First, because, as "the principle is in him, he chose to drink; and second, for the harm done while he was drunk." In any case, his being drunk "causes his ignorance" (1113b 32–34), and his inebriation is caused by his decision to drink. Thus, not only is the drunk not irresponsible, he is in fact doubly responsible. One is responsible *for being* irresponsible; one has chosen to put oneself in a state in which one is no longer able to choose. However, not being able to choose refers to an earlier and more primordial capacity to choose—namely, the voluntary. Aristotle thus reduces irresponsibility to responsibility.

Still, with respect to the inattention of the agent, one might argue for an irresponsibility that could not be derived from a more primordial responsibility. There again, Aristotle takes sides, as it were, favoring the voluntary and relativizing the involuntary: "But presumably he is the sort of person who is inattentive. Still, he is himself responsible for becoming this sort of person, because he has lived carelessly" (1114a 3–4). One notes here again the reference to character, which as we just saw is *up to us* for Aristotle. One is responsible for irresponsible acts because one is responsible for the kind of person one is, and has *let* oneself become someone of bad character. Ultimately, irresponsible acts all seem to point to an earlier voluntary decision. "Similarly, an individual is responsible for being unjust, because he has cheated, and for being intemperate, because he has passed his time in drinking and the like: for each type of activity produces the corresponding sort of person" (1114a 5–8).

Drawing on an interesting distinction between actions and states— potentially an objection—Aristotle states that actions and states are not voluntary in the same way. We are in control of our actions, he maintains, "from the beginning to the end" (1114b 31); whereas in the case of our states, we are indeed in control of its beginnings but not of its end, for we cannot predict what the "cumulative effect of particular actions will be" (1115a 2–3). Thus for the case of the state of our body, our health: Surely one does not get sick by will, nor does one actually recover one's health willfully. Nonetheless, insists Aristotle, the sick person "is sick willingly, by living incontinently and disobeying the doctors . . . At that time, then, he was free not to get sick" (1114a 16–17). Once he does get sick, after years of smoking for instance, he cannot make himself "unsick," just "as it was up to someone to throw a stone, since the principle was up to him, though he can no longer take it back once he has thrown it" (1114a 18–19). The state of our health and our "bodily vices" are *up to us* in that sense, and our body is thus also in some sense "up to us," subject to our will.

In the end, in Aristotle's construction of the concept of responsibility, it has been a matter of securing the domain of what is *up to us* and voluntary, which is "in us." This domain would constitute the sphere of responsibility as the accountability of the agent, a sense that will prove dominant in the history of philosophy. However, the reference to what is "up to us," as that which is "in us," remains obscure: What does the "in us" actually refer to? It is the unsupported cornerstone that supports everything else, and yet its phenomenological content remains dubious. Was it sufficiently determined? It will be a matter of establishing it more securely and fully. One sees in Kant the attempt to elaborate on the notion of agency as the seat of the voluntary. He will describe it in terms of the capacity to begin absolutely out of transcendental freedom, i.e., in terms of an absolute spontaneity. This will lead to an account of responsibility based upon the supposition of the subject, the position of a *subjectum*. Responsibility will then be conceived as imputability or accountability of such subject.

TWO

Kant: Responsibility as Spontaneity of the Subject

Personhood and Responsibility

Kant situates responsibility within the sphere of rational agency, within the horizon of subjectivity. A certain conception of freedom (as *causa sui,* self-determination, and autonomy) makes possible such responsibility, and Kant's philosophical reflection on responsibility takes place within the horizon of the freedom of the subject, further specifying what Aristotle had metaphorically designated as the "paternity" of the act. Here agency, the principle of the act, is further determined in terms of freedom and spontaneity, freedom being defined as "absolute spontaneity," a capacity by the subject to begin absolutely a new series of causes. For it is indeed the subject—the *subjectum,* the spontaneous I—that is the causal foundation and absolute beginning (transcendental freedom) here, and which Kant designates in the *Critique of Pure Reason* as the locus and basis of responsibility as *imputability* (*Imputabilität*). Responsibility is understood in terms of the *subjectum* that lies at the basis of the act.

Kant determines responsibility as imputation, based on the freedom of the subject, and claims further that responsibility as *self-responsibility* defines personhood as such. Ultimately, Kant privileges the notion of personhood within his interpretation of subjectivity, personhood actually being defined by responsibility and self-responsibility. The Kantian determination of the essence of subjectivity is indeed threefold, corresponding to the three determinations of the I that he retains: There is the I in the sense of the determining I (the "I think" or transcendental apperception);

the I in the sense of the determinable I (the empirical I, the I as object); and the I in the sense of the moral person (the end in itself). But this threefold determination of subjectivity in Kant can in turn be divided into two fundamental senses: On the one hand, there is the broad formal concept of the ego in general, in the sense of *self-consciousness,* whether as transcendental consciousness (the I-think) or as empirical consciousness (the I-object), that is, personality taken in the sense of *rationality;* on the other hand, there is the strict and proper concept of personality, namely, that of the moral person who is defined by *responsibility.*

Kant follows the traditional definition of man as rational animal. However, the union of animality and rationality does not suffice to fully define the essence of personality or personhood, through which man is not only considered as a particular entity among others, but as capable of freedom and self-responsibility. Strictly speaking, personality applies to the subject *only* as it is recognized as capable of responsibility or imputation, that is, responsible for itself. The essence of the person is self-responsibility. The practical subject enjoys a certain preeminence over the theoretical subject, because unlike the theoretical determination of the I, deemed "impossible" by Kant in the Paralogisms, the *practical* determination of the subject alone is capable of establishing a positive account of personhood, as end in itself and self-responsibility. For instance, the person's being an "end in itself" (*Selbstzweckhaftigkeit*), such as it is displayed in the Kantian theory of the moral person, could be posited as one of the most fundamental determinations of the human being, as Kant situates the ultimate ends of man in morality. In fact, the characterization of the subject as *moral,* with its distinction between *persons* and *things,* is determinative for the notion of responsibility, or more precisely, of imputation: As person, the human being is understood as a being who is capable of imputation, as a being who is responsible for itself.

The Foundation of Responsibility in Transcendental Freedom

Responsibility indeed constitutes for Kant the differentiating feature between persons and things, the defining characteristic of personhood. In contrast to things, Kant asserts, a person is a subject that is capable of imputation. In his *Doctrine of Right,* Kant explains that a person is "a subject whose actions can be *imputed* to him," whereas a "thing is that to which nothing can be imputed."[1] This capacity to be a subject as ground of imputation is owed to the faculty of freedom, taken as "transcendental freedom," which determines the possibility of responsibility and moral responsibility. In the *Critique of Practical Reason,* Kant insists that freedom is the ground for all subsequent responsibility, writing that "the question of freedom . . . lies at the foundation of all moral laws and accountability to them," which means that "without transcendental freedom in its proper meaning, which is alone *a priori* practical, no moral law and no accountability to it are possible."[2] Responsibility rests upon the subjectivity of the free subject. Kant states that an

> action is called a *deed* insofar as it comes under obligatory laws and hence insofar as the subject, in doing it, is considered in terms of the freedom of his choice. By such an action the agent is regarded as the *author* (*Urheber*) of its effect (*Wirkung*), and this, together with the action itself, can be *imputed* to him, if one is previously acquainted with the laws by virtue of which an obligation rests on these.[3]

As we will see, transcendental freedom is the foundation of responsibility.

One finds in Kant a crucial development on transcendental freedom, and on the imputation of the acting subject, in the *Critique of Pure Reason,* in the Third Antinomy in the Transcendental Dialectic ("Third Conflict of the Transcendental Ideas"), also known as the "cosmological" antinomy. The imputability of the subject is indeed both a moral/juridical notion and a cosmological/metaphysical one, and both aspects involve a fundamental philosophical interpretation of subjectivity, which is approached here as transcendental freedom. One cannot stress enough the importance of the role of transcendental freedom in this account of responsibility, as well as for the entire critical system, as Kant wrote famously that "The concept of freedom, in so far as its reality is proved by an apodictic law of practical reason, is the keystone of the whole architecture of the system of pure reason and even of speculative reason."[4] The discussion of freedom as a cosmological concept in the Third Antinomy is determinative for Kant's thinking on the imputation of the act and on responsibility. As Henry Allison notes, the third antinomy "is not only the locus of the major discussion of the problem of freedom in the *Critique of Pure Reason,* it is also the basis for Kant's subsequent treatments of the topic in his writings on moral philosophy."[5] It is therefore necessary to focus on this passage for an understanding of Kant's philosophy of responsibility and freedom. More precisely, it provides an account of imputability, which is grounded on the faculty of freedom. The basis for imputability is the spontaneity of the agent as subject, that is, a power "which could start to act from itself, without needing to be preceded by any other cause that in turn determines it to action according to the law of connection."[6]

Responsibility, taken here as imputation of the subject, is discussed within the context of an *antinomy* between freedom and natural determinism. Freedom, in turn, is discussed within a general discussion of causality.[7] Kant presents this aporetic structure through an opposition between a thesis and an antithesis. This is the thesis, which provides the basis for an imputability of the act: "Causality in accordance with laws of nature is not the only one from which all the appearances of the world can be derived. It is also necessary to assume another causality through freedom in order to explain them" (CPR, 484, A 444/B 472). Counter to this is the antithesis: "There is no freedom, but everything in the world happens solely in accordance with laws of nature" (CPR, 485, A 445/B 473). The burden of proof is on the possibility of admitting a free causality, as natural causality is assumed by Kant as a given and not in dispute. As Henry Allison rightly stresses in *Kant's Theory of Freedom,*

> Both parties to the Third Antinomy assume the validity within experience of "causality in accordance with laws of nature," that is, the mode of causality affirmed in the Second Analogy. In dispute is whether it is also necessary, or even permissible, to appeal to another conception of causality, transcendental freedom, defined as "the power [*Vermögen*] of beginning a state spontaneously [*von selbst*]" (A 533/B 561) in order to account adequately for any given appearance. (Op. cit., 14)

The question of freedom, of the responsibility that it grounds, is discussed in the Third Antinomy in the context of a cosmological discussion. It is as a notion both cosmological and ethical, as I alluded to above, that Kant approaches the question of imputability. "Cosmological," because the reflection takes place within the context of a discussion on causality in nature; and "ethical," because of the appearance in this causal network of a freedom of the human being—*another causality,* as Kant states—which will constitute the subject as subject of imputation. Another causality than that of nature would determine the free subject as a person, as personhood, as self-responsibility; a dignity is given to us in the cosmos by virtue of this free causality, or "causality by freedom."

There are thus two causalities for Kant, and only two—natural causality, and causality by freedom—because there are for him two fundamental categories of beings. On the one hand, there are things, which obey the universal determinism of nature; and on the other hand, there are persons, which follow a different kind of causality, a causality through freedom, or free causality. Kant explains in the *Critique of Pure Reason,* in "Resolution of the cosmological idea of the totality of the derivation of occurrences in the world from their causes": "In regard of what happens, one can think of causality in only two ways: either according to nature or from freedom" (CPR, 532, A 532/B 560). "In only two ways" (we recall that for Aristotle, things could happen in three ways: through necessity, through fortune or chance, and through our voluntary action) and only through two causalities: mechanistic causality (in Kant's sense of a mechanism of nature), and freedom. For Kant, there are thus only two ways for things to happen: either by necessity (they could not have happened any other way), following the universal laws of nature by which each thing is as it were "pushed" or determined by a preceding cause; or else from freedom, a kind of spontaneity or free surge that does not follow the universal laws of nature (at least, as we will see, not in causality, although it does follow it in time, following a distinction Kant makes which I will return to shortly) and is therefore not "pushed" by some preceding cause that would determine it. Kant presents it as a sort of originary capacity to begin, absolutely, "from itself," i.e., spontaneously: "By freedom in the cosmological sense, on the contrary [to the causality of nature], I understand the faculty of beginning a state *from itself* (*von selbst*), the causality of which does not in turn stand under another cause determining it in time in accordance with the law of nature" (CPR, 533, A 533/B 561). Let us clarify from the outset—both causalities are operative *in* the world, in a singular intertwining. Yet they are nonetheless said to be radically distinct as causalities, in a classic Kantian dualism.[8]

Our focus will bear mostly on so-called causality by or through freedom, as it is the one which is instrumental in Kant's definition of responsibility. Kant first and provisionally characterizes freedom negatively as a sort of "lawlessness" (CPR, 485, A 447/B 475), a rebelliousness to universal determinism, a leaping out of natural causality. Indeed, in one sense (the negative sense), freedom is independence *from* the laws of nature, a "liberation from coercion" or "from the guidance of all rules." Freedom in this context is identified with lawlessness. Kant for instance speaks of the "lawless faculty of freedom" (CPR, 489, A 451/B 479), and he goes so far as to claim that "transcendental freedom is contrary to the causal law" (CPR, 485, A 445/B 473). Freedom seems to be inimical to rules and laws as nature is structured according to them, to such an extent that Kant adds pleasantly, "if freedom were determined according to laws, it would not be freedom, but nothing other than nature" (CPR, 485, A 447/B 475). With transcendental freedom we are, as it were, leaping out of causality, that is to say, out *of nature,*[9] if not out of the world. Such a faculty of freedom is indeed "out of this world," since it cannot appear in the field of appearances as a spatio-temporal given and is for that very reason termed "transcendental." Kant explains that freedom taken in the cosmological sense—that is, as the faculty of beginning a state from itself—"is a pure transcendental idea, which, first, contains nothing borrowed from experience, and second, the object of which cannot be given determinately in any experience" (CPR, 533, A 533/B 561). Such a faculty is noumenal, since it cannot appear in a spatio-temporal causal network. In the *Critique of Practical Reason,* Kant returns to the question of freedom in its relation to natural causality, and makes a clarification. As established with the phenomenal/noumenal distinction, and in order to solve the apparent contradiction between freedom and the mechanism of nature as intertwined in one action, Kant stresses that the "concept of causality as natural necessity, unlike the concept of causality as freedom, concerns only the existence of things as far as it is determinable in time, and consequently as appearances in contrast to their causality as things-in-themselves" (CPrR, 97–98). However, with respect to the free agent, we enter another realm than the mechanical causality of nature, a realm in which the same subject considers his existence not as subject to time-conditions, but as determinable by laws which he gives himself through reason. In such an existence, nothing precedes the determination of his will.

Kant begins by developing the aporias involved in the antithesis, which claims that there is no freedom and that everything in the world happens only in accordance with the laws of nature. If we assume that there is only the causality of nature, then the consequence is that "everything *that happens* presupposes a previous state, upon which it follows without exception according to a rule" (CPR, 484, A 444/B 472). Now the same necessity applies to that previous state as well, which has also arisen from a previous state that caused it ("But now the previous state itself must be something that has happened . . ."). The notion of a universal causality of nature presupposes this temporal antecedence, as "the causality of the cause through which something happens is always something *that has happened,* which according to the law of nature (*nach dem Gesetz der Natur*) presupposes once again a previous state and its causality, and this in the same way a still earlier state, and so on" (CPR, 484, A 444/B 472).[10] The aporia of natural causality as the sole causality begins to appear: There is no way to interrupt or escape the ineluctability of this infinite regress, so that one could never reach the beginning of the series, the "first" beginning and cause.[11] Kant explains: "If, therefore, everything happens according to mere laws of nature, then at every time there is only a subordinate but never a first beginning" (CPR, 484, A 444/B 472). Now, without such a beginning one could never have arrived at this present state, which of course is an impossibility—hence, a first aporia. But most importantly, the impossibility of finding a first cause would signify that no completeness of causes can be reached, which would contradict the principle of sufficient reason, which precisely demands such a completeness: "But now the law of nature consists just in this, that nothing happens without a cause sufficiently determined *a priori*" (CPR, 484, A 446/B 474), and therefore an absolutely first beginning provided by a first cause. This is why Kant insists that by following the mere causality of nature one could never attain a "completeness of the series on the side of the causes descending one from another" (CPR, 484, A 446/B 474). This aporia signifies the impossibility of the antithesis ("There is no freedom"), which precisely claimed that there was only one causality, the causality of nature. Such causality cannot provide the first beginning that would ensure the completeness of causes and thus satisfy its own requirement. Kant then concludes that "the proposition that all causality is possible only in accordance with laws of nature (*nach Gesetzen der Natur*), when taken in its unlimited universality, *contradicts itself, and therefore this causality cannot be assumed to be the only one*" (CPR, 484, A 446/B 474; my emphasis).

As a consequence, another causality must be admitted, one in which "something happens without its cause being further determined by another previous cause" (CPR, 484, A 446/B 474). That implicit reference to the motif of a first cause, and thus of the *causa sui,* is presented by

Kant in terms of spontaneity, i.e., that which begins from itself, an "*absolute* causal *spontaneity* beginning *from itself*" that Kant also names "*transcendental freedom*," transcendental insofar as it transcends the course of nature, even though it alone provides the possibility of a completeness of the series of appearances on the side of the causes.[12] An intelligible freedom must be assumed, although "no insight into it is achieved" (CPR, 486, A 450/B 478) since it is not a part of the phenomenal world.[13] It can thus only be assumed, as an outside *of* the world, and yet this outside makes the world possible by securing the completeness of causes. The completeness of the world, and thus its possibility, rests upon this noumenal, outer-worldly freedom. Such is the enigma presented by Kant: The completeness of the world lies outside the world, and yet this outside constitutes the world; it is literally the outside *of* the world.

Transcendental freedom, Kant explains, is the capacity of a cause to produce a state spontaneously, or "from itself" (*von Selbst*) (CPR, 533, A 533/B 561). A transcendentally free cause would be a "first cause," that is, without a prior cause. The whole determination of responsibility as imputation will revolve around the possibility of such a *causa sui*. Kant justifies this claim by appealing to a requirement of reason, going back to the ancient tradition of the prime mover:

> The confirmation of the need of reason to appeal to a first beginning from freedom in the series of natural causes is clearly and visibly evident from the fact that (with the exception of the Epicurean school) all the philosophers of Antiquity saw themselves as obliged to assume a *first mover* for the explanation of motions in the world, i.e., a freely acting cause, which began this series of states first and from itself. (CPR, 488, A 450/B 478)

The first instance of a free-acting cause is thus the first mover, which allows one to conceive of an origin *of* the world. The origin *of* the world cannot be *in* the world. Yet, as we saw, the world as a totality is only possible on such a basis. In fact, nature and freedom are for Kant thoroughly intertwined. Absolute spontaneity is said to begin, "from itself," "a series of appearances that runs according to natural laws" (CPR, 484, A 446/B 474), this already indicating that free causality, although independent from natural causality, is intertwined with it. Just as natural necessity rests on transcendental freedom, freedom in turn produces effects in the world. We will return to this intertwining shortly. At this stage, it suffices to posit that natural causality does not give us a first cause; the causality of freedom does, thus satisfying the principle of sufficient reason.

Kant recognizes that so far he has only established the necessity of a first beginning of a series of appearances from freedom "only to the extent that this is required to make comprehensible an origin of the world" (CPR, 486, A 448/B 476), which clearly for Kant does not apply to us. However, he insists, because "the faculty of beginning a series in time entirely on its own is thereby proved" (while he immediately recognizes, as we alluded to above, that this proof gives us no insight into it, since such a faculty is transcendental and never to be observed within a field of appearances), then "we are permitted," he continues, "also to allow that in the course of the world different series may begin on their own . . . and to ascribe to the substances in those series the faculty of acting from freedom" (CPR, 486, A 450/B 478). Kant thus allows for an analogy between the transcendent creator of the world and rational agents operating in the world by virtue of this capacity to begin absolutely—i.e., to be a spontaneous free cause, cause of itself or *causa sui*. Through this analogy with the prime mover, in the context of a discussion on the aporia of natural causality, Kant proves the possibility of freedom, which can thus be admitted as operating *in* the world. Further, Kant warns us not to be "stopped here by a misunderstanding, namely, that since a successive series in the world can have only a comparatively first beginning, because a state of the world must always precede it, perhaps no absolutely first beginning of the series is possible during the course of the world" (CPR, 488, A 451/B 479). This is only a misunderstanding, "for here we are talking of an absolute beginning not, as far as time is concerned, but as far as causality is concerned" (CPR, 488, A 451/B 479). There is the origin *of* the world, and there is also an origin *in* the world. It will be possible to speak of an absolute beginning *in* the world, thanks to this distinction introduced by Kant between beginning in time and beginning in causality.

Indeed, Kant posits the freedom of the will in terms of the spontaneity of the act, which itself rests on the notion of *causa sui*. Now this concept traditionally only applies to God, and Kant makes explicit reference to the tradition of the prime mover. However, such a first cause only pertained to the origin *of* the world. The issue here is determining how can there be also an origin *in* the world—and how can one reconcile such a free spontaneity with universal determinism, or the causality of nature? How does one begin absolutely when every event must presuppose a prior event that causes it? How can there be an origin within the causal network of nature? Kant himself recognized the difficulty in admitting a free cause that would operate within the world, that is, within a chain of causes, for all that has been established so far is the necessity of a first beginning of a series of appearances from freedom as it pertained to the origin of the world, while "one can take all the subsequent states to be a result of mere natural laws" (CPR, 486, A 448/B 476). This is the antinomy of pure reason, this idea of a free cause or unconditioned causality constituting for Kant "the real stumbling block for philosophy" (CPR, 486, A 448/B 476). Kant attempts to resolve this problem by distinguishing a beginning *in time* from a beginning *in causality,* the latter applying to free agency operating in the world. As (transcendentally) free agents, we can never begin in time, but we can begin in causality, hence providing a basis for responsibility. Only in the case of divine creation are beginning in time and beginning in causality merged. For our own free actions, the beginning is only in causality (as we are not origins *of* the world but origins *in* the world). In the causality of freedom (the beginning in causality), no antecedent cause determines my actions, which can in no way "be regarded as simple causal consequences of the antecedent state of the agent." *In the midst of the world, and within the world and in the course of time itself, certain events somehow happen as absolute beginnings,* that is, from "a faculty of absolutely beginning a state" (CPR, 485, A 445/B 473). To the potential objection that no absolute beginning can happen in the world, Kant replies that there can be a *comparatively* first beginning, and thus that there can be an absolute beginning (in causality) occurring *in medias res.* Kant is explicit on this point, namely, that there is an origin *of* the world, but there are also origins *in* the world, writing that "we are permitted also to allow that in the course of the world different series may begin on their own as far as their causality is concerned" (CPR, 486, A 450/B 478). Even though freedom can only take place within the causal network of the world, it remains nonetheless absolute and uncaused; Kant insists that an absolute first beginning of a series is possible during the course of the world.

Thus, on the one hand, the capacity to begin a new series of causes from oneself is absolute (though it is an absolute beginning in causality, not in time), and on the other hand this capacity is still inscribed within the fabric of the world and its causal laws. We introduce something new in the world, out of our own spontaneity,[14] but what we introduce is something new *in the world,* which then gets taken up in natural causality. Whatever I decide to do out of this spontaneous, transcendental freedom, still has to take place in the world. The new that I introduce is absolute (otherwise it would not be "new"), but that absolute happens in the conditioned world (this is why Kant spoke of a "comparatively first beginning"). All I can do is begin a new series of causes, which are themselves inscribed in nature. This is why Kant establishes that one must assume a first uncaused beginning, but along with it, "its natural consequences to infinity," consequences of the free act which follow purely natural laws (CPR, 488, A 450/B 478). In a sense, the act is both free or uncaused *and* part of natural determinism, according to Kant's distinction between a beginning in time (natural determinism) and a beginning in causality (freedom). To take Kant's example:

> If (for example), I am now entirely free, and get up from my chair without the necessarily determining influence of natural causes, then in this occurrence, along with its natural consequences to infinity, there begins an absolutely new series, even though as far as time is concerned this occurrence is only the continuation of a previous series. (CPR, 488, A 450/B 478)

With respect to free decision and action, natural causes exercise no determining influence whatsoever. A free action does indeed "follow upon them" but it "does not follow from" them (*die zwar auf jene folgt, aber daraus nicht erfolgt*).

Now, what is significant in such "absolute spontaneity of an action" or transcendental freedom—which lies in the "intention" or "resolution" (*Entschliessung*) and the act, Kant specifies—is that it will be determined as ground for imputability, that is, for the very possibility of responsibility as accountability of the subject. This power or performativity of transcendental freedom—as we recall, it was defined by Kant as the *power* (*Vermögen*) of beginning a state spontaneously, or from oneself (*von Selbst*)—provides a ground, as a decision to act which is outside of natural causality. In the "Remark on the Third Antinomy," Kant clarifies that the originary capacity of initiating a causal series gives itself as the "ground" of what he terms *Imputabilität*, or imputability. It appears here that responsibility as imputability rests upon a ground (a basis, a *subjectum*), and in fact requires it. Kant's account of responsibility, i.e., the imputation of the act, as articulated in the Third Antinomy, thus relies on an ontology of the *subjectum,* for it is because there is a *subjectum* at the foundation of the act that the latter can be imputed or ascribed to an agent. A certain conception of the human agency is here proposed, which consists in understanding it as subject and *subjectum.*[15] The infinite chain of causes stops in a first cause, allowing for the ultimate ground of the act to appear (as the colloquial expression has it, "the buck stops here"). The infinite chain of antecedent impersonal causes gives way to an author-subject who is the first cause of the act and the ground of imputation. The search for reasons can proceed infinitely, but the search for the *author* of the act is finite, and stops when the "who" of the act is identified, as ground of the act. Responsibility thus means here the imputation of a free subject. Kant writes:

> The transcendental idea of freedom is far from constituting the whole content of the psychological concept of that name, which is for the most part empirical, but constitutes only that of the absolute spontaneity of an action, as the real ground of its imputability (*Imputabilität*); but this idea is nevertheless the real stumbling block for philosophy, which finds insuperable difficulties in admitting this kind of unconditioned causality. (CPR, 486, A 448/B 476)

This absolute freedom, understood as the power to make a first beginning in causality, is then the ground of responsibility, that is, of an agent as free cause of its actions. Responsibility now means: An act can be grounded absolutely, and a foundation of the act can be displayed—this is the freedom of the subject. The spontaneity of freedom constitutes the intervention of the agent in the world, its introducing new events in the world, and causing changes within it, changes that can be traced back to the agent as free cause. Hence, "the absolute spontaneity of an action" constitutes "the real ground of its imputability."

Responsibility as Autonomy

This sense of freedom as ground of imputability opens the space of personhood and autonomy. As we saw, apart from a negative understanding of freedom as foreign to law and contrary to causality, another, more positive sense appeared in the notion of self-causation (*causa sui*). As Kant stresses, the notion of a freedom that is foreign to causality and "lawless" is only the negative account of it, one that merely emphasizes that freedom is independent from "foreign causes" (FMM, 285). Kant explains in the beginning of the third section of *The Foundations of the Metaphysics of Morals* that the "preceding definition of freedom [as independence from causes] is negative and therefore affords no insight into its essence. But a positive concept of freedom flows from it which is so much the richer and more fruitful" (FMM, 285). Understood *positively*, freedom is not foreign to law but is indeed *another kind of causality*. For, as Kant explains, "freedom is by no means lawless even though it is not a property of the will according to the laws of nature" (FMM, 285). On the contrary, it must be thought of as a different kind of causality, a causality according to immutable laws, if it is the case that the concept of causality "entails that of laws according to which something (i.e., the effect) must be established through something else which we call cause" (FMM, 285). Freedom will be taken as a causality ("Otherwise a free will would be an absurdity"), and thus it is "by no means lawless," but it will be a causality of a peculiar kind (FMM, 285). While natural causality presents a *heteronomy* of efficient causes, freedom presents an *autonomy*, that is, the power of the will to be a law for itself.[16] In fact, Kant clarified that as a kind of causality of living beings so far as they are rational, "freedom would be that property of this causality by which it can be effective independent of foreign causes determining it" (FMM, 285). What is at issue here is the notion of a heteronomy of causes ("foreign causes"), and not causality as such. Whereas natural necessity is defined by Kant as "a heteronomy of efficient causes" (FMM, 285), the freedom of the will is identified with autonomy: "What else, then, can the freedom of the will be but autonomy (i.e., the property of the will to be a law to itself)?" (FMM, 286). The positive sense of freedom will thus be determined as a causality of autonomy. Kant understands this sense as the act of giving oneself the law that is to be followed, a kind of causality which is defined by an "ought" and not by the necessity (a "must") of nature. Freedom as freedom *from* causality supposes a freedom as *self-causation* and autonomy: As free from all laws of nature, the person is "obedient only to those laws which he himself gives" (FMM, 278).

If freedom means acting *independently* from external causes ("heteronomy of efficient causes"), my actions cannot be said to be regulated by some heteronomical principle. Rather, I act freely when I follow my own principles, as freedom is the "faculty of determining oneself from oneself"

(CPR, 533, A 534/B 562). Despite the common view that freedom is not subject to the law, and despite Kant's own formulations in the Third Antinomy according to which freedom seems "contrary to causal law," in fact freedom is the act of *giving oneself the law* that is to be followed. The will cannot be thought of except as some kind of causality producing effects. Whereas everything in nature works according to laws, a rational being has the power to act according to its conception of the law, that is, according to principles: "this conception is the will" (FMM, 263). Rational agents posit an end, more precisely posit themselves as an end, and to that extent are called persons. Consequently, the agent is free and responsible as an *autonomous* being. Kant defines personality as autonomy: It rests upon the freedom of the will as autonomous, and therefore a person is only subject to the laws he posits himself. This determines the moral person in terms of autonomy, autonomy being the cornerstone of such an ethics of freedom. This ethics is revealed in the feeling of respect.

Kant writes in *Foundations of the Metaphysics of Morals:*

> Beings whose existence does not depend on our will but on nature, if they are not rational beings, have only relative worth as means, and are therefore called "things"; rational beings, on the other hand, are designated "persons" because their nature indicates that they are ends in themselves (i.e., things which may not be used merely as means). Such a being is thus an object of respect. (FMM, 273)

Respect thus reveals the *dignity* of the person, through which man gives himself to himself. Self-worth grounds a morality of autonomy, and autonomy becomes the ground for the dignity of the person. "A thing has no worth other than that determined for it by the law. The lawgiving which determines all worth must therefore have a dignity," that is, an unconditional worth. For such a being, "only the word 'respect' is suitable" (FMM, 278). This dignity lies in the fact that man never exists merely as a means, but also as an end (that is, as an absolute value), precisely to the extent that, in the feeling of respect, he gives himself to himself and belongs to himself as responsibility for himself. The moral person exists as its own end; it *is* itself an end. Respect reveals that the person exists for the sake of itself, that it is an end for itself, and that the self exists for the sake of itself.[17] What is categorically imperative is no longer a divine command, for that would still be heteronomical; rather, autonomy is the basis for dignity and respect, and moral worth. Self-worth is the fundamental content of morality. This is why Kant stresses that autonomy is the "basis of the dignity of both human nature and every rational nature" (FMM, 278).

The famous fundamental principle of morality states: "Act so that you use humanity in your own person as well as in the person of everyone else never merely as a means but always at the same time as an end." As a result, Kant places the principle of morality in the autonomy of the subject, stressing that in pure morality man is not bound to external laws, but is subject only to his own. "The moral principle I will call the principle of *autonomy* of the will in contrast to all other principles which I accordingly count under *heteronomy*" (FMM, 276). As he articulated in the *Critique of Pure Reason,* the rational being has two points of view from which it can regard itself: First, as belonging to the world of sense, and thus being subject to laws of nature (heteronomy); and second, as belonging to the intelligible world, under laws which are independent from nature and are based in reason alone. As belonging to the intelligible world, man can never conceive the causality of his own will except as free and as independent from the causes of the sensible world. Thus the concept of freedom is indistinguishable from that of autonomy.

A law that proceeds from a self-legislating rational will—and not from a heteronomical principle—obligates us only through *respect.* Since it is the rational will that is the author of this law, it is, in a deeper sense, *the rational will* that is the object of respect. Rational nature can be seen not only to be an end in itself (i.e., to have fundamental objective worth), but to have *dignity* (i.e., to have absolute or incomparable worth). Respect here is respect for the moral law. Kant describes this law as first being negative in its effect, for it tears one away from one's inclinations, tendencies, and "sensible feelings." It "humiliates" our self-conceit, "repulses" feelings, and thus has a negative effect on them. However, just as in Spinoza, an emotion can only be overcome by another emotion, and the repulsed sensible feelings will give way to a *positive* feeling, that of respect. The feeling of respect, arising against the background of the humiliation of the sensible, is therefore not itself sensible; it is *a priori,* intellectual. Kant writes: "And as *striking down,* i.e., humiliating, self-conceit, [the law] is an object of the greatest respect and thus the ground of a positive feeling which is not of empirical origin."[18]

Respect *for* the law should also reveal the self which feels respect for itself in its Being, and in an *essential* way. In the feeling of respect, the self is immediately revealed to itself, not in an empirical mode, but in a non-sensible, *a priori* way. Reason freely gives itself over to the moral law; it produces, as it were, the feeling of respect for the law: Respect for the law is the active ego's respect for itself as the self which is responsible. To the extent that it is both *a priori* and self-produced, the feeling of respect is a *self*-affection, and respect, as submission before the law, is a *self*-submission. By submitting to the law, I in fact submit to *myself*, and thereby am revealed to myself as freedom, self-determination, and *self-responsibility*. In subjecting myself to the law, I subject myself to myself as pure reason, that is, in this subjection to myself I raise myself to myself as a free, self-determining being. Respect reveals the self as responsibility, to itself and for itself. Respect thus manifests an essential characteristic of the person: In responsibility for itself, the person is appropriated to itself in its own proper self; respect engages the responsibility of a self that in each case I have to be. In respect, I raise myself "up" to myself, I "own up" to myself, I answer for myself by taking the responsibility myself. This concept of self-responsibility will become the very meaning of enlightenment for Kant, as he proclaimed in the essay "What is Enlightenment?"

The Ideal of Self-Responsibility

One knows that famous passage from *Foundations of the Metaphysics of Morals* in which Kant writes:

> Here we see philosophy brought to what is, in fact, a precarious position, which should be made fast even though it is supported by nothing in either heaven or earth. Here philosophy must show its purity, as the absolute sustainer of its laws, and not the herald of those which an implanted sense or who knows what tutelary nature whispers to it.

This passage is (as it were) echoed by Nietzsche, who writes in *Twilight of the Idols:* "For what is freedom? Having the will to be responsible to oneself."[19] Responsibility becomes identified with an ideal of self-responsibility as autonomy. For Kant, the principle of autonomy requires that reason "must regard itself as the author of its principles, independent of alien influences" (FMM, 287). Autonomous self-responsibility is thus opposed to heteronomous determinations. To that extent, and in contrast to the "causality of all irrational beings" that are determined by the influence of foreign causes, we are defined in terms of responsibility, that is, autonomous self-responsibility. In his 1784 essay "What is Enlightenment?"[20] (the full title reads, "Beantwortung der Frage: Was ist Aufklärung?"), answering the question posed by the Reverend Johann Friedrich Zöllner (an official in the Prussian government) and published in the *Berlinische Monatsschrift* (*Berlin Monthly*), Kant famously defines enlightenment as a way out of immaturity and dependency—that is, out of a state of irresponsibility—and as a call to (self-)responsibility. As Michel Foucault has noted, the way Kant poses the question of *Aufklärung* is entirely different from other accounts of an historical era, in that it is first characterized negatively: *Aufklärung* "is neither a world era to which one belongs, nor an event whose signs are perceived, nor the dawning of an accomplishment. Kant defines *Aufklärung* in an almost entirely negative way, as an *Ausgang,* an 'exit,' a 'way out.'"[21] That exit is from irresponsibility, and enlightenment is thus the process that releases us from such irresponsibility. Indeed, in the opening lines, Kant declares that "Enlightenment is man's release from his self-incurred tutelage (*Unmündigkeit*)." Here *Unmündigkeit* designates immaturity and dependence, and "not being of age." What tutelage? What immaturity? What irresponsibility? Kant defines it as "man's inability to make use of his understanding *without direction from another*" (E, 462; my emphasis). Irresponsibility is thus the state of being determined in one's judgment by another, that is, heteronomy. Significantly, Kant claims that this dependence on others, this being ruled by others, is self-imposed (as Kant speaks of a "self-incurred" tutelage), as if humans were ultimately responsible for their own irresponsibility and immaturity.[22] This indicates that responsibility represents for Kant the essential nature and vocation of man, and that such a responsibility will be conceived outside of and against the intervention of the other. There lies the subjectivist enclosure of the concept of responsibility, and the privileging of a self-responsibility which is conquered against the presence of otherness in selfhood. Responsibility would then be the autonomous practice of one's reason without the direction of others, that is, the very overcoming of heteronomy.

Further, Kant stresses that in this situation of irresponsibility, the issue is not a lack of understanding but of *courage,* namely, the courage to use one's judgment on one's own. As Foucault makes clear, "Enlightenment is defined by a modification of the preexisting relation linking will, authority, and the use of reason."[23] To that extent, responsibility as the autonomous practice of one's own reason is not a matter of knowledge but of the courage to use it autonomously. Responsibility as autonomous practice thus proves to be a matter of *power*, as Nietzsche would recognize when he wrote, "Independence is for the very few; it is a privilege of the strong" (BGE, 41). Responsibility is the power to act autonomously and affirm one's independence. "Self-incurred is this tutelage when its cause lies not in lack of reason but in lack of resolution and courage to use it without direction from another. *Sapere Aude!* 'Have courage to use your own reason!'—that is the motto of enlightenment" (E, 462). One notes here how responsibility is associated with the thematics of power and self-legislation, and how such power arises out of a rupture with any heteronomical principle, that is, a rupture with the reliance on the other. Responsibility represents the position of the power of the autonomous self, the auto-positioning of a sovereign subjectivity. For its part, irresponsibility (immaturity) is thereby defined as a (self-incurred) fleeing in the face of this self-determination. By calling human beings back to their responsibility, i.e., the courage to think and act on their own, Kant also articulates a call to autonomy, *responsibility now being defined strictly as autonomy*. In turn, the human being in its proper personality is approached in terms of freedom and self-responsibility.

The whole argument, in a sort of self-fulfilling or self-positing circle (recalling the self-position of power that we noted in Aristotle's account of responsible decision), develops on the assumption of a primacy of responsibility *as self-positing of the self*, with irresponsibility described as a derivative mode of it. As we just saw, the state of immaturity is for Kant a self-induced situation, for, as he notes, humans beings remain in such an irresponsible state "after nature has long since discharged them from external direction (*naturaliter maiorennes*)" (E, 462). They do so, we are told, out of "laziness and cowardice"—out of a weak will, we might add. They remain "under lifelong tutelage," thus inviting guardians to step in and take over their subjectivity; this abdication is what explains "why it is so easy for others to set themselves up as their guardians" (E, 462). Not being responsible is easy ("It is so easy not to be of age"), while being responsible is hard ("the step to competence" is "arduous").[24] One is thus not simply immature and irresponsible, one yields to the easy way, one *wants to be* irresponsible, one *makes oneself* irresponsible. The paradox of this situation is patent: One is responsible for not being responsible. The only account for the very possibility of this paradox is that there is no radical, irreducible irresponsibility, but only instead a responsibility that attempts (and by definition fails) to escape itself. Irresponsibility arises out of a certain yielding of responsibility, which Kant designates by the terms "laziness" and "cowardice": "Laziness and cowardice are the reasons why so great a portion of mankind . . . nevertheless remains under lifelong tutelage" (E, 462).

The weight that one must carry (responsibility) and that is so tempting to avoid and flee from is thus the weight *of oneself* (hence the task of autonomy and self-responsibility). That weight must be borne by oneself without having another relieving us of it. I must not rely on the other, I must rely solely on myself. Kant hereby takes issue with the following of heteronomical principles, the reliance on external authorities—be that the authority of knowledge, of religion, or of technical and scientific expertise. "If I have a book which understands for me, a pastor who has a conscience for me, a physician who decides my diet, and so forth, I need not trouble myself. I need not think, if I can only pay—others will readily undertake the irksome work for me" (E, 462). One can associate this passage with the very thrust of Kant's critical project, and it is clear that the project of a critique of pure reason supposes a seizing by reason itself of its own powers, and thus supposes the space of autonomy. These three examples, according to Michel Foucault, mirror Kant's three critiques:

> Kant gives three examples: we are in a state of 'immaturity' when a book takes the place of our understanding, when a spiritual director takes the place of our conscience, when a doctor decides for us what our diet is to be. (Let us note in passing that the register of these three critiques is easy to recognize, even though the text does not make it explicit).[25]

The move to self-responsibility is not only difficult, it is also inherently subversive: It is not by accident that those rulers who seek power over others always seek before anything else to infantilize those they rule. "That the step to competence is held to be very dangerous by the far greater portion of humanity . . . —quite apart from its being arduous—is seen by those guardians who have so kindly assumed superintendence over them" (E, 462). The ruled are made to feel infantile, to believe themselves to be in need of protection. Fear is used in order to discourage people to become responsible, and the guardians "show them the danger which threatens if they try to go alone" (one can think here of how certain political administrations have used and manipulated public trauma and fear in order to establish control). People are made to feel incapable of being on their own. However, as Kant stresses, "this danger is not so great, for by falling a few times they would finally learn to walk alone" (E, 462).

One's irresponsibility and immaturity is thus chosen, although, as Kant notes, it then becomes second nature: "For any single individual man to work himself out of the life under tutelage which has become almost his nature is very difficult." In fact, one could say that one chooses such a nature. Irresponsibility is the choice, through freedom, to become irresponsible (or rather, remain immature) by nature; this is an impossible wish, but that is the content of irresponsibility for Kant. One wants to stay in this immature state, as one "has come to be fond of this state" (E, 462). It is a matter, in re-seizing one's responsibility, of reengaging the risk of a free existence by abandoning the false security of nature, of rules and formulas—"mechanical tools of the rational employment, or rather misemployment," to which Kant opposes "the dignity of men" who are "now more than machines" (E, 467). This re-appropriation of one's freedom can take place, Kant clarifies, "slowly," as a matter of education and experience, and he warns against a revolutionary spirit that may overthrow autocratic despotism but could never amount to "a true reform in ways of thinking. Rather, new prejudices will serve as old ones to harness the great unthinking mass" (E, 463).

The most powerful element, the most revolutionary and emancipatory, is in the end nothing but freedom itself. As Kant states: "For this enlightenment, however, nothing is required but freedom" (E, 463). What freedom? The freedom to use one's mind, and to do so publicly; the freedom "to make public use of one's reason at every point" (E, 463). There are of course many examples of restrictions on such freedom and Kant gives a list: "But I hear on all sides, 'Do not argue!' The officer says, 'Do not argue, but drill!' The tax-collector: 'Do not argue, but pay!' The cleric: 'Do not argue, but believe!'" A more pernicious way of negating freedom is to allow for speaking one's mind, to allow for so-called "freedom of conscience" as long as it is not followed by any effect, as long as it can be ignored ("Argue as much as you will and about what you will, but obey!"). After the events of September 11, 2001, when there were expressions of disagreement with policies of the Bush administration, oftentimes one would hear the president say: "Those people have a right to speak, this is democracy—they can say what they want." Yet in fact, what was said was: "Speak all you want, your opinions will be allowed but ignored—allowed *as* ignored!" This is why what matters is that this using of one's reason be truly performative, i.e., be *practical*. It must, in other words, be not only a private matter, but a public expression involving others, the whole community: "Everywhere there is restriction on freedom. But what sort of restriction is an obstacle to enlightenment, and what sort is not an obstacle but a promoter of it? I answer: The public use of one's reason must always be free, and it alone can bring about enlightenment among men."

It is at this juncture that Kant introduces the crucial distinction between the private and public uses of reason. "By the public use of one's reason I understand the use which a person makes of it as a scholar before the reading public. Private use I call that which one may make of it in a particular civic post or office which entrusted to him" (E, 463). Reason must be free in its public use (as a member of the whole community or the society of world-citizens), and can tolerate restrictions in its private use, i.e., within a role in society in a professional setting. Kant privileges the public use of reason, speaking out "before the public for judgment" (E, 464): One uses one's reason *without subjecting oneself to any authority*. Such is the sense of autonomy. Clearly, in some technical capacities one must not argue, but obey. In the private use of reason, one must obey because one is playing a specific role in society. Yet, as a member of the reasonable community, as a citizen, as "a scholar," as Kant puts it, one can indeed argue. "While it would be ruinous for an officer in service to quibble about the suitability of a command given to him by his superior, he must obey; but the right to make remarks on errors in the military service and to lay them before the public for judgment cannot equitably be refused him as a scholar" (E, 464). One must pay one's taxes, but as a scholar one can publicly express one's doubts regarding the justice of these taxes. A preacher's use of reason for the sake of his congregation "is merely private," for Kant, "because this congregation is only a domestic one." As a priest one is not free, but as a scholar the same cleric "has complete freedom" and "enjoys unlimited freedom to use his own reason and to speak in his own person" (E, 464).

Any attempt to preclude the future enlightenment of the human race through submission to religious authority is condemned by Kant as impossible. That would be, he adds, a "crime against human nature," as freedom, autonomy, and thus responsibility are humanity's essential vocation and destiny. Humanity's vocation is to be responsible for itself, a self-responsibility that lies in autonomy. This is why Kant adds that the "touchstone of everything that can be concluded as a law for a people lies in the question whether the people could have imposed such a law on itself" (E, 465). The monarch cannot impose his law on the people in a despotic way, for "his lawgiving authority rests on his uniting the general public will in his own." Such a vocation is in progress for Kant, which explains why he clarifies that we do not live in an enlightened age, but rather in an age of enlightenment. "If we are asked, 'Do we now live in *an enlightened age*?' the answer is, 'No,' but we do live in an *age of enlightenment*" (E, 465). Man's self-responsibility is the task and regulative idea of our age. "As things now stand, much is lacking which prevents men from being, or easily becoming, capable of using their own reason in religious matters correctly, with assurance and free from outside direction" (E, 465–466), yet the way is opened for men to remove the obstacles to enlightenment. The spirit of freedom must expand, so that self-responsibility as self-determination and self-legislation becomes the future of humanity.

The Kantian philosophy of responsibility thus rests on a philosophy of freedom as transcendental faculty of the subject, on the notion of the autonomy of the person, and on the self-responsibility of man. I am responsible for what I have done myself, as a rational free agent, and I am responsible as autonomous being. Furthermore, the call to responsibility as self-responsibility engages the human to take over its own destiny; it is a self-empowering act. Kant thus also reveals the historicity of responsibility, by making of self-responsibility a *task* of humanity. However, precisely as self-grounding, autonomy will prove itself ungrounded, and the more it seeks to posit itself on its own, the deeper the abyss will open beneath it. Autonomy, as self-grounding, deconstructs itself and opens onto its own groundlessness. Such groundlessness will be exposed—indeed, explored— in Nietzsche's historical genealogy of accountability, with radical consequences for the concept of responsibility.

THREE

Nietzsche's Deconstruction of Accountability

One has thereby attained to the knowledge that the history of moral sensations is the history of an error, the error of accountability, which rests on the error of freedom of will.

HUMAN, ALL TOO HUMAN

The Fiction of Responsibility

RESPONSIBILITY AS HISTORY

One of the most decisive features of Nietzsche's critique of the Western tradition is his claim that its inherited concepts are essentially constructs ("fictions" or "lies"), as opposed to accurate grasps of an objective essence. There will thus not be a "natural" or "objective" concept of responsibility. We already noted, in particular with respect to Aristotle, the performative character of the traditional account of responsibility, and how the predominant sense of responsibility was constituted as a sphere of control over events. Aristotle secured such a sphere through his careful and strict distinguishing of the voluntary from the involuntary and by emphasizing the voluntary in one's actions. With respect to Kant, we saw how a problematic notion of transcendental freedom—a freedom that is not of this world— was made the foundation of responsibility understood as the imputability of a subject, and further characterized as autonomous self-responsibility, that is, within the egological horizon that is reductive of alterity (under the rubric of "heteronomy").

Nietzsche exposes such features further by stressing how the traditional concept of responsibility rests on the constructs—indeed the *fictions*—of agency, causality, free will, intentionality, and subjectivity. Hence Nietzsche's destructive genealogy of those concepts, of those idols, which for him means as much the exposure of their fictive nature as an attack on the values they subtend and carry. This is indeed the goal of Nietzsche's *genealogy of responsibility*, namely, to return to the origins of its (pathological) formations in order to determine how its concept has been *constructed*, for what purpose and with what motives. In such a genealogical—literally de-constructive—return to the history of responsibility, another path is opened, another fate and another future of our being-responsible. The Nietzschean genealogical destruction of the concept of responsibility, far from leading to a nihilism of values, in fact opens new possibilities, which come to be explored in various ways in contemporary continental thought.

It is important to stress at the outset that Nietzsche's genealogy of the tradition is not, as is at times claimed, a nihilistic attack on morality. This claim is based on the flawed notion that is similar to what Merleau-Ponty remarked, "From the simple fact that I make of morality a problem, you conclude that I deny it."[1] Interestingly, Nietzsche had already objected to such a reading,[2] and clarified that it was a matter for him of reengaging our tradition and its concepts, an attempt at reevaluating its values, that is, reevaluate the value of its values: It is a matter of questioning the value of moral values. It is thus crucial to distinguish here between a positive examination of the value and origins of morality (Nietzsche's genealogy) and a unilateral attack on morality. Nietzsche himself stressed the positive dimension of his enterprise, for instance in §345 of *The Gay Science* (book 5). The title of the section reads, "Morality as a problem," which already suggests quite plainly that it is a matter of *problematizing* morality and its value, that is, of *questioning* it, as opposed to taking it for granted and leaving it unquestioned. Nietzsche explains:

> Even if a morality has grown out of an error, the realization of this fact would not as much as touch the problem of its value. Thus nobody up to now has examined the *value* of that most famous of all medicines which

is called morality; and the first step would be—for once to *question* it. Well then, precisely this is our task.[3]

This task is all the more necessary given that, as Nietzsche notes, such a questioning approach—asking about the meaning and values of morality—is cruelly lacking. In *Beyond Good and Evil*, he takes issue with the so-called "science of morals" in which there is always something lacking, "strange as it may sound: the problem of morality itself; what was lacking was any suspicion that there was something problematic there" (BGE, 98). As he insists in *The Gay Science*, "It is evident that up to now morality was no problem at all," or "I see nobody who ventured a *critique* of moral valuations" (GS, 284).

What does Nietzsche mean by making morality into a problem? What does he mean by "critique"? Not a negative enterprise, as *critique* for Nietzsche is not an attack against morality but rather an inquiry into the history of the origins of morality; it is a matter of attempting to explore "the history of the origins of these [moral] feelings and valuations," which is neither a merely historical account nor a merely negative critique. In a parentheses, Nietzsche clarifies that this 'history of origins' is "something quite different from a critique," as well as being different from a simple history of ethical systems. In *The Will to Power,* in a section titled "Critique of Morality," we read: "The inquiry into the origin of our evaluations and tables of the good is absolutely no way identical with a critique of them, as is often believed." Further, Nietzsche clarifies that such an inquiry seeks instead to evaluate the value of morality, that is to say, *for life.* "What are our evaluations and moral tables worth? What is the outcome of their rule? For whom? In relation to what?— Answer: for life."[4] A "for life" that quickly becomes a "from life," from the perspective of life. One should stress here that when Nietzsche speaks of values, as he puts it, we speak "under inspiration," under the perspective of life, which compels us to posit values. In such a return to the origins of morality *in life,* Nietzsche seeks to reconstitute what in the second essay of the *Genealogy of Morals* he calls the "history of the origins of responsibility" (*Geschichte der Herkunft der Verantworlichkeit*),[5] in an expression we have chosen as the guiding thread for this work. Here as elsewhere, de-constructive genealogy will be synonymous with the opening of new possibilities—of a future.

THE CRITIQUE OF CONCEPTUALITY

Taken negatively, Nietzsche's genealogy represents a radical challenge to the values of the tradition of responsible agency, and in particular its supporting concepts (free will, causality, intention, agency, autonomy, and subjectivity). Before we engage in such deconstruction, it is crucial to recall Nietzsche's understanding of what a concept is, for his critique of responsibility is before anything else a critique of the *conceptuality* of responsibility—of responsibility as a concept—and even a critique of conceptuality as such.

As we alluded to above, a concept for Nietzsche is never the objective grasp of some essence, of some transcendent given or fact, but rather an all-too-human invention, a creation of our mind that is then accepted by convention. A concept has, by definition, no objective validity, no "truth-claim." In a sense, a concept is from the outset, as a concept, something "false"—what Nietzsche would call a "lie." Concepts are arbitrary conventions or inventions, and not objectively true forms. As David Allison explains, "Words, terms, meanings, propositions, and concepts, for Nietzsche, are generalized constructs of human invention—they merely serve as momentarily agreed-upon fabrications, as the conventional fictions of a given culture and its language."[6] This recognition cannot but cast a doubt on our traditional beliefs in our concepts (in their objectivity) and consequently the concept of responsibility, *as a concept,* also falls under suspicion. The reliance upon the traditional concept of responsibility and its senses, the reliance on its objectivity and truth, finds itself shaken: The concept of responsibility, heretofore taken as fact, is beginning to appear as a belief, as a construct. There is no objectivity of concepts, but we *believe* that concepts are objective, i.e., representations of reality. For Nietzsche, this is the whole matter: There is no objectivity of concepts, but a *belief* in the objectivity of concepts, the belief in reason and its categories, the belief that a concept unconditionally would designate the essence of things. In book 1, §11 of *Human, All Too Human,* Nietzsche thus explains that "man has for long ages believed in the concept and names of things as in *aeternae veritates,*" and man "really thought that in language he possessed knowledge of the world."[7] Of course, as he adds, only much later did it dawn on humans that "in their belief in language they have propagated a tremendous error," and that we do not possess categories that would give access to a world in itself. This passage indicates the intimate relation between the formations of concepts and the constitutive role of language in such formation. It is thus important to dwell on the question of language as it affects the constitution of the concept of responsibility.

In the 1873 essay, "On Truth and Lie in an Extramoral Sense," Nietzsche engages the question of knowledge and, in particular, that of conceptuality. Nietzsche begins the essay by re-inscribing knowledge in its factical, even accidental, situation and concrete history, as opposed to giving it a transcendent origin. "Once upon a time," he writes, "in some out of the way corner of that universe which is dispersed into numberless twinkling solar systems, there was a star upon which clever beasts invented knowing."[8] What Nietzsche seeks to stress in this passage is the accidental nature of the phenomenon of knowledge (human invention), its completely unnecessary (contingent) character, since one "might invent such a fable, and yet he still would not have adequately illustrated how miserable, how shadowy and transient, how aimless and arbitrary the human intellect looks within nature" (TL, 79). In these beginning paragraphs, Nietzsche emphasizes how knowledge is an invention, a construction. "As a genius of construction man raises himself far above the bee in the following way: whereas the bee builds with wax that he gathers from nature, man builds with the far more delicate conceptual material which he first has to manufacture from himself" (TL, 85). Man, the "genius of construction," the inventor, creates a form that is ultimately a form *of himself.* Knowledge is thus an anthropomorphic construction deprived of any objectivity, an anthropomorphization of the real. This is why Nietzsche continues by stressing that such a creation "is a thoroughly anthropomorphic truth which contains not a single point which would be 'true in itself' or really and universally valid apart from man" (TL, 85). Knowledge is not the conceptual grasp of reality, but an anthropomorphizing of reality, for the sake of power and appropriation of the real by man: "At bottom, what the investigator of such truths is seeking is only the metamorphosis of the world into man. He strives to understand the world as something analogous to man, and at best he achieves by his struggles the feeling of assimilation" (TL, 85–86). This notion of knowledge as assimilation or "making something familiar," making the world something more familiar *to us,* is also developed in §355 of *The Gay Science,* where knowledge is removed from a problematics of objectivity and truth, and brought closer to appropriation (power) and subjectivity or anthropomorphism (GS, 300); and in §112 of the same work, Nietzsche qualifies science as an "attempt to humanize things" (*Anmenschlichung der Dinge*) (GS, 172–173). The phenomenon of knowledge, far from giving access to an objective transcendent world, is entirely dependent on human hermeneutical constructions and is radically contingent, given the temporary and fleeting character of human existence. Knowledge is but a *product* of that existence and cannot outlast it;[9] as immanent to human life and creativity, knowledge did not exist before it and will not survive it. "There were eternities during which it did not exist. And when it is all over with the human intellect, nothing will have happened. For this intellect has no additional mission which would lead it beyond human life" (TL, 79). Knowledge is thus a phenomenon entirely *immanent* to life. In turn, life is for Nietzsche *the* ultimate phenomenon, a radically subjective experience that is not anchored in some problematic "objective" realm. This is why the intellect is not concerned with an objective realm, but fulfills a need that arises out of life itself. It can also be used as a tool of deception for the sake of the preservation of the individual or, out of boredom and from the need to exist socially ("herd-fashion"), used as a kind of peace-treaty with others in the guise of a drive to truth. The name "truth" is the designation of such conventional agreement deposited in language. "That which shall count as 'truth' from now on is established. That is to say, a uniformly valid and binding designation is invented for things, and the legislation of language likewise established the first laws of truth" (TL, 81).

THE LINGUISTIC BASIS OF THOUGHT

Knowledge, concepts, truth itself, are here referred back to language, conceived of as a sort of symbolic activity performed for the sake of life's needs. What matters in truth is precisely not disinterested knowledge, but what it can provide for life. "It is in a similarly restricted sense that man now wants nothing but truth: he desires the pleasant, life-preserving consequences of truth. He is indifferent toward pure knowledge which has no consequences" (TL, 81). We are twice removed from objectivity: First as life, which as lived is radically subjective; and second as language, which Nietzsche understands as the material basis of thought, and as far from any referentiality to some objective external reality. The link between language and a corresponding objective reality finds itself severed, as it immediately appears in Nietzsche's questions: "And besides, what about these linguistic conventions themselves? Are they perhaps products of knowledge, that is, of the sense of truth? Are designations congruent with things? Is language the adequate expression of all realities?" (TL, 81). Clearly, for Nietzsche, the answers to such questions must be negative. Conceptuality will prove to be a linguistic phenomenon, and language a material, physiological production, as Nietzsche clearly states: "What is a word? It is the copy in sound of a nerve stimulus" (TL, 81). Language is resolutely rooted in physiology, and this materiality of the word, *of sense,* simply cannot be referred to an outside reality that would function as its metaphysical substrate. Nietzsche makes clear that "the further inference from the nerve stimulus to a cause outside us is already the result of a false and unjustifiable application of the principle of sufficient reason" (TL, 81). The origin of language is thus not an ideal sphere of intelligibility, but a material production, a radically subjective phenomenon. "Truth" and "objectivity" can no longer serve as principles regulating our linguistic productions, our production of sense: "If truth alone had been the deciding factor in the genesis of language, and if the standpoint of certainty had been decisive for designations, then how could we still dare to say 'the stone is hard,' as if 'hard' were something otherwise familiar to us, and not merely a totally subjective stimulation!" (TL, 81–82).

Indeed, for Nietzsche, a word is the copy or image in sound of a nerve stimulus. In this one statement he has affirmed both the material basis of language (nerve stimulus) and the metaphoricity of sense (copy or image). This metaphoricity of sense is as it were unhinged, for sense is no longer anchored in any proper, literal, ideal meaning. The referentiality or transference inherent in metaphor (*this* word *for* another) is not one connecting a word with a reality, but one binding heterogeneous and always subjective realms. "To begin with, a nerve stimulus is transferred into an image: first metaphor. The image, in turn, is imitated in a sound: second metaphor. And each time there is a complete overleaping of one sphere, right into the middle of an entirely new and different one" (TL, 82). Between these spheres, there is no relation of causality, nor even one of expression; it is rather a relation of artistic invention and metaphorical production:

> For between two absolutely different spheres, as between subject and object, there is no causality, no correctness, and no expression; there is, at most, an *aesthetic* relation: I mean, a suggestive transference, a stammering translation into a completely foreign tongue—for which there is required, in any case, a freely inventive intermediate sphere and mediating force. (TL, 86)

What is also important to note here is the radical absence of any necessity (whether natural or otherwise) in this transference. Nietzsche is very clear on this point, and goes as far as to state that "even the relationship of a nerve stimulus to the generated image is not a necessary one" (TL, 87). Echoing Hume on this issue, Nietzsche understands any idea of necessity to be the result of repetition and habit:

> But when the same image has been generated millions of times and has been handed down for many generations and finally appears on the same occasion every time for all mankind, then it acquires at last the same meaning for men it would have if it were the sole necessary image and if the relationship of the original nerve stimulus to the generated image were a strictly causal one. (TL, 87)

Both the material basis of language as well as the metaphoricity of sense collapse the possibility of an ideal objective sense for, on the one hand, language only refers here to physiology, and on the other hand, its process of signification takes place in an arbitrary (metaphorical) transference from a nerve stimulus to a word. This is why Nietzsche is able to state that to infer from the nerve stimulus a cause outside of us is a prejudice of reason, of the principle of sufficient reason: Only such a prejudice would demand such a leap. Staying faithful to the genesis of language reveals instead the absence of objective sense as correlate of language. Hence the entirely conventional nature of language and conceptuality: No natural connection whatsoever with sense is here allowed. This will account for the fact that there cannot be a "natural" concept of responsibility.

Nietzsche emphasizes further this radical arbitrariness of language. For instance, relying on the gendered nature of the German language, he notes: "We separate things according to gender, designating the tree as masculine and the plant as feminine. What arbitrary assignments!" (TL, 82). Any cognitive distinction rests on such arbitrary decisions. The very plurality of languages is an argument for the non-naturalness of language, its independence from any reality or some "thing in itself": "The various languages placed side by side show that with words it is never a question of truth, never a question of adequate expression; otherwise, there would not be so many languages" (TL, 82). Arbitrary designations are mistakenly taken to be the exact descriptions of the things themselves. However, when one returns to the material genesis of language and sense, one can no longer invoke such thing in itself. "The 'thing in itself' (which is precisely what the pure truth, apart from any of its consequences, would be) is likewise something quite incomprehensible to the creator of language and something not in the least worth striving for," concludes Nietzsche (TL, 82).

Language, then, is a metaphorical activity, a copy of a copy, without proper meaning—and *so is thinking*. The way we think is a metaphorical activity. The very process of thought, indeed conceptual thinking, is structured metaphorically. If one thinks of the mechanisms involved in the formation of a concept (gathering resemblances, cutting differences, collecting similarities, comparing and contrasting markedly different cases, etc.), one can see how it displays a metaphorical activity as a bringing together of scattered elements, as a transference overleaping domains. In David Allison's words, this is "a shifting process of displacement and transference," so that "metaphor is an instrument *for* thinking and not an end-point or terminus of thought" (op. cit., 77). We may believe that through our linguistic designations, through our concepts, we know things as they truly are, as if we could know "something about the things themselves when we speak of trees, colors, snow, and flowers"; in fact, "we possess nothing but metaphors for things—metaphors which correspond in no way to the original entities" (TL, 83). The X of the thing in itself first appears as the nerve stimulus, then as an image and as a sound, an X each time crossing out objective sense in the crossing to another realm. There is no faithful representation from the X to the word or the concept, as language "is not derived from the essence of things." In fact, the affirmation of the metaphoricity of sense, as it forbids any positing of a proper meaning, leads to a radical change in the conception of the Real. For Nietzsche, the Real is no longer what tradition formerly held it to be, and which it never was. Nietzsche, writes Allison,

> no longer conceives reality according to the model of a stable, essentially static, or even law-governed, order. Nor does he claim that the real is itself rational or logical, much less that the natural order is reasonable or purposive. For Nietzsche, there is no enduring, fixed, absolutely stable form

of reality either outside ourselves, in the world, outside our own thought, or even within the confines of our thought. (Op. cit., 77)

In other words, there is no reality as an objective order to conform to or correspond to. Rather, "reality" becomes the constructed *result* of our *metaphorical* activity.

CONCEPTS AND METAPHORS

It is in this context that Nietzsche reengages the question of conceptuality. What is a concept for Nietzsche and how does he understand what he calls the "formation of concepts"? A concept, he tells us, is the result, the trace or residue of a metaphor, and the formation of concepts is an artistic creation.

> Anyone who has felt this cool breath [of logic] will hardly believe that even the concept—which is as bony, foursquare, and transposable as a die—is nevertheless merely the *residue of a metaphor,* and that the illusion which is involved in the artistic transference of a nerve stimulus into images is, if not the mother, then the grandmother of every single concept. (TL, 85)

In what sense? A concept is a dead metaphor, and in that sense its oblivion and negation. By definition, a concept must erase the individual experience from which it was formed. As a general representation, it necessarily negates "the unique and entirely individual original experience to which it owes its origin" so that "we obtain the concept, as we do the form, by overlooking what is individual and actual" (TL, 85). This implies that in the process of rationalization, the image is schematized into a concept. The rational person "universalizes all these impressions into less colorful, cooler concepts, so that he can entrust the guidance of his life and conduct to them. Everything which distinguishes man from the animals depends upon this ability to volatilize perceptual metaphors in a schema, and thus to dissolve an image into a concept" (TL, 84). A concept kills and mummifies metaphorical life, and it has been the philosophers' "idiosyncrasy" to essentialize, de-historicize, and eternalize metaphorical life. In *Twilight of the Idols,* Nietzsche thus claims that all that "philosophers have handled, for thousands of years now, has been conceptual mummies," and that they have been the worshippers of conceptual idols (TI, 18). This negation of life through concepts takes place precisely as the concept also *embraces* and includes within it "countless more or less similar cases—which means, purely and simply, cases which are never equal and thus altogether unequal" (TL, 83). This inclusion is a negation (and a sort of de-realization, as what is singularly real in experience is being abstracted from), for each concept "arises from the equation of unequal things" (TL, 83), abstracting from the differential uniqueness of experience. In fact, as Nietzsche emphasizes, "one leaf is never totally the same as another," which is another way of saying that the concept "leaf," as any concept, does not exist and thus only has an *imaginary* existence. The greatest paradox, of course, is that such a non-existent notion is then taken to be what is *most real*! Nietzsche points to this paradox when he notes that

> the concept "leaf" is formed by arbitrarily discarding these individual differences and by forgetting the distinguishing aspects. This awakens the idea that, in addition to the leaves, there exists in nature the "leaf": the original model according to which all the leaves were perhaps woven, sketched, measured, colored, curled, and painted—but by incompetent hands, so that no specimen turned out to be a correct, trustworthy, and faithful likeness of the original model. (TL, 83)[10]

David Allison narrates the story of Goethe's "pathetic" attempt one day to retrieve in a public garden the "ideal plant," the so-called "primal plant," the "archetypal 'essence' of all plants" (op. cit., 266 n. 14). Of course, in such a quest, Goethe had to go to a *specific* garden (the Public Gardens of Palermo) where, while looking for *the* unique plant, he found himself surrounded by a wild and anarchic *diversity* of countless, different, and very *real* plants! Ultimately, a concept is such an imaginary entity. In *The Gay Science,* Nietzsche makes the claim that over "immense periods of time," the intellect "produced nothing but errors" (GS, 169), and that such a concept as that of causality, that is, the duality of cause and effect, "probably does not exist" (GS, 172; translation modified).

One can thus see how, ironically, it is the activity of the mind that invented such fictions as "objectivity," "essences," and "causes" precisely on the basis of this *forgotten* metaphorical activity of the mind. In other words, a metaphor is taken to be a non-metaphor, and this oblivion results in what is called a concept! Man "forgets that the original perceptual metaphors are metaphors and takes them to be the things themselves" (TL, 86). One recalls Nietzsche's celebrated passage on truth, where truth is declared nothing but a fluid complex of metaphors:

> What then is truth? A movable host of metaphors, metonymies, and anthropomorphisms: in short, a sum of human relations which have been poetically and rhetorically intensified, transferred, and embellished, and which, after long usage, seem to a people to be fixed, canonical, and binding. Truths are illusions which we have forgotten are illusions; they are metaphors that have become worn out and have been drained of sensuous force, coins which have lost their embossing and are now considered as metal and no longer as coins. (TL, 84)

What all this amounts to is that there are no essences of things, and that concepts are not the grasp of such essences. An abstract concept does not and cannot have a corresponding referent in the world.[11] There is not even a basis for the very notion of a correctness of perception. It is a difficult thing for man, according to Nietzsche,

> to admit to himself that the insect or the bird perceives an entirely different world from the one that man does, and that the question of which of these perceptions of the world is the more correct one is quite meaningless, for this would have to have been decided previously in accordance with the criterion of the *correct perception,* which means, in accordance with a criterion which is *not available.* But in any case it seems to me that the correct perception—which would mean "the adequate expression of an object in the subject"—is a contradictory impossibility. (TL, 86)

In the very arbitrary nature of these customary metaphors called "truth," there is a sort of obligation to conform, to believe, that is, to *forget* that these are lies. "From the sense that one is obliged to designate one thing as 'red,' another as 'cold,' and a third as 'mute,' there arises a moral impulse in regard to truth" (TL, 84), and one places one's behavior, as it were, under the control of abstractions. These abstractions— concepts—are ways for humans to secure a stable "conventional" construct of reality on the basis of a forgetting of the primal unstable and creative metaphoricity of life:

> Only by forgetting this primitive world of metaphor can one live with any repose, security, and consistency: only by means of the petrification and coagulation of a mass of images which originally streamed from the primal faculty of human imagination like a fiery liquid, only in the invincible faith that *this* sun, *this* window, *this* table is a truth in itself, in short, only

by forgetting that he himself is an *artistically creating* subject, does man live with any repose, security, and consistency. (TL, 86)

The Error of Responsibility

GENEALOGY AS SYMPTOMATOLOGY

This apparent digression on Nietzsche's genealogy of conceptuality has in fact taken us to the heart of the matter. For responsibility, the concept of responsibility, as it has been constructed in the tradition, is not "accurate" and cannot be so. Like all concepts, it is a construct, an invention, a fiction, what Nietzsche calls an "error." By "error," of course, Nietzsche does not mean a falsehood or untruth that could be corrected. Rather, this description points to the *fictitious nature* of any concept whatsoever, and thus a genealogy of morality consists in revealing and exposing such fictitiousness. Ultimately, Nietzsche would stress the fictitious nature of life itself, which unfolds through and through as a creation of fictions. Nietzsche's critique thus does not consist in denouncing the falsity of a concept or a judgment; rather, it is to expose the lie *as a lie*. In *Ecce Homo,* he writes: "I was the first to *discover* the truth by being the first to experience lies as lies—smelling them out."[12] Not necessarily in order to reject them but to evaluate their purpose and utility for life and its health, since errors can be conditions of life. In *Beyond Good and Evil,* Nietzsche makes that point clearly while recognizing the utter novelty of his approach and how it could be misunderstood by the reader:

> The falseness of a judgment is not necessarily an objection to a judgment; in this respect our new language may sound strangest . . . The question is to what extent it is life-promoting, life-preserving, species-preserving, perhaps even species-cultivating . . . To recognize untruth as a condition of life . . . and a philosophy that risks this would by that token alone place itself beyond good and evil. (BGE, 11–12)

One is thus asked to put into question the belief in the objectivity of morality, including the traditional insistence on establishing a rational foundation for morality, a task which Nietzsche derides (BGE, 97). In such a task, morality is taken for granted, and in fact these attempts are nothing but a manifestation of a faith in the prevalent established morality. However, when Nietzsche calls for a philosophizing beyond good and evil, he first of all demands that the philosopher abandons the belief in the fiction of moral judgment. This follows from Nietzsche's insight that there are *"no moral phenomena at all"* (BGE, 85), that morality is merely an interpretation of phenomena, and more precisely, a *"mis*interpretation" (TI, 38).[13] Morality itself is nothing but a fiction. This is why moral judgments are never to be taken literally; they should instead be seen as symptoms of a certain state of life, and perhaps as a reaction against life, an opposition to life, if it is the case that the "true world" "has been constructed by contradicting the actual world (this 'true world' is in fact an apparent world, insofar as it is just a *moral-optical* illusion)" (TI, 21). In §258 of *The Will to Power,* Nietzsche speaks of his "attempt to understand moral judgments as symptoms and sign languages," themselves rooted in life itself, as these symptoms reveal the "processes of physiological prosperity or failures" (WP, 149). Moral values rest on physiological processes: Pity and love of mankind are said to rest on the "development of the sexual drive," justice on the development of "the drive to revenge," virtue on "pleasure in resistance," and honor on the "recognition of the similar and equal-in-power" (WP, 148). If applied to "the specific Christian-European morality: Our moral judgments are signs of decline, of disbelief in life, a preparation for pessimism" (WP, 149). Morality only has a semiological value, and should be approached in terms of a symptomatology that calls for interpretation: "Morality is just a sign language, just a symptomatology" (TI, 38), and Nietzsche goes so far as to speak of morality in *Beyond Good and Evil* as "a sign-language of the affects" (BGE, 100). With respect to the Kantian motif of respect, for example, respect is analyzed as "what deserves respect in me is that I can obey," and you "ought not to be different from me" (BGE, 100)![14]

This genealogy as symptomatology requires an investigation into the origins of our concepts, through what Nietzsche calls in the beginning of *Human, All Too Human,* a historical philosophizing.[15] Engaging a genealogy of the formation of the concept of responsibility will reveal how such a concept has been constructed on the basis of the categories of causality, subjectivity, intention, autonomy, agency, and free will—the "superstition" of free will, as Nietzsche terms it in *The Gay Science* (GS, 285), or also the "fable of intelligible freedom" (HH, 34) and the "fantastic concept of so-called intelligible freedom" (HH, 35). These fundamental concepts are in the end nothing but fictions, inventions, fabrications, without any correspondence to anything that exists. Conceptuality, along with the "fictions of logic," rest for Nietzsche on assumptions "with which nothing in the real world corresponds" (HH, 16), as, for instance, the assumption of the equality of things, the identity of the thing, causality or the I-cause, free will, agency, intention, and accountability—notions that have been the bedrock of the traditional concept of responsibility. These categories, which have become idols of worship and belief in the Western tradition—along with the other prejudices of reason that force us "to posit unity, identity, duration, substance, cause, thinghood, being," thus making us "entangled in error, *forced* into error" (TI, 20)—will be exposed as fictions by way of a deconstructing genealogy. The idealistic, metaphysical edifice built upon them will be dismantled, that is to say, exposed as a lie. In the *Twilight of the Idols*, Nietzsche states that Heraclitus will always be in the right "for saying that being is an empty fiction. The 'apparent' world is the only world: the 'true world' is just *added to it by a lie*" (TI, 19). Thus, the destructive or deconstructive genealogy of responsibility will consist in dismantling idealistic fictions in order to uncover[16] the processes at play within them, allowing for reevaluation of their values. Let us follow this deconstruction step by step.

THE "FABLE OF INTELLIGIBLE FREEDOM" AND THE *CAUSA SUI*

We recall how for Kant responsibility was wed to the position of a *subjectum* as absolute beginning and transcendental freedom as a capacity which, although it operated in the world, was not connected to the phenomenal laws of nature and was called "intelligible" for that very reason. (Whereas Nietzsche, in the second essay of *The Genealogy of Morals*, argues that responsibility arises out of a very concrete history—i.e., a contract between a creditor and a debtor!) We also recall how this faculty of spontaneity was understood as unfolding without a prior determining cause, as *escaping* the natural network of causes, not because it was simply "lawless," but because it was ultimately self-caused, a *causa sui*. A spontaneous act is not caused by another prior cause because *it causes itself,* spontaneously, of itself. Now, it is on this alleged capacity that Nietzsche focuses his critiques. Nietzsche is particularly severe, to say the least, with regard to the notion of *causa sui,* a bedrock of the concept of accountability. In §21 of *Beyond Good and Evil*, Nietzsche presents the concept of *causa sui* in the following way: "The *causa sui* is the best self-contradiction that has been conceived so far, it is a sort of rape and perversion of logic" (BGE, 28). Now we know that the very concepts of freedom and responsibility as accountability—indeed, the very concept of moral ascription—rest for Kant upon the possibility of a free, absolute beginning as self-caused, i.e., as *causa sui*. For Nietzsche, the belief in *causa sui* and freedom is first a matter of pride and arrogance, "the extravagant pride of man" that "has managed to entangle itself profoundly and frightfully with just this nonsense" (BGE, 28)—namely, the "nonsense" of a faculty of free will that is conceived of (so Spinoza described it) as an empire within an empire. The proud belief in free will is duplicated in the belief in our responsibility for our actions, as if we were their authors, as if we owned them. The history of the concept of responsibility has been, for Nietzsche, the history of such a metaphysical desire and arrogance (to be the author of one's actions, to originate oneself) and it is all encapsulated in the motif of *causa sui:* "The desire for 'freedom of the will' in the superlative metaphysical sense, which still holds sway, unfortunately, in the minds of the half-educated; the desire to bear the entire and ultimate responsibility for one's actions oneself, and to absolve God, the world, ancestors, chance, and society involves nothing less than to be precisely this *causa sui*" (BGE, 28). As if, through this motif of the *causa sui,* one could "pull oneself up into existence by the hair, out of the swamps of nothingness" (BGE, 28) in an act of self-origination, the prejudice being that "origination from something else counts as an objection that casts doubt on the value of what has thus originated" (TI, 20), and that all things of value must *not* have become. One also sees here how responsibility is understood within the context of this metaphysical dream, raising the human being to the level of a God (we recall how for Kant *causa sui* was shared by both God and us, as rational agents).

Nietzsche pursues his critique of such a metaphysics of noumenal freedom by emphasizing that the *causa sui* is the name for a de-historicized reality, which is then idealized insofar it supposedly has not grown from something else. Indeed, a prejudice which is typical of metaphysical thought structures the concept of *causa sui;* this is the inversion of values in terms of what is most important and valuable, an "idiosyncrasy" of the philosophers, which "consists in confusing what is first with what is last" (TI, 19). The most abstract abstractions are made to be the first and highest levels of reality. Philosophers put first "what comes at the end—unfortunately! For it should never come at all!—the 'highest concepts,' that is, the most universal, the emptiest concepts, the final wisp of evaporating reality—these they posit at the beginning *as* the beginning" (TI, 19). The end-result of an abstraction is confused with the beginning. In this inversion, there is the accompanying valorization of a reality that would not have become, which would not have roots in anything considered lower. To have evolved is considered to be a lack and a fault. "The higher is not *permitted* to grow out of the lower, is not *permitted* to have grown at all . . . Moral: everything of the first rank has to be *causa sui*," and Nietzsche adds, "That's where they get their stupendous concept 'God'" (TI, 19–20). According to Nietzsche, the belief in *causa sui* rests upon the belief that we must have "'been at home in a higher world at one time'—(instead of *in a far lower one,* which would have been the truth!)—'we must have been divine, *since* we have reason!'" (TI, 21). In fact, not only have we never dwelt there, but we now have strictly no access to some noumenal realm. Reason is nothing but a metaphysics of language, a "crude fetishism" with respect to language. "In its origin, language belongs to the time of the most rudimentary type of psychology: We encounter a crude set of fetishes when we become conscious of the basic presuppositions of the metaphysics of language— or, to put it plainly, *reason*" (TI, 20). The Kantian reliance on the *causa sui* betrays both this metaphysics of language and its theological orientation. "'Reason' (*die Vernunft*) in language: oh, what a tricky old woman she is! I'm afraid we're not rid of God because we still believe in grammar" (TI, 20). Intelligible, self-causing, transcendental, this concept of freedom is an error. "What can be *our* doctrine alone?—That nobody *gives* human beings their qualities, neither God, nor society, nor their parents and ancestors, *nor they themselves* (the nonsense of this last notion we are rejecting was taught by Kant as 'intelligible freedom', and maybe was already taught by Plato as well)" (TI, 36). For Nietzsche, the notions of *causa sui,* free will, and transcendental freedom are nothing but errors, and his genealogy of these terms will lead to the deconstruction of the concept of responsibility *understood as the accountability of the subject.* At the beginning, there is no spontaneity of the will. Indeed, there is no such thing as a "first beginning." At the beginning, "there stands the great and fatal error of thinking that the will is something *effective*—that will is an *ability* . . . Today we know that it is just a word" (TI, 20). The foundation of the *causa sui* finds itself deconstructed.

In terms of action, this foundation took the name of (willful) intention, as Nietzsche clarifies that "the origin of an action was interpreted in the most precise terms as itself originating in an *intention*" (BGE, 44). For Nietzsche, intention—the "morality of intention" (BGE, 44)—is a prejudice, "something on the order of astrology and alchemy," and "in any case something to be overcome" (BGE, 45). The myth of intention as origin of the act (a "calamitous new superstition") was introduced by traditional morality, moral judgments being possible on the basis of such intentions: "The intention as the whole origin and prehistory of an action—almost to the present day this prejudice dominated moral praise, blame, judgment, and philosophy on earth" (BGE, 44). However, is this reliance on intention, our belief in it, sufficient to quiet what Nietzsche describes as a "suspicion" with respect to intention, namely, how do we know for certain that intention exhausts the act? Is consciousness the totality of the field of experience? Is an action caused by a willful intention? In fact, "Today at least we immoralists have the suspicion that the decisive value of an action lies precisely in what is *unintentional* in it" (BGE, 44).[17] By raising a doubt on the belief in consciousness and intention, by reintegrating the unintentional (the involuntary!) into the fabric of the act, Nietzsche suggests that so-called willful intention is nothing but a "symptom" of something else, comparing it to the skin of an unknown body, which betrays something but conceals "even more." The deconstructive genealogy of responsibility takes here the form of a reversal of a skin, of a surface.

Further, this critique of free will and intention as the ground of action, of what Nietzsche calls "intention-morality," leads him to approach intention thus: "In short, we believe that the intention is merely a sign and symptom that still requires interpretation" (BGE, 44). Its apparent simplicity conceals many struggling, contradictory forces, whose momentary issue is called an "event" or "action." It would be overly simplistic to believe in some linear causal source located in a sovereign willful agent. The seemingly simple concept of free will conceals a plurality of conflicting forces as well: Free will is "something *complicated*," "a plurality of sensations" (BGE, 25). In the belief in the concept of conscious intention, there has been a shift, a sort of confusion between cause and effect through which one takes the effect (the accompanying effect called "consciousness") for the cause of the act. This raises the question of causality, which is operative in the concept of intention—and hence of responsibility.

THE ERROR OF CAUSALITY

For Nietzsche, causality does not represent an objective order of things, does not structure some objective order. One should not reify cause and effect. In fact, cause and effect, as well as the concept of *causa sui,* are not in the least properties of things. They are not to be used, says Nietzsche, but not for explanation: "one should use 'cause' and 'effect' only as pure *concepts,* that is to say, as conventional fictions (*conventioneller Fiktionen*) for the purpose of designation and communication—*not* for explanation" (BGE, 29). This is why Nietzsche's critique of free will does not take him to some deterministic position; he is just as opposed to the naïve simplistic *belief* in unfree will. As is the case with free will, "'unfree will' is mythology" (BGE, 29), for as he explains further, "in real life" there are only strong or weak wills. The concept "unfree will" amounts to a misuse of cause and effect, as it maintains the belief in the objectivity of causality, thus sharing the same common prejudice with the proponents of free will, at the very moment it thinks it rejects it. There is thus no free will and there is no causality as some objective order or lawfulness. It is not that they do not exist; rather, they do not exist *in this way,* as they are *fictions we have invented.* "It is *we* alone who have devised cause, sequence, for-each-other, relativity, constraint, number, law, freedom, motive, and purpose; and when we project and mix this symbol world into things as if it existed 'in itself,' we act once more as we have always acted—*mythologically*" (BGE, 29). Free will is a mythology, as is unfree will. These concepts are not to be believed, but to be taken as symptoms we must interpret.

In §112 of *The Gay Science,* Nietzsche emphasizes the artificial character of cause and effect "explanation," stressing how one separates in the flux of life "two separate things," cause and effect, whereas there is but "a manifold one-after-another." Nietzsche sees the flux of becoming whereas metaphysical rationalist thought invented a causal order, that is, the abstraction of a cause distinguished from the effect. However, causality *does not exist*: "Cause and effect: such a duality probably never exists; in truth we are confronted by a continuum out of which we isolate a couple of pieces, just as we perceive motion only as isolated points and then infer it without ever actually seeing it" (GS, 173). Ultimately for Nietzsche, the cause and effect structure is a construct concealing the manifold continuum of life, an artificial construct that we impose on the flux of life:

> The suddenness with which many effects stand out misleads us; actually, it is sudden only for us. In this moment of suddenness there is an infinite number of processes that elude us. An intellect that could see cause and effect as a continuum and a flux and not, as we do, in terms of an arbitrary division and dismemberment—would repudiate the concept of cause and effect and deny all conditionality. (GS, 173)

Causality, in fact, explains nothing, because with such concepts, we are dealing with nothing but imaginary beings. "But how could we possibly explain anything! We operate only with things that do not exist: lines, planes, bodies, atoms, divisible time spans, divisible spaces" (GS, 172). Knowledge is not explanation but an imposition of forms—our human, all-too-human form—onto the flux of life: "how should explanations be at all possible when we first turn everything into an *image,* our image!" (GS, 172). Science is an attempt at humanizing things. The causal order thus constructed reflects our anthropomorphizing of life as we impose our form on the flux of becoming. We have therefore constructed an imaginary world to live in, by inventing the concepts (lies) of bodies, lines, planes, causes and effects. Morality and religion are nothing but an imaginary construct of causes and effects, i.e., the construct of an imaginary world: "In Christianity neither morality nor religion come into contact with reality at any point. Nothing but imaginary *causes* ('God,' 'soul,' 'ego,' 'spirit,' 'free will'—or 'unfree will'): nothing but imaginary *effects* ('sin,' 'redemption,' 'grace,' 'punishment,' 'forgiveness of sins')" (AC, 137). Nietzsche thus reveals the connection between imaginary beings, an imaginary natural science, an imaginary psychology, and an imaginary teleology—all leading to an imaginary world, a "purely fictitious world" invented out of hatred for the actual one.

One of the constitutive errors of the metaphysical tradition of responsibility is the reliance on causality, the imposition of causes on every existence, on every event, as their *substratum:* Causality is the alleged substrate of the event. The very notion of imputability rests upon the belief in causality as substratum. "Being is thought into things everywhere as a cause, is *imputed* to things" (TI, 20). We have *created* a world of causes, a world of wills, and a world of spirits. All happening is considered a doing, all doing is supposed to be the effect of a will; the world is understood as a multiplicity of doers; a doer or subject "was imputed to everything that happened" (TI, 32). Yet Nietzsche insists that one cannot attach a doer to deeds: "there is no 'being' behind doing, effecting, becoming," and the doer "is merely a fiction added to the deed" (GM, 45). This position of a cause-ground is what allows for a system of accountability—and therefore of punishment—to be set up. For Nietzsche, such a position is an error in several senses. First, there is the confusion or inversion of cause and effect. In the opening lines of "The Four Great Errors" in *Twilight of the Idols*, Nietzsche insists that, "There is no error more dangerous than *confusing the effect with the cause*" (TI, 30), an inversion which of course is the symptom of a more fateful inversion of values with respect to life, an inversion that condemns life and "affirms" the negation of life. This confusion of cause and effect, which Nietzsche calls "the genuine corruption of reason" and one of "humanity's oldest and most contemporary customs," historically bears the names of religion and morality. Religion and morality rest upon such an inversion: "*Every* statement formulated by religion and morality contains it" (TI, 30). The example that Nietzsche gives, that of Cornaro's diet, betrays that it was not free will that caused Cornaro's healthy life, but a healthy life that was the basis for his "skimpy diet."[18] The argument presented in this example is that an artificial construct is mistakenly taken to be the basis and cause for living, when the so-called cause was in fact the effect of a life-disposition. Once again, the mistake is the denial of the material basis of life and the idealization of an abstract principle which is constructed after the fact and mistakenly (retroactively) posited as cause and origin. The inversion of cause and effect reflects the inversion of material existence into an ideality—an inversion that Nietzsche, in turn, seeks to invert! Based on such inversion and abstraction, causality is made to play the role of the foundation of events, allowing for the corresponding concept of responsibility as accountability of the subject to be established. How does this happen? Through the imaginary hypostatizing of a cause beneath the event, through the retroactive imputing of such cause to the event. Judith Butler stresses this retroactive assigning of a cause in the constitution of responsibility: "For Nietzsche, the self as 'cause' of an injurious action is always retroactively attributed—the doer is only belatedly attached to the deed. In fact, the doer becomes the causal agent of the deed only through a retroactive attribution that seeks to comply with a moral ontology stipulated by a legal system."[19] Of course, and I will return to this question shortly, one needs to bear in mind that the doer as such is also a fiction, and that in fact the very opposition between a doer and a deed is a lie. This error itself rests upon what appear here as a retroactive attribution, that is, an inversion of temporality.

THE INVERSION OF TEMPORALITY

The second error of causality pertains to that phenomenon of the retroactive assigning of the cause to the event, to what Nietzsche describes as an "inversion of temporality," an *Umkehrung der Zeit*. The focus of Nietzsche's analysis bears on the peculiar temporality of cause-assigning, and the reversal of temporality that takes place in the process of an *a posteriori* imputation of a cause. Nietzsche calls this phenomenon the error of "false causality," once again pointing to the invention of an imaginary causality to give an account of the event. Causality, and in particular the inner causality of the will, is a pure invention: "In every age we have believed that we know what a cause is: but where did we get our knowledge, or more precisely, our belief that we have knowledge about this? From the realm of the famous 'internal facts,' none of which has up to now proved to be factual" (TI, 31). This delusion lies in the retroactive assigning of a cause, presenting the paradoxical temporality of an after-the-fact (re)construction that is then posited as having existed *before* the event! "I'll begin with dreams: a particular sensation, for instance, a sensation due to a distant cannon shot, has a cause imputed to it (*untergeschoben*) afterwards (*nachträglich*)" (TI, 32–33).[20] Once the cause has been introduced *after the event,* it is then said to exist prior to the event, an event that has now been transformed into necessity and meaning—a meaning that we have introduced: "In the meantime, the sensation persists in a kind of resonance: it waits, as it were, until the drive to find causes allows it to come into the foreground—not as an accident anymore, but as 'meaning'" (TI, 33). As Nietzsche explains, the sensation then becomes part of "a whole little novel in which precisely the dreamer is the protagonist." The event has been reconstructed and is now said to be happening *according to causality* (one recalls here Kant's "Analogies of Experience," in which it is "deduced transcendentally" that events occur according to the law of causality). Of course, the cause was produced afterwards, and then re-injected as that from which the event occurred.

The cannon shot shows up in a *causal* way, and time seems to flow backward. What comes later, the motivation, is experienced first, often with a hundred details that flash by like lightning; the shot *follows* . . . What has happened? The representations *generated* by a certain state of affairs were misunderstood as the cause of this state of affairs. (TI, 33)

This inversion of temporality satisfies a certain drive (the "drive to find causes"), arising out of a need. Far from being the objective order of things, causality rests on a subjective need.

CAUSALITY AS NEED

Indeed, Nietzsche claims that causality arises out of a need. The drive to *produce* a cause is first a need to *assign* a cause, and this need immediately betrays, one should note, that there is a perception of a lack that needs to be supplemented. In other words, the drive to find causes supplements . . . a lack of cause! The cause itself is lacking. An event, in its eventfulness and givenness, is indeed a happening *devoid* of a cause: It happens first, from and as itself. Phenomenologically, the event happens in a non-causal way, in an anarchic irruption which disrupts any order (we recall here how Kant described freedom as rebellious to causality, as lawless), with a meaning that is either missing, partial or delayed, still to come, *en souffrance*. The response to this "suffering" is the drive to find causes, or rather, as we will see, causal *interpretations* (but *not* causation). Nietzsche sees a lack at the root of all our cause-seeking:

> Most of our general feelings—every kind of inhibition, pressure, tension, and explosion in the play and counterplay of the organs, and in particular the state of the *nervus sympaticus* [sympathetic nervous system]—arouse our drive to find causes: we want to have a *reason* for feeling that we're in *such and such* a state—a bad state or a good state. (TI, 33)

It is not enough, he concludes, to simply stay with the fact that has occurred. Some *groundlessness* is being felt, and it is then felt as a *lack*. What is lacking is a reason, a ground, a cause, for our existence and our feelings. What is felt is then nothing else than the groundlessness of existence itself, and a cause would provide a ground that could provisionally suture the lack. In fact, the event manifests the lack of cause in such a way that we are driven to seek it at all costs. The pure "that" (i.e., facticity) of the event is the locus of anxiety: "It's never enough for us just to determine the mere fact *that* we find ourselves in such and such a state: we admit this fact—become *conscious* of it only if we've given it some kind of motivation" (TI, 33). A cause then becomes the place-holder of the lack of cause, the place-holder of . . . a nothing.

However, as I alluded to, we never "find" actual causes (there are no such things), but rather invent causal (mis)interpretations which are ultimately nothing but memories and mental associations of other past events. Causality becomes a remembering. "Memory, which comes into play in such cases without our knowing it, calls up earlier states of the same kind, and the causal interpretations that are rooted in them—but *not* their causation" (TI, 33). The faith in these representations, in causality, is reinforced and secured out of habit and custom. However, the real cement of the recourse to and faith in causality lies in our need for it, which is itself based on a fear. If causality is rooted in the drive to find causes, this in turn drive responds to a fear, and finding a cause calms our fears. A distress is felt before the lack of cause, so that any explanation is better than none. Finding a cause allows us to supplement the lack, to provide a basis and security to the uncanniness of existence. This is why Nietzsche insists that knowledge seeks to make the unfamiliar familiar, reducing the uncanny of the pure event and thereby increasing our sense of control. The drive to causality is the drive to transform something unfamiliar into something familiar, a motivation that lends itself to a psychological analysis and genealogy by Nietzsche:

> *A psychological explanation of this error.*—Tracing something unfamiliar back to something familiar alleviates us, calms us, pacifies us, and in addition provides a feeling of power. The unfamiliar brings with it danger, unrest, and care—our first instinct is to *do away* with these painful conditions. First principle: some explanation is better than none. (TI, 33)

What is considered to be "true" is most often what makes us feel good, and the first representation that explains the unknown as familiar feels so good that one considers it true. "Proof of *pleasure* ('strength') as criterion of truth" (TI, 33). In *The Gay Science,* Nietzsche further characterizes this making-familiar of knowledge as an increase in the feeling of power. In §355, for instance, titled "The origin of our concept of 'knowledge,'" Nietzsche asks: "What is it that the common people take for knowledge? What do they want when they want 'knowledge'? Nothing more than this: something strange is to be reduced to something *familiar*" (GS, 300). Even in the philosophical tradition, Nietzsche insists, knowledge is a factor of appropriation of the unknown, i.e., the unfamiliar. "And we philosophers—have we really meant *more* than this when we have spoken of knowledge? What is familiar means what we are used to so that we no longer marvel at it, our everyday, some rule in which we are stuck, anything at all in which we feel at home" (GS, 300). What could drive such a quest? Clearly no longer in this context some disinterested concern for knowledge as objective truth about things in themselves! Rather, a fear before the unknown and a desire for the security of the familiar, what Nietzsche calls the "instinct of fear":

> Look, isn't our need for knowledge precisely this need for the familiar, the will to uncover under everything strange, unusual, and questionable something that no longer disturbs us? Is it not the *instinct of fear* that bids us to know? And is the jubilation of those who attain knowledge not the jubilation over the restoration of a sense of security? (GS, 300–301)

Causality is then a lie created out of fear: "the drive to find causes is conditioned and aroused by the feeling of fear" (TI, 34). The question 'why?' is an expression of that fear, and a cause is sought to alleviate that fear.

A proof of this is that the cause given is always something familiar, something we already know, so that "the new, the unexperienced, the alien, is excluded as a cause" (TI, 34). And the "fact that something already *familiar,* something we have experienced, something inscribed in memory is posited as the cause, is the first consequence of this need" (TI, 34; translation modified). As Nietzsche pleasantly explains, the banker thinks right away about "business," the Christian about "sin," the girl about "love." What matters is to suppress the feeling of the strange and new; in other words, *with the position of causality, what matters is the suppression of the eventfulness of the event as ungrounded. Causality suppresses the uncanniness of being.* Finding a cause suppresses the anxiety of the uncanny, establishes a sphere of security in an "at-home." Echoing Descartes's title for the Second Meditation, where he famously asserts that the mind is better known than the body, Nietzsche claims that this privileging of the known over the unknown establishes the belief in so-called "internal facts," such as free will, a kind of inner causality as the main site of truth.

> When they [men of knowledge] find something in things—under them,
> or behind them—that is unfortunately quite familiar to us, such as our
> multiplication tables or our logic, or our willing and desiring—how happy
> they are right away! For "what is familiar is known": on this they are
> agreed. Even the most cautious among them suppose that what is familiar
> is at least *more easily knowable* than what is strange; and that, for example,
> sound method demands that we start from the "inner world," from the
> "facts of consciousness," because this world is *more familiar to us*! Error
> of errors! (GS, 301)

Exposing this Cartesian prejudice, that the mind is better known than
the body, Nietzsche also exposes the ensuing myths of the "I," of "inner
facts," of the internal causality of the will in the subject, all of which
myths are constitutive of the belief in agency as ground for the sense of
responsibility as accountability of the subject.

THE SUPPOSITION OF THE SUBJECT

Responsibility rests on a threefold belief, namely, that motives are the
antecedents of an act, that thoughts are caused, and that the I is such a
cause. In §17 of *Beyond Good and Evil,* Nietzsche analyzes the supposition of a subject under its thinking and denounces it as a fiction. First,
in a quasi-phenomenological observation, describing a "small terse fact,"
Nietzsche notes that a thought does not come from some I-substrate but
instead originates *from itself,* and that it comes when it comes. "With
regard to the superstitions of logicians, I shall never tire of emphasizing
a small terse fact, which these superstitious minds hate to concede—
namely, that a thought comes when 'it' wishes, and not when 'I' wish"
(BGE, 24). It is false, even unphenomenological, to state that the I is the
condition of thinking, or that the I is in a position of subject. The notion
of the "I think" as principle and foundation, as it has been established
in modern philosophy since Descartes, is said by Nietzsche to be contrary to the *facts:* "it is a *falsification* of the facts of the case to say that
the subject 'I' is the condition of the predicate 'think'" (BGE, 24). Even
the "it" (in the expression, "a thought comes when 'it' wishes") is misleading, for it might suggest that there is some entity, that is, *some substrate* at the basis of thinking. "It thinks: but that this 'it' is precisely the
famous old 'ego' is, to put it mildly, only a supposition, an assertion, and

assuredly not an 'immediate certainty'" (BGE, 24). The notion of an underlying subjectivity is thus contrary to the facts, an unphenomenological construction.

The alleged "simplicity" of the "I think" is likewise deceiving, a seduction of words. Nietzsche challenges the reliance on the notion of an immediate certainty (the immediacy and evidence of the 'I think'). In *Beyond Good and Evil,* Nietzsche speaks of the belief of those "harmless self-observers" in the superstition of the "I will" or the "I think," "as though knowledge here got hold of its object purely and nakedly as 'the thing in it self,' without any falsification on the part of either the subject or the object" (BGE, 23). However, the very expressions "immediate certainty," "absolute knowledge," and "thing in itself" all involve a contradiction in terms (*contradictio in adjecto*) since all certainty is constructed, all knowledge is for us and therefore not absolute, and the thing in itself cannot be "in itself" since that would mean absolutely independent from us, to the point where we would not even notice it! When one analyzes the process that is expressed in this sentence, 'I think,' one would find many claims therein that are impossible to establish, much less prove,

> for example, that it is *I* who think, that there must necessarily be something that thinks, that thinking is an activity and operation on the part of a being who is thought of as a cause, that there is an "ego," and, finally, that it is already determined what is to be designated by thinking—that I *know* what thinking is. (BGE, 23)

Unlike what Descartes asserted, the 'I think' is anything but "simple." In fact, these "simple truths" are more like *decisions:*

> for if I had not already decided within myself what it is, by what standard could I determine whether that which is just happening is not perhaps "willing" or "feeling"? In short, the assertion "I think" assumes that I *compare* my state at the present moment with other states of myself which I know, in order to determine what it is; on account of this retrospective connection with further "knowledge," it has, at any rate, no immediate certainty for me. (BGE, 23)

Instead of immediate certainties, we have the following questions: "From where do I get the concept of thinking? Why do I believe in cause and effect? What gives me the right to speak of an ego, and even of an ego as cause, and finally of an ego as the cause of thought?" (BGE, 24). All these are constructs for Nietzsche, which he understands in terms of the constitutive role of language in thinking. The subject will appear as a linguistic construct.

An underlying substantial ego is not a phenomenological fact but a metaphysical idol, and ultimately for Nietzsche a *linguistic* prejudice: The substantialist egology of modern Cartesian philosophy is a reliance on the implicit metaphysics of grammar! "One infers here according to the grammatical habit: 'thinking is an activity; every activity requires an agent; consequently—.'" (BGE, 24), so that Nietzsche can state, "formerly, one believed in the soul as one believed in grammar and the grammatical subject" (BGE, 67). This is why, as Lawrence Hatab explains, Nietzsche's critique of free agency rests upon a linguistic analysis of the "seduction of language." He writes that Nietzsche "notes 'the seduction of language' that tempts us to distinguish an agent from its deed by way of the grammatical difference between nouns and verbs . . . Nietzsche believes that the very notion of agency is a fiction born from such linguistic constructions."[21] Nietzsche clarifies this dependency of a metaphysics of subjectivity on language in *The Will to Power*. Starting with a critique of the positivists' view that "there are only facts," Nietzsche recalls that precisely all there is are not "facts," but interpretations. The very statement that claims that everything is subjective is also an interpretation (this is why, we should note in passing, the statement "there are only interpretations" does not mean "everything is subjective," and that Nietzsche's perspectivism is not a subjectivism or a relativism).[22] By claiming that all there is, is interpretation, and that even the subjective is an interpretation, Nietzsche is also casting doubt on the belief in the subject. This is why he continues by stating that an interpretation does *not* require an interpreter. "Finally, is it necessary to posit an interpreter behind the interpretation? Even this is invention, hypothesis" (WP, 267). The subject is indeed "not something given," i.e., not a fact. What is the subject in this case? It is, we are told, "something added and invented and projected behind what there is" (WP, 267).

In the following paragraphs, Nietzsche writes on the subject as both the Cartesian metaphysical cause of thought and as a word, i.e., the linguistic "I," by stressing their fictitious nature. He states that, "However habitual and indispensable this fiction [of the subject] may have become by now—that in itself proves nothing against its imaginary origin" (WP, 268). However, ultimately, the metaphysical notion of subjectivity as substrate rests upon the linguistic motif of the subject, and not the other way around: "The concept of substance is a consequence of the concept of the subject: not the reverse!" This means that the metaphysicians' notion of substance is a linguistic construct, since the subject is a linguistic construct. Nietzsche had previously established that the "I" is a word that we set up "at the point at which our ignorance begins," a horizon of our knowledge and not a truth. This is why, after recalling the metaphysical Cartesian motif of (and belief in) substantiality—"'There is thinking: therefore there is something that thinks': this is the upshot of all Descartes's argumentation. But that means positing as 'true a priori' our belief in the concept of substance"—he adds that such a belief "is simply a formulation of our grammatical custom that adds a doer to every deed" (WP, 268). A subject as cause of its effects, an agent as cause of its actions, a doer as cause of its deed, these would be grammatical-metaphysical fictions; we are prejudiced by what Nietzsche characterizes in *The Genealogy of Morals* as a "seduction of language," along with the "fundamental errors of reason that are petrified in it" (GM, 45). Just as the "popular mind" distinguishes the lightning from its flash, just as it reifies the "it" in the "it rains," just as it conceives of the event as an action requiring a subject (as if behind the manifestation of strength, there was an indifferent substratum that would have the freedom to be manifest strength or not), just as it "doubles the deed" ("it posits the same event first as cause and then a second time as its effect"), the metaphysician distinguishes a subject from its effects. In fact, Nietzsche proclaims forcefully: "there is no such substratum; there is no 'being' behind doing, effecting, becoming; the doer is merely a fiction added to the deed—the deed is everything" (GM, 45). "The deed is everything," this expression would require and call for another conception of the event, in which such an event (i.e., a "deed") would no longer be anchored in a cause-substrate and no longer ascribed as an action to an imputable agent, but would be recognized as happening from itself and yet happening to someone. It would require, thus, another conception of responsibility, no longer as the accountability of the subject, but rather in terms of a responsiveness to the event. We will return to this.

Indeed, the traditional concept of responsibility requires the (sup)position of a subject, and participates in an ontology of substantiality and causation. For Nietzsche, as one would say 'I,' one would immediately posit a subject, and 'thinking' would become the predicate of such subject-cause. The subject and the substantial 'I' are only *habits*, and Nietzsche writes that "perhaps some day we shall accustom ourselves, including the logicians, to get along without the little 'it' (which is all that is left of the honest little old ego)" (BGE, 24). The 'I,' the 'it,' are interpretations added to the event. In *Twilight of the Idols*, Nietzsche stresses the fictitious nature of the ego, which is only a word: "And as for the 'I'! That has become a fable, a fiction, a play on words: it has completely and utterly ceased to think, to feel, and to will!" (TI, 32). Nietzsche recalls that these concepts are products of our invention: "There are simply no mental causes at all! . . . We have invented a world of causes, a world of will . . . we have constituted the ego as a cause" (TI, 32). Events are constructed as actions; actions, constructed as deed, are distinguished from doers. A doer is then constructed as subject; an agent which is distinct from the act is invented. All happening "was a doing, all doing the effect of a willing; for it, the world became a multitude of doers, a doer (a 'subject') was imputed to everything that happened" (TI, 32). This belongs to the prejudices of reason, which "sees actors and actions everywhere" (TI, 20), which "believes in the will as an absolute cause," which believes in the 'I,' etc. Ultimately, an ontology of causation is enforced everywhere, by which "Being is thought into things everywhere as a cause, is *imputed* to things" (TI, 20). Imputation is here a concept that is determinative of the metaphysical sense of responsibility, and it is here shown to belong to an ontology of substance, to be mere product of a habitual (mis)use of language. Its deconstruction will go through a critique of the concept of free will, long thought to have a causal efficacy.

THE ERROR OF FREE WILL

In "The Four Great Errors" of *Twilight of the Idols*, Nietzsche shows that belief in the fictions of consciousness or the ego as "internal fact" rests upon the belief in the will as an efficient cause. Of all these myths regarding such internal facts, Nietzsche singles out the belief in the will as cause, "Of these three 'internal facts' which seemed to vouch for causality, the first and most convincing is the 'fact' of *will as cause*" (TI, 32), the so-called internal causality. Ultimately, the issue for Nietzsche is "whether we really recognize the will as *efficient*, whether we believe in the causality of the will" (BGE, 48). But Nietzsche states that "Today we don't believe any word of all that anymore" (TI, 32); the so-called internal world is a world of illusions and mirages, and "the will is one of them." The will is now just a word, a word that no longer has any power to convince or to move—an epiphenomenon, a mere superficial accompaniment. "The 'internal world' is full of optical illusions and mirages: the will is one of them. The will no longer moves anything, so it no longer explains anything either—it just accompanies events, and it can even be absent" (TI, 32). The will thus also loses its role as motive to become a surface-phenomenon, an accompanying thought: "The so-called 'motive': another error. Just a surface phenomenon of consciousness, an accessory to the act, which conceals the *antecedentia* of an act rather than representing them" (TI, 32). A similar inversion as that of the belief in causality is at play in our belief in the will as cause. Nietzsche explains that we believe ourselves to be "causal in the act of willing; there, at least, we thought that we were *catching causality in the act*" (TI, 31).

Philosophers, Nietzsche tells us in reference to Schopenhauer, "are accustomed to speak of the will as if it were the best-known thing in the world." Whereas Schopenhauer claimed that we know the will absolutely, he in fact only borrowed a "*popular prejudice* and exaggerated it" (BGE, 25). The will is in fact very complicated ("Willing seems to me to be above all something *complicated*"), something that has unity in name only, "and it is precisely in this one word that the popular prejudice lurks" (BGE, 25). Beneath the name of "will," there is for Nietzsche a plurality of *sensations,* the will being described in these pages of *Beyond Good and Evil* in extraordinarily physical terms:

> In all willing there is, first, a plurality of sensations, namely, the sensation of the state "*away from which*" and the sensation of the state "*towards which,*" the sensation of this "from" and "towards" themselves, and then also an accompanying muscular sensation, which, even without our putting into motion "arms and legs," begins its action by force of habit as soon as we "will" anything. (BGE, 25)

Sensations make up the actual "ingredients" of the will, along with what Nietzsche calls the phenomenon of a "ruling thought" ("in every act of the will there is a ruling thought") so that one can no longer abstract a pure will from thought. In addition to a complex of sensations and thoughts, the will is an affect, and more precisely, the affect of command or superiority. Nietzsche points to a physiology of power within the will. "That which is termed 'freedom of the will' is essentially the affect of superiority in relation to him who must obey: 'I am free, "he" must obey'—this consciousness is inherent in every will" (BGE, 25). Also present is the focus of attention, the aiming at a goal, "the unconditional evaluation that 'this and nothing else is necessary now,' the belief that obedience will be achieved ... A man who *wills*—, commands something within himself that renders obedience, or that he believes renders obedience" (BGE, 26).

The peculiar aspect of such a command—indeed, "what is strangest about the will," concedes Nietzsche—is that we "are at the same time the commanding *and* the obeying parties" (BGE, 26). However, we are used to deceiving ourselves by ignoring this duality, and we construct the myth of a simple subject through the synthetic concept of the 'I,' and draw erroneous conclusions from it, "to such a degree that he who wills believes sincerely that willing *suffices* for action." The one who wills believes that will and actions are one, and he ascribes "the success, the carrying out of the willing, to the will itself." In the end, the affirmation of the will is the increase in the sensation of power. "'Freedom of the will'—that is the expression for the complex state of delight of the person exercising volition, who commands and at the same time identifies himself with the executor of the order—who, as such, enjoys also the triumph over obstacles, but thinks within himself that it was really his will itself that overcame them" (BGE, 26). In all willing there is essentially a question of commanding and obeying, that is, an experience of power. The notion of "free will" thus needs to be approached in terms of power. In this passage from *Beyond Good and Evil,* Nietzsche describes it in highly personal, psychological terms, giving a psychological account of freedom. There is no free will, but there are weak or strong wills. The weak-willed invest notions such as necessity, causal connections, out of a compulsion to obey. Discussions on the "unfreedom of the will" can be seen from two perspectives. On the one hand, "some will not give up their 'responsibility,' their belief in *themselves,* the personal right to *their* merits at any price (the vain races belong to this class)." However, "others, on the contrary, do not wish to be answerable for anything, or blamed for anything, and owing to an inward self-contempt, seek to *shift the blame* for themselves somewhere else." These are the weak-willed, who indulge in pity and the religions of human suffering.

FREE WILL AS A "MAKING-RESPONSIBLE"

Ultimately it appears that agency, causality, free will, and an underlying ego, far from being the conditions of responsibility, were in fact constructed *in order to constitute* responsibility. They were invented in order to posit an agent as responsible and accountable, since this agent is then declared to be cause and origin of its actions. The belief in the will gives us the certainty that we are the cause of our actions, thus giving rise to our belief in responsibility—that we are responsible for our actions. In other words, responsibility is not the consequence of free will; rather, free will as a concept was invented to make responsibility possible: "Likewise, we never doubted that all the *antecedentia* of an action, its causes, were to be sought in consciousness and could be discovered there if we looked for them—discovered as 'motives': otherwise, the actor would not have been free *for* the action, responsible *for* it" (TI, 31–32). Far from being some objective fact, free will is here a construct built with the certain purpose of making humans responsible.

Under the heading "The Error of Free Will," in *Twilight of the Idols*, after having declared that we today have no "sympathy" anymore for the concept of free will, Nietzsche calls this will "the most disreputable of all theologians' tricks, designed to make humanity 'responsible' in the theologians' sense, that is, *to make them dependent on them*" (TI, 35). Free will was invented in order to constitute humanity as responsible, and responsibility is here traced back to a making-responsible *for the sake of a power*. After having shown how the alleged unity of 'the will' was nothing but a complex of sensations structured through a problematics of power, Nietzsche prolongs his critique of free will in terms of the motives behind its institution. Of what complexes is free will (and *causa sui*) the symptom? Positing accountability, demanding accountability, making-responsible, all require the belief in free will, in order to punish. This is what Nietzsche calls the "psychology" of all making-responsible—i.e., making others guilty and thus dependent. "Here I am simply offering the psychology of all making-responsible.—Wherever responsibilities are sought, what tends to be doing the seeking is the instinct of *wanting to punish and rule*" (TI, 35). In the process, one deprives *becoming* of any innocence, instead tracing linkages to so-called agents, intentions, wills, and purposes. The *institution of responsibility* expresses the desire to find guilty parties by identifying agent-causes to whom one can impute guilt. In short, the doctrine of the will would have been "essentially invented for purposes of punishment, that is, for purposes of *wanting to find people guilty*" (TI, 35). The whole of traditional psychology, for Nietzsche, lies in priests' desire to create for themselves the right to punish. Human being are said to be free "so that they could be ruled, so that they could be punished—so that they could become *guilty*: consequently, every action *had* to be thought of as willed, the origin of every action had to be thought to lie in the consciousness" (TI, 35). One can see here how free will is not the basis of responsibility, but was invented after the fact in order to constitute responsibility, as a making-responsible. Nietzsche's "epistemological" critique of free will and causality is here expanded into a symptomatological genealogy.

Nietzsche's genealogical critique of the will thus emphasizes the connection between the philosophies of free will and the problematic of *punishment*. In §23 of *The Wanderer and His Shadow*, titled "Have the adherents of the theory of free-will the right to punish?" Nietzsche explicitly approaches free will in terms of the needs of prosecutors to constitute someone who can be punished. Those who judge and punish as a profession need first and foremost to establish "whether an ill-doer is at all accountable for his deed" (HH, 312). So-called "scientific," "objective" studies in contemporary psychology on the accountability of youngsters or "mentally challenged" individuals are not as neutral as they claim, for their conclusions on the accountability of the subject have an immediate impact on a system of punishment. If the "subjects" of such clinical research are said to be accountable, i.e., legally responsible, they can be punished. The more accountability, the more punishment can be applied. Those scientific studies in fact serve a purpose that is already established, namely, the increase of the possibility of punishment; they simply provide the *a posteriori* rationalization for such punishment. How does one establish accountability and thus the possibility of punishment? By the position of free will. Was the "evil-doer" acting deliberately? Was he able to use his intelligence, acting for reasons and not under compulsion? Does he display will and rational choice? "If he is punished, he is punished for having preferred the worse reasons to the better: which he must therefore have *known*. Where this knowledge is lacking a man is, according to the prevailing view, unfree and not responsible" (HH, 312). But more than intelligence (Aristotle's rational deliberation), it is free will that comes to the fore as the genuine cause for the act. "The *intelligence* is not the cause, because it could not decide against the better reasons? And here one calls 'free will' to one's aid: it is *pure willfulness* which is supposed to decide, as impulse is supposed to enter within which motive plays no part, in which the deed, arising out of nothing, occurs as a miracle," and it is therefore such willfulness which is punished. "Thus the offender is punished because he employs 'free-will'" (HH, 313). Nietzsche proceeds to demonstrate how this theory self-deconstructs, or at the very least betrays its own arbitrariness, since such will decides "without motive, without origin, something purposeless and non-rational," so that the adherents of the theory of free will in fact "have no right to punish" as their own principles deny them that right. Still, it remains that what is called for in order to punish is the accountability of the agent provided by its free will. Free will is the instrument and condition of punishment, constructed and secured *for the sake* of punishment. The more accountability, the more punishment and control are possible.

For Nietzsche, the origin of responsibility lies in the drive to punish, through guilt-assigning if not guilt-producing, for *guilt is produced.* As Nietzsche writes in *The Gay Science,* "Although the shrewdest judges of the witches and even the witches themselves were convinced of the guilt of witchery, this guilt nevertheless did not exist. *This applies to all guilt"* (GS, 216; my emphasis). Ultimately, it is the spirit of *ressentiment* and a quest for revenge which produce the concepts of guilt and responsibility, which concepts themselves make necessary the further invention of concepts such as free agency, intention, causality, etc. One is called "free" in order to be found responsible, held guilty. The origins of guilt, in the sphere of obligations, are "soaked in blood" (GM, 65); the categorical imperative "smells of cruelty" (GM, 65); and as for Christian ethics, it is the "metaphysics of the hangman" (TI, 36)! As we know, Nietzsche attempts to counter this *ressentiment,* "to get the concepts of guilt and punishment back out of the world, and to purge psychology, history, nature, social institutions and sanctions of these concepts," so as to get rid of the moralist world-order which infects the innocence of becoming by means of punishment and guilt. This requires the destruction of the very concept of accountability, which will lead Nietzsche to proclaim the unaccountability of all things.

THE UNACCOUNTABILITY OF ALL THINGS

In book 2 of *Human, All Too Human*, in a section titled "The Fable of Intelligible Freedom," Nietzsche returns to what he names the "error of accountability" (*des Irrthums von der Verantwortlichkeit*), which itself rests on the error of free will (HH, 34). Nietzsche reconstitutes the history of this error within a history of the moral sensations ("The principal stages in the history of the sensations by virtue of which we make anyone accountable for his actions, that is to say, of the moral sensations . . ."). First, one calls individual actions good or bad quite irrespective of their motives but in terms of their useful or harmful consequences; oftentimes, Nietzsche observes, one calls actions "evil" when in fact they "are only stupid" (HH, 58). Nietzsche makes the claim that so-called good actions are "sublimated evil ones" and that evil actions are "brutalized good ones" (HH, 58), and that between good and evil actions there is only a difference of degree, not of nature. One then forgets the origin of these designations and believes that good and evil are inherent in the actions themselves, abstracting a concept of good and evil, and thus repeating the same mistake that is singled out in "Truth and Lie in an Extramoral Sense"—forgetting the metaphoricity of language and believing that the stone is itself hard, the tree is itself green, "that is to say . . . taking for cause that which is effect" (HH, 34). Still in line with this inversion of cause and effect, one then attributes the good or evil to the motives. One goes further yet and attributes good and evil, not only to the motives of the act, but to the whole nature of man. That way, one has invented the concept of accountability, and in that way "successively makes men accountable for the effects they produce, then for their actions, then for their motives, and finally for their nature" (HH, 34). However, just as he did in *The Wanderer and His Shadow*, Nietzsche is quick to show that this position of accountability leads to its own self-deconstruction, for the nature of man proves unaccountable, being the product of so many past and present influences. *The cause (human nature) proves itself unaccountable*. Nietzsche concludes that one finally discovers that "man can be made accountable for nothing . . . that is to say . . . not for his nature, nor for his motives, nor for his actions, nor for the effects he produces" (HH, 34). "Accountable for nothing," as a statement, can of course be taken in two ways: Either as the affirmation of the unaccountability of humans, or as the claim that one is accountable for (the) nothing as such, as Sartre will argue. We will see how for Sartre, one is responsible out of the nothing and for the sake of the nothing in the guise of an ungrounded freedom. Nietzsche here simply points to the groundlessness of accountability, the unaccountability on which it rests, and the error that it therefore represents. "One has thereby attained to the knowledge that the history of the moral sensations if the history of an error, the error of accountability, which rests on the error of freedom of will" (HH, 34).

Further in book 2 of *Human, All Too Human*, in a section titled "Unaccountability and Innocence" (*Unverantwortlichkeit und Unschuld*), Nietzsche speaks of the "complete unaccountability of man for his actions and his nature" (*Die völlige Unverantwortlichkeit des Menschen für sein Handeln und sein Wesen*), a fact that is "the bitterest draught the man of knowledge has to swallow" (HH, 57), accustomed as he is to think of himself in terms of accountability. We recall how responsibility and self-responsibility represented for Kant the very essence of the person. However, for Nietzsche, the belief in the accountability of man "rested upon an error" for "it is absurd to praise and censure nature and necessity" (HH, 57). Nietzsche invites us to think away from accountability and guilty, and rather in terms of necessity *and innocence*. He writes, "Everything is necessity: this is the new knowledge, and this knowledge itself is necessity. Everything is innocence: and knowledge is the way to insight into this innocence" (HH, 57). Even the actions of man are taken as escaping the false ideology of accountability. So that just as "he loves a fine work of art but does not praise it since it can do nothing for itself, as he stands before the plants, so must he stand before the actions of men and before his own" (HH, 57). One can admire their strength, their beauty, but not find any "merit" in them. Indeed, so-called free will is a conflict of forces within oneself: "the chemical process and the strife of the elements, the torment of the sick man who yearns for an end to his sickness, are as little merits as are those states of distress and psychic convulsions which arise when we are torn back and forth by conflicting until we finally choose the most powerful of them" (HH, 58). Or rather, Nietzsche adds in a remarkable way, "until the most powerful motive *chooses us*" (HH, 58; my emphasis)! The "free agent" of the tradition is more *acted* than acting, more inhabited by forces than deciding the course of an act. At the basis of the act, there is no causal agent with motives and intentions. Guilt is thereby indeed driven out of this world, and Nietzsche proclaims the innocence of becoming: "Everything is innocence (*Unschuld*)."

Nietzsche clarifies these claims of the unaccountability of all things and the innocence of becoming in *Twilight of the Idols*. In the last paragraph of "The Four Great Errors," after his deconstruction of imaginary causes (intentions, subjects, etc.), Nietzsche is able to question the very notion of authorship, whether divine or human, and declares that there is no author of who we are. Existence simply displays a radical absence of agency. "What can be *our* doctrine alone?" he asks, and immediately answers, "That nobody *gives* human beings their qualities, neither God, nor society, nor their parents and ancestors, nor they *themselves* (the nonsense of the last notion we are rejecting was taught by Kant as 'intelligible freedom,' and maybe was already taught by Plato as well)" (TI, 36). It is thus not simply divine authorship that is denied, but also the authorship that could be claimed by humans themselves, under the guise of autonomy and *causa sui*. There is simply no author, whether divine or human. "*Nobody* is responsible for being here in the first place, for being constituted in such and such a way, for being in these circumstances, in this environment" (TI, 36). Nietzsche also rejects the old myths of intention and an allegedly divine purpose or essential vocation of man: "We are not the consequence of a special intention, a will, a goal; we are not being used in an attempt to reach an 'ideal of humanity,' or an 'ideal of happiness,' or an 'ideal of morality'—it is absurd to want to *divert* our essence towards some goal" (TI, 36). There are no transcendent goals or purposes, except the ones we invent. In fact, we are the ones who have invented the very concepts of ends, purposes, and agents: "*We* have invented the concept 'goal': in reality, goals are *absent*" (TI, 36). Nietzsche thus denies the possibility of a transcendental freedom positing *from out of the world* an intention, and he insists that one "belongs to the whole," that "one *is* in the whole," which implies that "there is nothing outside the whole!" (TI, 36).

Nietzsche sees this critique as "the great liberation" (*einer grossen Loslösung*) from the Christian theology of guilt-assigning, and opening onto the tragic "innocence of becoming" and life (TI, 36). It is the liberation from the metaphysical concept of accountability, if it is the case that "wherever responsibilities are sought, it is usually the instinct of *wanting to judge and punish* which is at work. Becoming has been deprived of its innocence when any being-such-and-such is traced back to will" (TI, 36). However, "nobody is made responsible anymore":

> no way of being may be traced back to a *causa prima* [first cause] ... —*only this is the great liberation*—in this way only, the *innocence* of becoming is restored ... The concept "God" was up to now the greatest *objection* against existence ... We deny God, and in denying God we deny responsibility: only *thus* do we redeem the world. (TI, 36–37)

"We deny God," that is, the notion of an author-subject of the world, and in *that* sense "we deny responsibility," that is, the metaphysical interpretation of responsibility as *accountability* of the agent-subject. It indeed seems that the very basis of responsibility—as accountability—finds itself denied, due to this radical lack of agency and authorship. That critique of agency and subjectivity, of authorship, indeed goes against the grain of the prevailing philosophical and common understanding of responsibility. However, it only denies *accountability, which is but the subjectivist and moral interpretation of responsibility.* Nietzsche only takes issue with the model of accountability resting on causes, intentions, and agents, and it is not certain that this closes off the possibility of another sense of responsibility (which is distinct from accountability) to emerge. Nonetheless, it is clear that the critique bears on negative and pathological constructs: It is a matter of restoring the innocence of becoming, of redeeming the world, of freeing human existence from guilt-assigning philosophies of accountability. In that freeing, another sense of responsibility would emerge, not based on subjectivity, but on the task of affirming life and carrying the weight of a Godless, abyssal existence, a task of overcoming nihilism and a future that Nietzsche assigns to the "overman."

As we have seen, Nietzsche destroys the metaphysical concept of responsibility, exposing it as a "fiction" that was invented for the purpose of guilt-assigning out of a self-hatred of life. However, the innocence of becoming that he proclaims could be said to open a new sense of responsibility, far from its traditional sense of accountability, as the taking on of the tragic innocence of a life that one must affirm. One sense of responsibility, as it were (and which remains to be explored), replaces another. This is why the charge that Nietzsche's genealogical critique of morality would lead to irresponsibility is actually the opposite of what occurs. Nietzsche does take leave of accountability, but not with all sense of responsibility. His critique of the nihilistic traditional concept of responsibility leads to a new *origin of responsibility,* which is no longer based on guilt but on the givenness of an a-theological existence coming into its own. To be more precise, this new sense of responsibility actually emerges *out of* the destruction of accountability: There is on the one hand the proclamation of the complete unaccountability of all things, since there is no author, agent, or cause; but paradoxically, it is this very agentless and authorless existence that responsibilizes us, putting us in the position of having to take over such groundlessness *in an extra-moral sense.* The idols of metaphysics are dismantled in order to deliver us to our groundless freedom—to our groundless responsibility. This deconstruction places us in the position of having to (obligation) carry this weight (responsibility). Nietzsche's destruction of idols in this sense is therefore a call to responsibility, a responsibility that becomes infinitized by the very groundlessness of existence, the absence of authorship and agency. It is not by chance, as we will see, that Sartre, placing himself explicitly in the wake of Nietzsche's philosophy of the death of God, developed a philosophy of absolute freedom and responsibility on the basis of the nothing.

In this transition between accountability and responsibility, and out of the groundlessness of existence, we are placed in the position of taking on this groundlessness and become the creators of the (meaning of) the world, the creator of values: "Revaluation of all values: that is my formula for an act of supreme coming to-to-oneself on the part of mankind" (*Ecce Homo,* in GM, 326; translation modified). The task of overcoming nihilism demands that we "*create values*"; "*Genuine philosophers . . . are commanders and legislators:* they say 'thus it *shall* be'" (BGE, 136). Consecrating the appropriation and destruction of Kantian autonomy within a problematics of power—"Independence is for the very few; it is a privilege of the strong" (BGE, 41)—Nietzsche calls for the "free spirits" to come, for a figure of the new philosopher as the bearer of the greatest responsibility, who would be capable of "enduring" the "weight of such responsibility" (BGE, 117) and who is described as "the man of the most comprehensive responsibility," "always destructive as well as creative and form-giving" (BGE, 72). Such free spirits "say, '*thus* it *shall* be!' They first determine the Whither and For What of man . . . With a creative hand they reach for the future, and all that is and has been becomes for them, an instrument, a hammer. Their 'knowing' is *creating,* their creating is a legislation, their will to truth is—*will to power*" (BGE, 136).[23] However, this commanding is not provided by the control of the voluntary and the decision of rational agency, but paradoxically by the absence of such fictions, by the withdrawal of essence and theological foundation. Therein lies the paradoxical character of Nietzsche's thought of responsibility: The boundless power of responsibility is here given by the lack of foundation in existence. This is also the paradoxical situation of Nietzsche's thought in this history of responsibility we are trying to reconstitute. On the one hand, he accomplishes a destruction of that tradition, yet on the other hand, one cannot help but note how certain features of that tradition, such as the very motif of power, of legislation and self-legislation, are brought to a paroxysm. We will follow this paroxysm more closely with Sartre. It must suffice to state here that Nietzsche's genealogy, which is often portrayed as simply critical of responsibility, should be viewed instead as opening the way for a transformation of the senses of responsibility, as well as enhancing its scope and reach. Nietzsche's deconstruction of accountability leads to a paradoxical absolutizing of responsibility—the explicit task of Sartre's existentialism, in the wake of the death of God. That is the "great liberation" (*grossen Loslösung*) of which Nietzsche speaks in the preface to *Human, All Too Human*,[24] a freedom and a responsibility which will constitute the heart of Sartre's thought, and which calls for an enhanced sense of responsibility as creation and self-creation.

FOUR

Sartre: Hyperbolic Responsibility

The Phenomenological Origins of Responsibility

EXISTENTIAL RESPONSIBILITY

Sartre's philosophy of responsibility is marked by a constitutive paradox, as it develops a post-metaphysical sense of responsibility while leading the metaphysical tradition to a paroxysm. Indeed, Sartre's thought reflects the peculiar merging of a phenomenological and post-theological account of responsibility with the Cartesian paradigm of subjectivity and will.[1] I will attempt in the following pages to highlight the phenomenological and ontological origins of responsibility as Sartre thematizes them—existence as prior to, and indeed without essence; original freedom and original choice as opposed to free will; responsibility as identified with existence itself; the determinative role of the nothing in Sartre's concept of responsibility; the invention of law in ethical decision, i.e., in a decision that takes place without norms; the absolutizing of responsibility and the overcoming of facticity; the problematics of authenticity and bad faith—in short, an *original or ontological responsibility.* But it will also be necessary to mark the hermeneutical limits of this account of responsibility, due to Sartre's dependence on the Cartesian tradition. Responsibility in Sartre derives from the unique hermeneutical situation of his philosophy, and thus relies on existential phenomenology (in the wake of the Nietzschean thought of the death of God) no less than on a Cartesian stress on subjectivity and the primacy of the ego and its will. Sartre thus marks a sort of turning point in the history of responsibility we are following, in which the modern tradition of willful subjectivity—and the motif of authorship, in Sartre's thinking of responsibility—is brought to a paroxysm, while at the same time new possibilities come into the open. That is, Sartre both prefigured and announced, if he did not fully exploit, a situation clearly described by Derrida in this way:

> To take up the question of responsibility again, even if one does not agree with the Sartrean metaphysics of freedom, there is nonetheless, in his analysis of decision, of a responsibility left to the other without criterion, without norm, without prescription, in the undecidable alone (cf. *L'existentialisme est un humanisme*), there is something there that can be separated from a Cartesian metaphysics of freedom, of free will.[2]

These new possibilities, explored and developed in his phenomenological ontology, remain limited by Sartre's heavy dependency on Cartesianism and his insufficient distance from this inheritance. Nowhere does this tension appear more clearly than in his thinking of responsibility. On the one hand, Sartre takes a phenomenological approach to philosophical questions, that is, emphasizes a new attentiveness to the givenness of phenomena, by turning away from the metaphysical and theological constructs dismantled by Nietzsche. Attending to the structures of an essence-less existence, Sartre renews our understanding of responsibility by giving us access to its phenomenological origins. On the other hand, he relies on the traditional motifs of authorship, subjectivity, and will. Sartre thus undertakes to develop an ontological analysis of responsibility, based on original freedom and a post-theological analysis of existence, and yet he still retains a very classical definition of responsibility based on willful subjectivity and authorship. As one can read at the beginning of the chapter on freedom and responsibility in *Being and Nothingness,* Sartre is still relying on that traditional sense when he provides his definition of responsibility, the only definition he ever gave: "We are taking the word 'responsibility' in its ordinary sense as 'consciousness (of) being the incontestable *author* of an event or of an object.'"[3]

Certainly, as we will see, that sense of authorship differs from the traditional accountability for one's actions (and is even paradoxical as it includes not only what I have *not* done but also perhaps what exceeds my capacities), since we are dealing here with an authorship with respect to my being, and to the whole world as a way of being. But in a sense this is precisely the problem, as the classical definition of responsibility is thus brought to a paroxysm, becoming a hyperbolic responsibility. Nonetheless, a paroxysm is always paradoxical, exceeding itself, and this hyperbolic inflation of responsibility as accountability will in fact lead to the exceeding of that tradition, opening onto other senses, if one understands that Sartre extends the scope of authorship so far that he ends up deconstructing it.[4] For instance, Sartre's philosophy retrieves existential origins of responsibility that are distinct from the mere authorship of an agent-subject. Responsibility arises out of that event named 'the death of God,' and Sartre attempts to draw the most radical consequences of this event, explaining that by existentialism, "we mean only that God does not exist and that we have to face all the consequences of this."[5] This is why Sartre states that the existentialist "thinks it very distressing that God does not exist, because all possibility of finding values in a heaven of ideas disappears along with Him" (HE, 40). By stating that God is dead, one is no longer able to justify one's actions by appealing to an *a priori* table of values, or even to a human nature; no transcendent values or commands could legitimize one's decisions and responsibilities. Will this situation imply some impossibility of ethics as such, and of responsibility, since there is no longer a way to rely on *a priori* values in our decisions? Not so for Sartre, for he does not claim that there are no values (that indeed would be nihilism), but rather that there are no *transcendent, given, a priori, objective* values. For Sartre, values are not transcendent, because they are immanent to existence itself and express its very freedom. They are not given *a priori* because they are created, invented, and chosen (and once chosen, they are not established once and for all but are to be chosen again and again). They are not objective, because they express subjective life, Sartre insisting that existence is subjective through and through. Subjectivity is the impassable horizon of existence according to Sartre. Doesn't he claim that "it is impossible for man to transcend human subjectivity" (HE, 37)?[6] It is in fact ironic that some critics of Sartre reproach him for not relying on objective *a priori* values to guide one's moral choices,[7] thereby assuming that values are what would grant an *objectivity* to morality, and thus ignoring the fact that the very concept of "value," as Heidegger has shown, already displays a subjective component: It is a subjectivist bias that focuses on values, on how being is evaluated from the perspective of a subject granting value to objects. In other words, a value already supposes an evaluation, and that evaluation supposes a subject making that determination, which for Sartre rests on a free choice. Values are therefore never objective! For Sartre, one's ethical values are not given in a transcendent and objective sphere, but must be invented in the motion proper to existence. Ethics thus becomes the praxis of one's very freedom, and its justification ultimately lies in such a praxis. For Sartre, freedom consists in having to make choices, and not being able to avoid making such choices. One chooses values, and one also chooses how one chooses values.

The core of existentialist ethics is responsibility because existentialism recognizes that human beings invent who they are and the values they live by, a responsibility that will be defined by Sartre as universal, hyperbolic, and even absolute. Ethics is the heart of human existence; "to be" means to be responsible because to be is to be free. As he states in *Being and Nothingness,* "there is no difference between the being of man and his *being-free*" (BN, 25). Responsibility is thus radicalized, from a responsibility for one's actions to a responsibility identified with being itself. Sartre develops the concept of a responsibility for being and the meaning of being, and not simply for one's actions—an ontological responsibility—thus radicalizing the subject-based philosophy of accountability. Far more radical than stating that one is responsible for one's actions is the claim that one is responsible for one's own being; far more radical than stating that the agent has free will, is the claim that to be means to be responsible; far more radical than claiming that the rational subject has control over its domain, is the claim that we are free from the depths of our being. For Sartre, it is not a matter of free will but of a freedom that is, as he writes, "more profound" than the will (BN, 583). Freedom is originary to our very being. Finally, more radical than stating that our responsibility ensues from free will, is the claim that we are responsible insofar as we are the authors of our very being, in the sense of inventing each time our being in an act of freedom. Sartre argues that the possibility of ethics—the absolute responsibility of an essenceless existence for itself and for all that is—is the consequence of the death of God. That means, at every moment and without any support, man must invent man. To that extent, he is absolutely responsible, not only for what he does but above all for what he is. Consequently, far from being annulled by Sartre's condemnation of theological thinking, responsibility in fact arises out of this withdrawal of theological principles. Ethics is here situated at the heart of existence as absolute responsibility, and is based on the absence of any *a priori* table of values, any "ethical scripture." Such a responsibility is for Sartre absolute, overwhelming, excessive or infinite, as well as universal. Let us examine such an ethics of absolute responsibility step by step.

ESSENCELESS EXISTENCE

It is well known that Sartrean existentialism took as its motto the following expression, "existence precedes essence." That proposition, to which we will return shortly, could also be taken as meaning that existence has no essence, since one could argue that in such a reversal, essence itself is deconstructed! It indicates at the very least that existence lacks a basis, that it can only be accessed as a sheer *fact*, a bare given. The givenness of existence, *as existence*, first requires that its connection with essence be shattered. This is of course brilliantly described in *Nausea*, which shows the original givenness of pure presence, of being without meaning (essence), of presence as a sheer given. As if for the first time, one realized that existence is not identical to its signification or concept (essence), that a glass of beer, as Sartre writes, exists first outside the concept of the glass of beer. Things are first given outside of their concepts, even outside the concept of "existing things," outside the very concept of existence. Existence exceeds its concept. Originally, the pure fact of a "that" is not covered over, determined, preceded or justified by a "what." Things exist first, prior to and without having a meaning.

Precisely because being is what is given first, because it is what first comes, that fact presents itself without any sense or meaning. At the moment of the givenness of existence, there is a radical senselessness, which does not necessarily preclude or foreclose the possibility of meaning but, rather, allows for a futural opening, a sort of promise to fulfill and enact. Consequently the meaning *of* existence (as a subjective genitive), is opened as a possibility by the factical givenness of existence. It is always a meaning to-come, always futural, and always a responsibility. One has to provide, invent, imagine, and construct such a meaning, and all of these are nothing but an original responsibility for meaning. Meaning opens in such originary responsibility. This is how Sartre describes the origins of responsibility, as arising out of the essencelessness of existence.

Sartre's philosophy of existence or, as he labeled it himself, existentialism, explicitly places itself within the horizon of Nietzsche's critique of traditional philosophy and theology, and understands itself as a consequence of what Nietzsche called the death of God. As I mentioned above, Sartre explains in "The Humanism of Existentialism" that by existentialism, "we mean only that God does not exist and that we have to face all the consequences of this" (HE, 40). At the end of the essay, Sartre reiterates this perspective and concludes with these words: "From these few reflections it is evident that nothing is more unjust than the objections that have been raised against us. *Existentialism is nothing else than an attempt to draw all the consequences of a coherent atheistic position*" (HE, 62; my emphasis).[8] We will see how, falling back on a classical undeconstructed humanism, Sartre concludes from this event of the death of God that our world is only a human world, which allows him to proclaim the humanism of existentialism. The title of his lecture reads *L'existentialisme est un humanisme*, which could thus be translated "Existentialism is a Humanism," more literally than "The Humanism of Existentialism."

However, it will also appear that existentialism above all needs to be understood in its ethical scope. For the withdrawal of theological foundations and principles frees existence as a responsibility for itself, indeed as an absolute, infinite, or boundless responsibility for itself and for the world. "Absolute responsibility," Jean-Luc Nancy writes, "has come to us with the absolute infinity of foundations and ends . . . with the death of God and the birth of the world. That is to say, with existence delivered over to our absolute responsibility."[9] A few lines further on, Nancy emphasizes that "existence is responsibility for existence" (RE, 8), a statement that Sartre would certainly not disavow. Responsibility here is not simply the consequence of free will but indeed defines the very being of humans.[10] Responsibility becomes identified with existence itself as soon as existence can no longer be measured against some pre-given authority, norm or fate. This frees responsibility from the calculation of a measure and launches it into the immeasurable of existence itself. Responsibility with Sartre would become boundless, as it arises out of the groundlessness of existence.[11] In other words, the more ungrounded it finds itself to be and the more it is delivered to the incalculable, the more responsibility would increase. This shows the extent to which Sartre conceives of ethics not in terms of some theoretical principles to apply, but as the very unfolding of human existence, an existence absolutely freed from any theological foundation and determinism. This is why responsibility in Sartre's work tends to be identified with existence itself, that is, with freedom, and no longer confined to the operations of a subject of imputation. This claim of an intrinsic ethicality of Sartre's existentialism seems to go against what he himself confessed at the end of *Being and Nothingness,* namely that he had not written an ethics and that he needed to expand his thought from a purely reflexive level to the ethical plane: "All these questions, which refer to a pure and not an accessory reflection, can find their reply only on an ethical plane. We shall devote to them a future work" (BN, 798), we are told. Now, notwithstanding the fact that such a future work never saw the light of day (with the exception of the posthumously published *Notebooks for an Ethics*), one could argue here that Sartre did not need to add an ethics to his volume of phenomenological ontology because the ethical itself was already inscribed in this ontology. He admitted as much when he wrote that even though ontology is unable to formulate ethical imperatives, it nonetheless allows "us to catch a glimpse of what sort of ethics will assume its responsibilities when confronted with a *human reality in situation*" (BN, 795).[12] This passage strongly suggests that if ontology cannot provide a morality or an ethics *per se,* it nevertheless articulates what one may call here the ethicality of ethics, the very possibility of ethics. When Heidegger was asked in his "Letter on Humanism" why he did not write an ethics to supplement his fundamental ontology, he replied famously that the thinking of being was an originary ethics. Such is clearly also the case with Sartre, as I will try to make explicit in the following pages. Sartre develops an understanding of existence that immediately engages ethics in its very possibility, and is thematized as absolute responsibility.

In his lecture on "The Humanism of Existentialism," Sartre defines existentialism as that philosophy which claims that existence precedes essence. The self-confessed goal of that lecture was to answer Sartre's critics, who had claimed that existentialism was a philosophy of despair, pessimism, and fatalism that emphasized the negative side of life—in short, a nihilistic philosophy. Such was, for example, the Marxists' charge, which maintained that Sartre would end up with a petit-bourgeois contemplative philosophy. To these charges, Sartre insists that his conception of existentialism leads to activism and is in a certain sense a philosophy of hope—a hope, however, which is immanent to existence and to action, and not in relation to a transcendent realm. For instance, Sartre writes, "The doctrine I am presenting is the very opposite of quietism, since it declares, 'There is no reality except in action'" (HE, 47). A few pages below, we read: "When all is said and done, what we are accused of, at bottom, is not our pessimism, but an optimistic toughness" (HE, 49). Optimism, because we invent and choose our being at every moment; but toughness, because this freedom takes place against the background of the nothing and the absence of God. In the end, existentialism is a philosophy of action, and *to that extent, of hope*. In fact, it is the indulgence of metaphysical dreams that would ultimately lead us to despair:

> Thus, I think we have answered a number of the charges concerning existentialism. You see that it cannot be taken for a philosophy of quietism, since it defines man in terms of action; nor for a pessimistic description of man—there is no doctrine more optimistic, since man's destiny is within himself. Nor for an attempt to discourage man from acting, since it tells him that *the only hope is in his acting and that action is the only thing that enables a man to live*. Consequently, we are dealing here with an ethics of action and involvement. (HE, 50; my emphasis)

The death of God does not lead to despair but opens the space for freedom, a freedom opened by the absence of any foundation for existence, and thus leads to action, engagement, and thereby, to responsibility. From the Christian perspective, the charge has been that Sartre's existentialism leads to the impossibility of morality, under the belief that "if we reject God's commandments and the eternal truths, there no longer remains anything but pure caprice, with everyone permitted to do as he pleases and incapable, from his own point of view, of condemning the points of view and acts of others" (HE, 32; translation modified).

As we know, Sartre attempts to answer these charges by emphasizing the humanism of existentialism, a humanism that will be understood as a subjectivist atheism. Sartre writes, "In any case, what can be said from the very beginning is that by existentialism we mean a doctrine which makes human life possible and, in addition, declares that every truth and every action implies a human setting and subjectivity" (HE, 32). Here we note what I alluded to above as the maintaining of a metaphysical humanism, and how a novel way of philosophizing does not preclude the persistence of classical metaphysical motifs within it, which are simply left unquestioned. For there is simply no necessity to infer from the death of God the primacy of the subject, unless of course one replaces, as Sartre does, a theocentrism with a structurally parallel anthropocentrism. This inference is a leap, itself made possible by the way in which Sartre has anthropologized Heidegger's Dasein, incorrectly translating the term as "human reality" (*réalité humaine* was Henri Corbin's translation of Dasein, a translation borrowed and (mis)used here by Sartre). This passage reveals Sartre's misunderstanding clearly: "This being," namely, the being for whom existence precedes essence, "is man or, as Heidegger says, human reality" (HE, 35). This is clearly a twofold misunderstanding, for not only is Dasein not human reality, but Heidegger also never wrote that existence precedes essence, and I will return to this last question. Nonetheless, for Sartre, as he stated famously (something Heidegger would answer and challenge explicitly in his "Letter on Humanism"), "the fact is we are on a plane where there are only men" (HE, 41). *Being and Nothingness* is much further from *Being and Time* than Sartre would have imagined.[13]

What is existentialism? For Sartre, its meaning can be defined in two ways. In this 1945 essay he distinguishes between Christian existentialists, such as Jaspers and Gabriel Marcel (one might add Emmanuel Mounier as well), and atheistic existentialists, of which he is the main representative (in which category he also places Heidegger and French existentialists whom he does not name). According to Sartre, what they have in common "is that they think that existence precedes essence," or, he adds in a very significant way, "if you prefer, that subjectivity must be the starting point" (HE, 34). One notes once again the subjectivist bias: Sartre, from the outset, equates the essencelessness of existence (phenomenological ontology) with the primacy of subjectivity (Cartesian motif), thereby merging, as we indicated above, a phenomenological attention to the phenomena with a Cartesian philosophy of the primacy of the ego. But it is in no way clear how the fact that existence precedes essence implies that subjectivity must be the starting point! For instance, when Heidegger writes, "The 'essence' of Dasein lies in its existence" (*Das "Wesen" des Daseins liegt in seiner Existenz*), he in no way signifies a return to subjectivity! Sartre's statement, existence *precedes* essence, is therefore not only an inaccurate citation of Heidegger's passage, but it also conveys a misinterpretation which is repeated many times in *Being and Nothingness*. And where Sartre writes, for instance, "We must say of it [freedom] what Heidegger said of the Dasein in general: 'In it existence precedes and commands essence'" (BN, 565), he attributes to Heidegger a statement that is not his, and this error will have major and unfortunate consequences. In fact, the statement "existence precedes essence" first means that there is no God to provide an essential justification for our existence, depriving it of any model such as a human nature, which might suggest that the very form of humanism might self-deconstruct in the withdrawal of theology. Sartre even comes close to recognizing this, when he writes: "Thus, there is no human nature, since there is no God to conceive it" (HE, 36). The withdrawal of foundation should have motivated Sartre to question anthropocentrism as well, the very values of authorship and subjectivity as ground. However, this is not what occurred.

For Sartre, there may not be a human nature but there is nonetheless a primacy of human subjectivity. In this lecture, Sartre draws a principal distinction between beings that are produced and human existence, recalling somewhat Heidegger's famed distinction in *Being and Time* between beings that are Dasein-like and beings that are either present-at-hand or ready-to-hand. The model of production thus plays, for Sartre, the role of an ontological divider. For produced beings, essence precedes existence. Sartre gives the example of a paper-cutter, "an object which has been made by an artisan whose inspiration came from a concept" (HE, 35). For the paper-cutter, essence precedes existence. For humans beings, existence precedes essence, because we are not produced (created) following a prior plan. Certainly, in an inappropriate ontology, we too can be conceived of on the model of these objects, as we too might be said to be "produced" by a God-artisan. Indeed, Sartre insists, when we think of God we think of God as "the creator," that is, the *producer* of all things, including ourselves. Thus "the concept of man in the mind of God is comparable to the concept of a paper-cutter in the mind of the manufacturer, and, following certain techniques and a conception, God produces man, just as the artisan, following a definition and a technique, makes a paper-cutter" (HE, 35). In such an analogy—the analogy of production—each individual is the actualization of a prior conception, lodged in the mind of God. And even if we dispense with God, continues Sartre, we can still retain the notion of an *a priori* essence of man in terms of human nature, as was done in the writings of the eighteenth-century *philosophes*. The notion of a human nature, with its reliance on an *a priori* universal humanity, is but a secularized version of the theological account of the human being *and therefore still remains itself a theological notion.* "Thus, here too the essence of man precedes that historical existence that we find in nature" (HE, 35).

Sartre seeks to break with both the traditional Christian model and the Enlightenment atheism of the eighteenth century, which in the end are less distant from one another than is usually assumed,[14] as they both posit the precedence of essence over existence. Sartre proclaims a radically *atheistic* existentialism in which existence is immediately identified as *human* existence. Here the human being is no longer referred to as a human nature but is approached as a future of itself, that is, as a self-invention. To be human now means to invent oneself. Responsibility will be conceived in terms of such self-invention.

It is indeed in the motifs of an essenceless existence and a free self-invention that the concept of responsibility will originate. As we have seen, Sartre seeks to draw all the consequences of the death of God. It would be pointless to declare that God is dead if one still retained a theological framework, whether in the guise of a human nature or a universal code of values. For Sartre, the death of God means the withdrawal of essence, and this withdrawal constitutes existence: The withdrawal of essence *is* the emergence of existence. This is why Sartre stresses that atheistic existentialism "states that if God does not exist, there is at least one being whose existence precedes essence" (HE, 35). To be precise, Sartre does not say that existence has no essence, rather he claims that it comes *before* essence. We must account for this nuance, starting with the proposition at the background of this entire discussion, that is, Heidegger's statement in §9 of *Being and Time* that we alluded to above: "The 'essence' of Dasein lies in its existence" (*Das "Wesen" des Daseins liegt in seiner Existenz*) (SZ, 42). This statement was Heidegger's way of immanently dissolving essence into existence. The "whatness" (*essentia*) of the entity that we are ("insofar as one can speak of it at all," Heidegger adds significantly) must necessarily be conceived of *as* existence. But this means, then, that Dasein has no essence, and thus does not exhibit "'objectively present attributes' [*Eigenschaften*] of an objectively present being" (SZ, 42). Dasein's selfhood is a *"way of existing"* (Weise zu existieren) and therefore not a being present-at-hand (SZ, 267). If Dasein is an existence (distinguishing this term, as Heidegger invites us to do so, from *existentia*[15]), that is, a pure potentiality-for-being, it will not be able to answer the question "*what* is it?" but only the question "*who?*" "We gain access [*Zugang*] to this Being only if we ask: *Who* is it? [wer *ist es*] The Dasein is not constituted by whatness but—if we may coin the expression—by *who-ness* [Werheit]" (GA 24, 169).

As we just saw, with Heidegger "essence" (which the German thinker put in quotation marks, indicating clearly that the word is no longer operative and is used only provisionally, if not rhetorically) is identified with existence. How does Sartre understand the relation between essence and existence? For him, essence is placed *following* existence, in a mere *reversal* of the traditional relation between essence and existence. One might then argue that his gesture is less radical than Heidegger's since it maintains the hierarchy between essence and existence, albeit in an inverted way. In Sartre, the traditional senses of existence and essence are maintained, whereas Heidegger deconstructs the *existentia-essentia* distinction altogether. Sartre simply reverses their relation. Essence will be said to come after our free existence, in the guise of the concepts or definitions that we can provide for ourselves; as for existence, it is retained as a unitary concept (*existentia*), although Heidegger distinguished the existence of things (*existentia* or *Vorhandenheit*) from the existence of Dasein (*Existenz*). Sartre's failure to distinguish clearly between these two senses of existence explains why the concept of facticity can pertain for him both to the givenness of things in their materiality and to the givenness of our existence. There too, Heidegger had distinguished between the facticity (*Faktizität*) of Dasein and the factuality (*Tatsächlichkeit*) of intra-worldly entities, which Sartre does not do explicitly, as he tends to conflate facticity with the concept of contingency (an ontical concept that is foreign to Heidegger's thought of existence). For instance, in *Being and Nothingness*, in the chapter on "The Facticity of the For-Itself," Sartre speaks of the facticity of the for-itself in terms of the fact of a *contingency*, a term that includes both the for-itself and the in-itself. He writes that the for-itself "*is* as pure contingency inasmuch as for it as for things in the world, as for this wall, this tree, this cup, the original question can be posited: 'Why is this being exactly such and not otherwise?'" (BN, 127). Sartre understands facticity as contingency, that is, in terms of causality and of a foundation in reason.[16] Contingency names a lack of necessity and justification in one's existence, and that contingency applies to both the for-itself and the in-itself. Facticity and factuality are thereby conflated. This is why Sartre gives this definition of facticity: "This contingency of the for-itself, this weight surpassed and preserved in the very surpassing—this is *facticity*" (BN, 173). The identification of facticity with contingency will not permit a sufficient problematization of the senses of existence.

On the basis of this inversion of the relation between existence and essence, Sartre characterizes the human being as the "being who exists before he can be defined by any concept" (HE, 35). The 'that' of existence is prior to its 'what.' How does Sartre describe this priority, and in what sense does this priority constitute the origin of responsibility? Sartre writes, "What is meant here by saying that existence precedes essence? It means that, first of all, man exists, turns up, appears on the scene, and, only afterwards, defines himself" (HE, 36). The 'that' appears first, it is what gives itself first, and it gives itself without or before meaning. It is first a 'nothing.' At first, human reality is 'nothing,' and therefore *the original fact is (the) nothing*. "If man, as the existentialist conceives him, is indefinable, it is because at first *he is nothing*" (HE, 36; my emphasis).[17] Let us be clear, this 'nothing' is a nothing of potentiality. It is nothing defined, nothing yet, which will afterwards be something—a 'what' that will be *chosen*. "Only afterwards will he be something, and he himself will have made what he will be" (HE, 36).[18] That 'will,' it should be noted, does not designate free will but is instead the manifestation of an deeper sense of freedom, which Sartre called in *Being and Nothingness* "original freedom." For Sartre, freedom "is not a faculty of the human soul to be envisaged and described in isolation" (BN, 60), like free will, but it is original freedom, i.e., it has to be considered in terms of man's being. We are free to the point that one's very *being* has to be chosen. We are what we choose to be. This is why he explains that, "the will, far from being the unique or at least the privileged manifestation of freedom, actually—like every event of the for-itself—must presuppose the foundation of an *original ontological freedom* in order to constitute itself as will" (BN, 571). With freedom, it is not a matter of free will, of establishing the possibility of voluntary acts (as with Aristotle), but of an existential freedom, a freedom that is "a more profound freedom than the will" (BN, 583). Freedom could be described as the *existence* of the will. Such freedom is originary to our very being (to be is to be free) and at the foundation of all our comportments. This, indeed, is the main claim of *Being and Nothingness*, that freedom, as Sartre put it, "is identical with my existence" (BN, 572). Insofar as this original freedom is identified by Sartre with the nihilating power of a nothing—"freedom can be nothing other than this nihilation" (BN, 567)[19]—and humans are defined in terms of such freedom, Sartre can state that nothing is given for the human being, or that what is given at the outset is the nothing that humans are. Nothing exists prior to the projection of freedom. Therein lies our original responsibility, which finds itself grounded in the nothing of human existence as originary freedom. One's own being must be invented, in a kind of originary and ungrounded praxis. For Sartre, the first principle of existentialism is: *Human beings are nothing but what they make of themselves.* One is *responsible* for one's own being. As Sartre states: "But if existence really does precede essence, man is responsible for what he is" (HE, 36). Consequently, existentialism's "first move is to make every man aware of what he is and to make the full responsibility of his existence rest on him" (HE, 36). Let us consider more closely the existential features of such responsibility.

THE GROUNDLESSNESS OF RESPONSIBILITY

The most salient character of this responsibility is that it arises, as we noted, out of a lack of foundation, out of a groundlessness. The withdrawal of ground has an immediate ethical impact, although it precludes the possibility of any *a priori* morality. However, for Sartre, ethics itself—the ethical as such—arises out of this lack of an *a priori* morality. This absence of ground compels us to rethink what is meant by ethics, to reconsider ethics from the ground up. For if there is no God to provide transcendent values to found our ethical comportment, then it is the very meaning of ethics as traditionally conceived that finds itself subverted. Indeed, Sartre insists that he does not want to propose a "secularized" version of a theological account of morality, through which one would seek "to abolish God with the least possible expense" (HE, 40). One can easily conceive of a philosophy that would proclaim its atheism while retaining within it theological structures and motifs, that would deny the existence of God while continuing to appeal to an *a priori* set of values one could draw from. However, "the existentialist ... thinks it very distressing that God does not exist, because all possibility of finding values in a heaven of ideas disappears along with Him" (HE, 40). For Sartre the death of God means that there is no longer an *a priori* Good or other *a priori* values, whether these lie in an a-temporal human nature or in the structure of pure reason. There is no intelligible heaven, "since there is no infinite and perfect consciousness to think it" (HE, 41). Opposing any type of secular moralism that would in fact keep the traditional theological structure in place, Sartre mentions the attempts that consist in conceding that God does not exist but which maintain nonetheless that "in order for there to be an ethics, a society, a civilization, it is essential that certain values be taken seriously and that they be considered as having an *a priori* existence" (HE, 40). The obligations to be honest, not to lie, cheat, steal, etc., would require an *a priori* value. However, as we saw, Sartre seeks to draw the most radical consequences of the death of God; hence his statement, "Dostoievsky said 'If God didn't exist, everything would be possible'; that is the very starting point of existentialism" (HE, 41)—namely, the impossibility of having recourse to *any priori* values. Nowhere, he states, is it "written that the Good exists, that we must be honest, that we must not lie," echoing what he already wrote in *Being and Nothingness*: "*nothing*, absolutely nothing, justifies me in adopting this or that particular value, this or that particular scale of values" (BN, 76). This is the case because "it is I who sustain values in being" (BN, 77), and because freedom is the *only* foundation of values: "My freedom is the only [*l'unique*] foundation of values" (BN, 76; translation modified). Far from being grounded on some metaphysical suprasensible realm, the ethical finds itself resituated at the very level of existence itself, with the groundlessness of its freedom and the facticity of its phenomenological givenness. Ethics, "if it exists," to use here an expression often employed by Derrida, and indeed the very notions of good and evil, need to be first situated in this newly revealed phenomenological context. For Sartre, obligation, responsibility, ethics itself and its categories, must be situated in existence itself, and in its contingent character. In the late interviews with Benny Levy, Sartre stresses how he attempted to distinguish his approach from Kant's, from the idea of a well-ordered world and the notion of a free reality penetrating necessary reality. What Sartre wanted was a "free reality to appear in a contingent reality. And the commands that it could give would manifest themselves in flaccid and doughy transcendence" (HN, 49). Sartre thus draws the most radical consequences of Nietzsche's dismantling of theological idols by emphasizing the *groundlessness* of values, or their grounding in an abysmal freedom, in the "Nothing." This "Nothing" will prove constitutive of ethical decision and choice.

Sartre insists on the situation of choice and decision as happening without any support, with nothing as a foundation; for instance, "man, with no support and no aid, is condemned every moment to invent man" (HE, 41). We should note from the outset that this motif of invention opens the space of the future as incalculable. One must invent because there is the incalculable. Citing the poet Francis Ponge, who wrote that "man is the future of man," Sartre explains that the future is not laid up in heaven, not known in advance by God, not already written, as it would then no longer be a future (HE, 42). Further, Sartre stresses that in inventing our ethics, we always encounter the "unforeseeable" (HE, 59). A leap is thus inscribed in the act of ethical decision, a leap into (and within) the incalculable. This is why voluntary deliberation, Sartre argues, "is always a deception." Relying upon so-called rational deliberation for one's choices would be bad faith, as the upsurge of freedom occurs "beyond causes, motives, and ends" (BN, 581), beyond the whole "cause-intention-act-end" structure (BN, 564). This is where Sartre breaks decisively with the tradition of situating freedom in the context of causality, as we saw it in Kant. Here freedom, Sartre tells us, "has no essence" (BN, 565), and arises out of the nothing that insinuates itself "between motives and act" (BN, 71). In *War Diaries: Notebooks from a Phony War,* Sartre reiterates that the motives are always separated from the possible by "a hiatus of nothingness," leading him to claim that, "the origin of responsibility is this primary fact that we realize ourselves as a discontinuity between the motives and the act."[20] Indeed, freedom is the manifestation of this hiatus, of this nothing. Freedom is a kind of rupture, for the for-itself a "nihilating rupture with the world and with himself" (BN, 567). The justification of a choice is also an act of freedom, ungrounded on some transcendent table of values. As Sartre explains, the "illusion" that causes and motives guide the act "stems from the fact that we endeavour to take causes and motives for entirely transcendent things," when in fact "causes and motives have only the weight which my project— i.e., the free production of the end and of the known act to be realized— confers upon them" (BN, 581). When I deliberate, he concludes, "the chips are down" (*les jeux sont faits*), which indicates that the decision has already been made, freely, or that at the very least the decision was never *founded* on some deliberation.

Existence thus has no basis. It is founded on nothing, and yet it has to project itself—indeed, invent itself—from such an absence of foundation.

We will return below to this "invention" or inventiveness, but let us stress from the outset the original situation: The existing self must take on such groundless existence, and take responsibility for it. To "take" or "seize" one's responsibilities already indicates that it is always an ungrounded act, the act of making oneself the ground of a groundless existence. This is indeed the meaning of anxiety for Sartre: "My freedom is anguished at being the foundation of values while itself without foundation" (BN, 76). Making oneself the foundation without oneself having a foundation, in other words, taking on one's groundlessness and projecting it as ground of one's freedom, this is how Sartre describes original responsibility. Indeed, the loss of essence and foundation, far from de-responsibilizing the subject, in fact responsibilizes it. *As deprived of foundation,* our responsibility is not suppressed but originates therein, along with its inventiveness. My very obligation arises out of this groundlessness: If there is neither a God nor an *a priori* table of values, I am unable to justify my actions on any a-temporal register, nor can I explain away my actions by reference to a given human nature. Unable to rely on some standard, I am then *obliged* to supply such a lacking ground, obligated to and responsibilized for the choices I make. Such is the meaning of obligation, and thus of ethics, if it is the case that for Sartre, ethics is defined by "the dimension of obligation" (HN, 69).[21] It is the existence of an *a priori* morality that would de-responsibilize me. The groundlessness of values, the very absence of an *a priori* morality, responsibilizes me. Situating human existence in the nothing is not nihilism, but paradoxically *the origin of ethics and the origin of responsibility.* Everything takes place as if responsibility were made possible by the very extent of the *absence* of moral norms one could rely upon; as if ethics, as Derrida will insist, is rebellious to norms;[22] as if, paradoxically, the obligation of ethical responsibility arose from a lack of normativity, in a sort of duty beyond duty ("hyper-duty") that will be thematized by both Levinas and Derrida.

And this may arguably be the greatest misunderstanding of Sartre by his critics. It is usually believed—assumed!—that moral norms must be given *a priori,* i.e., that their givenness is what constitutes morality, and that the absence of these norms would constitute the collapse of morality. It is thus generally assumed that if 'right' and 'wrong' were chosen, they would lose their normativity.[23] Now, Sartre makes the claim that values are not given *a priori* (since there is no God), and that appealing to such values amounts to appealing to something that does not exist. One could also argue that it is from a lack of *a priori* norms that ethical responsibility emerges in the first place, and that the very problem of right and wrong can first arise. 'Right' and 'wrong' are a matter of choice and decision, they are not given *a priori*. The very meaning of 'right' and 'wrong' is not given *a priori,* and is thus also a matter for decision; it is a matter to be problematized, as we saw in Nietzsche. In a word, 'right' and 'wrong' are a matter for our responsible decision. Conforming to ready-made norms or applying an *a priori* moral program would in fact be the height of irresponsibility, as no actual decision would be made. Here lies what Derrida would call the aporia, that is, the paradoxical or impossible possibility, of ethical decision: It lacks a norm, a rule, that would give it *a priori* the way to decide, and yet this lack is its condition. Derrida would go so far as to claim that for "there to be a decision, I must not know what to do . . . The moment of decision, the ethical moment, if you will, is independent from knowledge. It is when 'I do not know the right rule' that the ethical question arises."[24] Sartre makes an analogous claim, for instance through the example of the student that will be discussed in a moment. Sartre argues that there is no established *a priori* universal ethics that can provide the right way to decide, concluding that, "There is *no way* of judging" (HE, 58–59; my emphasis). Yet Sartre maintains, as Derrida will, that this non-way of aporia is in fact the original situation of ethics, the only way for a possible decision, and that we have to decide out of this aporia.

THE IMPURITY OF ETHICS

At this point, we recognize that the absence of any given *a priori* value-system means the absence of determinism and humans' radical freedom— their utterly abandoned or thrown responsibility. This notion of abandonment is crucial. Sartre uses the term *déréliction,* which is rendered in English as "forlornness" or "abandonment." That the term is in fact Sartre's translation of Heidegger's *Geworfenheit* ("thrownness"), this passage indicates: "When we speak of forlornness, a term Heidegger was fond of, we mean only that God does not exist, and that we have to face all the consequences of this" (HE, 40). Nowhere does this abandonment, that is, the groundlessness of existence, appear so vividly than in the moment of choice. Sartre indicates this: "Forlornness implies that we ourselves choose our being"

(HE, 45). Original choice reveals thrownness, and our ontological abandon is an abandonment *to responsibility,* a responsibility that is groundless through and through. That groundlessness of ethical responsibility is manifest in the radical absence of determining factors, as well as of any *a priori* values and norms. As an example of this abandonment *to freedom (and to responsibility),* Sartre tells the story of a student of his, who came to him with the following problem: His father was at odds with his mother and was a collaborator; his elder brother had been killed by the Germans, and the student wanted revenge. His mother was living alone with him, and needed him. His choice was either to go and fight by joining the Free French Forces in England (thereby leaving and sacrificing his duty to his mother), or to stay with his mother (thereby sacrificing his commitment to a broader problem). On the one hand, the student could take a concrete action directed toward one individual, or on the other hand he could take an action directed toward a national collectivity. Two kinds of morality are delineated—an ethics of empathy, of personal devotion, and an ethics with a broader scope. He had to choose one between the two. How? On the basis of what ethical system? Sartre would show how they all are inadequate.

First, the Christian doctrine commands us to be charitable, to love our neighbors, to deny ourselves for others. But such commands cannot help in this decision—for how would we decide between the love for country and the love for one's mother? Should one help only one individual, or the collectivity? Sartre's answer is eloquent in its aporetic simplicity: "Who can decide *a priori?* Nobody. No book of ethics can tell him" (HE, 43). This is why, second, Kantian ethics will also prove useless. The Kantian ethics commands us never to treat another as a means, but always as an end. If the student helps his mother, he would treat her as an end, and the others as means; if he helps the freedom fighters, he would treat them as ends, but then would neglect his mother and thus treat her as means.

What both Christian ethics and Kantian ethics have in common, and what makes both of them inadequate, is their very *universality.* They "are always too broad for the concrete and specific case that we are considering" (HE, 43). A universal ethical doctrine is structurally inadequate for ethical decision, for the way in which such a decision *happens.* Let us note that the situation described by Sartre deconstructs the very possibility of a pure ethics, of a pure Good, not only because there is no norm to provide a guidance to the judgment, but above all, because by choosing a good one actually produces an evil, in a sort of self-betrayal of ethics. The purity of ethics finds itself impossible: It is not possible to choose a good without at the same time choosing an evil, as if performing one duty makes one betray another. Sartre thus reveals the radical impurity of ethics, and thus casts doubt on the very possibility of what is called "a right action." Ethics is impure, not only because of the inadequacy of a universal ethics (its principles being always too *general,* too abstract), but also because of the self-sacrifice (i.e., the aporia) implied in the ethical decision. There is no possibility of following duty alone, as Kant would require of us, since there are several conflicting, antinomical, duties in play. In addition, one does not know how the act will turn out, the perverse effects that always affect a decision and its "rightness," and yet *one* is responsible for carrying out that act, without knowing what the right course of action is.

"Trusting one's instincts" is also inadequate, for there too one would have to make a decision, and there too it would not be determined or guided by *a priori* principles. Furthermore, feelings are formed by the deeds that one does, and therefore I cannot treat them as guides for action. "And that is to say that I can neither seek within myself the true condition which will impel me to act, nor apply to a system of ethics for concepts which will permit me to act" (HE, 44). The guidance sought by going to one's teacher is a guidance *sought* from someone whom one chose, anticipating—and approving in advance—what they would say. Thus to choose an adviser is already to commit *oneself* by choice. If the adviser is Jean-Paul Sartre, the answer will be the following: "Therefore, in coming to see me he knew the answer I was going to give him, and I had only one answer to give: You're free, choose, that is, invent" (HE, 44–45). Invent! Because "no general ethics can show you what is to be done; there are no omens in the world" (HE, 45). Ethical responsibility is thus a matter of *invention,* not of application of some precepts or rules. Even if one were to simply apply a rule, that person would still have to interpret its meaning and approve it. Accordingly, "The existentialist does not think that man is going to help himself by finding in the world some omen by which to orient himself. Because he thinks that man will interpret the omen to suit himself. Therefore he thinks that man, with no support and no aid, is condemned at every moment to invent man" (HE, 41). With respect to interpretation, then, one bears the entire responsibility. That is what responsibility means, namely, that we ourselves choose our being, and that such a choice happens in an ungrounded way.

THE INVENTION OF THE LAW

For Sartre, what constitutes the value of a value is never an *a priori* ideal meaning, a "transcendental signified," but the *act* itself that affirms and posits such value. The only way to determine the value of a value is to "perform an act which confirms and defines it" (HE, 44). There is a performativity of ethical valuation, wherein ethics becomes the matter of a making, or of an invention. This accounts for the crucial analogy Sartre draws between responsibility, ethics, and the work of art. The first element of this analogy is the motif of *invention*. To the objectors who allege that existentialism does not propose a worthy ethics because its values are "merely" chosen, Sartre replies first that it is not for concrete, actual ethical decision to conform to an abstract and dubious construction, but the other way around! He writes, "You've got to take things as they are" (HE, 60). The fundamental situation of ethics is that it is to be *invented,* out of a lack of an *a priori* moral norm. With respect to the aporetic nature of this situation, Sartre writes: "My answer to this is that I'm quite vexed that that's the way it is; but if I have discarded God the Father, there must be someone to *invent* values" (HE, 60). The invention of ethics and values arises out of the disappearance of God, and with it, the disappearance of any possible reference to a given in the positing of values. If nothing is given, then everything has to be created or invented.[25] This constitutes the second element of the analogy with the work of art. Each finds an absence of *a priori* rules. For "to say that we invent values means nothing else but this: life has no meaning *a priori.* Before you come alive, life is nothing; it's up to you to give it a meaning, and value is nothing else but the meaning that you choose" (HE, 60). Ethics is created, not discovered in some ready-made table of laws. It is in this context that Sartre draws the analogy with the work of art. One "chooses without referring to pre-established values, but it is unfair to accuse him of caprice. Instead, let us say that moral choice *is to be compared to the making of a work of art*" (HE, 55; my emphasis). This analogy does not lead to some kind of aestheticism, but rather aims at revealing the performativity of ethics; and not aestheticism, since Sartre insists that his claim must be taken only as a comparison or as an analogy. Just like the person having to make an ethical choice, the artist, as Sartre explains it, paints a picture without following rules established *a priori.* There is no pre-defined picture or painting for the artist, prior to the act of creation; rather, "the artist is engaged in the making of his painting," and the painting "to be made is precisely the painting he will have made" (HE, 55). There are no *a priori* aesthetic values. These appear afterwards, that is, after the creation of the work of art, in "the coherence of the painting, in the correspondence between what the artist intended and the result" (HE, 55). One cannot judge a painting until it is done, and Sartre concludes: "The same holds on the ethical plane" (HE, 60). As is the case with the work of art, morality lacks *a priori* rules, and places us in the same creative position, such that in the end there is no ethical reality except in making and acting.

What makes the analogy between art and morality possible is that both are creations, inventions without *a priori* rules. In both cases, "we can not decide *a priori* what there is to be done" (HE, 55–56). This situation appears very clearly in the example of the student asking for guidance—no ethical doctrine could provide an answer to the ethical problem or dilemma he was facing. That young man was obliged to invent the law for himself, because man is "choosing his ethics" (HE, 56). Responsibility means having the obligation to invent one's ethics, against the background of the non-givenness of essence and of *a priori* rules, since "man makes himself; he isn't ready made at the start. In choosing his ethics, he makes himself, and force of circumstances is such that he can not abstain from choosing one" (HE, 56). To choose an ethics means to project a value, and the value of that value is not given prior to the projecting but needs to be justified in the act of projecting, and in that sense must be chosen over and over again.

Hyperbolic Responsibility

FROM INDIVIDUAL TO UNIVERSAL RESPONSIBILITY

Responsibility for Sartre is clearly situated at the level of the individual, as one must begin with the subjective: *I* am responsible. Responsibility is always individualized, is each time mine. Each individual must take over his or her own existence, because no one is categorized on the basis of a pregiven "nature" or "essence." Existence is irreducibly singular—existence is *my own* to be and to invent. There is thus a radically *individuating* quality to essenceless existence. Sartre is very clear on this point, precisely by stressing the irreducible subjectivity of existentialism: "Man is nothing else but what he makes of himself. Such is the first principle of existentialism. It is also what is called subjectivity, the name we are labelled with when charges are brought against us" (HE, 36). It is in this sense that man is a subjective life, "rather than a patch of moss, a piece of garbage, or a cauliflower" (HE, 36). Existentialism makes each of us responsible for our own being. Further, Sartre states that there is no event in the world that does not in fact concern me, which is not mine to take on. Responsibility is each time mine as it engages my own existence (as mine alone) *and* the meaning of the world that I carry on my shoulders.

Yet, Sartre will immediately refer this mineness of responsibility to a *universality,* and my own existence to "all men." For "when we say that a man is responsible for himself, we do not only mean that he is responsible for his own individuality, but that he is responsible for all men" (HE, 36). *I* am responsible, and I *alone,* but nevertheless I am responsible for *all* men. Individual responsibility would thus have a universal reach, while remaining mine alone, in the sense of what Sartre would later call a "singular universality."[26] Certainly, in the background of these claims and of this discussion is Sartre's thesis that there is such a thing as a universal human condition. There is no common *essence,* no human nature, but there is a shared *condition.* A condition is not based on an essence, but on the features of an existence, which as we know has no essence. In fact, one could define a condition as the situation of not having an essence! Contrasting nature and condition, Sartre states that although "it is impossible to find in every man some universal essence which would be human nature, yet there does exist a universal human condition" (HE, 52). By "condition," Sartre understands "the a priori limits which outline man's fundamental situation in the universe" (HE, 52). Although historical situations vary, what "does not vary is the necessity for him to exist in the world, to be at work there, to be there in the midst of other people, and to be mortal there" (HE, 52). Thus, "condition" for Sartre echoes Heidegger's notion of "existential," as distinct from categories. One indeed recognizes in Sartre's enumeration the following existentials of *Being and Time:* being-in-the-world, the *Umwelt* of work, *Mitsein,* and being-toward-death. As a consequence of such shared a condition, every individual choice has a universal scope for Sartre, and individual responsibility has an immediate universal reach. This is why

Sartre realizes that "our responsibility is much greater than we might have supposed" (HE, 37).

Indeed, individual responsibility does not mean a "private" responsibility, for it exists in the world and has to articulate itself in the element of a world with others. Individuality is not synonymous with privateness. Individuality is in the world, always existing with others there. The very term "existence," the key concept of Sartre's philosophy, as its Latin root *ex-istere* suggests, means to stand outside, to stand forth *in a world*. One exists in the world by acting in the world, and engaging others in one's choices. The world, and others, are thus involved in my existence. Sartre retrieves Heidegger's insight that Dasein—which is each time mine—is a being-in-the-world-with-others. "Of course, freedom as the definition of man does not depend on others, but as soon as there is involvement, I am obliged to want others to have freedom at the same time that I want my own freedom. I can take freedom as my goal only if I take that of others as a goal as well" (HE, 58). Sartre is very clear on this point: The subjectivity he conceives of is not a strictly individual subjectivity, for one discovers in the *cogito* not only himself, but others as well. Thus subjectivity is essentially intersubjectivity. Contrary to the philosophies of Descartes and Kant, Sartre understands the "I think" as reaching "ourselves in the presence of others," to the point that "the others are just as real to us as our own self" (HE, 51). Others are even the condition of our own existence, insofar as I access myself through them. "Thus, the man who becomes aware of himself through the cogito also perceives all others," and he "realizes that he cannot be anything . . . unless others recognize it as such" (HE, 51). In short, to reach a truth about myself, I must go though the mediation of others, and "one makes a choice in relationship to others" (HE, 56). Hence, Sartre concludes forcefully: "Let us at once announce the discovery of a world which we shall call intersubjectivity" (HE, 52). The world *is* intersubjectivity, although Sartre ultimately retains the privilege of the individual self in this intersubjective world, as he betrays when he writes: "this is the world in which man decides what he is *and what others are*" (HE, 52; my emphasis). Responsibility thus remains on the side of the ego, a philosophical position that Levinas would object to by proposing a more radical way of overturning (destituting, deposing) the subject toward the other in order to let otherness itself affect and transform the very concept of responsibility. We will return to this.[27]

As we have seen, Sartre rejects *a priori*, given values—values that would impose themselves on *all* humans. He thus rejects an *a priori* universality of man. However, he does not advocate some kind of relativism since, on the contrary, our responsibility extends to all human beings. Furthermore, freedom is a universal condition of being human that transcends particular states or historical periods for Sartre. He then advocates a universality of choice.[28] This universality is not something given *a priori*, but something chosen: "In this sense we may say that there is a universality of man; but it is not given, it is perpetually being made. I build the universal in choosing myself; I build it in understanding the configuration of every other man, whatever age he might have lived in" (HE, 53). In what sense? Sartre first clarifies the meaning of subjectivity (or subjectivism), which, we recall, he posited as the first truth of existentialism. Human subjectivity is the horizon of Sartre's reflections. Human subjectivity means that my individuality involves *all men*. When I choose a value, I choose a form, a concept or an ideal, a notion that I project as a value to be embraced by all; I project a universal horizon, or rather a horizon of universality, to also be chosen by others. In elevating this model for ourselves, *we implicitly extend it as a model for others;* thus in *Hope Now,* Sartre explains that by existing "we are struggling . . . to arrive at a definition of what is human" (HN, 67). When we act morally, we act in the name of some value, some principle, some ideal: There is therefore a universal scope of values for Sartre, not because they are objective, or given *a priori,* but because we project with our values a universal horizon in which we engage others. There is a universality, but it is neither given nor objective. It is chosen and subjective, intersubjective: I exist in the dimension of the universal, but this universal can only exist as chosen. He writes,

> When we say that man chooses his own self, we mean that every one of us does likewise; but we also mean by that that in making this choice he also chooses all men. In fact, in creating the man that we want to be, there is not a single one of our acts which does not at the same time create *an image of man* as we think he ought to be. (HE, 37; my emphasis)

Sartre gives the example of a worker who chooses a Christian course rather than a Communist trade union. In that choice, a philosophy is embraced, values are chosen, and therefore this choice involves all. If I choose an apparently quite private course, such as getting married, even though this decision is strictly mine, I am also embracing the value of marriage and monogamy. In that sense, I am responsible both for myself *and* for all men, since I am creating a certain image of man. In creating myself, I create man. To choose this or that course is to choose, to affirm the value of what we choose, and affirming the value of an action places me in the universal: I choose it because I believe it is good for all men, as Sartre believes with Socrates that "we can never choose evil. We always choose the good, and nothing can be good for us without being good for all" (HE, 37).

In a strikingly Kantian style, responsibility becomes lodged in the universal, if we understand that this universal is projected from an individual subjectivity, and chosen or projected as a possible horizon for co-existence. However, Sartre clarifies his difference from Kant on this question of universality. He first recognizes his debt to Kant for this stress on a certain universality in ethics and an ethics of freedom: "though the content of ethics is variable, a certain form of it is universal. Kant says that freedom desires both itself and the freedom of others. Granted" (HE, 58). However, he then breaks with Kant, by stating that whereas Kant "believes that the formal and the universal are enough to constitute an ethics," Sartre *"on the contrary"* believes that

> principles which are too abstract run aground in trying to decide action. Once again, take the example of the student. In the name of what, in the name of what great moral maxim do you think he could have decided, in perfect peace of mind, to abandon his mother or to stay with her? There is no way of judging. (HE, 58–59)

Sartre thus breaks with Kant on the motif of the abstractness of the universality of ethics, gesturing toward another conception of the universal. As we noted above, Sartre reveals the aporia in ethical judgment, the very same one that Derrida would unveil in the structure and logic of decision. However, it is not a matter for Sartre of stressing the undecidability of decision, but rather the *concreteness, unpredictability, inventivity,* and in the end the *freedom* of ethics: "The content is always concrete and therefore unforeseeable; there is always the element of invention. The one thing that counts is knowing whether the inventing that has been done, has been done in the name of freedom" (HE, 58). "In the name of freedom," such is the very sense and direction of his ethics.

Freedom is the ground of ethics, and ethics is for the sake of freedom. For Sartre, in and through particular circumstances, "we want freedom for freedom's sake" (HE, 57). We can thus identify what separates Sartre from Kant: (1) the difference in their conception of universality (*a priori* or chosen, based on the law or on a negation of any norm); (2) the concreteness versus abstractness of ethics; (3) the aporia of ethical decision versus the conformity to law and duty; and (4) the singularity of the ethical moment, and its unbridgeable gap with universal form, since principles, as Sartre puts it, "break down." It remains that Sartre keeps the horizon of universality in his thinking of ethics and responsibility. In a sense, every act I perform is an exemplary act. An act for Sartre is always an example, for all to follow: "For every man, everything happens as if all mankind had its eyes fixed on him and were guiding itself by what he does" (HE, 39). In a quasi-Kantian formulation, echoing the famous universalizing imperative of morality, Sartre states that every man, every singular individual, when acting, must at the same time ask him or herself: "Am I really the kind of man who has the right to act in such a way that humanity must guide itself by my actions?" (HE, 39).

ABSOLUTIZING RESPONSIBILITY

In fact, for Sartre, responsibility is not only universal but indeed absolute. He often writes of the absolute character of our responsibility. For instance, he refers to his own conception of responsibility as "absolute responsibility" (HE, 64), evokes the "absoluteness of choice" (HE, 53), refers to "the absolute character of free involvement" (HE, 53), and describes each person as being "an absolute choice of self," or "an absolute upsurge at an absolute date" (HE, 66). Responsibility is absolute because of Sartre's very conception of existence as absolutely free. One should stress here that this absolute responsibility strictly flows out of Sartre's claim regarding the absolute freedom of the for-itself, and he clearly states that "this absolute responsibility . . . is simply the logical requirement of the consequences of our freedom" (BN, 708).[29] Responsibility is also said to be absolute because of its very boundlessness, a responsibility that is rendered infinite or boundless by the groundlessness of existence. Because there is no essence, my responsibility knows no bounds. *Let us note the paradoxical character of this responsibility. It is absolute to the extent that it is based on nothing.* Responsibility becomes absolute to the extent of such groundlessness; it is *as* ungrounded, that existence becomes responsible for itself, absolutely, and without any support other than itself. This is why to be responsible means to be responsible for that very responsibility—even if I was thrown into it, even if I am *not* responsible for it. I am responsible for my very irresponsibility with respect to my responsibility, I am responsible for the fact that I am not responsible for my responsibility.

We find in Sartre a kind of hyperbolic inflation, or paroxysm, of responsibility—an inflation through which responsibility becomes excessive,[30] if not overwhelming. My responsibility embraces the whole world, *the meaning of the world as shared by all.* Does Sartre not state that when a man commits himself to anything, he is not only choosing what he will be, but is "also a lawmaker who is, at the same time, choosing all mankind as well as himself" (HE, 38)? In such a choice, our responsibility becomes total, radical, and inescapable, and occurs in anxiety. This anxiety manifests the groundlessness of our freedom. "In anguish freedom is anguished before itself inasmuch as it is instigated and bound by nothing" (BN, 73). This groundlessness leads to the unavoidable nature of our responsibility as well as its overwhelming character, since I literally have the meaning of the world on my shoulders![31] This hyperbolic inflation of responsibility becoming absolute will lead Sartre to claim that facticity—that is, the very order of the not chosen, such as birth, and therefore what could represent a limit to my responsibility—is a matter for my responsibility, and is in a sense chosen too. My responsibility becomes absolute in this reduction of any determinism and of facticity itself. However, another important aspect of this discussion on the absoluteness of responsibility should be kept in mind. Sartre speaks of the absolute character of our responsibility also out of his own admitted Cartesianism, to which I will return at the end of this chapter. We will see how he connects the absoluteness of responsibility with the absoluteness of the Cartesian truth.

This inflation of responsibility implies that responsibility reduces, overcomes or appropriates the irresponsibility that seems to haunt and threaten it at every step, starting with the very irresponsibility of a non-chosen freedom—indeed, a non-chosen responsibility!—and extending to the power of feelings, emotions, and passions; to the facticity of our environment and situations; to accidents and events which happen to me from without, events of which I am not the cause, etc. I will be said to be responsible for all of these.[32] With respect to the non-chosen freedom and responsibility, Sartre suggests that such irresponsibility, in the guise of the impossibility of justification and groundlessness of responsibility, is at the origin of responsible action. "We are condemned to be free," that is, we are *not* responsible for our responsibility, we are *not* free to be free. Let us analyze this singular phenomenon. First, Sartre breaks with the notion of a transcendental freedom; our responsibility is irresponsible with respect to itself, because it is *thrown* to its own abandonment. Herein lies the radical difference between Sartre's thought of freedom and Kant's notion of transcendental freedom. Whereas for Kant, freedom was given a quasi-theological basis—being understood on the model of the divine *causa sui*—for Sartre, on the contrary, freedom arises out of the disappearance of God and divine principles, as a *thrown freedom* ("we are *condemned* to be free"). Sartre explicitly marks his distance with Kant on this motif of the *causa sui*, remarking that "the ethical modality implies, at least at that level, that we stop wanting to have being as a goal, we no longer want to be God, we no longer want to be *ens causa sui* [our own cause]. We're looking for something else" (HN, 59). Freedom is no longer *causa sui*, no longer a transcendental freedom but a thrown freedom. This reveals a certain irresponsibility or non-responsibility at the origin of responsibility: I am unfree to be free, irresponsible or unaccountable for my responsibility, in which I am thrown and that *I cannot justify*. I am not free to be free. However, as Sartre remarks in *Being and Nothingness,* the for-itself is not free to be unfree: To be free to decide upon our being-free or not-free would imply that we are already free! Therefore we are not free to be free or unfree: We *are* free, as a fact; such is "the facticity of freedom" (BN, 623), which implies that the irresponsibility of our responsibility is but the fact of this responsibility.

As we mentioned above, this absolute responsibility must nonetheless attempt to appropriate any instance of irresponsibility that might threaten it. Sartre focuses on those instances of irresponsibility that are so many "deterministic excuses," such as "the power of passion," and more generally all that can be classified under the general rubric of "facticity," of what is received as a fact because not-chosen. Any appeal to a determinism is denounced as a lie: "If we have defined man's situation as a free choice, with no excuses and no recourse, every man who takes refuge behind the excuse of his passions, every man who sets up a determinism, is a dishonest man" (HE, 57). One could rephrase this passage as follows: Anyone who claims to be irresponsible in some fashion is lying. Why? Because for Sartre *there is no real irresponsibility,* because irresponsibility is impossible. Even the irresponsibility of our very responsibility, as we saw, was revealed as the irreducible fact of my freedom. The irresponsibility alleged by subjects are declared expressions of bad faith, failed attempts to escape inescapable responsibility. Irresponsibility is thus a lie for Sartre. Irresponsibility becomes nothing but the attempt at escaping responsibility, as in the case of bad faith, which is ultimately a failure because I *cannot* de-responsibilize myself.

Thus, Sartre argues against the so-called power of passion. The existentialist "will never agree that a sweeping passion is a ravaging torrent which fatally leads a man is swept to certain acts and is therefore an excuse" (HE, 41), because man is not capable of being determined, cannot be made unfree. He writes emphatically that "there is no determinism, man is free, man is freedom" (HE, 41). One is thus responsible for his or her passion. Another target is of course the appeal to circumstances in one's fate. People may complain that circumstances have been against them, that they were worthy of something much better, that they had a "bad break." Sartre rejects this reasoning as making the individual irresponsible, and as denying the fact that "reality alone is what counts" (HE, 48)—that is, the reality of our actions, our praxis. Once again drawing an analogy from the work of art, Sartre insists that the genius of Proust consists in the totality of the *works* of Proust; and similarly the genius of Racine is the series of his tragedies, outside of which there is nothing. Why should we attribute to Racine the *capacity* to write *yet another* tragedy, when that is precisely what he did *not* write? The individual is nothing but the sum of his undertakings, the ones he chose and for which he is responsible (HE, 64). Therein lies the futility of complaints, for Sartre: I cannot complain since I am the author of my being, and it would be "senseless to think of complaining since nothing foreign has decided what we feel, what we live, or what we are" (HE, 64). The existentialist, when portraying a coward, shows him as responsible for his cowardice. He is not a coward through his physiology or psychology; he has made himself a coward by his choices and actions. Cowardice lies in the *act* of giving up or giving way. Humans' *being* lies in their actions, and hence a coward is defined by the deed that he or she has done. The coward *makes him or herself* cowardly, the hero *makes him or herself* heroic; one is responsible for one's temperament and feelings.

Continuing to draw the consequences of this thesis of an absolute responsibility, and attempting to reduce facticity, Sartre maintains that there are no accidents in life, and that we are responsible for the event, for what happens to us. This might seem paradoxical, as one might note here an antinomy between event and responsibility. Isn't the event that which exceeds the subject of responsibility? Hence Jacques Derrida asks the following question: "are we ever responsible for what happens?" and clarifies: "Alternative of the same question: isn't a decision always unjustifiable? Can we or not answer for an event? For a singularity, for its singularity"? He then describes the aporia of event and responsibility:

> can we be responsible for the happening/arrival [*l'arrivée*] of something which, as such, as the happening/arrival of some thing (what we call ordinarily the event) must be unpredictable, exceed the program and naturally surprise not only the addressee but also surprise the subject to whom and by whom it is supposed to happen? *Can one be responsible without neutralizing the eventfulness of the event? To be responsible for an event, isn't that neutralizing its very surge [irruption] as an event? In other words, isn't there something like an aporia between the concept of responsibility and the concept of event?*[33]

Sartre would in fact negate that aporia, by attempting to reduce the surprise of the event, which is immediately to be taken on by our responsible engagement. What happens, he explains, happens *to me,* and what happens to me, he continues, happens *through me.* The event is thus immediately taken on by the subject; the event is the immediate mobilization of my responsibility. What happens, happens to me because everything concerns me, and what happens to me happens through me because I am the one by whom the world takes on a meaning. Here responsibility means, not simply the accountability of the subject, but the fact that I am *concerned* by the meaning of the world. When something happens in the world, I am called to respond and to answer for it: I am responsible for it. Any event becomes a call to my responsibility, and is thus not antinomical to it: I am engaged by the event. Even a war declared by others becomes mine. If war is declared, I can either join it or fight it, I can always desert or even commit suicide if I do not want to be drafted, but I have to choose and in a sense for

Sartre "everything takes place as if I bore the entire responsibility for this war" (BN, 709). Everything which happens is mine, says Sartre, and nothing human is foreign to me: "By this we must understand first of all that I am always equal to what happens to me qua man, for what happens to a man through other men and through himself can only be human" (BN, 708). There is no non-human state of things, he continues, reasserting the humanism of existentialism. I can decide on the non-human, but "this decision is human, and I shall carry the entire responsibility for it" (BN, 708). Sartre posits here responsibility as the appropriation of all foreignness for the subject, a movement that Levinas will try to overcome through responsibility as expropriation by otherness. Let us recall here Aristotle's distinction between what is up to us and what is not up to us; for Sartre, *everything* is up to me, that is, to the extent that everything is reduced to the human. Any event is immediately mine and taken over by my freedom, and there are thus no accidents without my appropriating them and making them my own. "Thus there are no *accidents* in life," and "anyway you look at it, it is a matter of a choice" (BN, 708).

OVERCOMING FACTICITY? THE QUESTION OF BIRTH

Finally, it is facticity itself that is reduced, as in the example of birth, the most extreme example of what has not been chosen. What is significant in Sartre's discussion of birth in *Being and Nothingness* is indeed that it represents *the* fact par excellence, the very figure of facticity: Not simply having been born as male or female, in this or that condition or situation, in this country or another, but having been born *at all*. Birth would seem to be an unsurpassable limit to the project or dream of a remainderless, absolute responsibility through which I could be the *author* of my being. Yet Sartre will argue that I am responsible for my birth. In the chapter titled "Freedom and Responsibility" in *Being and Nothingness*, Sartre begins by stating that as condemned to be free (this is what he calls the facticity *of* responsibility, the facticity *of* freedom), man "carries the weight of the whole world on his shoulders," and that "he is responsible for the world and for himself as a way of being" (BN, 707). In every respect I bear the responsibility of the choice which, in committing myself, also commits the whole of humanity. Sartre stresses that as being without excuse, "I carry the weight of the world by myself alone (*je porte le poids du monde à moi tout seul*) without anything or any person being able to lighten it" (BN, 710). As we noted above with respect to this last motif, Sartre is very close to Levinas who, citing Dostoevsky, claims that I am more responsible than others. We will return to this dissymmetry, but let us already note here that in contrast to Levinas, the excessive *and individuating* weight of responsibility for Sartre lies in my carrying the weight of the whole world on my shoulders, as I am the author of the meaning of the world. (Sartre stresses that we are responsible for the meaning of being, not for the existence of the world, recalling Heidegger's thematization in *Being and Time* of the meaning of being as sole access to being.) Indeed, Sartre defines responsibility as authorship. At the beginning of this chapter, we cited Sartre's definition of responsibility, perhaps the "only definition of 'responsibility' that Sartre ever ventures."[34] This definition reads as follows: "We are taking the word 'responsibility' in its ordinary sense as 'consciousness (of) being the incontestable *author* of an event or of an object'" (BN, 707). This authorship, as Sartre thus admits, is the ordinary or received sense of responsibility as imputability or accountability, and his borrowing it shows Sartre's insufficient deconstruction of that tradition, despite his proclaimed intent to draw all the consequences of the death of God, which would imply the deconstruction of authorship as such! As Jean-Luc Nancy observes, the death of God should also lead to the disappearance of the very notion of authorship. In *Being Singular Plural,* within the context of a discussion of his notion of the "creation of the world" as *ex nihilo,* Nancy explains that the "concept of the 'creation of the world' represents the origin as originarily shared, spaced between us and between all beings. *This, in turn, contributes to rendering the concept of the 'author' of the world untenable.*"[35] The creation of the world, as Nancy understands that expression—that is, in a non-theological way—supposes a break with any reliance on the semantics of authorship, divine principle and *causa sui*. "In fact," Nancy adds, "one could show how the motif of creation is one of those that leads directly to the death of God understood as author, first cause, and supreme being" (BSP, 15).[36] Sartre does not undertake a deconstruction of authorship, and in fact he brings that tradition to a paroxysm, by claiming that our responsibility arises out of our original freedom, which is but the radicalized existential version of free will.

As we know, Sartre's early philosophy of responsibility and freedom operates under an all-or-nothing logic: Either one is free, and one is free absolutely, or one is simply not free.[37] It is in this context that Sartre engages the question of facticity as it enters the discussion of responsibility. Sartre begins by recalling that since the for-itself is the one by whom there is a world, then "whatever may be the situation in which he finds himself, the for-itself must wholly assume this situation" (BN, 707). That signifies that the for-itself must make himself responsible for his own facticity. And he must "assume the situation with the proud consciousness of being the author of it" (BN, 707). There seems to be a contradiction here, for how could I be the author of a situation in which I find myself (thrown), of which I am not the author? Sartre replies that my situation only takes on meaning through my projects, and that "my" facticity (is it ever mine? for Sartre it is) takes on meaning through my transcendence and cannot be experienced except in terms of my transcendence, such that I am in a sense the author of my being. We have no essence, we have to invent our being, and to that extent we are its "authors." Ultimately, my absolute responsibility means that nothing is foreign to me, and that I am the author of the whole world in the sense that I have to make myself the author of what I have not authored!

In such a logic, in which my facticity must be reduced to my responsibility, birth must also be reduced to my freedom. This is what Sartre attempts to do, beginning by addressing the objection of an imaginary interlocutor who would object, "I did not ask to be born." Sartre immediately counters that this is "a naïve way of placing the emphasis (*mettre l'accent*) on our facticity" (BN, 710; translation modified). It will be a matter of putting more weight, more "emphasis," as it were, on the other side of the equation, that is, on transcendence. "I am responsible for everything," insists Sartre, conceding that the only thing I am not responsible for is—my responsibility itself. I am responsible for everything, "except for my very responsibility, for I am not the foundation of my being" (BN, 710). As we saw, this is not a limit for Sartre, because it simply means that I am not free *not* to be free, and thus that I am all the *more* free! He will thus argue that the facticity of my birth, my very thrownness, is up to my free choice. How does he proceed?

Sartre first insists that forlornness or abandonment, that is, thrownness, is an abandonment *to freedom*. As soon as I exist, I exist as free; at the same time, I am thrown into that freedom. Thus "everything takes place as if I were compelled to be responsible" (BN, 710). I am as it were abandoned to a responsibility, abandoned to action, and not abandoned as simply lying there as a dead weight. "I am abandoned (*délaissé*) in the world, not in the sense that I might remain abandoned and passive in a hostile universe like a board floating on the water," but rather in the sense that I find myself alone, without help, and yet engaged in that condition in a world "for which I bear the whole responsibility without being able, whatever I do, to tear myself away from this responsibility for an instant" (BN, 710). Sartre then adds, significantly, that I am even responsible for my very desire to flee or escape my responsibility: There is no possibility of irresponsibility. Just as irresponsibility would be reducible to responsibility, facticity could be reduced to freedom. If I am thrown into a responsibility for being, facticity would not necessarily be a limit for such responsibility.

This can be seen in the phenomenon of birth itself, which Sartre approaches from various angles. First he addresses the question of suicide, which is the most radical way of attempting to "undo" birth. Sartre insists that suicide is one mode among others of being-in-the-world, that is to say, it is a choice of my free being-in-the-world; he has already stated that "suicide, in fact, is a choice and affirmation" (BN, 616). Suicide is a possibility, namely the possibility of choosing to end a life that has begun: Suicide is a free relationship to birth. Second, he maintains that one cannot be passive in life; so that I either affirm or deny life. But affirming life means *affirming one's birth*, and negating life, as we saw, signifies comporting oneself toward birth, albeit negatively. So by affirming or negating life, I comport myself toward birth; I "act" upon it, I "choose" my birth in some way. Third, birth presents the peculiar characteristic of being "directly inapprehensible and even inconceivable," as "this fact of my birth never appears as a brute fact" (BN, 710). Indeed, birth seems to radically elude our grasp, our recollecting; seemingly forever ungraspable, inappropriable, birth thus constitutes a "hard limit" or impossibility for the reach of any responsible engagement. As we noted above, Sartre here again identifies or confuses facticity with factuality, with the "brute fact" of factuality, even if to then null our access to it by calling it "inaccessible." In a passage from *Being and Nothingness*, Sartre states that, "It is impossible to grasp facticity in its brute nudity, since all that we find of it is already recovered and freely constructed" (BN, 132). Sartre denies the possibility of grasping facticity "in its brute nudity." This is, to be sure, a paradoxical sense of facticity—a fact that never appears as a brute fact, a fact that eludes grasp, a fact that is forever absent! But this is not just any fact—it is *the* fact of our very coming into being, a fact that never appears as *a* fact! Sartre even goes so far as the state that facticity is "everywhere, but inapprehensible" (*partout, mais insaisissable*). Interestingly, it is this identification of facticity with the brute fact of a factuality that will allow Sartre to ultimately reduce it to our responsibility. This evasiveness of facticity indeed implies that "I never encounter anything except my responsibility" (BN, 710).[38] Sartre thus literally exploits the elusiveness of birth to dissolve it entirely into our responsibility, our current projects: "Yet I find an absolute responsibility for the fact that my facticity (here the fact of my birth) is directly inapprehensible . . . for this fact of my birth never appears as a brute fact but always across a projective reconstruction of my for-itself" (BN, 710). My birth is inapprehensible directly, but it gives itself indirectly through my free reconstruction.[39] Birth gives itself *from* my free constructs and projects, *a posteriori or after the fact*. That original fact is irremediably gone, and only appears, "after the fact," *through* my freedom; it is never a past, isolated, absolute fact. I *do* have access to my birth indirectly, through my own free projects, and thus I am responsible for it. That access is only mediated through my present and reconstructed from there. "I am ashamed of being born or I rejoice over it, or in attempting to get rid of my life I affirm that I live and I assume this life as bad." Sartre concludes: "Thus in a certain sense I *choose* being born" (BN, 710).

Facticity has thus been reduced to the transcendence of responsibility, and Sartre concludes by observing that my abandonment, that is, my facticity, "finally . . . consists simply in the fact that I am condemned to be wholly responsible for myself" (BN, 711). The facticity of my birth is inaccessible, and hence I encounter nothing but my responsibility. Birth means being thrown to my responsibility. Responsibility arises out of this abandonment and, in turn, one might suggest that I am responsible for this very abandonment. The authentic person is the one who—in anguish—realizes that his or her condition is to be thrown into a responsibility which extends to their very abandonment: I am responsible for my abandonment, that is, I am responsible for the fact that I am not responsible for my responsibility. The human being is "no longer anything but a freedom which perfectly reveals itself and whose being resides in this very revelation" (BN, 711), Sartre conceding nonetheless (the chapter ends with this thought) that most of the time, we exist as fleeing from such anguish; we exist in what Sartre would call "bad faith." As we will see, that fleeing is doomed to fail (responsibility is inescapable), especially since, as Sartre claims, "I am responsible for my very desire of fleeing responsibilities" (BN, 710).

THE PARADOX OF AUTHENTICITY: THE EXAMPLE OF BAD FAITH

As we have seen, Sartre develops a thinking of an absolute responsibility, a responsibility that falls on my shoulders alone, even if it has a universal reach. Even when it involves others, responsibility remains mine alone to carry: The war I have not chosen is mine, stresses Sartre, "*I am* this war" (BN, 707). I choose for all men, but *I* choose, and I *alone* choose. I carry the weight of the whole world on my shoulders, and I also carry the weight of my infinite responsibility itself. I am responsible for my very responsibility, responsible for its absence of foundation. The weight of such hyperbolic responsibility is obviously unbearable for the individual; it is impossible. Such absolute responsibility cannot but be anxiety-producing, overwhelming, unbearable or "insupportable" (*accablante*) (BN, 707). This is why, according to Sartre, most often people try to escape such angst by taking refuge in irresponsible behavior *and thinking*. Certainly, Sartre admits, "there are many people who are not anxious"; however, he insists, "we claim that they are hiding their anxiety, that they are fleeing from it" (HE, 38). In denying one's anxiety, one avoids *the anxiety of responsibility*, and takes refuge in what Sartre calls "bad faith," which is nothing but the doomed attempt to escape one's (inescapable) responsibility. Bad faith is a comportment that seeks to suppress anxiety, *which is the fundamental mood of responsibility*, and indeed, of the originary human condition. Since Sartre has defined the situation of man as one of free choice, without excuse and without help, and anyone who takes refuge in the excuse of passions, or by inventing some deterministic doctrine, is indulging in self-deception. Bad faith is a kind of lie or self-deception, but Sartre clarifies that bad faith is no "cynical lie" or a "knowing preparation for deceitful concepts," but more precisely means a fleeing before "what it cannot flee" (BN, 115). This reveals that our responsibility is inescapable, and that irresponsibility is impossible, or only a negative mode of responsibility.

The motif of bad faith recasts Heidegger's famed thematic of authenticity. This authenticity, however, is not without paradox, as it manifests a radical *impropriety* within human existence: As for-itself, I am what I am not, and I am not what I am, so that an irreducible duplicity is inscribed in the every structure of my being. To that extent, the goal of authenticity can only be subverted; to be authentic can no longer mean conforming to a model of oneself, since the self is never identical to itself. To be an authentic self will involve an inescapable duplicity, the very duplicity implied by the non-coincidence to itself of the for-itself. Presence to self, clarifies Sartre, "supposes that an impalpable fissure has slipped into being" (BN, 124). There is no self-identical self but there is a presence to self, which implies a non-coincidence or non-identity with oneself. Authentic being will prove paradoxical, never without a relation to an inappropriable, an impossible, which Sartre calls "transcendence," or the impossibility to ever coincide with oneself. This will appear in the notion of play, of playing at being one's self, in the analyses of bad faith, as Sartre maintains that "we can be nothing without playing at being" (BN, 131).

Let us unfold this paradox of authentic being. Sartre stresses that to exist authentically consists in owning up to our condition, which as we know is one of infinite freedom and responsibility: Authenticity consists in acting *in the name* of freedom and *for the sake* of freedom, and to recognize oneself as a no-thing. The authentic person is the one who, as a free being, cannot but *will* his or her freedom in any circumstances. To exist inauthentically, on the contrary, consists in existing as if one were *determined,* like a thing—seeking to hide from oneself the wholly voluntary nature of one's existence and its absolute freedom. To exist inauthentically, or in bad faith, thus consists in attempting to abdicate one's responsibilities, to disburden oneself of the weight of freedom. This self-deception "is obviously a falsehood because it belies the complete freedom of involvement" (HE, 57). It is also impossible, for one cannot make oneself unfree and irresponsible, and because one is ultimately responsible for this self-deceit. It is as if, in such self-denial, we were trying to congeal into an in-itself. Clearly this is impossible, and thus we are not only responsible for our irresponsibility (since we *choose* this escapist attitude), but ultimately we are not even able to be irresponsible, because irresponsibility as such has been reduced to being a derivative mode of absolute responsibility. Sartre argues that I am responsible for relinquishing my irresponsibility, reduced to being a deficient mode, thus privileging responsibility over irresponsibility. Inauthenticity would thus seem to be a mode, and a mode only, of authenticity. However, we will see how authenticity in turn is inhabited by an irreducible inauthenticity, on account of the duplicity of the for-itself.

Bad faith consists in attempting to be what one is, to be identical with oneself. Hence the café waiter tries to *be* a café waiter. However, he can only *play* at being one, for no one can be any actual identity of any kind, due to our transcendence, that "divine absence" of which Sartre speaks, evoking Paul Valéry (BN, 103). I am never any one of my acts, "perpetually absent to my body, to my acts . . . I cannot say either that I am here or that I am not here . . . On all sides I escape being" (BN, 103). Now, therein resides the paradox or aporia of this discussion: On the one hand, irresponsibility is said to be only an inauthentic fleeing from authentic responsibility, but on the other hand, bad faith reveals the original lack of self-identity in the for-itself. It thus reveals the impossibility of identity, such that authenticity can never be the conformity to an authentic self. The self is marked by a fundamental duplicity and lack of self-identity. This explains why, if bad faith is impossible (unsuccessful), good faith also proves impossible. Such is the sense of Sartre's critique of sincerity, the ideal of sincerity as "an ideal of being-in-itself" (BN, 115). Sincerity (along with the *esprit de sérieux*) is impossible, due to the duplicity of the for-itself. I cannot be in good faith, since being "escapes me on all sides and annihilates itself" (BN, 111). I cannot be in good faith any more than I can be in bad faith, and Sartre concludes that "in the final analysis the goal of sincerity and the goal of bad faith are not so different" (BN, 110)! Both good faith and bad faith are comportments of irresponsibility, for each attempts to deny the freedom and transcendence of the for-itself. Authentic responsibility would thus not be some adequation to some ideal self, but rather maintaining the gap at the heart of the subject—being what one is not, not being what one is. By maintaining the lack of self-coincidence with oneself, responsibility would affirm the impossibility of coincidence, and be a responsibility to the impossible. Authentic responsibility is a responsibility *toward this impropriety of existence. One is responsible on the basis of this impropriety, and for it.* Authenticity will consist in assuming the play of being. Lacking an identity, one can only *play* at being what one is (like the waiter):

"The good speaker is the one who *plays* at speaking because he can not *be speaking*" (BN, 103). Bad faith is not simply playing but trying to make of that play a reality, like the waiter playing at *being* a waiter and trying to forget it is a role-playing. The waiter tries to be a waiter, in the mode of the in-itself. To be authentic thus consists in playing, but without attempting to *be* what one plays. One plays against the background of the groundlessness of this absence of being—the play is originary. Due to a radical absence of self-coincidence of the for-itself, the self is itself in the mode of not-being it. "I am a waiter in the mode of *being what I am not*" (BN, 103). Authenticity can be re-described here as responsibility toward this non-coincidence, responsibility toward the transcendence of existence. Play is the mode of such existence, in an irremediable ex-appropriation. We will return to this impropriety of responsibility.

SARTRE'S CARTESIANISM

For all of its phenomenological insights, Sartre's philosophy of responsibility brings to a paroxysm the tradition of will and subjectivity that has defined modern philosophy since Descartes. While situating his thought in the wake of phenomenology and Heidegger's analytic of existence (as witnessed in his massive borrowing of the terminology of *Being and Time*), Sartre ultimately remains a Cartesian philosopher and his account of responsibility as authorship (however expanded and radicalized) remains indebted to the traditional enclosure of responsibility, i.e., to its egological enclosure and its foundation on the will. Heidegger himself would note the Cartesian character of Sartrean philosophy, by identifying the motif of "project" in Sartre's existentialism as a sign of subjectivism. Already in "Letter on Humanism," but also in his last seminars, Heidegger explains that Sartre's notion of "project" makes it "all too possible to understand the 'project' as a human performance. Accordingly, project is then only taken to be a structure of subjectivity—which is how Sartre takes it, by basing himself upon Descartes."[40] This Cartesianism of Sartre's thought appears in his characterization of responsibility as absolute, which we noted above. What is most significant is that he connects this absoluteness with the absoluteness of the Cartesian truth. He even claims, following Descartes in an almost indistinguishable way, that "before there can be any truth whatsoever, there must be an absolute truth" (HE, 51). The implicit presence of Husserl is also unmistakable, as Husserl speaks in *Ideas I* of transcendental consciousness as absolute.[41] For Sartre, the truth of the Cartesian cogito is an absolute, a first undeniable truth. Let us read this eloquent and solemn declaration: "There can be no other truth to start from than this, *I think, therefore I exist*. There we have the absolute truth of consciousness becoming aware of itself" (HE, 50–51). Sartre embraces this Cartesian tradition, while bending it to his philosophy of existential freedom—existentializing Descartes, as it were—going as far as to write the following: "In this sense you may, if you like, say that each of us performs an absolute act in breathing, eating, sleeping or behaving in any way whatever. There is no difference between being free . . . and being absolute" (HE, 53). We saw how for Sartre, the point of departure is the subjectivity of the individual, how this is the first truth of existentialism, just as the cogito was the first certainty with Descartes. Outside of Descartes, outside of the Cartesian cogito, Sartre writes, "all objects are no more than probable," such that "any doctrine of probabilities which is not attached to a truth will crumble into nothing."

Sartre assumes the necessity of an absolute foundation of thought; for there to be any truth whatever, there must be an absolute truth, and that is the *ego cogito*. Sartre understands this certainty as providing a basis for ethics, as it grants a dignity to the human being; it is, he states, the only theory that "gives man dignity, the only one which does not reduce him to an object" (HE, 51). Sartre continues in this vein by assuming an idealism, rejecting all materialisms as philosophies that treat of man as an object, as a set of pre-determined reactions. Against such materialist philosophies, Sartre proclaims, "We definitely wish to establish the human realm as an ensemble of values distinct from the material realm" (HE, 51). Even transcendence is made to conform to this radical subjectivism. The human is defined as a self-surpassing, a transcendence, but the horizon thus reached remains that of the self: "Man is constantly outside of himself . . . and, on the other hand, it is by pursuing transcendent goals that he is able to exist; man, being this state of passing-beyond, and seizing upon things only as they bear upon this passing-beyond, is at the heart, at the center of this passing-beyond" (HE, 61). For Sartre, subjectivity is the horizon of transcendence, whereas in Heidegger transcendence takes us to the element of being. For Sartre, transcendence is simply the *being of subjectivity*. Our self-surpassing makes us exist in a human universe, as opposed to a world of things. This is what he calls the humanism of existentialism: This relation of transcendence (transcendence as passing beyond, not as the transcendence of God) is constitutive of man and subjectivity, "in the sense that man is not closed in on himself but is always present in a human universe, is what we call existentialist humanism" (HE, 61). This is the humanism of Sartrean responsibility, "because we remind man that there is no lawmaker other than himself; and that in his forlornness he will decide by himself" (HE, 61). (For Heidegger, we are on a plane where there is being, whereas with Sartre we are on a plane where there are only men.) This self-responsibility lies in the fact that we are what we make, that we are literally the authors of ourselves. To that extent, Sartre continues the tradition of authorship, subjectivity, and will as causality that has circumscribed the concept of responsibility in our tradition. Significant in this regard is the following passage from *Being and Nothingness,* which we cited above. Sartre first notes that "*nothing,* absolutely nothing, justifies me in adopting this or that particular value, this or that particular scale of values" (BN, 76), and then immediately adds, "it is I who sustain values in being" (BN, 77). What is the necessity for passing from the nothing of values to the I as subject and author of these values? There is none, except a subjectivistic bias. It will take a veritable overturning of subjectivity to reopen responsibility as an experience of otherness, a gesture that is performed in Levinas's great reversal of responsibility.

FIVE

Levinas's Reversal of Responsibility

Responsibility toward the Other

Levinas's corpus, comprising one of the greatest ethical thoughts of the twentieth century, presents an extraordinary revolution in the thinking of responsibility—a peculiar "reversal," to use his term, of the concept of responsibility. One finds in Levinas's thinking of responsibility a sustained attempt to overcome the very horizon of egology. Indeed, far from assigning responsibility to the actions of an agent on the basis of the freedom of the subject, following an entire tradition, Levinas breaks with such a horizon—indeed, breaks with the very concept of horizon in philosophy—and re-conceptualizes responsibility as a being "for-the-other." As Levinas explains in *Ethics and Infinity*: "Usually, one is responsible for what one does oneself. I say, in *Otherwise than Being or Beyond Essence*, that responsibility is initially *a for the other*,"[1] a for-the-other that expresses the structure of subjectivity as *"the other in the same"*[2] and which is so radical that Levinas would give it the meaning of a being-hostage to the other. No longer a responsibility for oneself or for one's actions, but a responsibility for the other and for the sake of the other; no longer following the freedom of the subject, but arising out of the other's demand on me—the other, for Levinas, "is above all the one I am responsible for."[3] Responsibility is no longer the responsibility of a free agent, as Levinas approaches it as a responsibility "that could not have begun from me," not begun with freedom, but before freedom and in a sense *before me* as well. This is why Levinas writes that responsibility "is not mine" (AE, 252), anticipating what Derrida would write on as a responsibility and a decision "of the other."[4] It is in this revolution of the concept of responsibility, in which the classical "responsibility for oneself and for one's actions" shifts toward another sense, that Levinas undertakes his key movement with respect to the concept of responsibility. As Jacques Derrida explains in *The Gift of Death,*

> Levinas wants to remind us that responsibility is not at first responsibility of myself for myself, that the sameness of myself is derived from the other, as if it were second to the other, coming to itself as responsible and mortal from the position of my responsibility before the other, for the other's death and in the face of it.[5]

We will return to all of these motifs, but let us first stress that this reversal targets in particular the Cartesian tradition in modern philosophy from Descartes to Husserl, that is, the primacy of egology and the predominance of the will, both of which Levinas seeks to overturn. Levinas seeks to exceed the egological enclosure of the concept of responsibility, exceed and reverse the free subject that is responsible for its actions. The concept of egological responsibility finds itself inverted in Levinas's emphasis on the primacy of the other over the ego; the I is itself inverted from a nominative position to the passivity of the accusative (already the accusation or persecution of the subject). Responsibility no longer designates the subject's authorship over its actions within a closed egological economy, but rather designates the other's demand on me. The author becomes the respondent: I am not responsible for my own actions, but first and foremost I am responsible for the other.

One sees immediately that this new thinking of responsibility is accompanied by, indeed strictly follows, an overturning (or expropriation) of the subject from its masterful position as agent toward its assignation to the call of the other, the other for whom it is now responsible. Responsibility is no longer situated within the sphere of the ego, but arises out of the alterity of the other (what Levinas terms the "astonishing alterity of the other"[6]) calling me to responsibility. The call comes from the other, deposing the ego from its posture or position of mastery into the destitute place of being the respondent of such a call of the other. This is why Levinas displaces the I from the nominative position it has occupied to the accusative "me" which reveals the ego as addressed, as a respondent, addressed by the other's call.[7] Leaving its position of power, the now deposed or deposited subject is overturned into the subjected (that is, subject to the address of the other). This extraordinary revolution in thought thus enacts a movement of overturning of the egological tradition, and to that extent Levinas's thought could be characterized as the symmetrical opposite of Sartre's philosophy of responsibility. For both, the I carries the weight of the world on its shoulders,[8] but for exactly opposite reasons! For Sartre, it is due to the absolute character of the self's freedom whereas for Levinas, it is due to the overwhelming character of the alterity of the other. Whereas Sartre places all the weight on the self and its freedom, Levinas empties such a free subject and expropriates it in favor of the other itself.

At the same time, however, we will see that reversing a tradition is not necessarily the same as freeing oneself from it, and that Levinas's revolution owes perhaps more than it would like to admit to the egological tradition that it seeks to reverse, *precisely insofar as it determines itself as its reversal.* It might prove to be necessary, in order to retrieve the phenomenological origins of responsibility, to decisively break with the egological enclosure, that is, to break also with its mere reversal, and begin altogether outside of egology. Paul Ricoeur argues in this regard that the very vocabulary of Levinas's philosophy, in its very desire for rupture, in its exasperation as it were, still attests to the egological tradition that secretly determines its itinerary. An anti-egological thought, such as Levinas develops, would thus still be tributary to egology, and another beginning might be necessary if one seeks to think responsibility outside of the egological enclosure of modern Cartesian thought. Before returning to these limits of Levinas's thought, it is important to follow how his thought of responsibility has attempted to *escape* (a crucial term in Levinas's work, as we will see) such an egological tradition.

Access to the Ethical: On Escape

THE ESCAPE FROM ONTOLOGY

As Levinas recounted in several late autobiographical texts or interviews,[9] he was first a student of Husserl's phenomenology and Heidegger's fundamental ontology, and began his philosophical career as a commentator on their works; indeed, Levinas introduced Husserl and Heidegger in France.[10] However, these were references from which he broke decisively as he began to develop his own *ethical* thought. One of the key features of such a departure, in addition to the rupture with the paradigm of totality, was the break with ontology as such (and with a certain phenomenology of intentionality and consciousness), as exemplified in Levinas's early texts on the "there is," and in his seminal 1951 text, "Is Ontology Fundamental?" (in EN, 1–11). For Levinas, the access to ethics (which for him should be elevated to first philosophy) and *to responsibility* took place in a break with ontology, that is, in a break with Heidegger. Far from being included as one moment in being, as one existential in the analytic of Dasein for instance (being-with), and far from being inscribed within the element and horizon of being, ethics is situated in the relationship to the other person, in the "intersubjective," a relation which for Levinas takes place, as he puts it, "beyond being." The intersubjective relation is the original experience, i.e., it is not mediated by being. Levinas insists that the origin of meaning is not Dasein's relation to being, not the understanding of being displayed by Dasein, but lies in the intersubjective relation. He writes that, "My main point in saying that [the face of the other is perhaps the very beginning of philosophy,] was that the order of meaning, which seems to me primary, is precisely what comes to us from the inter-human relation, so that the face . . . is the beginning of intelligibility" (EN, 103).[11] This claim already places the ethical—the relation to the other—as prior to the order of knowledge and the element of being, and situates Levinas in opposition to traditional ontology and the privilege of epistemology in Western philosophy. This privileging always reduces the other to a problematic of cognition, under the authority of identity, or of "the Same," and is therefore for Levinas an act of violence, a "murder" of the other: "with regard to beings, understanding carries out an act of violence and of negation" (EN, 9). Levinas aims at reversing the traditional hierarchy in which ethics is reduced to being a branch of ontology and epistemology, and seeks to raise ethics to the level of first philosophy. Ethical responsibility will take place for Levinas beyond knowledge, indeed beyond being, as Levinas will speak in *Otherwise than Being or Beyond Essence* of a "responsibility beyond being" (AE, 31).

Levinas's critique of Heidegger begins by putting the "primacy of ontology" into question; that is to say, the primacy of ontology *over ethics*. For Levinas, ontology, the thinking of being, as it has defined the entirety of Western philosophy from Parmenides *to Heidegger*, is a thinking of the Same (*le Même*), a *logos* of being that reduces otherness to the Same by the very power of its theoretical com-prehensiveness. Levinas understands *theoria* as a negation of otherness. "Theory also means intelligence—*logos* of being—that is to say, a manner of approaching the known being in such a way that its otherness in relation to the knowing being vanishes."[12] Western philosophy, as ontology, is for Levinas "a reduction of the Other to the Same" (EE, 33–34). In opposition to the tradition of Western thought, defined in this way, Levinas attempts to go "beyond the Eleatic notion of being,"[13] to overcome ontology, and to move beyond being, toward the other, and more precisely, the other *human* (*l'autre homme*). "To me," he clarifies without ambiguity, "the Other (*Autrui*) is the other human being" (EN, 110; translation modified). Therein lies Levinas's undeconstructed, indeed assumed and proclaimed, humanism. Levinas is not interested in deconstructing humanism, and in fact he is very critical of the contemporary critiques of humanism and of the subject. He takes issue, for instance, with structuralist thought, with its appeals to impersonal principles—"what they want is a principle of intelligibility that is no longer enveloped by the human" (EN, 112); but also with the later Heidegger who places Dasein at the service of a neutral and impersonal power—"What *scares me* a little is also the development of a discourse in which the human becomes an articulation of an anonymous or neutral intelligibility" (EN, 116; my emphasis). He goes on to criticize Merleau-Ponty's touching-touched chiasm as an example of a thought where "man is only an aspect" (EN, 112) of a non-human reflexive structure ("it is as if space were touching itself through man"), and he interprets the contemporary mistrust of humanism in the following way—"they want the subject to appeal to a principle that would not be enveloped by concern for human fate" (EN, 112). With the terms "concern," and concern for the "human," we are already in the sphere of the ethical, a sphere that would be negated by contemporary critics of humanism. Far from attempting to overcome humanism and subjectivity, Levinas would seek to give them a new foundation, precisely no longer in the primacy of the ego but in the relation and responsibility to the other. "It is the other who is first, and there the question of my sovereign consciousness is no longer the first question" (EN, 112). It would be an *other* humanism, a humanism of the other (human), as Levinas states: "I advocate . . . the humanism of the other human" (EN, 112).[14]

In fact, it is in his definition of the human that Levinas breaks most decisively with Heidegger, for as he explains, "Man is not only a being who understands what being signifies, as Heidegger would have it, but also a being who has already understood and grasped the commandment of holiness in the face of the other man" (RB, 226). The human is not the place of the givenness of being (Dasein), but the for-the-other of responsibility. His conception of humanism is thus ethical through and through, as the human is defined in ethical terms. What makes humans humans is the ethical, as responsibility for the other human. Understood in this way, ethics represents what is truly human in human beings, a humanism of the other that breaks with ego-centered philosophies and opens onto the infinite character of the alterity of the other to whom I am responsible.

This movement beyond being and toward the other (human) constitutes the core of Levinas's thought, and he indeed would characterize it in a late interview as "the kernel of all I would say later" (RB, 46). One could in fact approach Levinas's thought as a whole from the effort to escape, exit or go beyond the same, toward an other that does not return to a same, that does not come back, and to that extent is infinite. Levinas's decisive early essay, *On Escape*,[15] thematizes a need to break with the "suffocating" horizon of being, with the "horror of the 'there is,'"[16] and in *Time and the Other*, with the isolation or solitude of existence. *Time and the Other*, he explained in a late interview, was a book that represented for him an attempt to escape "from this isolation of existing, as the preceding book [*Existence and Existents*] signified an attempt to escape from the 'there is'" (EI, 57).[17] Ultimately, it has been a matter of "escaping *from being*" (EI, 59), an escape that takes place in one's devotion to the other. Levinas clarifies that "the true exit from the *there is* is in obligation" (RB, 45), in responsibility for the other, in the sense of being concerned, not for my own self, but for the other. For anxiety is not about the possibility of death, but rather about *being*, "the horror of the *there is*, of existence. It is not the fear of death; it is the 'too much' of oneself" (RB, 46). This is why, and importantly, it is also a matter of escaping *from oneself*. Escaping from oneself, that is to say, going beyond oneself toward the other. "Leaving oneself," he writes in a striking formulation, "that is, *being occupied with the other*" (RB, 46; my emphasis). There is a (vicious) circle between being and oneself (Dasein is the concern for being and for oneself) that Levinas seeks to break. The horror of the *there is* "is close to disgust for oneself, close to the weariness of oneself" (RB, 46), and being encumbered with being is being encumbered with one's own being, with oneself: "Escape is the need to get out of oneself, that is, to break that most radical and unalterably binding of chains, the fact that the I [*moi*] is oneself [*soi-même*]" (OE, 55). *Le moi est haïssable*, Pascal famously wrote, and Levinas comments: "Here, the profound meaning of Pascal's line is revealed: The self is detestable" (EN, 130; translation modified). The exit from both the "there is" (impersonal being) and "oneself" (egology) require an opening onto the other. In the end, for Levinas, the true exit lies in responsibility for the other—to the point, as we will see, of a dying for the other.

This need to escape the horizon of being and the enclosure of the self accounts for Levinas's critique of totality and totalizing philosophies, for, according to him, "it is in fact the whole trend of Western philosophy," culminating with Hegel, that seeks totality, which has "this nostalgia for totality" and for a "panoramic vision of the real" (EI, 76). He understands that quest as an attempt to negate alterity, as the "attempt at universal synthesis, a reduction of all experience, of all that is reasonable, to a totality wherein consciousness embraces the world, *leaves nothing other outside itself*, and thus becomes absolute thought" (EI, 75; my emphasis). Levinas found the sources of his critique of totality first in Franz Rosenzweig's critique of Hegel (but also in moments in the history of philosophy such as Plato's Good beyond being, or Descartes's Third Meditation with its idea of God as infinite), but he conceives of it in terms of the inappropriability—or as he terms it, exteriority and infinity—of the other. The encounter with such an inappropriability of the other is the original experience—before knowledge, since knowledge presupposes such an encounter, and before ontology, since being as such presupposes the encounter with the specific being—and is the original meaning of ethics as what cannot be totalized. "The irreducible and ultimate experience of relationship appears to me in fact to be . . . not in synthesis, but in the face to face of humans, in sociality, in its moral signification . . . First philosophy is an ethics" (EI, 77). Ethics breaks totality, opening onto an irreducible exteriority and otherness, a non-synthesizable which for Levinas is the face to face: "The relationship between man is certainly the non-synthesizable par excellence" (EI, 77). There is simply no context (being, world, horizon) that would include the face to face with the other, as the face "originally signifies or commands outside the context of the world" (EN, 167). There is no third unifying term that could provide a reduction of that relationship (even the notion of the third in Levinas confirms the irreducibility of the face to face, as it is defined from the perspective of the face to face, a face to face that is the "irreducible and ultimate experience"). The face to face is transcendence, and "the face breaks the system" (EN, 34). This relationship is primary, and since for Levinas the relationship with the other is essentially ethical (indeed, the very definition of ethics!) as it implies the prior recognition of the other as other, ethics is first philosophy. Ethics is thus opposed to ontology, which for Levinas is a thinking of the Same and a progressive negating of alterity.

There is of course much to be said concerning this characterization of ontology as a "thought of the Same," and as negating alterity. One might object, with respect to Heidegger (the clear target of Levinas's critique of ontology), that he was the one who subjected Western metaphysics to an unprecedented phenomenological *destruction* which brought out the difference between being and beings, a difference long-ignored by metaphysics in its enterprise of substantification of being. In short, was it not precisely Heidegger who undertook the overcoming or abandonment of "Western onto-theo-logy," and who certainly attempted to overcome traditional ontology? Not for Levinas. On the contrary, the phenomenological thought of Heidegger would in fact be the "imperialist" culmination of the dictatorship of the Same (EE, 35). Levinas's judgment is severe, as for instance in the opening pages of *Totality and Infinity,* where he defines ontology as a philosophy of power:

> As a philosophy of *power,* ontology, as first philosophy, which does not put the Same into question, is a philosophy of *injustice.* Heideggerian ontology, which subordinates the relation with the Other to the relation with Being in general . . . leads fatally to . . . *imperialist domination,* to *tyranny* . . . Being before beings, is . . . a movement within the Same, without regard for any obligation to the Other. (EE, 38; my emphasis)

Now, this disregard for the other, we should note, is what defines evil for Levinas, so that ontology itself is evil! "Evil," Levinas writes, "is the order of being pure and simple" (EN, 114). Evil is the disregard for the other in the persevering into being (ontological thought). Levinas draws an analogy between the solidity of the solid, the hardness of the hard, and the cruelty of a being "absorbed in its *conatus essendi*" in the struggle for life (EN, 202). On the contrary, ethics will constitute the concern for the other, that is, a "concern for the other man, a care for his food, drink, clothing, health, and shelter" (EN, 212).

What could be the basis of such charges?[18] For Levinas, by positing the priority of being over beings, Heidegger would have only accentuated the all encompassing character of being, and thereby the reduction of the entity that is other to the Sameness of being. Let us scrutinize this claim. In "Is Ontology Fundamental?" Levinas describes fundamental ontology as "the knowledge of Being *in general*" (EN, 1; my emphasis). This is a first decisive interpretation on Levinas's part, one that will prove crucial to his subsequent thinking on ethics. First, he identifies ontology with knowledge, and a conceptual knowledge; and second, he identifies being with the generality or universality of beings. Levinas conceives of being as the *horizon* of beings and of any relation to beings. Horizon plays a role analogous for Levinas to that of the *concept* in classical idealism. Being is analogically identified with a concept: Beings emerge against a background that includes them, as the individual cases against the background of the concept. This is a second crucial interpretative decision on Levinas's part: Being is understood as *conceptual* generality. He claims that the understanding of being "rejoins the great tradition of Western philosophy" insofar as to understand the particular being "is already to place oneself beyond the particular. To understand is to relate to the particular, which alone exists, through knowledge, which is always knowledge of the universal" (EN, 5). One must therefore say that, just as individual cases fall under their concept, all beings and relations to beings fall within being. All relations to beings fall under being, "except for the other" (EN, 5), exclaims Levinas! The relation to the other, that is, is the other person, the other human, "exceeds the confines of understanding" (EN, 5). Why? Because we do not *encounter* the other by way of a concept; the other "does not affect us on the basis of a concept" (EN, 5; translation modified). The other is not a concept, and does not appear within a concept. Rather, the other "is a being and counts as such" (EN, 5; translation modified). As other, it is not mediated by the horizon of being, a horizon that neutralizes the alterity of the entity: If the relation to beings takes place within the horizon of being, then the relation to the other person is *included within* being, that is to say, subjected to being as a neutral essence. Being as conceptual generality *neutralizes* the alterity of the other, its eventfulness. In Levinas's reading, Heidegger conceives of the relation to the other entity as included within the horizon of being: "Being-with-the-other-person—*Miteinandersein*—thus rests on the ontological relation" (EN, 9). However, for Levinas the relation with the other does not occur against the *background* of the ontological relation.

It is this alleged dependency that Levinas vehemently rejects. All entities fall within being *except for the other,* as it is not in terms of being in general that the other comes toward me. The other is not a possible case of a relation to entities; the other escapes the ontological horizon, does not let itself be circumscribed by a thinking of the Same. In fact, Heideggerian ontology cannot do justice to the other because "as soon as I have grasped the other within the opening of being in general, as an element of the world where I stand, I have apprehended it at the horizon. I have not looked it in the face, I have not encountered its face" (EE, 21). The comprehension of being cannot comprehend the relation to the other; it "cannot *dominate* the relation with the other" (EE, 39). One must in fact invert the hierarchy, "invert the terms" (EE, 38). It is the relation with the entity—with the other entity—which commands and precedes the relation with being. Levinas draws a contrast between two modes of speech, one in which one names something (*appeller quelque chose*), and another by which one speaks to someone (*en appeller à quelqu'un*). The first is a violence, as in such naming it takes possession of the entity. The understanding names things, does not invoke them: "And thus, with regard to beings, understanding carries out an act of violence and of negation. A partial negation, which is a violence" (EN, 9). With respect to the other, the situation is different as "I do not possess him" (EN 9). I thus do not name the other in the sense of thinking *about* him or her, but speak *to* him or her. One must leave the universal dimension of the concept to enter the inter-personal relation, which is outside conceptuality. This is why Levinas adds: "I have spoken to him, that is, I have overlooked the universal being he incarnates in order to confine myself to the particular being he is" (EN, 7). The relation to the other hence precedes the horizon of conceptuality and being. The relation to the other is not ontology—it escapes ontology, and it precedes ontology. Since for Levinas the relation with the other is what rigorously defines "ethics," then we must say that ethics precedes ontology, and not the inverse.

THE CRITIQUE OF EGOLOGY

This radical critique of ontology, as a thinking of being *in general,* is accompanied by a critique of egology, as *solipsism.* This solipsism would appear, for instance, in what Heidegger calls the "mineness" (*Jemeinig-keit*) of Dasein. Ontology as the thinking of the Same will inevitably culminate in a solipsistic egology, and Heidegger's notion of a mineness of being seems to bear this out. Levinas then attempts to counter the *Jemeinigkeit* of Dasein with a more primordial "being for the other." We could note a tension here, if not a contradiction: How can one affirm, on the one hand (and in order to reproach Heidegger), the *generality* or neutrality of ontology, and on the other hand speak of (and reproach Heidegger for) the irreducible *mineness* of that same ontology? However, the contradiction is perhaps only apparent, for it is precisely because ontology is a thinking of the Same—that is, a negation of otherness— that it also takes the form of an egoistic and solipsistic thought. Here sameness and mineness are indissociable, as Levinas writes: "*The Other becomes the same by becoming mine*" (EE, 37).

We know that for Heidegger, being is "each time mine" (*je meines*), that "mineness" belongs constitutively to Dasein.[19] We also know that it is Heidegger himself who speaks of an "existential solipsism" in order to characterize the analytic of Dasein. Levinas will thus interpret, with some justification it seems, the fundamental character of mineness as the sign of an enclosure upon oneself of a "mine" if not of an ego—i.e., as the indication of the enclosure of ontology in an egology that reduces alterity. For if being is each time delivered over to Dasein, such that it takes it on authentically and responsibly by projecting itself toward death as its most extreme and proper possibility, that seems to be at the price of a radical exclusion of the other. Is not the other dismissed in Heidegger's analysis of Dasein's authentic assumption of death? To be convinced of this, one simply needs to read side by side the deprecating analyses of everyday being-with, on the one hand, and the interpretation of authentic existence, on the other hand, which seems only capable of occurring in a radically solitary *metaphysical* individuation. My death is mine alone, I am alone in being faced irrevocably with death, which is never death in general nor *the death of others*, but above all mine, "my" death. The verb "to die," which for Heidegger defines the being of human beings, is declined exclusively in the first person singular. In this primacy of my death, all relations to other Dasein fade. Levinas states: "An authenticity of the most proper potentiality-of-being and a dissolution of all relations with the other!" (EN, 214; translation modified). Levinas thus understands mineness as an "original contraction of the me . . . in terms of a *belonging to self* and *for self* in their inalienable co-belonging" (EN, 226). What is important in this reading is Levinas's understanding of mineness as a reduction of the other to the ego, or to the Same—the terms are now practically synonymous. This allows Levinas to explicitly associate Heidegger with the modern egoistic and subjectivist tradition. In "Diachrony and Representation" (1985), he thus writes of "the egology of presence affirmed from Descartes to Husserl, and *even in Heidegger,* where, in Section 9 of *Being and Time,* Dasein's 'to be' is the source of *Jemeinigkeit* and thus of the I" (EN, 161; translation modified).

Levinas follows this interpretation further yet, and on the basis of it, opposes to "solitary mineness" a being-*for*-the-other that would be more authentic and which is *defined in terms of responsibility.* In his effort to give thought to an experience of alterity that cannot to be reduced to the Same, Levinas rejects the Heideggerian primacy of mineness based on death. It is a matter of leaving "the *Jemeinigkeit* of the *cogito* and its immanence construed as authenticity" (EN, 221). Levinas describes this experience as the face to face with the other, in which I am faced with the destitute and vulnerable nature of the other. Now, this vulnerability expresses the mortality or irremediable exposure to death of the other, and the responsibility that is engaged is not for oneself, but for the other insofar as he or she is mortal: I am called to care for the other and to attend to the other as other. This is why Levinas challenges death in Heidegger as egoistic and solipsistic, and opposes to it a death that would be more primordial, namely the death of the other. The death of the other, as Levinas puts it, is "the first death." I would be concerned for the other's death before my own death, and the concern for the other's death would be more authentic than Heideggerian death as a solitary, solipsistic dying. Levinas explains that for him it is a matter of a genuine "alternative between, on the one hand, the identical in its authenticity, in its *own right* or its unalterable *mine* of the human, in its *Eigentlichkeit,* independence and freedom, and on the other hand being as human devotion to the other" (EN, 211; my emphasis).

Levinas considers that the thinking of being is a solipsistic thinking which negates the other, that is, a thinking of the Same. Certainly, we know that for Heidegger Dasein is essentially *Mit-sein,* being-with; he emphasized in *Being and Time,* "Dasein is essentially being-with" (*wesenhaft an ihm selbst mit Sein*) (SZ, 120), and this "with" is an existential and not an accident. For Levinas this makes no difference. Why? On the one hand, because it is precisely in that same being-with that Dasein "begins to identify with the being of all others and to understand itself from the impersonal anonymity of the 'they,' to lose itself in the averageness of the everyday or to fall under the dictatorship of the They" (EN, 213; translation modified)—in sum, to be inauthentic. Is it an accident that, when Heidegger seeks to describe the inauthenticity of Dasein, he often does so by referring to being-with? For Levinas it is no accident; it springs from "Heidegger's very philosophical project" (EN, 213), a project in which "the relation to the other is conditioned by being in the world, and thus by ontology." But on the other hand, and more radically, it is the very conception of the other implicit in Heidegger's work that is problematic: He indeed understands the other as being-with, but this "with," with its meaning of "a reciprocal being with one another" (T, 19), is still for Levinas in one sense a neutral term. Being-together is a communion or a collectivity around something in common. Now the relation to the other, for Levinas, is not a communion, or a togetherness. Such togetherness would reproduce a logic of the same, and it is that logic that Heidegger maintained when he treated of the other, or rather, of being-with. "We hope to show, for our part," writes Levinas, "that the proposition with [*mit*] is unable and inapt to express the original relation with the other" (T, 19).[20]

The true relation to the other is not a being-together in a shared world, but lies in a face to face encounter without intermediary, without mediation, and outside of the concept, which Levinas refers to as the "insurmountable duality of beings" (EI, 67). This thinking will be developed through Levinas's elaboration of another conception of the self, no longer a subject nor even a Dasein, but a "hostage to the other" in primordial responsibility for the other. This being-hostage, that is, a nonchosen responsibility for the other—in Levinas's compact expression, "Condition of hostage—not chosen" (AE, 214)—testifies, as Derrida shows in his *Adieu à Emmanuel Lévinas*,[21] to the radical dispossession or expropriation of the subject in Levinas's work. The subject is no longer a self-identity, an ego, a self-consciousness, nor even an authentic self or Dasein, but is now a pre-originary openness to the other ("pre-originary" since this openness precedes the subject), a welcome of the other, in the subjective genitive sense.

Pre-Originary Openness to the Other

ETHICS BEYOND ETHICS

In *Adieu à Emmanuel Lévinas,* Jacques Derrida presents the ethical thought of Emmanuel Levinas as a profound work on hospitality. In fact, it is the motif of ethics itself that is to be approached in terms of hospitality. Indeed, Derrida claims that Levinas's thought *as a whole* should be approached from the motif of *hospitality.* Although, as Derrida admits, "the word does not occur frequently and is not emphasized, *Totality and Infinity* is an immense treatise on hospitality" (*Adieu,* 49). Taking stock of Levinas's relation to ethics—the way in which one finds in his thought the elaboration of "another thought of ethics, of responsibility, of justice, of the state, etc., another thought of the other itself" (*Adieu,* 14)—Derrida singles out one of the most determinative questions in Levinas's thinking, that is, subjectivity as it is expropriated through the pivotal notion of a pre-originary openness to the other, or *hospitality.* Furthermore, Derrida insists that "Levinas's entire thought is and wants to be a teaching on ... what 'to welcome' or 'to receive' *should* mean" (*Adieu,* 153). At stake in this account is an entire re-conceptualization of ethics, of the ethical itself, and as well a new thinking of responsibility. In the background of this emphasis on hospitality is a certain contemporary political and social context, and Derrida refers specifically to the problems of immigration, the precarious status of illegal immigrants, but also to all the populations in transit, all the displaced peoples such as migrant workers, exiles, and others who are "without a home." This homelessness echoes the expropriated subject that is theorized by Levinas, an expropriation or deposing of the subject which, for Derrida, affects and transforms our understanding of "hospitality," of "being at-home," of "identity," and of being one's own. For Derrida, this situation calls for no less than "a mutation of the socio- and geo-political space, a political and juridical mutation, but above all calls for ... an *ethical* conversion" (*Adieu,* 131; my emphasis). Indeed, this situation transforms what is meant by responsibility.

What does "to welcome" or "to receive" mean? The answer to this question would give us access to the very meaning of ethics in Levinas's work. Levinas offers us a genuine ethics of hospitality, that is to say, an ethics *as* hospitality. Hospitality, here, is not a "regional" question, for instance a political or juridical issue, or even a specific question within the field of ethics; instead, it pertains to ethics itself in its most authentic sense. Hospitality is not a mere region of ethics, but designates ethicality itself, which is what Levinas is ultimately concerned about. This is why the very word "ethics" is not, for Levinas, the final word, in spite of what a certain philosophical *doxa* would suggest. What matters is not ethics, taken as a certain normative discipline, but rather the *ethicality* of ethics—what Levinas called at times an "ethics beyond ethics." Levinas referred to such ethics beyond ethics with the term "holiness" (*sainteté*), designating the yielding of priority from the self to the other.[22] In fact, Levinas was weary of the Hellenic and metaphysical term "ethics," and was attempting instead to give thought to the event of the other occurring in the ethical. He named this the "holy," and in a late interview he explained: "The word ethics is Greek. More often, especially now [in 1986], I think about holiness, about the holiness of the face of the other or the holiness of my obligation as such" (RB, 49). Further, to the question "What is the ethical?" Levinas answered: "It is the recognition of holiness." And what is holiness? When "the fundamental trait of being is the preoccupation that each particular being has with his being"—when "plants, animals, all living things strive to exist," when for each one "it is the struggle for life"—holiness represents the moment at which, in the human, "lo and behold . . . the concern for the other breaches concern for the self. This is what I call holiness" (RB, 235). Now this reformulation of ethics in its very possibility (*as* holiness, as pre-originary openness to the other) opens the question of the responsible subject. Indeed, for Levinas, responsibility for the other arises out of this pre-originary openness to the other. Ethical responsibility does not arise out of the freedom of the subject or agent, but out of the subject's pre-originary openness to the other.

THE REVERSAL OF THE RESPONSIBLE SUBJECT:
FROM AGENT TO GUEST

This pre-originary openness to the other (hospitality to the other) involves nothing less than a radical reversal of the concept of the responsible subject. When Levinas defines the subject as *hôte*—in French, *hôte* means both host and guest, and this particular semantic situation will prove crucial to his discussion—this does not mean that the subject would have, among other faculties or attributes, the ability to welcome the other. More importantly, it means that the subject, *as such, is* a welcome of the other, an openness to the other, before any self-posited identity. There is not, first, the subject as a pre-given substantial identity that would constitute the basis for a capacity to welcome. Hospitality is not an attribute of a pre-constituted ego, but the constitutive structure of subjectivity as openness to the other, as assigned to the other. The subject does not pre-exist the encounter with the other, but is pre-assigned to the other, a relation which Levinas understands as one of responsibility. This is why in *Ethics and Infinity,* he explains: "I speak of responsibility as the essential, primary and fundamental structure of subjectivity. For I describe subjectivity in ethical terms. Ethics, here, does not supplement a preceding existential base; the very node of the subjective is knotted in ethics understood as responsibility" (EI, 95). That "knot" in subjectivity or *of* subjectivity is the hold of the other on the same, as Levinas explains in *Otherwise than Being or Beyond Essence:* The "knot knotted in or as subjectivity (*en subjectivité*) . . . signifies an allegiance of the Same to the Other" (AE, 47). The knot signifies that there is not, first, a self-relation or self-affection, and only then a relation to an other: The self is, *as* a self, a relation to the other *as* a *responsibility* for the other. Responsibility for the other is thus co-extensive with that pre-originary openness of the subject, whose identity is fractured and opened by the irruption or invasion of the other. The first *revolution* brought about by the thought of hospitality, then, concerns the concept of responsible subjectivity. The subject is no longer a self-identity, an ego, a consciousness, or an intentional consciousness with a responsibility based on its freedom and agency. Far from the traditional willful agency that owns up to its actions, the subject is here an openness to the other, a "convocation" of the subject by the other. I would like to unfold briefly this "revolution" of the concept of responsibility, the term "revolution" having to be understood also in the literal sense of a spatial turning around or reversal, the concept of the subject being "turned upside down," expropriated. I will single out four fundamental features.[23]

The first characteristic is that the openness to the other is an openness to an infinite. The subject welcomes the other *beyond its own finite capacities of welcoming.* The welcoming of the other, understood as a receiving, exceeds or overflows the capacity to receive. The "faculty" of welcoming is exceeded by what it welcomes, in a dissymmetry what Marion would call a "saturated phenomenon" (although the more proper way of designation would be to speak of a saturated subject, since it is the phenomenon that saturates the welcoming subject). It is to this extent that responsibility is excessive, hyperbolic, overwhelming—not because, as Sartre believed, my freedom is boundless, but on the contrary because the subject is open to an other which is greater than itself. Hence the welcome is a welcome of an infinite. The subject here designates the hospitality of a finite threshold that opens onto the infinite. The subject is exhausted in the welcome of the other; it neither pre-exists nor survives it. This is why the subject must be conceived of as the welcome of the other, that is to say, precisely, the welcome of the infinite.

Second, this welcome of the other (as openness to the other) in the *objective* genitive sense, should be understood as being first a welcome *of* the other in the *subjective* genitive sense. The welcome *of* the other in the objective genitive sense is already an answer to a more prior welcome, that *of* the other in the subjective genitive sense. Hospitality is not an act performed by a sovereign subject at home in its domain. Hospitality names the pre-originary openness to the other that the subject is. The other has always already "arrived." This is why the "yes" *to* the other is a response to the "yes" *of* the other. Being responsible for the other arises out of my welcome of the other in the subjective genitive sense. This response "is called *as soon as* the infinite—always *of/from* the other—is welcomed" (*Adieu*, 51). The other comes first, and the subject only comes later, as recipient of the event and arrival of the other: "*One must begin by responding*" (*Adieu*, 53). Responsibility arises out of this event, and not from the self-positing of a subject (rather, responsibility is its *de-position*). Derrida cites this sentence from Levinas: "It is not I—it is the other that can say *yes*" (*Adieu*, 52). One can draw the consequences of this situation with respect to the concepts of decision and responsibility, traditionally attributed to the egological subject. Taking seriously the priority of the yes *of* the other over the yes *to* the other would lead to an entirely different approach to the question of decision and responsibility, which would no longer be the development of an egological immanence. In fact, as Derrida stresses, a theory of the subject is incapable of accounting for any decision—just as autonomy, we could echo, is incapable of accounting for responsibility as the experience of a responding to the event of alterity. Here responsibility can no longer be identified with accountability, for it is no longer based on the free project of a spontaneous subject. In fact, ethical responsibility arises out of the interruption of the spontaneity of the self, and it is this experience of the interruption of the work of identification of the ego that Levinas calls the ethical experience. "One calls this putting in question of my spontaneity by the presence of the other, ethics" (EE, 33). Another thought of responsibility and decision, outside of the tradition of autonomous subjectivity, is here being sketched. The Levinasian definition of the subject as "subject of the welcome" amounts to a complete reversal and destruction of the Kantian tradition of the autonomous responsible subject.

Third, to the extent that the welcoming only welcomes beyond the capacity of the I—because, in other words, of this abyssal or immeasurable dissymmetry—responsibility cannot be understood as an appropriation but as a dissymmetrical expropriation. The thought of the welcome (*accueil*) is thus in opposition to Heidegger, to the themes of gathering together or recollection (*Versammlung, receuil*), of a collecting (*colligere*) that would be accomplished in recollection in an "at home." Levinas reads Heidegger's notions of concern or care as a gathering of being, in which "being precedes and *gathers itself* [*se recueille*] in thought in its own way, in the guise of a concern for being, proper to its 'event' of being" (EN, 209; my emphasis). Here the gathering of the *at-home* (*recueil*) already supposes the welcome (*accueil*). To welcome does not mean to "collect" or "recollect," "gather" or "appropriate," but to be exposed to an other who is "higher" than oneself. The welcome makes possible the recollection of the at-home, such is rigorously the meaning of the infinite for Levinas: To possess the idea of the infinite is to have already welcomed the Other. Appropriation is here reversed as expropriation, and responsibility becomes the site of such an expropriation, which is assigned to the locus of the other.

And finally, this structure of hospitable subjectivity involves a paradoxical situation with respect to the status of the subject as *host,* a peculiar reversal—a revolution, once again—of the meaning of the host. If the subject is from the outset a host in an originary or pre-originary way, if it is not *prior* to this opening to the other, then there is no longer an "at-home" or an ownership on the basis of which one would be responsible. For Levinas, the reference to a home, the claim to a "place in the sun," is the "usurpation" par excellence: "I cannot forget Pascal's thought: 'My place in the sun. There is the beginning and the prototype of the usurpation of the whole world'" (EN, 231). As I alluded to earlier, responsibility is not a capacity or a power. The welcome *of* the other is a subjective genitive. Therefore, the subject as host (*hôte*) immediately turns into a subject as guest (*hôte*). Here, *the host is first and foremost a guest,* for there is no "at-home," no proper place, from which the subject is able to welcome the other. Levinas opposes the understanding of hospitality that assumes, as Derrida puts it, that in order "to be able to welcome, perhaps one supposes that one is at-home, that one knows what one means by being at-home, and that at-home one hosts, one receives or one offers hospitality, thus appropriating a place in order to *welcome* the other, or worse, *welcoming* the other in order to appropriate a place" (*Adieu,* 39–40). Against this conception of hospitality as a capacity or power of the subject on the basis of a self-assured, proper place, one notes with Derrida the originality and radicality of the Levinasian expropriation of the subject: "I have the feeling that Levinas tries to break with a possible conception of hospitality, which links it to ipseity [*l'ipséité*], that is, with a conception of the same, of the hospitable self [*soi-même,* literally: self-same] who asserts power over the other."[24] Since the gathering of the at-home already supposes the welcome of the other in the subjective genitive sense, then the host as a master in his or her "own" home becomes the guest as a stranger in that home. If the at-home with oneself of the dwelling is an *at-home with oneself as in a land of asylum or refuge,* then the inhabitant dwells there also as a refugee or an exile, as a guest and not a proprietor.

RESPONSIBILITY AS EXPROPRIATION OF THE SUBJECT

This is what Derrida calls the "implacable law of hospitality":

> The host who welcomes, the one who welcomes the invited guest, the welcoming host who believes himself the owner of the house is in reality a guest welcomed in his own home. He receives the hospitality that he offers *in* his own home, he receives hospitality *from* his own home—which ultimately does not belong to him. The host, as *host,* is a *guest.* (*Adieu,* 79)

The inhabitant is a refugee, an exile, a guest, and not an owner. On the basis of all these motifs, one can identify the radical expropriation that the subject undergoes. The sovereign ego is de-posed in its pre-originary openness to the other, overturned from host to guest. The "home" is in fact a "land of asylum," and hospitality designates "that originary dispossession, the withdrawal that, expropriating the 'owner' of what is most his own, and expropriating the *self* of itself, makes of his home a place of transit" (*Adieu,* 79). The "at-home" becomes henceforth a "response to a wandering or errancy, a phenomenon of errancy which it stops" (*Adieu,* 164). In an extraordinary formulation, the meaning of which is destined to remain undecidable, Derrida writes: "the subject of the welcome is *chez lui chez l'autre,* i.e., is in his own home in the home of the other" (*Adieu,* 173). This sentence can mean simultaneously that the subject is at home in the other, or that the subject, at home, is in the other. One can follow this radical expropriation of the responsible self in Levinas's most extreme, paroxystic formulations. The subject as host/guest will be further radicalized (in particular, in the later text *Otherwise than Being or Beyond Essence*) as persecuted, as *hostage* of the other. Such are the two figures of the Levinasian ethics—hospitality without propriety, and the persecuted obsession of the hostage. One can follow the passage between these two definitions of the subject, the subject as host and the subject as hostage. A logic of *sub*stitution will take the place of a logic of subordination or subjection. But it follows the same movement undertaken in *Totality and Infinity,* while radicalizing further the destruction of the concepts of intentionality, activity or will, already challenged in the thought of the subject as host and hospitality. The persecution, substitution, accusation, the putting in question of the subject still designate the situation of the subject as host/guest, but now understood as "persecuted in the very place where it takes place, at the place where, as an immigrant, exile, stranger, perpetual guest, it finds itself assigned to a place before being able to take up one" (EE, 104). The host becomes the hostage, evoking the traumatic invasion that any hospitality—if it is the welcome *of* an other in the subjective genitive—must already presuppose.

These motifs reveal the radical expropriation of the self by the other, the peculiar extenuation or exhaustion of subjectivity defined in such a way. For it is indeed an expropriation that is at the basis of the de-posing of the ego: "Is the human I first? Is it not he who, in place of being posed, ought to be de-posed?" (RB, 97). The reversal of the egological-subjectivist tradition is also an expropriation of the subject. This logic of expropriation allows us to account for Levinas's fundamental categories. Hence the notions of the "host," the "hostage," the subject as "persecuted," the "other as infinite," all these notions can be traced back to a radical *dispossession* and *destitution* of the subject, the *ex-propriation* of any sense of "home," of "ownership," of "proper dwelling." It also accounts for the way in which the subject is said to be understood in ethical terms. For "as host or as hostage, as other, as pure alterity, a subjectivity analyzed in this way must be stripped of every ontological predicate, a bit like the pure I that Pascal said is stripped of every quality that could be attributed to it" (*Adieu,* 191). This stripping of predicates or accidents does not give access to some pure, substantial egohood; on the contrary, the I itself is also stripped of all proper substantial identity, to become nothing but the mark or trace of the other. This is why Derrida also remarks that Levinas's introduction of transcendence at the core of the immanence of the subject "has to do with this pre-originary ex-propriety or ex-appropriation that makes of the subject a host/guest and a hostage, someone who finds him/herself, *before* any invitation, elected, invited *and* visited in his/her home as in the home of the other, who is in his/her own home in the home of the other (*chez lui chez l'autre*)" (*Adieu,* 173).

This radical expropriation of any proper self occurs in the experience of responsibility for the other. Responsibility registers for Levinas the expropriation of the subject, expropriated toward the other for whom it is now obligated. No longer situated within the egological sphere (accountability of the agent), responsibility emerges in my encounter with the alterity of the other. This is the first decisive break with the tradition in Levinas's understanding of responsibility; it no longer designates an activity of the subject, but manifests an essential passivity. Levinas associates the experience of responsibility to *passivity,* as he reverses the classical activity or spontaneity of the subject into the passivity of an obligated for-the-other. In *Otherwise than Being or Beyond Essence,* he thus speaks of responsibility as escaping freedom, as the defeat of the cogito and of "the originary *activity* of all *acting,* source of the *spontaneity of the subject,* or of the subject as spontaneity" (AE, 220). The I, interrupted and called by the other, as it were emerges from the other, for there is no pre-constituted self that only subsequently would relate to an other, or open up to an exteriority. The other is always already preceding me, interrupting the egological attempt to close itself.[25] I am thus interrupted: *My being, myself* are interrupted (both egohood and ontology are here overturned); responsibility is severed from the entire tradition of will or free will, from the predominance of the motifs of action and agency. Far from being the consequence of a willful agency, responsibility expresses the passive exposure of the self to the experience of an alterity that lays claim upon me. I am exposed to an other, not unfolding an egological content that is somehow "free" of any disturbance from an alterity. This exposure is what Levinas describes as the experience of the face of the other, an experience that will prove to be the origin of responsibility.

The Origins of Responsibility: The Face

THE POVERTY OF THE FACE: ETHICS AND VIOLENCE

Levinas indeed describes the *experience* of responsibility as the face to face with the other, which for Levinas is the irreducible form of relation to the other: The relationship with the other can only be an encounter, never a synthesis or a communion. The origin of responsibility is here an *experience*—the experience of an encounter with the other, *face to face*. For Levinas, this encounter is essentially of an ethical nature, and is rooted in the phenomenon of a responsibility for the other. Ethical responsibility is a relation to the other, and not to some objective transcendent Good. As Derrida explains in *The Gift of Death*, responsibility is possible on the condition "that the Good [can] no longer be a transcendental objective, a relation between objective things, but [rather] the relation to the other, a response to the other" (GD, 50). The originary encounter with the face of the other, with the other as "presenting" a face (although we will see that for Levinas the face is not a presentation), is ethical. Before being an affective relationship, I am first situated in an ethical relation of obligation. What does Levinas mean by the face (*visage*)?[26] In one word, vulnerability. A human vulnerability—or better, vulnerability as the very humanity of man. As we will see, this vulnerability opens for Levinas the following alternative or paradox—violence or non-violence, ethics or its negation, respect or defacing. The *vulnerability* of the other is thus the origin of ethics and responsibility (but also of violence), recalling Hans Jonas's characterization of the fragile and the vulnerable as ground of a renewed understanding of responsibility (although Jonas spoke of a vulnerability of nature in a rupture with anthropocentric ethics,[27] while Levinas stays within the inter-human relation). In the encounter with the face, I am faced with the destitute and vulnerable nature of the other, and called to be responsible for him or her.

In the late interviews gathered in *Ethics and Infinity,* Levinas returns to the question of the face. He begins by noting that the face is not an object of perception, a perceptual phenomenon—indeed it is perhaps not even a phenomenon, if a phenomenon is what appears and becomes present. The face, as it were *seen from beyond the visible,* has a proximity, but it is not a present phenomenon. In *Otherwise than Being or Beyond Essence,* Levinas specifies in this respect that the face escapes presentation and representation, that it is indeed "the very defection of phenomenality" (AE, 141). And this is so not because it would be an excessive phenomenon (as with Marion's "saturated phenomenon" or "excess of givenness"[28]), but on the contrary due to its poverty, its weakness: The face is "a non-phenomenon because 'less' than the phenomenon" (AE, 141). Phenomenology is here exceeded by default or by excess of poverty, and Levinas does state that his work exceeds the confines of appearance in being (*l'apparoir de l'être*), and therefore "ventures beyond phenomenology" (AE, 281). One may compare this gesture with what Heidegger called in a late seminar a "phenomenology of the inapparent,"[29] or contrast it with what Marion designated as a phenomenology of the "saturated phenomenon."[30] I would suggest here that Levinas does not so much move beyond phenomenology as point to an excess which inhabits it. In fact, despite what some commentators have hastened to claim with respect to a theological nature of Levinas's discourse, Levinas has clearly maintained the phenomenological status of his discourse, stressing that his vocabulary, even when at times it borrows from a religious tradition, takes on a phenomenological meaning. For instance:

> The terminology I use sounds religious: I speak of the uniqueness of the I on the basis of a *chosenness* that it would be difficult for it to escape, for it constitutes it; of a debt of the I, older than any loan. This way of approaching an idea by asserting the concreteness of a situation in which it originally assumes meaning seems to me essential to phenomenology. It is presupposed in everything I have said. (EN, 227)

Even the absolute of which Levinas speaks, the absoluteness of the other, is for Levinas a phenomenological notion: "The absolute—an abusive word—could probably take place concretely and *have meaning only* in the phenomenology, or in the rupture of the phenomenology, to which the face of the other gives rise" (EN, 167; my emphasis). Thus religious vocabulary is given a phenomenological status in Levinas's work, and religious concepts become phenomenological notions and need to be approached as such. Levinas often speaks of the interruption of phenomenology—which remains an interruption affecting and displacing phenomenology, an interruption that phenomenology undergoes.[31]

Interrupted by the in-visibility of the face, phenomenology itself is transformed from a phenomenology of the present being, of perception, to a phenomenology which is assigned to the givenness of the otherness of the other in the face. It is in this sense that Levinas states, "one can say that the face is not 'seen'" (EI, 86), is not the object of a thematic gaze. What is being seen in the face is its own invisibility, that is, its absolute alterity—or what Derrida would call the "secret" of the other—its transcendence. This break with a phenomenology of perception appears clearly when Levinas states that the best way of encountering the face "is not even to notice the color of his eyes" (EI, 85). In fact, this way of looking at the face would be a kind of defacement, and the face seen in this perceptual way would then be "defaced," as in the French *dévisager*. To *dé-visager* someone is tantamount to a de-facing; and this is why Levinas specifies that "Defacement occurs also as a way of looking, a way of knowing, for example, what color your eyes are. No, the face is not this" (RB, 144–145). The face does not *present* a countenance or a form, but exposes a nakedness and a passivity: "The disclosure of the face is nudity—non-form—abandon of oneself, aging, dying; more naked than nakedness: poverty, wrinkled skin" (AE, 141). The face expresses a poverty and a vulnerability. To this extent, the access to the face is not perceptual but *ethical*: "I think rather that access to the face is straightaway ethical" (EI, 85). Indeed, the face displays a kind of uprightness, upstandingness or straightforwardness, as *droiture* in French designates both a physical characteristic of being upright, and a moral signification: Someone who is *droit*, "straight," is someone who is direct or honest. This straightforwardness and frankness is also the naked exposure of a vulnerability, an exposure without defense; "there is first the very uprightness of the face, its upright exposure, without defense" (EI, 86). The face is "straight" because it is unable to conceal its naked presence. *That exposure is an originary honesty*—not an intentional honesty, but an honesty of exposure. It is "straight" because exposed, and vulnerable because exposed. This radical exposure of the face is radically stripped of protection, defenseless: The face is defenselessness itself, and Levinas states that the rectitude of the face indicates a movement forward, "as if it were exposed to some threat at point blank range, as if it presented itself wholly delivered up to death" (RB, 126–127). Extreme exposure, beyond or before all human intending—"as to a shot at 'point blank'," *à bout portant* (EN, 145)! I stressed above the pre-originary openness to the other of the subject. Here openness is described as exposure, and exposure to injury, that is, already, to death. *The face is above all exposure to death.*

Levinas describes further the moral aspect of the face, in his analysis of the poverty of the skin (*la peau*) as opposed to the flesh (*la chair*). The skin of the face, he tells us, "is the most naked" (EI, 86), a nakedness that is described in its moral dimension. In *Otherwise than Being or Beyond Essence,* Levinas also provided a phenomenological analysis of the skin, the "contact of a skin," emphasizing its thinness (*minceur*), thin surface, "almost transparent," already pointing to the face's poverty and lack of substantiality. The skin is thought of in terms of the exposure and poverty of the face, its nakedness (AE, 143). Being naked and being physically nude are two different things. Levinas adds that nakedness is "with a decent nudity." It is not pornographic or obscene, but is a *moral nakedness,* that is an exposure of poverty and vulnerability. Levinas speaks of the "poverty" of the face, as "there is an essential poverty in the face" (EI, 86). It is *only* what it is, it has no riches, a (non)phenomenon, a poverty emphasized by our attempts to cover or disguise it, or simply by our attempts to *present* a face. It is as if the face was by itself not presentable, not providing a form; one then puts on make-up, makes a face or takes a countenance, *to give it an intentionality,* attempting to adorn the essential poverty of the face, to make up for its poverty. That poverty, that nakedness, that exposure to death of the face is an invitation. It is an invitation to violence, specifies Levinas, who is very clear on this point: "The face is exposed, menaced, as if inviting us to an act of violence" (EI, 86). That negation of the other which is violence is thus in a sense inscribed in the face itself. Levinas writes that there is in the face of the other "always the death of the other and thus, in some way, an incitement to murder, the temptation to go to the extreme, to completely neglect the other" (EN, 104). Vulnerability or weakness, the cynics tell us, is "provocative," although one would need here to draw a distinction between vulnerability and weakness: Weakness, as opposed to strength, is a term that is operative within a problematics of power, whereas vulnerability has a moral connotation, and for Levinas is operative within the context of the ethical. This is why, for Levinas—and against what some Nietzschean critics might claim—heteronomy, subjection, and obligation are not synonyms of submissiveness, slavery or bondage. I will return to this when treating of heteronomy. The command of the other "entails no humiliation" (EN, 35), but opens the space of respect: An ethics of the other is not another slave morality.

Levinas writes that the vulnerability of the face is in one sense an invitation to violence.[32] And yet—and this is what is most peculiar, most paradoxical—this very vulnerability which invites violence is *at the same time* a call to the suspension of violence, to non-violence, and thus already to ethics. Levinas writes, "The face is exposed, menaced, as if inviting us to an act of violence. *At the same time,* the face is what forbids us to kill*" (EI, 86; my emphasis). *At the same time:* In a dangerous proximity which threatens its very purity, if not possibility, ethics is rooted in an experience that also constitutes the possibility of violence. The separation between ethics and violence is dangerously thin, if not undecidable: There is even a violence *of* ethics or done *in the name* of ethics, which Levinas seems to recognize and accept when confronted with the problem of the executioner's face. In this case, he specifies, the executioner "is the one who threatens my neighbor and, in this sense, *calls for violence* and no longer has a face" (EN, 105; my emphasis). Conversely, violence "can involve justice" and "one cannot say that there is no legitimate violence" (EN, 106). In any case, ethics is defined by Levinas in relation to violence: "the face is what forbids us to kill." Ethics is thus the interruption of violence, its suspension; and violence, in turn, is also defined in terms of ethics, as the negation of the face, which supposes that the face in its inviolability has already given itself: Violence supposes the face, and thus ethics. Paradoxically, it is that inviolable character of the other that can give rise to the desire to kill, as the "other is the only being I can want to kill" (EN, 9), that is, to negate completely. This desire is doomed to fail, for Levinas, and there is an inherent aporia in murder: One can only want to kill that which cannot be killed, so that Levinas speaks of "the temptation and impossibility of murder" (EN, 11). Murder is an attempt to negate an irreducible. Levinas makes this point: "The face is what one cannot kill, or at least it is that whose *meaning* consists in saying: 'thou shalt not kill'" (EI, 87). The prohibition against killing "does not render murder impossible," because the ethical command not to kill is "not an ontological necessity" (EI, 87). Killing is ontologically *impossible*, ethically *forbidden*, all the while happening every day, incited by the other's exposure and a desire arising out of the very inviolability of the other. This impure origin of ethics, the intertwining between ethics and violence (ethics is the suspension of violence, violence is the negation of ethics) will always represent a continual threat to the integrity of ethics. Levinas would tend to sever that knot and give a priority to ethics, to the ethical pre-originary openness to the other over violence, whereas Derrida would attempt to enter the aporia further. As we saw, violence is not strictly speaking the absence of ethics, but its negation: It thus requires that the ethical dimension is opened in its very possibility. This is why Levinas would stress that war supposes a prior ethical peace: "War supposes peace, the prior and non-allergic presence of the other; war does not constitute the first event of the encounter" (EE, 218). This is why, as he puts it, "I even think that the good is older than evil" (RB, 55).

THE FACE AS DISCOURSE

As we have seen, Levinas distinguishes the face from the domain of vision and perception, refuses "the notion of vision to describe the authentic relationship to the Other" (EI, 87–88). The authentic relationship to the other is in language, in discourse, which for Levinas is a response, and already a responsibility. In the words of Jean-Luc Marion, "The face does not appear; it manifests itself by the responsibility that it inspires in me."[33] The origin of ethical responsibility lies in the vulnerability of the other, which calls to me insofar as "the face speaks" (EI, 87). The face is above all a language. It speaks to us, it is a saying (as opposed to a said, following Levinas's distinction between saying and said, *le dire* and *le dit*) to which I must respond. Discourse is an *address*. Whereas understanding only names things, gives them designations, original language as saying is an "instituting sociality" (EN, 7). Such original language lies in the fact that "before the face I do not simply remain there contemplating it, I respond to it" (EI, 88). In encountering the other, I am in that dimension of the saying, in which original sociality is instituted through the greeting: "Man is the only being I cannot encounter without my expressing this encounter to him. That is precisely what distinguishes the encounter from knowledge. In every attitude toward the human being there is a greeting—even if it is the refusal of a greeting" (EN, 7; translation modified). It is "difficult," insists Levinas, to "be silent in someone's presence" (EN, 7). In greeting someone—and I can only greet someone (saying) before saying something to him or her (said)—I have already answered them and answered for them: I am responsible for them. The saying is indeed a way of greeting the other, "but to greet the Other is already to answer for him" (EI, 88). The greeting is thus a response. Any communication, any content being exchanged, presupposes this prior call of the other in its saying. "It is necessary to speak of something, of the rain and fine weather, no matter what, but to speak, to respond to him and already to answer for him" (EN, 7). Such an originary language, or saying, "is prior to the statements of propositions communicating information and narrative" (EN, 166). The face speaks, and is a discourse to which we respond, a response that is straightaway a responsibility, an originary responsibility: "it is discourse and, more exactly, response or responsibility which is the authentic relationship" (EI, 88).

From the start, the original encounter with the other is one of my responsibility for him or her. This explains why for Levinas the authentic relationship to the other is not affective or emotional, for even in love what matters is not the erotic or desire—"Love does not begin in the erotic" (RB, 229)—but the ethical. Levinas stresses that the "positive definition of love of the neighbor is distinguished from everything that is erotic and concupiscent" (RB, 127). In "Philosophy, Justice, Love," Levinas rethinks the idea of "love for one's neighbor," the love without concupiscence of which Pascal spoke, in terms of a more primordial "responsibility for the other," that is, in terms of a certain non-indifference to the other, or care. In the light of such responsibility, love is to be approached in its ethical sense, as betrayed in this passage from "Intention, Event and the Other" where Levinas speaks of love "or responsibility" (RB, 143). The meaning of love is responsibility to the other.

> That is the responsibility for my neighbor, which is, no doubt, the harsh name for what we call love of one's neighbor; love without Eros, charity, love in which the ethical aspect dominates the passionate aspect, love

without concupiscence. I don't very much like the word love, which is worn-out and debased. Let us speak instead of the taking upon oneself of the fate of the other. (EN, 103)

The most authentic relation to the other is thus for Levinas ethical, and the ethical lies in our responsibility for the other—in taking upon ourselves the fate of the other.

FROM UNIQUE TO UNIQUE: FEARING FOR THE OTHER

What does the face say? It commands, as Levinas tells us. It is an order, and more precisely, an order not to kill. "The first word of the face is 'Thou shalt not kill.' It is an order" (EI, 89). The face commands us, "as if a master spoke to me," from above. However, this height of obligation—this categorical imperative that is the face, this vertical command—emanates from someone who is poor and destitute: "it is the poor for whom I can do all and to whom I owe all" (EI, 89). One notes here how the categorical imperative refers not to the law, but to a singular other. Levinas breaks here decisively with the Kantian formulation of respect and universality, for as he explains, "To respect is to bow down not before the law, but before a being who commands a work from me" (EN, 35). One has to answer for someone, "not by appealing to the abstraction of some anonymous law, some juridical entity" (EN, 144): Ethics is not a relation to a universal but to the unique. Levinas distinguishes his approach from Kantian universalism in this way: "My manner of approaching the question is, in effect, different. It takes off from the idea that ethics arises in the relation to the other and not straightaway by a reference to the universality of a law" (RB, 114). In fact, responsibility arises out of a relation to the unique, while its overlooking or neutralization would lead to unethical calculations.

What is the unique for Levinas? The unique is first "what is refractory to the concept" (AE, 218), what escapes conceptuality and genre. For Levinas, the non-generic character of the I does not imply that it is the *unique* example of a genus. Rather, the I is not of the order of generic conceptuality and its individual counterpart: "The uniqueness of the I consists not only in the fact that it is encountered as a unique exemplar, but in the fact that it exists *without a genus*, without being the individuation of a concept. The selfhood of the I consists in the fact that it re-

mains outside the distinction between the individual and the general"
(EE, 90; my emphasis). The uniqueness of the I is given in the experience
of responsibility and its intransferability—a responsibility that cannot
be refused. There lies for Levinas the ultimate principle of individuation.
However, one needs to stress here that uniqueness is above all the uniqueness of *the other,* who is outside genus, conceptuality, law, and universality: "When I speak of uniqueness, I am also expressing the otherness of
the other" (EN, 205); and the unique, we should note, is "of the other,"
and not primarily located in the I. The unique (of the other) is what does
not belong to a genus. "The unique is the other in an eminent way: he
doesn't belong to a genus or does not remain within his genus" (EN, 205).
The relation to the other is a relation to such a unique, a relation and
responsibility "to the other man as unique" (RB, 114). The other gives
itself, thus, apart from any social role or genus; the other is "incomparable." This explains why Levinas writes that the face is signification
without context, and not "a character within a context" (EI, 86); that it
is "meaning all by itself" (EI, 86). Significantly, this uniqueness of the
other seems to call for my own uniqueness, as if my uniqueness pro-
ceeded from the uniqueness of the other, "from the unique to the unique"
(RB, 108). Indeed, the uniqueness of the self does not come from some
substantial identity; rather, the I is unique as the one who is called and
elected to respond—without possible escape—to the uniqueness of the
other! "He for whom one is responsible is unique, and he who is responsible cannot delegate his responsibility. In this sense, he is also unique"
(RB, 214). The other concerns *me:* In this accusative I am revealed as
unique and irreplaceable in my responsibility for the other, a uniqueness
as it were granted by the other, granted by my responsibility for the other,
since it is "as responsibility and in responsibility that the 'me' gains its
uniqueness."[34] This is why Levinas speaks of an uniqueness of chosenness. The human I "is neither the substantial identity of a subject nor the
Eigentlichkeit in the 'mineness' of being . . . but the I of the one who is
chosen to answer for his fellowman and is *thus* identical to itself, and
thus the self. A uniqueness of chosenness!" (EN, 217).

In this break with universality, ethical responsibility is assigned to the
uniqueness of the other human. It is a relation, not to the universal, but to
the unique other in his suffering. Ethics is not grounded on the universal
moral law, but on the suffering of the other person. Indeed, responsibility

arises out of a *fear for the other:* I fear for the death of the other, I fear for someone who is in great peril. That is *my* fear, although it is not, Levinas clarifies, a fear *for oneself.* "Fear for the other, fear for the death of the other man is my fear, but it is in no way a fear for *oneself*" (EN, 146). Rather, it is *my* fear *for another.* This fear (which recalls Hans Jonas's notion of a "heuristic of fear" in his thinking of responsibility[35]) is for the other's suffering, but also for my own potential violence as a being-in-the-world who can establish a home expulsing and excluding all others in some third (or developing!) world, in other words, a fear "for all the violence and murder my existing . . . can bring about" (EN, 144). Levinas goes so far as to raise this suffering of the other to the level of the "supreme principle of ethics"! Referring to the tragedies of the twentieth century, Levinas explains in the essay "Useless Suffering," how history has transformed the very meaning of ethics. "Emerging at the end of unspeakable suffering . . . the unjustifiable suffering of the other," ethics is reoriented toward the inter-human (and away from the abstractness of the law), and "it is this attention to the suffering of the other that, through the cruelties of our century (despite these cruelties, because of these cruelties) can be affirmed as the very nexus of human subjectivity, *to the point of being raised to the level of supreme ethical principle*" (EN, 94; my emphasis). It is thus a suffering, a poverty, and a vulnerability that command and call me. And who am I? "I am he who finds the resources to respond to the call" (EN, 94).

THE FACE AS THE MORTALITY OF THE OTHER

The other's vulnerability, ultimately, reveals his or her mortality. For if the face is what can be outraged, defaced, done violence to, it is because the other is mortal, already exposed to death. What is an injury, is not the announcement of death? Levinas speaks of the exposure of the face to death, to "an invisible death and mysterious forsaking" (EN, 145). This is precisely why the first command is: Thou shalt not kill! (Though this is a command that Levinas also specifies as 'Thou shalt not leave me alone in my dying!' Levinas allows for a being-with the other in death.) In "Philosophy, Justice, and Love," addressing the question "What is there in the Face?" and after having recalled that the face is "definitely not a plastic form like a portrait" (EN, 104), Levinas stresses that the relation to the face is a relation to the "absolutely weak," that is, to what is "absolutely exposed," bare, and destitute. And this "absolute," Levinas concedes, is "an abusive word," but none-theless it "could take place concretely and have meaning only in the phe-nomenology, or in the rupture of phenomenology, to which the face of the other gives rise" (EN, 167). And what is it that is laid bare, what is this rup-ture? The answer is death. Behind all the masks and defenses, the face *ex-presses* the death of the other:

> Face of the other—*underlying* all the particular forms of expression in which he or she, already right "in character," plays a role—is no less *pure expression,* extradition with neither defense nor cover, precisely the ex-treme rectitude of a *facing,* which in this nakedness *is an exposure unto death:* nakedness, destitution, passivity, and pure vulnerability. *Face as the very mortality of the human being.* (EN, 167; my emphasis)

Levinas thus retrieves Heidegger's celebrated analyses of death as the isolating, individuating event faced by each Dasein, with the following difference: It is not *my* death which is in question, but the death of the Other for whom I care, for "there is, consequently, in the Face of the Other always the death of the Other" (EN, 104). Ultimately, the face expresses the Other's dying. One finds here, once again, the aporetic structure of ethics, which is at once made possible by this mortality of the other ('Thou shalt not kill!') and threatened by a co-essential violence. For, as Levinas stresses, in the fact that the Other reveals itself as mortal—that is, as subject to the possibility of death—there is a kind of "incitement to murder," a perverse desire to "accomplish" that mortality, to "finish the other off": There is a "temptation to go to the extreme, to completely neglect the Other," in a word, to "kill" the other (EN, 104). *At the same time,* the face is the 'Thou shalt not kill!' which ultimately means, as we saw above, not to let the other die alone: "I cannot let the other die alone," writes Levinas (EN, 104); the other's dying is "like a calling out to me" (EN, 104). In "The Philosopher and Death," Levinas writes that the face "looks at me and calls to me. It lays claim to me. What does it ask? Not to leave it alone. An answer: Here I am" (RB, 127). Not letting the other die alone—aloneness, being alone, is not here simply being alone *in the world,* but also and primarily being alone *when facing death.* The relation to the face is a relation to "what is alone and can undergo the supreme isolation we call death" (EN, 167). Responsibility for the other is to accompany the other in its death, to not let the other die alone, to not be indifferent to his fate, to not become "an accomplice to that death" (EN, 169). The face signifies to me 'Thou shalt not kill!,' and if "one thinks this to the limit, one can say that I am responsible for the death of the other" (RB, 53). The I is called to answer for the death of that other.

The mortality of the other is thus what calls me to responsibility. The facing of the face in its mortality "summons me, demands me, claims me," as if "the invisible death faced by the face of the other . . . were 'my business'" (EN, 145). As we saw above, it is a matter of the other's death in my responsibility for him, as death "engenders something like an appeal from the other" (RB, 129). Levinas claims that "behind the countenance that it gives itself," the face "is like a being's exposure unto death: the without-defense, the nudity and the misery of the other" (RB, 48). Vulnerability means exposure to death, and it is this very defenselessness that paradoxically commands. "This face of the other, without recourse, without security, exposed to my gaze in its weakness and its mortality, is also the one that orders, 'Thou shalt not kill!' . . . *The face is wholly weakness and wholly authority*" (RB, 215; my emphasis). Responsibility is the taking care of the other insofar as it is mortal. "But through this mortality," Levinas adds, "an assigned task and obligation that concern the I—that 'concern me'—a coming face to face with authority, as if the invisible death to which the face of the other is exposed were, for that I that approaches it, his business, implicating him before his guilt or innocence, or at least without his intentional guilt" (EN, 167). Levinas here decisively severs responsibility from intention, as I am guilty before having done anything, guilty of the other's suffering. It is as if the death of the other concerned me even before my own death, as if it had priority over my death, as if the death of the other put me into question, as if I would be an accomplice if I did nothing! "The death of the other man puts me in question, as if in that death that is invisible to the other who exposes himself to it, I, through my eventual indifference, became the accomplice" (EN, 145–146). Responsibility for the other—non-indifference to the other—is not leaving the other die in his or her "death-bound solitude." I am responsible for the death of other in this first sense. It is also a responsibility in another sense, as heard in the command not to kill: "To be in relation with the other face to face—is to be unable to kill" (EN, 10). This is why Levinas claims that the death of the other is the "first death." I am responsible for the other's death before my own death: "it is for the death of the other that I am responsible, to the point of including myself in death"; or also, "Responsibility for the other to the point of dying for the other!" (EN, 173). I am responsible because of, and for, the other's mortality.

RESPONSIBILITY FOR THE OTHER

Let us unfold the features of Levinas's notion of a responsibility for the other. The authentic relation to the other, as we saw, is ethical, an ethicality that Levinas describes in this way: "The ethical attitude takes on a meaning that I call the face of the other man: nudity, exposure to death, and in the being of the I, infinite obligation and obedience to the imperative" (RB, 117; translation modified). The ethicality of ethics lies in responsibility. And for Levinas, responsibility is first and foremost a responsibility to the other. Levinas clarifies that responsibility is not some aspect of subjectivity, but rather its very constitution. Referring to *Otherwise than Being or Beyond Essence,* he explains that in "this book I speak of responsibility as the essential, primary and fundamental structure of subjectivity" (EI, 95). Indeed, responsibility is not the consequence of the faculty of free will, and is not even based on a pre-given self. Responsibility does not suppose a self-given identity. Responsibility does not even supplement an existential foundation. Rather responsibility structures subjectivity through and through, for, as Levinas stresses, "I describe subjectivity in ethical terms . . . the very node of the subjective is knotted in ethics understood as responsibility" (IE, 95). The subject is an ethical being, and its ethicality precedes its ontological constitution: The constitution of the subject is its 'for-the-other.' Such a responsibility is prior to being and to beings; it is not said in the ontological categories. In fact, it is no longer a self-responsibility: "I understand responsibility to mean responsibility *for the other*" (EI, 95; translation modified). "For the other"—that is, not a responsibility that ensues from my deed, not a responsibility based on my accountability for my actions. Levinas severs the traditional relation between responsibility and action: I have not done anything and yet I am responsible. The other has not done anything and I am responsible for him or her. Instead, as soon as "the other looks at me, I am responsible for him" (EI, 96). I do not even *take* responsibility for the other; rather, "his responsibility is incumbent on me. It is responsibility that goes beyond what I do" (EI, 96). Such responsibility occurs before action, before a free acting, expressing an originary one-for-the-other: "Usually, one is responsible for what one does oneself. I say . . . that responsibility is initially *a for the other*" (EI, 96). This is what Levinas calls "persecution": I have done nothing and yet I have always been accused, and thus persecuted. Levinas also severs the traditional relation between responsibility and the self, overcomes the egological enclosure of responsibility. No longer assigned to the interests of the ego, no longer about myself, I am now responsible for what is foreign to me, for "what does not even matter to me" (EI, 95). I am concerned for what does not matter to me because as such, as a matter of the other, it matters to me. Such is Levinas's conception of responsibility—it is a caring for what does not matter to me as a self, in the experience of the face. This experience is that of a being devoted to the other. "It is a relation to the other as other and not a reduction of the other to the same. It is a transcendence" (EN, 180).

This responsibility for the other is non-reciprocal, dissymmetrical or asymmetrical, infinite, and non-chosen; it is the experience of a being devoted to the other in the guise of a being "hostage" to the other. All concerns for reciprocity, contracts, and agreements with others are inadequate to capture my original responsibility to the other as pre-originary passivity before the infinite obligation to the other, and ultimately for Levinas are examples of (egoistic) calculative thinking. An ethics based on the reciprocity between moral subjects would negate the infinite transcendence of the other, and my obligation to such a transcendence. That responsibility does not arise out of a contract but out of a *non-indifference* to the other, whose importance in this thought of responsibility cannot be stressed enough: "Nonindifference—already responsibility," writes Levinas eloquently (RB, 55), and, he elsewhere speaks of non-indifference to the other as the very meaning of responsibility, "all the way to the substitution to the neighbor" (AE, 258). The humanity of man lies in this non-indifference, and the inter-human consists in that non-indifference of responsibility. The inter-human, he writes, "lies in a non-indifference of one to another, in a responsibility of one for another" (EN, 100). For Levinas, that non-indifference is constitutive of the inter-human relation. It is therefore not possible to *be* indifferent to the other. I can *feign* indifference, I can choose to be indifferent as a rule, but these presuppose the original affection of the other that calls me to respond. Non-indifference is originary, indifference is derivative. As he explains,

> To encounter, what does that mean? From the very start you are not indifferent to the other. From the very start you are not alone! Even if you adopt an attitude of indifference you are obliged to adopt it! The other counts for you; you answer him as much as he addresses himself to you; he concerns you! (RB, 50)

Non-indifference to the other is thus the fundamental "condition" of the human being, taking place before the establishment of an ethical system of reciprocity (where calculation of interests is present), before the reciprocity of responsibility can be formalized in "impersonal laws," prior to any contract, before the exchange of courtesies. It is a pure concern for the other, an asymmetrical concern which is oblivious of reciprocity; and herein lies the asymmetry of responsibility of which Levinas speaks. Against Buber, Levinas rejects the symmetry and reciprocity of the I-Thou. What the other does for me is *his business*. Levinas stresses that the I is without reciprocity, that I alone am the hostage, speaking of the "exceptional position of the I as the only one having to respond for the other" (RB, 230). I am responsible, *more* than the others, Levinas repeats like a leitmotif: "'We are each of us guilty with respect to all, and I more so than all the others,' says a character in Dostoevsky's *The Brothers Karamazov*, thereby expressing this 'originary constitution' of the I or the unique, in a responsibility for the neighbor or the other, and the impossibility of escaping responsibility or of being replaced" (RB, 229). This is less precisely the "human condition," as we formulated it above, than it is perhaps the *human incondition* (*l'incondition humaine*), as Levinas terms it so as to stress the destitute insubstantiality of the I hostage of the other.

RESPONSIBILITY AS OBSESSION

Levinas insists that I am responsible from the outset, as soon as I have encountered the other. The other does not even have to ask anything of me since its face is already, out of its naked vulnerability, a demand on me: "Positively, we will say that since the other looks at me, I am responsible for him, without even having taken on responsibilities in his regard" (EI, 96). Responsibility is thus pre-originary—prior to any free decision on the part of the subject,[36] but also independent of any particular attitude of the other. I do not *take* a responsibility for the other, I *am* responsible for him or her, *before* a decision of any kind: Responsibility for Levinas happens *before* any decision, that is, *before* freedom, in a "before" or a "past of the other" (EN, 115) which is absolute. It was never present and I was never present to it; it is an immemorial past which is nonetheless (and I will return to this) an election, which is never without "violence."[37] The infinite or limitless responsibility "in which I find myself comes from before my freedom, from a 'before-any-remembering'" (AE, 24), and in turn I am responsible for such a past, which is not the past of my deeds. I am assigned to the other before any engagement on my part, in a relationship before the act which Levinas calls *obsession*: Obsession signifies that the other has a hold on me before I can re-seize myself in an act of freedom. I am obsessed because I am not free to respond to the other or not, but *have* to; I am obsessed by the other without any possibility of re-appropriating myself from such a pre-originary hold of the other upon me. The I *belongs* to the other.

I am obligated before any vow, "before being present to myself or returning to self" (EN, 149), in a radical expropriation of the self that is at once an obligation to the other! Levinas describes this expropriation as a kind of defeat, a "defection from the unity of transcendental apperception, just as there is here a defeat of the originary intentionality in every act" (GDT, 172). It is as if, he explains, there was something before the beginning, hence the without-origin or "an-archy" of subjectivity which puts the spontaneous subject in question. I do not have my origin in myself. In a beautiful passage from "Diachrony and Representation," Levinas writes of the "ethical anteriority of responsibility," of an "an-archic responsibility" that de-structures temporality itself: "Here we have, in the ethical anteriority of responsibility (for-the-other, in its priority over deliberation), a past irreducible to a hypothetical present that it once was. A past without reference to an identity naively (or naturally) assured of its right to presence, in which everything supposedly began" (EN, 170). Such "an-archic responsibility" undoes the self-presence of the self, opening it to the for-the-other of responsibility: "Here I am in this responsibility, thrown back toward something that was never my fault or of my own doing, something that was never within my power or my freedom, something that never was my presence and never came to me through memory" (EN, 170).

This responsibility is beyond all reminiscence, retention, representation, presentation. Here lies Levinas's crucial break with the tradition: Responsibility is not the consequence of free will, and is altogether disconnected from freedom. It represents instead the passive experience of the presence of the face which obligates me before I can decide on it. I am responsible "for the faults or the unhappiness of others" (AE, 24); I am responsible out of my own non-freedom and extreme passivity even for the *freedom of others:* "Responsibility before any free engagement . . . would be responsibility for the freedom of others" (AE, 173). Responsibility is no longer based on freedom, but on the extreme passivity of the I. In opposition to the whole tradition of responsibility from Aristotle to Sartre, Levinas would claim that such a responsibility is "older" that any free decision, older than "any rememberable deliberation constitutive of the human" (EN, 114). Obligation is not preceded by a free decision, but is placed on me by the other's claim, following here the structure of subjectivity as a "for-the-other" reversing and expropriating the for-itself. "The conversion of the for-itself into the for-the-other of responsibility could not be played again within an autonomous *for-itself,* even in the guise of a simple discovery made by the 'I think,' inflexible but still reflecting on itself" (EN, 152; translation modified). Because subjectivity is from the outset such a being-for-the-other, "heteronomy is somehow stronger than autonomy" (EN, 111), leading to a radical de-posing of the ego. Heteronomy is stronger than autonomy, but as we noted, Levinas is quick to point out that heteronomy is not submission, servitude or bondage (see for instance EN, 111; RB, 172): "There is an extraordinary obedience—service without servitude!—to the uprightness of the face of the other man whose irrecusable imperative does not proceed from a threat" (RB, 283). Ethical subjection is not submission to a power, does not fall within a problematic of power and domination. Subjection is the opening of ethical responsibility and care for the other. It is not an alienation from the other, but is instead characterized as *inspiration:* Responsibility is "from the other and for the other, but without alienation: inspired" (AE, 181).

RESPONSIBILITY AS ELECTION

My responsibility—and it is always mine, even though it is for the other, as I am irreplaceable in my being-chosen by the other, and Levinas always maintained the irreducible place of subjectivity, albeit reversed in the accusative—is inescapable, inalienable. This is why Levinas speaks of a chosenness and election in responsibility, of an election which would not be a

privilege but "the fundamental characteristic of the human person as morally responsible" (EN, 108): I am chosen, elected by the call of the other to
responsibility. This chosenness marks my radical passivity, a passivity
which is unable to transform itself into an activity, into a free project. The
"despite oneself" (*le malgré soi*) is not a prior will frustrated by an obstacle.
Rather this "despite oneself" *is* the self, the "inassumable passivity of the
self" (AE, 91). One notes here how responsibility is paradoxically assigned
to an "inassumable," for it is out of the inassumable passivity of the self that
it then finds itself responsible . . . for that very inassumability! In fact, for
Levinas, this passivity is more passive than the opposition activity-passiv-
ity, and thus is a pre-originary passivity that cannot be assumed and reversed or overcome into an activity—i.e., it will remain passive. This re-
maining-passive defines subjectivity for Levinas and accounts for its
responsibility: "The subjectivity of the subject is precisely this non-reseiz-
ing of oneself," an increasing of a debt beyond the *Sollen* (AE, 93), an exposure to adversity. This chosenness at it were "singles me out," individuates
me as the one called, the one and only, "as though the I were elected and
unique—wherein the other is absolutely other, that is, incomparable" (RB,
219). Such chosenness represents the principle of individuation for Levinas.
Responsibility for the other is the principle of individuation. Contrasting
it with former models of personal identity (as the substantial ego, as I think,
as the mineness of Dasein, etc.), Levinas speaks of the "I" in terms of responsibility for the other, and "through that responsibility a human 'I' that
is neither the substantial identity of a subject nor the *Eigentlichkeit* in the
'mineness' of being," but "the *I* of the one who is chosen to answer for his
fellowman and is *thus* identical to itself, and *thus* the self" (EN, 217). I am
myself because chosen by the other. Responsibility for the other "is the
originary place of identification" (RB, 110). In a course from 1975, Levinas
returns to the question of the identity of the self, situating it in the tradition
of reflexive consciousness:

> How shall we think about the I in its identity, its uniqueness; or how shall
> we think about this uniqueness of the I? Can it be thought as a thing
> identified (the identity of the thing would be the series of views or inten-
> tions that confirm one another, or an accord of intentions)? Must the I be
> thought of as identification in the reflection upon self that assimilates the
> other to the self, at the price of no longer being able to distinguish it from
> the totality thus formed? (GDT, 20)

To this tradition, Levinas opposes an identity that comes, as it were, from the other—arises out of the other:

> Neither of these two solutions is appropriate, a third one is needed . . . The I [le Moi]—or "me" [moi] in my singularity . . . only surfaces in its uniqueness in responding for the other in a responsibility from which there is no flight, in a responsibility from which I could not be free. The "moi" [moi] is an identity of oneself that would come about by way of the impossibility of letting oneself be replaced. (GDT, 20)

The uniqueness of the I would thus "consist" in the hold, the gravity of the hold, that the other has on me. I am unique when I am responsible (chosen), and to that extent irreplaceable. "Where is my uniqueness? At the moment when I am responsible for the other I am unique. I am unique inasmuch as I am irreplaceable, inasmuch as I am chosen to answer to him" (RB, 66). I am irreplaceable because I cannot escape my responsibility and transfer it to someone else. Hence the weight of responsibility—it is mine alone to carry. Thus, "ethically, responsibility is indeclinable. The responsible I is irreplaceable, noninterchangeable, commanded to uniqueness" (RB, 66). The self is then always in the accusative, accused of some guilt or responsibility, summoned to answer, not for his or her sins, but for the other. The peculiarity of this identity of chosenness is that it emerges from the deposition of the ego. As de-posed, I come to myself as identical to myself, an identity of subjection, as it were: "it is a matter of saying the very identity of the human I starting from responsibility, that is, starting from this position or deposition of the sovereign I in self-consciousness, a deposition which is precisely its responsibility for the other" (EI, 100–101). This is the sense of the substitution that Levinas speaks about. I can substitute myself for everyone (responsibility for the other), but no one can substitute for me (uniqueness of chosenness).

RESPONSIBILITY AND SUBSTITUTION

Levinas defines his late work, *Otherwise than Being or Beyond Essence,* in the following way: "This book interprets the *subject* as *hostage* and the subjectivity of the subject as substitution breaking with the *essence* of being" (AE, 282). Substitution designates the asymmetrical for-the-other which structures subjectivity, the responsibility commanding the I, which Levinas calls expiation, obsession, "persecution" (RB, 100), and substitution. Substitution, we should stress, is asymmetrical: I substitute for the other, but the other does not substitute for me. "This responsibility for another is structured as the one-for-the-other, to the point of the one being a *hostage* of the other, a hostage in his very identity of being called irreplaceable, before any return to self. For the other in the form of one-self, to the point of *substitution* for another" (GDT, 172). It is a matter of recognizing that I am responsible for the other in a limitless way, as hostage to that other without any possibility of freeing my self from it. How does Levinas describe this? He explains for instance the following, with respect to this enigmatic "expiation for the other": Expiation must be understood in "the perspective of holiness, without which the human is inconceivable. This means that man is responsible for the other man and that he is responsible for him even when the other does not concern him, *because the other always concerns him*" (RB, 99; my emphasis). This "always" marks the radical, even excessive, clearly inexhaustible nature of such responsibility; "always" means that one can "never" be free of it. This is why it is bad faith to claim, "I did my duty," for I am never done with the other and because, ultimately, this ethics, as we saw above, is hyperbolic—an ethics beyond ethics, a duty beyond duty. Hence Levinas adds, "The other's face always regards me. And this is *de jure* limitless. At no moment can you leave the other to his own destiny. I sometimes call this *expiation,* extending all the way to substitution for the other" (RB, 99). Recognizing that there is in "expiation" a negative connotation, implying a suffering, Levinas is prompt to admit that responsibility for the other is not "pleasant." It can even be "something terrible," for "it means that if the other does something, it is I who am responsible" (RB, 216)—but it is Good! It is *the Good.*

My limitless responsibility thus exceeds any act I may have done. In fact, "The hostage is the one who is found responsible for what he has not done" (RB, 216). I have done nothing, I am guilty of nothing, and yet I am infinitely responsible for the other, hostage to the other. This would represent for Levinas a new style of the accusative—a guilt without faults, an indebtedness without loan—which he attempts to name with the term "substitution." This term does not mean that I would simply take the other's place by identifying with him or her, it "does not amount to putting oneself in the place of the other man in order to feel what he feels," and it does not involve "becoming the other" (RB, 228). I do not substitute for the other in the sense of Heidegger's notion of inauthentic "leaping in" in *Being and Time,* whereby I would take the other's responsibility away from him or her. Instead, substitution designates for Levinas responsibility itself as a way of accompanying the other, as being with and for the (mortal) other. Substitution "entails bringing comfort by associating ourselves with the essential weakness and finitude of the other" (RB, 228). In substitution, the emphasis remains on *my* responsibility. In being responsible for the other, I am not depriving the other of its responsibility; I am bearing his or her weight by sacrificing my self-interests so as to become, not the other, but *for the other.*

Critical Questions:
The Limits of Levinas's Reversal of Responsibility

AN EXIT FROM ONTOLOGY?

I would like to reflect in what follows on the significance and scope of this briefly reconstituted Levinasian reversal of the concept of responsibility, itself following the reversal and expropriation of the subjectivity of the subject toward the other, a movement that we have noted on several occasions. We may note the presence in such a reversal of a number of implicit assumptions that secretly govern Levinas's thought. I will try to single out some of the most determinative ones. The first bears on Levinas's definition of ethics. As we saw, the access to the ethical takes place, for Levinas, in a break with ontology. However, one may raise a few questions: Should the question of ethics be raised according to this alternative—the other or being? Is the other to be opposed to being? Can ethics be opposed to ontology, the thought of the other to the thought of being? Should one accept the equivalence that Levinas posits between being and the Same? Should the other as exteriority be opposed to the ego? (We recall for instance Levinas's attempt to draw an alternative between the identical in its authenticity, the mineness of the existent, and being as human devotion to the other.) Should the question of the other and therefore (for Levinas) of ethics only be raised "beyond being," beyond ontology? In Françoise Dastur's words: "Do we really have to choose between Lévinas, who asks us to contemplate 'otherwise than Being,' and Heidegger, who leads us to another way of thinking about Being?"[38] Does ontology necessarily represent the obliteration of ethical concern? Is there a possibility, despite Levinas's claims, of developing an *ontological* sense of ethics and of responsibility? Levinas has a tendency to conflate, if not identify, what he calls "Heideggerian ontology" with traditional ontology. Now this identification is untenable, not because ontology in Heidegger's work would differ from traditional ontology, but quite simply because *there is no* Heideggerian ontology: Heidegger's thought of being is *not* an ontology. Ontology is the science of beings as beings, it is the *logos* of what Heidegger calls "beingness" (*Seiendheit*). Now, Heidegger's entire thinking has consisted in putting into question the meaning and the truth of *being* itself, and not simply beingness. This is why, precisely, Heidegger has subjected ontology to a radical destruction or deconstruction, and decisively transformed the manner in which the thinking of being is to be conceived. For to bring out being *as being* is to manifest it in its *difference* from beings. It is in this sense that Heidegger could have said that being is the *Other* of all beings.

In her article, "Le temps et l'autre (Husserl, Heidegger, Levinas)," Dastur questions Levinas's opposition between being and the other, wondering whether "being or the other constitutes a credible alternative,"[39] a question which is to be taken in the following sense: "is there really an incompatibility between ontology and ethics, and must the other be irreconcilably opposed to being? Does not ontology itself already have a practical and an ethical dimension, which determines it in a fundamental way?"[40] Which ontology is Dastur referring to? Is it "the Greek or classical ontology, which posits Being outside or 'before' man—what for Heidegger is an ontology of substance, of presence-at-hand, of *Vorhandenheit*"?[41] Precisely not. It is fundamental ontology, which includes the properly human dimension, and most importantly, a practical dimension. Dastur would insist on this practical dimension of Heideggerian ontology, and in particular on its ethical scope. "For Heidegger, 'ontology' thus understood is always 'practical,' always 'engaged,' and thus bears an intrinsically ethical dimension."[42] Such ethicality—which Heidegger will call an "original ethics"—implies a relation to the other, to the other Dasein, to the other than Dasein, and to the otherness *of* Dasein (as given in the call of conscience). To that extent, there is a possibility of thinking ethics in relation to ontology, otherness in relation to being. To Levinas, who asks us to think, not "being otherwise, but otherwise than being" (AE, 13), we could respond—not otherwise *than* being, but otherwise *as* being, the otherness *of* being.

This ethical dimension of being can be seen in the phenomenon of being-with. Levinas claims that for Heidegger the other is only a "possible case" of the relation to beings, that being with-one-another (*Miteinandersein*) depends on the ontological relation. Now one might object here, first, that being is not the foundation of beings, and that therefore the relation to beings depends on *nothing*: Being is not the ground of beings, but gives itself on the same level as beings ("*à même* being," as Jean-Luc Nancy would say). Further, being is from the outset a relation to an alterity, from the outset a *being-with (others)*. *Sein* is constitutively *Mit-Sein*, and Heidegger stresses that being-with is not an accidental phenomenon but an irreducible feature and existential of Dasein. The "with" is coextensive with being, *so that the ethical is co-extensive with the ontological*. Nancy emphasizes this point in *Being Singular Plural* by insisting on the indissociability of being and the other. He writes, in opposition to Levinas, that "what he (Levinas) understands as 'otherwise than Being' is to be understood as what is 'most proper to Being,' precisely because *it is a matter of thinking being-with rather than the opposition between the other and Being*" (BSP, 199 n. 37; my emphasis, translation modified). The other, far from being opposed to being, becomes the very problem of being, "*the most proper problem of Being*" (BSP, 32).

One could question Levinas's interpretation further with regard to his understanding of being, which he takes to be the universal genre of beings. We recall Heidegger's statement that being is the *other* of beings, in which one finds the implicit refutation that being is the universal genre of beings. If that were the case, being would once again be identified with the whole of entities, with beingness. Being points to an alterity, and not to the sameness of universality. Heidegger stresses this irreducibility of being to universality in the very first paragraph of *Being and Time*. There, Heidegger reviews three traditional interpretations of the concept of being. The first states that being is "the most universal concept" (SZ, 3), and admittedly being possesses some sort of universality, since it determines *all* beings, everything that is: Being is that by which a being (entity) is a being. Yet Heidegger insists on the fact that this universality of being is not generic— "the 'universality' of being is not that of a *genre*" (SZ, 3). If it were the case, beings would be what is given first, and being would be the generalized abstraction of beings. Now this is not possible since beings *as beings* suppose being as their *a priori*. If being precedes beings, it cannot be under-

stood as a genre of beings. So when Levinas interprets fundamental ontology as knowledge of being *in general* and when he understands this "in
general" as a unifying concept of beings, as a conceptual generality, he is
in defiance of both *the spirit and the letter* of Heidegger's thinking with
respect to the meaning of being. The meaning of being, for Heidegger, is
not to be the genre of beings but the *openness* of beings, that is to say, the
event of presence in which beings come forth. What does this mean? Quite
simply, that being is the exposure and the disclosure of entities as a whole,
the disclosure of beings and nothing more. It is not situated above or below,
it doesn't unify anything, it is only the *es gibt* ("there is") of entities. This is
why the being who has an understanding of being, namely Dasein, is essentially characterized by Heidegger as an openness, a disclosure of being
unveiling the whole of what is. Heidegger often specifies this exposure to
all things in the following manner: Dasein is disclosed (exposed) to intra-
worldly entities, it is exposed to other Daseins, and it is exposed to the
entity that it itself is. As we noted above, the very concept of Dasein includes a primordial relation to the other—to the other entity, to the other
Dasein, and to oneself *as an other.* Being in Heidegger's sense thus cannot
be opposed to otherness. On the contrary, being is the openness of a relation to otherness. Is being not thought in Heidegger as transcendence, on
the basis of the ek-static, that is to say as a boundless ex-propriating exposure to the other? On this account, what are we to make of Levinas's attempts to go "beyond" being, if being is already the beyond? The consequences of this debate for a rethinking of responsibility cannot be
underestimated: Is there a need to exit ontology to access otherness? Is
ontology antinomical to ethics? These questions imply a reflection on the
phenomenological givenness of otherness in our being-responsible, to
which I will return in the next chapter.

WHAT CONCEPT OF OTHERNESS?

It is indeed around this question of otherness that one could raise another set of questions. One could question here Levinas's conceptualizing of otherness—his transforming it into a supra-category, into a
universal and encompassing genre. This is a gesture that actually runs
the risk of threatening the very meaning of alterity; in this Levinas runs
the risk (as Dastur astutely notes) of "otherness suppressing itself in be-

coming the same as itself."[43] Should otherness be raised to the level of a meta-category, be capitalized by Levinas ("the Other") and oppose the other meta-category of "the Same"? Should otherness be identified with exteriority? One may caution against the speculative "facility" that consists in generalizing and raising alterity to the level of a homogeneous genre. Alterity only gives itself in experiences of rupture, disruption, and dispersion. This is what the phenomenon of conscience reveals—an alterity to which the self is exposed. What matters is to think a self whose constitution is such that it can welcome "the at once frightening and marvelous alterity of a being at the origin of which we are not and which is also among other things—ourselves."[44] Instead of positing an infinite other beyond the self, one might attempt to grasp the self as a structure of receptivity, "a structure of receptivity without which no 'response' and no responsibility would be possible."[45]

Let us reconstruct this point. Selfhood means receptivity, and as Dastur puts it, alterity is in fact "the most intimate alterity of the self," as opposed to exteriority. One should not oppose a pure auto-affection to an absolute hetero-affection, but note the alteration of the self in conscience (and I will return to such hetero-affection in greater detail). One would then not access the otherness of the other through a break with the egological horizon, but through an analysis of the receptivity of the self.[46] Conscience attests to the finitude of the being-called as exposure to alterity—the alterity of the self, and also the alterity of the other. The alterity of the other is revealed in the alterity of conscience, and takes place in the alteration of the self. This is why alterity cannot be understood as exteriority, and the relation to the other as a separation. Rather, as Nancy states, the other is neither exteriority nor separation but intertwining or interlacement (*entrelacement*):

> The intertwining of the limit and of the continuity between the several *theres* must determine proximity not as pure juxtaposition but as *composition* in a precise sense, which must rest on a rigorous construction of the *com-*. This is nothing other than what is made necessary by Heidegger's insistence on the character of a *with* that cannot be reduced to an exteriority.

This implies that there is a permeability between self and others: "For the *being-with-the-there* there must be contact, thus also contagion and encroachment, however minimal, and even an infinitesimal derivation of the tangent between the openings in question."[47] The emphasis would thus shift, from the transcendent and infinite other, to the finite structure of receptivity of the self; from the infinity of transcendence to phenomenology as a thought of finitude; from a fleeing beyond being to a return to the things themselves and their givenness. In that case, alterity is not the absolute exteriority of which Levinas speaks, but the event of an encounter which intimately intertwines the self and the other. This last motif also casts a doubt on Levinas's opposition between the ego and the transcendent other.

We recall how Levinas identified Heidegger's notion of mineness with egohood, speaking of a solipsism of mineness. However, with mineness, it was a question of Heidegger showing that being is not a substance or an essence, but that it "is" each time at play or at issue in the entity that I am, that it is a "task of being." The intent is thus from the outset a departure from the subjectivist tradition: Mineness is determined, as early as *Being and Time,* on the basis of being itself and no longer as a form of the ego.[48] It is *being* that is each time mine. In §9 of *Being and Time,* after having posited that the being of entity that we are is each time mine, Heidegger explains, "It is being that, for that very entity, is always at issue" (*Das Sein ist es, darum es diesem Seienden je selbst geht*) (SZ, 41). Being mine thus means being itself, in the sense that it is each time at issue in the entity that I am. Mineness is not ontical individuality, worldless egohood, or a self-consciousness closed in on its *cogitationes,* but is rather to be understood in its meaning of being—that is, as the meaning of being. Mineness is that event of being that I have to be authentically. Since Dasein is understood as an openness to the other entity (being-in-the-word, being-with-others), its individuation cannot be understood to mean the exclusion of the other. The so-called "existential solipsism" does not indicate Dasein's closure on itself, but designates instead the solitude, isolation, or individuation of the *existent.* Now since the existent is defined by the *openness* to beings, it becomes necessary to think of the individuation of the self and the openness to the other being—and to the other—*at the same time.* Care supposes such an openness, and to that extent implies the relation to the other. This is why Dasein is constitutively being-with. *Existential* solipsism posits that Dasein, in its being-singular and in this very solitude, is being-with. It is as that singular entity that I am with the other. Heidegger writes: "Being-together is part of the essence of human existence, that is to say *of an always*

singular entity."[49] It is as if it is in the very separation of metaphysical solitude, that the relation to others opens. This separation opens the question
of death.

WHOSE DEATH?

Levinas opposes to the dying for oneself in Heidegger, a dying for the
other that would be more primordial. As he states in a lecture from January 1976, "The death of the other: therein lies the first death" (GDT, 48).
The motif of death as it operates in *Being and Time* is, for Levinas, what
indicates the solipsism of Heidegger's thought. According to Levinas,
"the fundamental relation of Being, in Heidegger, is not the relation with
the other, but with death, where everything inauthentic in the relation
with the other is denounced, since one dies alone" (EI, 51). Levinas challenges that privilege of a dying for oneself in Heidegger, its priority over
the concern for the other's death (the death of others is dismissed by
Heidegger in his existential analysis of death), and he attempts to imagine a dying (namely, a dying *of the other*) that would "concern me before
and more than my own death" (EN, 240). In his lecture titled "Dying
for . . . ," Levinas appeals to a sense of sacrifice that "would not fall within
the opposition between the authentic and inauthentic," and where "the
death of the other preoccupies human Dasein before its own death." This
death of the other would indicate "a beyond ontology" (EN, 214).

With respect to the charge of a solipsistic death, it is a fact that Heidegger himself stated that in the authentic relation to my death, "all relations to other Dasein are dissolved" (SZ, 250). Death, as my death alone,
becomes the ground for responsibility, as Jacques Derrida recalled: In
Being and Time, responsibility is tied to the singularity of my own dying,
since it is "from the site of death as the place of my irreplaceability, that
is, of my singularity, that I feel called to responsibility. In this sense, only
a mortal can be responsible" (GD, 41). One could nevertheless question
such a "solipsism" of death. For when Heidegger writes that "all relations
to other Dasein are dissolved," it is not so much the relation to the other
as other that is in question as a certain mode of relation to others, namely
substitution, which is an *inauthentic* mode of being with others. It is in
opposition to this model of "substitution" (not just any word in Levinas's
thought of responsibility) that Heidegger explains that authentic being-

with cannot be understood on the basis of an identification between the self and others in a common being. One must think being-together in a way that accommodates the fundamental solitude and singularity of existence. To that extent, it is death—insofar as it is always my death, insofar as it marks the interruption or absence of any relation to the other (*unbezüglichkeit*)—through which the singularity of Dasein is revealed, and which will prove paradoxically to be the very basis of any relation to the other. Everything happens as if it was on the basis of a certain *interruption* of being-in-common that the other can give itself *as other.* It is precisely this interruption of any relation which is that by which all relation can be opened. Without this interruption it is the dictatorship of the Same. The other gives itself here on the basis of the unique, singular, non-substitutable character of Dasein: The other, the very experience of otherness, gives itself on the basis of what cannot be shared. The relation to the other opens in the relation to death. It is on the basis of this abyss of what cannot be shared—namely, death—that the other can appear *as other.* Hence, despite what Levinas maintains— namely, that the thinking of death in Heidegger is an extreme individualism and solipsism, that it excludes the possibility of an authentic opening to the other—we must on the contrary recognize the constitutive character of being-toward-death for being-with.[50] For authentic being-toward-death does not dissolve being-*with* but only the possibility of *substitution,* which, we must insist, is an *inauthentic* mode of being-with. In its singularity and in this very solitude, Dasein is open to others. It is as this singular entity that I am with, and for the other.

Further, it could be argued that in order to be able to sacrifice oneself for the other, to die for the other, I must already be able to die *myself.* Death must already be, as Heidegger defines it, a possibility of *my* being; I must already be a mortal, that is, be capable of death. As Françoise Dastur argues, to state that the death of the other is the "first death," is "to give oneself in advance what it is precisely a matter of establishing. One can only be moved (*s'émouvoir*)[51] about the death of the other if one is *already* a self, if that structure of receptivity that selfhood is, the self, is already present, and it can only be present as a relation to one's own having-to-die" (HQA, 23). Furthermore, dying *for* the other does not mean dying *in its place,* if one understands this expression to mean to 'die the other's death.' I cannot take away the other's death; I can at most just delay it: No one can take the other's dying, wrote Heidegger; and Derrida is correct when he writes that I can give the other everything "except immortality," that I can die for the other

> in a situation where my death gives him a little longer to live, I can save someone by throwing myself in the water or fire in order to temporally snatch him from the jaws of death, I can give her my heart in the literal or figurative sense in order to assure her of a certain longevity. But I cannot die in her place, I cannot give her my life in exchange for her death. Only a mortal can give. (GD, 43)

Significantly, when Levinas describes one's responsibility for the death of the other, he always characterizes it as "not leaving the other die alone," as if to suggest that the closest I can be to the other's death is in accompaniment. Doesn't that suppose the individuation of death? The "mineness" of death? When I do sacrifice myself for the other, I do not take the other's death away from him or her, it is *I* who dies! In sacrifice, *I* die *for* the other but I do not die *in place* of the other. This is why Heidegger stressed that death only takes place in the first person singular. Death "in general" does not exist; there is only *my* death. It is in this sense that death is the supreme principle of individuation for Heidegger. He writes that "death, in so far as it 'is,' is each time essentially mine" (SZ, 240). All shared death, in a common fate—or all death for the other, in sacrifice—already supposes the unsubstitutable "mineness" of my death. Jacques Derrida explains in *The Gift of Death*:

> Giving one's life *for* the other, dying *for* the other . . . does not mean dying in the place of the other. On the contrary, it is only to the extent that dying—insofar as it "is"—remains mine, that I can die for another or *give* my life to the other. There is no gift of self, it cannot be thought of, except in terms of this irreplaceability. (GD, 42)

One notes the irreducible solitude of mortal existence. To care for or about the death of the other supposes the relation to death insofar as it is always *my* death. As Dastur shows, if Dasein "did not already *by itself* have a relation to death" (HQA, 23), it could not take upon itself the death of the other. Consequently each of us, "however surrounded one may be in one's agony, is inexorably condemned to dying alone" (HQA, 22).

Nonetheless, that solitude of dying is not exclusive of a relation to the other. In the first place, solitude or the absence of others not only cannot be opposed to being-with others, but actually supposes it. The experience of mourning shows this: The other is never so present than when he or she is gone; his or her absence makes him or her present *as* other. To be alone is in a sense to experience the presence of the other, in his or her very absence. The mineness of existence is thus in no way incompatible with our being-with others. Mineness is in fact the basis of being-with, "since what I share with others is precisely this untransferable character of existence which separates me abysmally from him or her" (HQA, 21). It is to that extent that Dastur is able to claim somewhat provocatively, in *La phénoménologie en questions,* that in *Being and Time* "it is a matter of the other everywhere," and that *Being and Time* is a work that would be unintelligible without this irreducible character of being-with. Outside of the relation to the other, Dasein is nothing. With and in the term Dasein, being-with is co-implicated. Responsibility is then duplicated, extended in Dasein, as at once a responsibility for oneself and for the other. I will return to this.

Instead of this opposition between a dying for oneself and a dying for the other, one could propose the notion of a *primordial mourning* in which the death of others concerns me to the extent that I exist as a self-for-the-other. The loss or death of the other is in a sense my loss, and my own death. Mourning would be a dying to the other undergone by those who remain, a dying to the one who is dead *that is essentially a dying to oneself.*[52] With the death of others, I too die. In that sense, the dying to oneself is indissociable from the dying of others: What dies for me in the death of others is my very self-for-the-other. This would require us to think the singular self as constituted by its being-with, and to rethink the relation of death to being-with. Nancy suggested in *The Inoperative Community* that "Dasein's 'being-toward-death' was never radically implicated in being-with—in *Mitsein*," and that "it is this implication that remains to be thought."[53] Death, he wrote, is indissociable from community, and it is "through death that the community reveals itself" (IC, 14). Death essentially exposes the *with* of existence—one always dies *to* the world, to life, to others. In fact, still drawing the consequences from Heidegger's claim according to which being-with belongs constitutively to Dasein (and extending all the way to include death itself), Nancy claims that death—as the most proper possibility of existence—should be taken "as a possibility of the with and as the with" (BSP, 90). It follows that nobody ever dies "alone," because "we are born and we die to one another" (BSP, 89; translation modified). Death is "my" possibility to the extent that "this mineness is delivered over to the singular plural of the always-other-mineness" (BSP, 91; translation modified).

THE DEFENSE OF SUBJECTIVITY

A key aspect in Levinas's thought of responsibility, and perhaps another limit, is his treatment of subjectivity. As we saw, Levinas reverses and expropriates the subject. However, that expropriation does not amount to a genuine overcoming of subjectivity, precisely because it is only a reversal; in fact, as overturned, the subject is maintained by Levinas, in its very destitute (de)position. As accused and persecuted, the subject is preserved. Levinas actually states in *Totality and Infinity* that his work is "a defense of subjectivity" (EE, 11)! A *defense* of subjectivity, even if it takes the paradoxical form of a subjection of the subject to the other, but precisely *as* destitute, as expropriated, the subject is maintained and indeed becomes the elected or chosen one! Levinas would go so far as to designate this destitute ego as the true *subjectum*. As he explains in *Of God Who Comes to Mind:* "The ego is no longer taken as a particular case of the Ego in general, it is the unique point which supports the universe ('supports' in both senses of bearing the unbearable, as suffering for, and supporting it)."[54] This is how Levinas rethinks subjectivity, the *subjectum*—which indeed, is that which is "thrown-underneath." Subjectivity is a being-subjected, a "subjection to all, as a supporting all (*un tout supporter*) and supporting of the whole (*un supporter le tout*)" (AE, 255). Levinas thus reinforces the position of ground of the *subjectum,* now rethought in terms of the accusation and passivity of the subject, as the persecuted subject of responsibility. In fact, such a reversal would have the perverse effect of reinforcing the subject. To state that the subject is subject*ed,* that it is always in the accusative position, and never in the nominative; to substitute for the "I think" the accusative *Me voici,* "here I am"; to state that the subject is "the called one," the "persecuted one"; does this not all of this precisely posit the I as the true *subjectum*? As the "elected one"? The other calls *me.* My hypothesis is that Levinas's thought could be characterized as an exploration of the *underpinnings* of the egological tradition, which he merely reverses. Is the maintaining of the subject not a limit of Levinas's overcoming of the tradition? Is a reversal of the modern tradition of will and subjectivity sufficient to deconstruct it? Instead of exploring the underpinnings of the egological tradition, and then simply replacing the absolute ego with the absolute other, egology by heterology, one could undertake an ontological interpretation of ethics and responsibility, far from any hyperbolic conceptuality which is still too dependent on Cartesian thought. One could attempt to *phenomenologically* retrieve the dimension in which the *givenness* of the other is only possible, in which something like otherness can *be*. It would be a question, therefore, not of opposing ethics to ontology, but of thinking the ethical resources of ontology, and the ontological senses of ethics.

Ultimately, this maintaining of the motif of the subject, of the *subjectum, even as reversed and subjected,* is perhaps still the Cartesian-Husserlian point of departure taken by Levinas. Being is put in brackets or "reduced" (since ontology represents the thinking of the Same), so that the analysis can begin with the I, with the subject. On the basis of this point of departure, Levinas *then* attempts to exceed the subject toward its outside, toward the other. We know that Levinas understands the other as *exteriority* (among numerous example, see for instance EN, 22). However, is otherness the same as exteriority? And exteriority to what, if not to the ego, the self-enclosed ego of the Cartesian tradition? It is striking in this respect to note that Levinas's constant reference throughout his work to designate the irruption or emergence of the other in its authentic sense is, of all possible examples, Descartes's idea of the infinite in the Third Meditation—that is, a context of absolute solipsism for the *ego cogito*. In the Third Meditation, Descartes attempts to retrieve the possibility of the external world through the only means he has left at his disposal, namely an investigation into the ideas present to his mind. The world having been judged "external" and dubious in the preceding meditations, the issue is to come out of the "inner sphere" of the ego to reach a problematic "outside." Now the idea of the infinite gives us such an access: Even though it is found in the ego as an innate idea, it nonetheless points to an outside of the ego, to an exteriority. It is in fact from a Cartesian perspective of the self-enclosure of the ego that the other can be taken as exteriority (to that ego). However, is exteriority a notion that is phenomenologically attested? Does it capture phenomenologically the givenness of the other? Or is it a conceptualization that still owes too much to the Cartesian tradition of consciousness? As Françoise

Dastur notes, "just as in the case of Sartre . . . in the last analysis, it was also a Cartesian motif that Levinas opposed to Heidegger's thought."[55] This would suggest that Levinas remains dependent on an egological, Cartesian thinking which he merely reverses. He retains the ego, and reverses it towards its other understood as exteriority. However, is there not a way to rethink responsibility outside of egology altogether?

Levinas attacks egology precisely to the extent that he remains dependent upon it. Therein lies the radical excess that is proper to his thinking: His attempts at exceeding the ego are proportionate to his pre-supposition of the ego, an ego that is never deconstructed but instead is subjected and maintained *as subjected*. This is the impossible position he finds himself in. In *Oneself as Another* among other places,[56] Paul Ricoeur argues that Levinas's thought is a *reactive* thought, a thought of rupture, of excess, of hyperbole, leading to the paroxystic formulations of *Otherwise than Being or Beyond Essence,* a kind of symmetrical reversal of the Cartesian and Husserlian tradition in philosophy, opposing it but never really questioning its foundations. Indeed, it is one thing to reverse this tradition, and quite another to no longer use it as a point of departure. For the Levinasian project, the result is a non-phenomenological conceptuality—as Dominique Janicaud argues in *Phenomenology and the "Theological Turn"*[57]—a sort of incantatory thinking that develops the concept of an "absolute alterity" which is devoid of any relation (see for instance EN, 167); or the notion of a face to face encounter taking place outside of the world, outside of any concrete and factical situation, outside of any context (EI, 86) and even apart from the other others, whom Levinas has to reintroduce artificially under the name of "the third."

In particularly revealing passages of *Otherwise than Being or Beyond Essence,* Levinas betrays the reactive dimension of his thought. He writes that the responsibility for the other *"goes against the grain* (à rebours) of intentionality and the will" (AE, 221), or again that the persecution of the subject "goes against the grain (*à rebours*) of intentionality" (AE, 177), and is "irreducible to intentionality . . . and will" (AE, 176). He evokes the saying as passivity of the exposure to the other, and concludes: "Hence the 'inversion' of intentionality . . . the abandonment of sovereign and active subjectivity" (AE, 81). He describes his account of the subject in opposition to the subject of the tradition, and states that the subject "thus is not to be described from the intentionality of the representational activity, of objectivation, of freedom and will. [The subject] is to be described from the passivity of time" (AE, 90). He often characterizes his thought in such a way. For instance, he writes of the "human inversion of the in-itself and the for-itself (of 'everyman for himself') into an ethical self, into a priority of the for-the-other," or of the "replacement of the for-itself of ontological persistence by an *I* henceforth unique . . . because of its chosenness for a responsibility for the other man" (EN, 202).

It appears quite clearly, in fact Levinas admits it often, that the definitions of the subject as a "welcome of the other," as "host," then as "hostage" have been forged through a peculiar reversal of the intentional willful subjectivity of the modern tradition in philosophy. Levinas explicitly presents his understanding of subjectivity as a reversal of the traditional subject. For instance: "Subjectivity as hostage. This notion *reverses* (*renverse*) the position from which the presence of the ego to itself appears as the beginning or the accomplishment of philosophy" (AE, 202; my emphasis). Among many instances of this reversal, let us mention the following: The subject is not a for-itself but a for-the-other; the subject is not a freedom but a passivity; the subject does not posit or constitute the meaning of the other, but is "affected" by the other. The subject does not intentionally structure the meaning of its world, but is exceeded by the other who affects it. The I is not a nominative but an accusative, a "me"; the subject does not initiate but can only respond. The subject is not a freedom, but a receptivity. The subject does not thematize, but is exposed to the transcendence of the infinite. The host does not receive, but is received in his own home, which then becomes a land of asylum, a place of transit. And finally, the subject is precisely not an active subject, a spontaneity, but is subjec*ted* to the other as a hostage. As we saw above, responsibility for Levinas no longer designates an activity of the subject, but is reversed into a symmetrical passivity. Responsibility for the other is "the defeat of the I think," the defeat of "the originary *activity* of all *acting,* source of the *spontaneity of the subject,* or of the subject as spontaneity" (AE, 220). As one can see, all the features of the Levinasian concept of the subject amount to a specific reversal of its traditional sense. Ultimately this situation—which provides both the radicality as well as the limitations of Levinas's thinking—reveals the Cartesian-Husserlian heritage of Levinas. Beginning with the I, he then proceeds to attempt to exceed it toward its outside, toward the exteriority of the other. However, as we noted, the other can be considered to be an exteriority only in relation to an already presupposed interiority of the subject.

Rather than begin from the ego in order to then attempt to leave it, by appealing to the only concept that remains—namely, that of exteriority, of the outside—it should be a question, as Ricoeur suggests, of going from the ego to the *self*, in order to see in it the givenness of the other in the constitution of a Same, but a Same in the sense of the *ipse* and not the *idem*. This subjection of the subject to an immeasurable and excessive obligation shows that the I is exposed to an irreducible otherness, that its authentic being-oneself is constituted in that very otherness. The I is constituted in an originary alteration of itself. Ricoeur underlines this rightly when he evokes the "verticality" of the call of conscience, the "dissymmetry" between the agency that calls and the self that is called. This verticality or dissymmetry manifests the hetero-affection of the I, and the otherness at the heart of self-appropriation. Instead of an opposition between the Same and the Other, one finds that the same constitutes itself in, by, and perhaps even *as* other (as Ricoeur wrote, "oneself as another"). *The self takes place at the place of the other.* What is an alterity if not in relation to a same, to a self? What is a self if not an openness to otherness? Levinas's conceptuality might serve to *prevent* a phenomenological analysis of these notions. As Dastur explains: "Ricœur also emphasizes that the hyperbole of the absolute exteriority of the other takes a paroxystic turn when, in order to affirm an unconditioned assignation of responsibility, Lévinas goes all the way to say in *Otherwise than Being or Beyond Essence* that 'selfhood in its *anarchic* passivity of identity is hostage'" (HPP, 95). Therefore, what "the hyperbole of an absolute heteronomy renders unthinkable—carving out an abyss between identity and alterity—is precisely what Ricœur wants to bring forth, namely, selfhood as a welcoming structure of the other, an other who is no longer 'scandalously' identified as an offender or as a persecutor" (HPP, 95–96). It would thus be an issue of no longer opposing, as the two great genres of being, the Same and the Other—of no longer opposing the egological, solipsistic subject to the subject as hostage of the other. The inappropriable which is revealed by the inscription of the other in the I in fact manifests that the I comes *to itself* in the place of the other. *Chez lui chez l'autre,* writes Derrida in his *Adieu à Emmanuel Lévinas,* gesturing toward a thought that would no longer oppose the appropriation of the egological subjectivity to the ex-propriation of the subject as hostage of the other: By speaking of the *ex-appropriation* of the subject, Derrida marks that from the expropriation of the other, the self appropriates itself.

Levinas posits that responsibility for the other represents the essence of subjectivity. Here we must raise a question: Does responsibility need to be tied to the figure of the subject? Does it not suppose, on the contrary, a non-subjective experience as openness to the other? And further, reversing subjectivity and responsibility leaves the question of the *being-responsible* still open: Only a being who *can* be responsible at all, that is to say, who is capable of answering to and answering for, can answer for the other. Levinas assumes what needs to be first established, namely the very possibility of *being* responsible. One would thus need to inquire about the ontological senses of being-responsible. If the gesture toward a 'beyond being' is rendered problematic, if not untenable, the question becomes: What are the ontological origins of responsibility? Heidegger claims that Dasein is a responsibility—for being, and for oneself. However, since for Heidegger the self is not the self-enclosed ego of the Cartesian tradition but an ekstatic opening, he also stresses that Dasein is responsible for the other entity, whether the entity is Dasein-like (the mode of *Fürsorge,* care for the other) or intraworldly (the mode of concern). *Dasein is a responsibility of being.* And such an *ontological* sense of responsibility takes place outside of egology. It will have the sense of an assumption of finitude, in an original *Schuldigsein* or being-guilty, taking on the sense of an appropriation of the inappropriable.

SIX

Heidegger's Originary Ethics

To stand under the claim of presence is the greatest claim made upon the human being. It is "ethics."

THE ZOLLIKON SEMINARS

Ethics as the Ground of Being

That Heidegger's work entails a major thinking of responsibility is a fact that has perhaps not been sufficiently recognized. This may be due in part to some assumptions regarding his relation to ethics, and a prevalent misunderstanding concerning his deconstruction of that tradition. I will attempt, first, to situate Heidegger's relation to ethics, and second, to unfold his philosophy of responsibility. Heidegger's thinking of ethics needs to be approached, from the outset, in terms of what he calls, in the "Letter on Humanism," an "originary ethics" (*ursprüngliche Ethik*).[1] The first significant aspect of such an expression is that it seeks to capture ethics in relation to being itself, for it is the thinking of being that is defined as an originary ethics. This already indicates that Heidegger's understanding of ethics and responsibility will develop in terms of being itself, and thus no longer in the tradition of subjectivity, will, and agency. The adjective "originary" is also indicative that it will not be an issue of ethics as an applied discipline or even as normative, but rather as an originary phenomenon.

Nevertheless, Heidegger has often been reproached for his alleged *neglect* of ethical issues, specifically his inability to provide or articulate an ethics, or even a perspective for practical engagement in the world. The simple fact that he never wrote an ethics, as he himself admits in his "Letter on Humanism," seems an eloquent fact in this regard. One also thinks here of the famous *Spiegel* interview and Heidegger's persistent and stubborn refusal, despite the increasingly desperate attempts by his interlocutor, to state how philosophy can be a guide for concrete affairs in the world. For, as he explains, "only a god can save us," and humans can only *ready themselves to be ready* for such an arrival—something that might take "at least 300 years," we are told.[2] The reasons offered for such a putative neglect of ethics vary. They include, for example, Heidegger's supposed "dismissal" of the intersubjective or collective dimension of human experience; his "contempt" for ontical or concrete affairs due to some undeconstructed Platonic theoreticism; his maintaining of a philosophy of "the Same" as opposed to an authentic thought of the Other; and last but not least, his own troubled relation to Nazism. Others have argued that Heidegger's thought of being suffers from a certain essentialism and is, as such, abstract, for instance through the ontological difference, i.e., the way in which Heidegger distinguishes being from the ontic. Whatever the reasons advanced, Heidegger's thought of being, it has been concluded, cannot contribute to ethics or to practical philosophy broadly conceived as a domain of action and of collective existence. I would like to reconsider these claims in light of a reflection on Heidegger's general relation to ethics.

It is true that Heidegger does not propose a system of morality, a body of prescriptive norms or values. It is also well-known that he takes issue with ethics as a discipline.[3] Hence it has been concluded by his critics that he does not offer a reflection on ethics. In an article titled "Heidegger's 'Originary Ethics,'" Jean-Luc Nancy states that "some have thought it possible to deny that there is any ethical dimension to Heidegger's thinking, basing their claim on his own objection to ethics as a 'discipline,' on the corresponding absence of a 'moral philosophy' in his work, and on his refusal of any moral interpretation of the analytic of Dasein."[4] However, Nancy suggests that this fact may mean something entirely unsuspected by these critics, namely that Heidegger does not propose a system of moral norms because of his very conception of the ethical: Heidegger does not propose moral norms, but attempts to re-think the very site of ethics; by way of a critique of the metaphysical tradition, he attempts to re-appropriate the phenomenological and on-tological origins of what has been called "ethics" in our tradition. As we alluded to above, in Heidegger's work the question of ethics is situated in and arises out of the very event of being and its givenness. Traditional accounts of ethics are indeed phenomenologically "destroyed" or decon-structed, but in order to retrieve a non-metaphysical, non-theological, more original sense of the ethical. For instance, when Heidegger takes issue with ethics as a metaphysical discipline in "Letter on Humanism," it is with the intent of uncovering a more originary sense of ethics as "authentic dwelling" and "standing-in" the truth of being. Even when, in *Being and Time,* he takes issue with the distinction between good and evil as "ontic," it is order to retrieve an original guilt (*Schuldigsein*) that is said to be more originary than good-and-evil morality and which provides an ontological foundation for morality (see SZ, 286). When Heidegger criticizes the theme of empathy, it is not in order to condemn an ethical motif as such, but to show how the problematics of empathy are still dependent on Cartesianism and ego-based philosophies. In-stead, Heidegger provides an ontological analysis of "being-with," that is, the originary being-with-others of Dasein that renders moot the ques-tion of accessing another mind through empathy.

Ultimately, for Heidegger, as he states in the "Letter on Humanism," the thinking of being is an originary ethics because being is not some substantial ground but an event that calls for a responsible engagement. His critique of ethics thus lies, not in some hatred for ethics or in some anti-ethical posture, but in his attempt to retrieve an ontological phe-nomenology of ethics. By returning to such ontological origins of ethics ("originary ethics"), Heidegger brackets out its metaphysical under-standing as a system of moral norms ("ethics"). Rather, he conceives of the ethical in terms of our relation to being—not as some theoretical principles to apply, but as the very unfolding of human existence. Ethics is understood in terms of being and of what Heidegger calls Dasein, that is, the human being conceived in its relation to being itself. In the words of Jean-Luc Nancy, "What is at issue is nothing other than the end of a metaphysico-theological foundation to morality to arrive at ethics as the ground of Being" (HPP, 73).

Dasein as an Ethical Notion

If only "those who have read Heidegger blindly, or not at all, have been able to think of him as a stranger to ethical preoccupations," as Nancy suggests (HPP, 65), then it becomes our task to articulate the ethical dimension of Heidegger's thought. It could be argued that this concern for ethics has been constant in Heidegger's thought, including when it is not explicitly addressed, because being displays its own ethicality. This is why Nancy also adds that "ethics constitutes, paradoxically, at once a discreet, unobstructive theme in Heidegger's work and a constant preoccupation, an orientation of his thinking" (HPP, 66). It is thus all the more important to make the ethical dimension of his thought explicit. First, the charge I mentioned above of a neglect of ethics in Heidegger's work may rest on a radical misunderstanding. One seeks in his work a *classical* problematic, does not find it, and then concludes that Heidegger ignored ethical questions. In that respect, his critics are absolutely right: Heidegger does not offer us a traditional understanding of ethics, and thus if one seeks it, one will not find it. As I alluded to above, Heidegger takes issue with traditional conceptions of ethics, and actually *rejects* ethics as a discipline in the metaphysical tradition. It is then concluded that his thought is an-ethical, if not anti-ethical. But his "rejection" of the tradition of ethics is done in the name of a rethinking of a more originary ethics that he attempts to pursue. For instance, with respect to the question of prescription in fundamental ontology, one can ask: Is it the role of philosophy to actually prescribe norms of ethics, to deliver a "morality" that would posit norms or values? Nancy insists, on the contrary, that "no philosophy either provides or is by itself a 'morality' in this sense. Philosophy is not charged with prescribing norms or values" (HPP, 66). Rather, philosophy's task is to think or rethink the ethicality of ethics, to engage in a reflection on the meaning of ethics, on what puts us "in the position of having to choose norms or values" (HPP, 66). Not indicating a choice but the situation of being "in the position of making a choice"; this resituates *ethics* in the concrete setting where it takes place, in the midst of factical existence itself, that is, in an essentially oriented openness.

A first characteristic of such originary ethics is its factical nature. Indeed, Heidegger's critique of traditional ethics is initially a critique of its *abstract* character. As early as 1921–1922, during his winter semester lecture course at the University of Freiburg titled *Phenomenological Interpretations of Aristotle,* Heidegger opposed the belief in "an absolute system of morality, a system of ethical value and value-relations that are valid in themselves." Instead, he writes of a concrete factical ethics, which he refers to as a "living morality."[5] This living morality would designate ethics as arising out of facticity, that is, in terms of existence as factically given. In *Being and Time,* Heidegger clarifies that no "values," no "ideal norms," float above factical existence, precisely because there is nothing above factical existence! There are no ideal norms above existence to which one can refer. As Nancy states: "In its principle, the ethics that thus announces itself refers to nothing other than existence. No 'value,' no 'ideal' floating above anyone's concrete, everyday existence provides it in advance with a norm and a signification" (HPP, 71).[6] When one considers, for instance, the *Eigentlich/Uneigentlich* alternative in *Being and Time,* one sees that it is a matter of an existence coming into its own, the immanent movement of a radically finite and open event, and not the "application" of rules, from above, to a previously an-ethical realm. We will see how Heidegger's characterizes Dasein's authenticity in terms of responsibility. Heidegger describes Dasein's authentic being as a being-responsible in the sense of responding authentically to the "call of conscience." That response involves one's own existence, indeed existence coming its own. Heidegger already made that claim in 1925, in "Wilhelm Dilthey's Research and the Struggle for a Historical Worldview." In relation to choosing oneself in resoluteness, Heidegger adds: "This choosing and this being resolved is the *choice of responsibility* for itself that Dasein takes one and that consists in the fact that in each instance of my acting I make myself responsible through my action. Choosing responsibility for oneself means to choose one's *conscience* as a possibility that the human being authentically is."[7] The very authenticity/inauthenticity opposition is founded upon a feature of existence and expresses an existential structure of Dasein. Dasein is defined as a possibility to be, and only that—with the original responsibility that it implies.

Dasein is an ethical being in the first sense that it is not a given "present-at-hand" being, but a task of being. As Heidegger pleasantly reminds us in his 1929–1930 lecture course, "We have forgotten that Dasein is not something one can cart around, so to speak, but something that man must take over on purpose."[8] As Heidegger wrote in *Being and Time,* "The 'essence' of Dasein lies in its existence" (*Das "Wesen" des Daseins liegt in seiner Existenz*), an "essencelessness" that leads to its definition as *potentiality-for-being*, as a being-free in which one's being is at issue for oneself. Heidegger thus explains that "Human Dasein, which has a world, is a being for whom its own existence is an issue, such that it chooses itself or renounces this choice. Existence . . . is a matter of our *freedom*."[9] Dasein does not *have* its possibilities in the manner of predicates; it is not some present-at-hand being to which a certain number of properties are appended. Dasein has no predicates because in each case it *is* its potentiality-for-Being. Precisely because Dasein's essence lies in its existence, because it has each time to be its being, because, in short, Dasein is a *way* of being, a "how" and not a "what," it can *modify* or *modalize* itself into authentic and inauthentic modes. Authenticity (being one's own) and inauthenticity (not being one's own) are inscribed in existentiality understood as possibility. This possibility is the possibility *to choose oneself* in one's being or *to flee oneself*. "Dasein always understands itself in terms of its existence—in terms of a possibility of itself: to be itself or not itself . . . Only the particular Dasein decides its existence, whether it does so by taking hold or by neglecting" (SZ, 12). For Dasein, to be means having-to-be. Having to be the being that it "is," Dasein can comport itself toward it in one way or another. More precisely, it can comport itself toward it *authentically* (which means, as its own) or *inauthentically*:

> In each case, Dasein *is* its possibility, and it "has" this possibility, but not just as a property, as something present-at-hand would. In addition, because Dasein is in each case essentially its own possibility, it *can,* in its very Being, "choose" itself and win itself; it can also lose itself and never win itself; or only "seem" to do so. (SZ, 42)

In the last analysis, in the authentic modality of existing, we do not go off to some plane which is distinct from factical existence. Authenticity has no other *content* than that of everyday existing; it is but a modified form of it: "Authenticity is only a *modification* but *not a total obliteration* of inauthenticity" (GA 24, 243/171). Authentic Dasein thus remains factical through and through. Its ethicality is hence factical as well, a feature of existence itself.

The ethical for Heidegger is situated in concrete, factical existence itself, in its specific motion and oscillation between the proper and the improper. Existence thus displays its own ethicality, is ethical through and through, and for that reason does not need to be "ethicized" from above. Instead of attempting to enframe Heidegger's thought of ethics in pre-established schemas, it should thus rather be an issue of understanding how he specifically approached the question of ethics in his thinking of being. The first gesture by Heidegger is to no longer separate ethics from existence, as if they constituted separate, independent spheres. Thought from the question of the meaning of being, ethics cannot be approached except in terms of the event of being. In a sense, for Heidegger, ethics is ontology itself; there is no need to "add" an ethics to an ontology that would have been presupposed as unethical. This is why Nancy writes: "In fact, we will have to show the extent to which the 'thinking of Being'—which is, after all, the principal, even exclusive title of this thinking—is nothing other than a thinking of what Heidegger called 'original ethics,' and that it is this throughout, in all its developments" (HPP, 66). It then appears that Heidegger did not so much neglect the ethical dimension of existence as radically transform the way that such a dimension is to be thought.

And indeed, recent publications of his early lecture courses in his *Gesamtausgabe* have made it clear that Heidegger developed his *own* thought through an appropriative reading of practical philosophy and its fundamental categories.[10] As early as 1919, in a Freiburg lecture course,[11] he thus spoke of "breaking the primacy of the theoretical," on the way to an originary phenomenology of the facticity of life, later renamed Dasein. In his 1924–1925 course on the *Sophist*,[12] he offers detailed interpretations of key passages from Aristotle's *Nicomachean Ethics,* and engages in an ontological and phenomenological appropriation of such notions as *phronēsis* and *aretē*. Other courses from this period also testify to the influence of practical-ethical categories in the genesis of Heidegger's thought and vocabulary. His (often neglected) re-appropriation of Kant's ethical philosophy also figures prominently in this respect, as in *The Essence of Human Freedom*,[13] where Heidegger proposes an ontological appropriation of Kantian freedom. Freedom is reinterpreted in terms of an analytic of Dasein, as the transcendence of Dasein. The structure of the moral law, similarly, is understood in the *Kantbuch* as the mark of the finitude of existence, assigned to the dissymmetry of the law and Kant's ethics is then reinterpreted in the perspective of an analytic of finitude.[14]

Apart from the task of tracing the genesis of Heidegger's ontological categories in the tradition of practical philosophy, one finds in *Being and Time* a practical-ethical understanding of Dasein. In its very definition, Dasein is determined as "care," a *caring* or a *concern* for its own being, that is, not in abstract theoretical terms, as the reflexive subject of the modern tradition, but in a radically practical-ethical sense. This ethicality is resolutely understood in its ontological sense: Dasein is "to be," that is, not a theoretical consciousness and self-consciousness, but a task of being, a possibility to be, *and nothing but that.* "Care" is an originary ontological-ethical category. This is why all the existentials of Dasein could and should be understood as ontological-ethical categories—they manifest Dasein's originary ethicality. One also thinks of the analyses of everyday being-in-the-world; the rethinking of intra-worldly beings in terms of the *prāgmata;* the genealogy of theoretical comportment, including the scientific *comportment,* in which Heidegger makes the point that *theoria* is a certain *comportment* of being-in-the-world, and being-in-the-world—whether in the narrow practical sense or the narrow theoretical sense—exhibits its own originary ontological-ethical sense.

This ontological ethicality, one should note, is prior to the traditional theory/praxis opposition, since both theory and praxis attest to it (they are both *comportments* of Dasein as being-in-the-world). It testifies, not so much to a simple priority of the practical over the theoretical, as we read sometime, but rather to an original dimension of being as ethical-practical that would no longer be situated within the traditional theory/praxis opposition. The metaphysical opposition of theory and praxis in fact presupposes that thinking, as *theoria,* is non-practical (i.e., contemplative) and that praxis is thoughtless (i.e., the application of theory). But thinking is no less practical than praxis is thoughtful; and this is why originary ethics occurs outside of, or prior to, the theory/praxis opposition. In the "Letter on Humanism," Heidegger makes the striking remark that "the deed of thinking [*das Tun des Denkens*] is neither theoretical nor practical" (BW, 263). In one sentence, he has stepped out of the theory/praxis opposition and re-inscribed another sense of ethicality at the heart of thinking—as the "adventure" into being. "Thus thinking is a deed. But a deed that also surpasses all praxis" (BW, 262). This passage testifies to an attempt at thinking the ethical-practical no longer within a metaphysical structure, but in its *ontological* sense. In "Letter on Humanism," Heidegger thus contrasts an ontical *praxis* (manipulation of entities, production of results under the law of efficiency, application of theoretical models) with an ontological-ethical engagement; this *poēsis* of being, in which the act of thought is accomplishment of the relation to being and a bringing forth of the useless, is in a word, originary ethics.

Ethics and the Useless

Heidegger points to this originary dimension (the site of an originary ethics) when he takes issue with the motif of application. For instance, in *Introduction to Metaphysics* Heidegger stresses the untimely nature of philosophy (as he would still do in the *Spiegel* interview), and claims that philosophy is in a certain essential sense "useless" (*Nutzlos*).[15] Philosophy, he states, "is not a kind of knowledge which one could acquire directly, like vocational and technical expertise, and which, like economic and professional knowledge in general, one could apply directly and evaluate according to its usefulness in each case" (IM, 9). It is due to its originary dimension that philosophy is not an applied discipline, that it is not instrumentalized. In *The Essence of Human Freedom,* Heidegger explained that, "Philosophy is not theoretical knowledge together with practical application," because philosophy "is more primordial than either" (GA 31, 18; EHF, 14), thereby suggesting that the conception of a theory along with its practical applications is a scientific model, pertaining to the sciences only, and foreign to philosophy. We might add that it is foreign to ethics as well, to the ethicality of ethics. According to Heidegger (IM, 12–13), asking for philosophy to have a result or a use is actually a demand of technological thinking, of what he calls in the *Beiträge* "machination" (*Machenschaft*). Does this conception of philosophy as untimely, and thus not for an immediate use, indicate the impossibility of philosophy? Heidegger does not seem to think so: "It is entirely correct and completely in order to say, 'You can't do anything with philosophy.' The only mistake is to believe that with this, the judgment concerning philosophy is at en end" (IM, 14). The absence of application does not necessarily mean the impossibility of ethics. In fact, ethics seems to be situated in the useless.

Originary ethics cannot be measured in terms of results, or the production of effects. Heidegger states that "such thinking has no result. It has no effect" (BW, 259). It has no effect, not because it is solely theoretical or contemplative—in fact, it "exceeds all contemplation" (BW, 262)—but because the ethics evoked here is no longer understood as the production of effects. The essence of thinking as originary ethics, Heidegger writes in the very first lines of "Letter on Humanism," is not that which causes an effect or is governed by the value of utility. In fact, in the *Beiträge* Heidegger makes the claim that genuine thinking is "powerless" in the sense that the "en-thinking of the truth of Being . . . does not tolerate an immediate conclusion and evaluation [i.e., closure], especially when thinking must . . . bring into play the entire strangeness of be-ing [i.e., openness]—thus when thinking can never be based on a successful result in beings."[16] This is all the more the case since as we know that any calculation of effects produced quickly proves . . . incalculable! The concern for results—the definition of ethics in terms of production of effects—in fact belongs to the imperative of technological thinking, which demands that everything be put to a use and exploited in an unconditional way and without reserve. In *The Verge of Philosophy,* John Sallis suggests that, "The genuine power of thinking consists in the capacity to undergo this displacement and to endure, as Heidegger says 'the strangeness of Beyng' . . . This endurance requires also enduring the apparent *powerlessness,* that thinking brings about no immediate effect on beings."[17] Sallis clarifies that such thinking "requires that one turn away from beings and all effectings upon them to Beyng in its strangeness" (VP, 147). Hence the site of originary ethics is not instrumental, is not the consequential mode of a subjective agency, but instead "requires the most radical loss of self, and it is in this madness that, properly attuned, one is drawn toward, opened to, the gift of Being" (VP, 147). The useless opens the space of ethics, while instrumentality closes it.

It is then clear that by originary ethics, Heidegger does not mean investigating how thinking can be applied to ontical issues. In other words, stressing the ethical dimension of Heidegger's thought does not mean a mere "application" of Heidegger's thought to various practical concerns, as though his thought—or thought in general, for that matter—could be used as some kind of tool, following an instrumental model. The current and growing development of so-called "applied ethics" in the curriculum conceals a peculiar and paradoxical blindness regarding the nature of ethics, and a neglect of a genuine philosophical questioning concerning the meaning of ethics, at the same time as it betrays an almost desperate need for ethics in our age. Yet this need arises out of the fact that ethics is left groundless; indeed, the notion of "application" provides a grounding for ethical precepts: Ethics is hereby guaranteed by a theoretical basis. However, ethical decision takes place in an ungrounded way. The concept of "applied ethics" is self-contradictory, an oxymoron of sorts. It leaves open the question of the nature of ethics, ignoring the ungrounded character of ethics through its reliance on norms. It represents a perfect example of un-phenomenological thinking, one that is entirely divorced from the matter at hand. Ethics occurs outside of reference to both ground and utility, from out of the useless.

Heidegger refers to the useless as the site of ethics when he speaks of the deed of thought in terms of the "humbleness of its inconsequential accomplishment" (BW, 262). What would thinking be if it were no longer understood as the contemplative *theoria* on the basis of which effects can take place? What would ethics be if it were no longer the act of mastering or manipulating entities?—when freed from the tyranny of utility, the tyrannical imperative to produce effects or results?—from the tyrannical imperative that all beings *have a use*? What would ethics mean if freed from the manic, frenetic race to exploit all resources, including "human" resources? In fact, thinking does not need to be put into action or put to a use, for when action is defined as the "accomplishment" of man's relation to being, then thinking becomes itself an act, the highest act: "Thinking acts insofar as it thinks" (BW, 217). It is in this sense that one can speak of an "originary ethics"—in the sense that Heidegger creates when he states that thinking is "*l'engagement par l'Etre pour l'Etre*" (engagement by Being for Being) (BW, 218; French in the original). A key feature of such an "originary ethics" is that it is identified with thinking itself, understood as the thinking of the truth of being.

Furthermore, Heidegger states that his thinking, as thinking which "inquires into the truth of being and so defines man's essential abode from Being and towards Being," is "neither ethics nor ontology" (BW, 259). Consequently, "the question about the relation of each to the other no longer has any basis in this sphere" (BW, 259). As I noted above, ontology and ethics are not different spheres. Ontology does not circumscribe some domain of principles which would then be "applied" to an ontical, ethical sphere. Ontology is (originary) ethics and ethics is ontological. Heidegger gives us a further insight into this originary ethics when he writes that "the name 'ethics,' in keeping with the basic meaning of the word *ēthos,* should now say that 'ethics' ponders the abode of man," and that the "thinking which thinks the truth of being as the primordial element of man . . . is in itself the original ethics" (BW, 258). Ethics understood in this way thus names human beings' sojourn on the earth, their very being as dwelling and inhabiting. Ultimately for Heidegger, ethics cannot be measured in terms of results and reduced to the production of effects on the basis of a theory within the end/means apparatus. Ethics is rather approached in terms of an incalculable finite dwelling of human beings, an authentic inhabiting in the openness of being, and designates humans' sojourn as mortals in the finite dimensionality of being. Ethics here becomes an ethics of finitude, of finite being.

De-subjectivizing Ethics

Being is thus not for a use, and neither is human existence for a use (we know how Kant situated the ethical itself in a break with instrumentality, in a refusal to reduce human beings to mere means). Another key feature of this original ethics, apart from its "uselessness," is its radically non-subjective nature. This appears in the motif of decision as it is treated in Heidegger's thought, indicating a radically non-subjectivistic approach to ethics. What was at stake in the critique of the theory/praxis opposition, as well as in the critique of the instrumental conception of ethics, was a freeing of ethics as the enactment of being as such. Ethics is no longer attached to the subject, but to the event of being; it is not the active manipulation of entities, but the enactment of being itself. Such an enactment, we should stress from the outset, cannot be the act of a subjectivity, because as Heidegger says of projection (*Entwurf*), it is always thrown (*Geworfen*), and therefore *before the subject*. Being is always already under way, always already in motion, "before" the will and before the subject. The "act" or "enactment" of being refers to such a motion *which we are*, but not as its authors. Rather, we are "en-owned" by it: "*This* throw is *thrown* in the resonance of en-ownment," Heidegger writes in a very compact sentence (CP, 320). Freedom, the "free throw," thus "never succeeds by mere human impetus [*Antrieb*] and human make up" (CP, 320). Humans do not initiate the free throw, they are the ones who, as Heidegger puts it, "always return from the free throw" (CP, 320).

In the *Contributions to Philosophy*, Heidegger's thinking increasingly turned toward the truth of be-ing as such (and no longer beingness), as it inquired into the truth of be-ing "out of be-ing *itself*" (CP, 3). This turning in his thought does not amount to an abandonment of the reference to the human being, but rather to its transformation, which will lead to a de-subjectivizing of thought. This is the case, first, because the turning in the question of being, from fundamental-ontological thinking to be-ing-historical thinking, does not mean that there would be two distinct questions. In fact, there is only one question, as Heidegger clearly states at several places—for instance, "the same question of the 'meaning of be-ing' is always asked, and *only* this question" (CP, 58, cf. 61). However, because it asks that same question ever more originarily, the "locations of questioning are constantly different" and the question "must transform itself from the ground up." With that *uniqueness* of the question of be-ing in mind—a uniqueness whose appropriation requires stumbling and change or a plurality of locations in the questioning—let us note that in the Thor seminar in 1969, Heidegger announced that his thinking of being has taken three essential formulations: as meaning of being, as truth of being, and as topology of being.[18] In this context, Friedrich-Wilhelm von Herrmann convincingly argues that "enowning-historical thinking originates from within the fundamental-ontological thinking of the question of being," and that therefore "Being-historical thinking becomes what it is from within a transformation (*Wandel*) of fundamental-ontological thinking—and not by turning-away from that first pathway of the question of being."[19] The shift from a questioning of the meaning of being to one out of the truth of be-ing itself means that there is a sort of dis-placing (*Verrückung*) of man into a dimension—which Heidegger calls the "between"—from which he becomes for the first time *himself*: "In the history of the truth of being Dasein is the essential *case of the between* (Zwischenfall), i.e., the case of falling-into that 'between' (*Zwischen*) into which man must be displaced (*ver-rückt*), in order above all to be *himself*" (CP, 223). In §227, Heidegger thus evokes a dis-placing of man into Dasein and evokes how, through this displacing *out of* the desolation of the abandonment of be-ing, man will come to stand in enowning and find "his abode in the truth of be-ing" (CP, 19). The origin of Dasein is thus the happening of be-ing itself, and the shift from fundamental ontology to be-ing-historical thinking implies a revolution of the site of the human being, as well as what is meant by "ethics."

How does Heidegger explain the shift from "meaning of being" to "truth of be-ing" in his thinking? In terms of a *turning* of the question of being, a turning that would have to part from a certain subjectivism and anthropocentrism which still threaten to affect the analyses of *Being and Time*. As he puts it: "In *Being and Time* Da-sein still stands in the shadow of the 'anthropological,' the 'subjectivistic,' and the 'individualistic,' etc." (CP, 208). The initial position of the question of being in *Being and Time* in terms of "meaning of being" and "understanding of being" suffers, Heidegger tells us in §138 of *Contributions*, from an excessive dependence upon the language of subjectivity (CP, 182–183). To that extent, it exposed itself to a series of misunderstandings, all sharing the same subjectivism: "Understanding" is taken in terms of the "inner lived-experiences" of a subject; the one who understands is taken in turn as "an I-subject"; the accessibility of being in an understanding is taken as an indication of the "dependency" of being upon a subject and therefore as a sign of idealism, etc. It is from this perspective that we are to understand Heidegger's moving from the expression "meaning of being" to that of "truth of be-ing." In 1969, Heidegger returned to this question in order to clarify it. In contrast with the metaphysical question concerning the beingness of being, Heidegger acknowledges that he attempted in *Being and Time* to pose the question concerning the "is-ness" of the "is" in terms of the *meaning* of being. For, precisely, metaphysics does *not* ask about the meaning of being, but only about the beingness of beings (itself ontically determined as ground). The expression "meaning of being" is thus to be taken as a first attempt to step out of the metaphysical conflation of being with beingness (*Seiendheit*):

> According to the tradition, the "question of being" means the question concerning the being of beings, in other words: the question concerning the beingness of beings, in which a being is determined in regard to its being-a-being [*Seiendsein*]. This question is *the* question of metaphysics [. . .] With *Being and Time*, however, the "question of being" receives an entirely other meaning. Here it concerns the question of being as being. It becomes thematic in *Being and Time* under the name of the "question of the meaning [*Sinn*] of being." (FS, 46)

Now, "meaning of being" is further clarified in *Being and Time* in terms of the project or projecting unfolded by the understanding of being: "Here 'meaning' is to be understood from 'project,' which is explained by 'understanding'" (FS, 40). At this point, Heidegger notes that this formulation is inadequate *because it runs the risk of reinforcing the establishment of subjectivity:* "What is inappropriate in this formulation of the question is that it makes it all too possible to understand the 'project' as a human performance. Accordingly, project is then only taken to be a structure of subjectivity—which is how Sartre takes it, by basing himself upon Descartes" (FS, 41). One recalls here the well-known passage from the *Nietzsche* volumes where Heidegger, discussing the unfinished or interrupted character of *Being and Time,* explained that, "The reason for the disruption is that the attempt and the path it chose confront the danger of *unwillingly becoming merely another entrenchment of subjectivity.*"[20] Heidegger thus engages in a turning that would de-subjectivize thought. He gives examples of such a "turning in thinking," when, for instance in §41 of the *Contributions,* he explains that the word "decision" can be taken first as an anthropological human act, "until it suddenly means the essential sway of be-ing" (CP, 58). Thinking "from *Ereignis*" will thus involve that "man [be] put back into the essential sway of be-ing and cut off from the fetters of 'anthropology'" (CP, 58). In other words, in the attempt to think the truth of be-ing, at issue is the "transformation of man himself" (CP, 58). Human Dasein is here de-subjectified, and the realm of ethics will have to be severed from the predominance of subjectivity.

In the *Contributions,* Heidegger is very careful to stress that "the projecting-open of the essential sway of be-ing is merely a response to the call" (GA 65, 56; CP, 39), and one sees here how the realm of the ethical—of originary ethics—is located in the space of a certain call, a call to which a response always corresponds (and we will return to this). It was thus in order to avoid the subjectivizing of the question of being, that the expression "truth of being" was adopted. "In order to counter this mistaken conception and to retain the meaning of 'project' as it is to be taken (that of the opening disclosure), the thinking after *Being and Time* replaced the expression 'meaning of being' with 'truth of being'" (FS, 41). Heidegger is then able to conclude that,

> The thinking that proceeds from *Being and Time,* in that it gives up the word "meaning of being" in favor of "truth of being," henceforth emphasizes the openness of being itself, rather than the openness of Dasein in regard to this openness of being. This signifies "the turn," in which thinking always more decisively turns to being as being. (FS, 41)

Freedom without Will

One of the key features of this rethinking of ethics as "originary ethics" is the re-seizing of freedom, away from the subjectivity and causality of the will, or "free will." For Heidegger, freedom is no longer understood as free will. Conversely, decision will no longer be the decision of a willful subject, but the "decidedness" of being. Heidegger has an important, positive thought of freedom. However, freedom is approached outside of the metaphysical constructs of free will, subjectivity, and causality, outside of the anthropological horizon, and in terms of the happening of being itself. As Heidegger writes in "On the Essence of Truth," freedom "is understood as letting beings be" (BW, 127), and therefore not as a faculty of the subject. We recall how, for Heidegger, existence is a matter of freedom. However, this freedom is not the free spontaneous project of a subject, resting on a pre-given self or a transcendental spontaneity. If this were the case, it would not be freedom: Freedom cannot be decided by a subject, but is rather "a freedom that breaks through in man and takes him up unto itself, thus making man possible" (EHF, 94). Man does not have freedom; rather, the very being of man lies in freedom. "Dasein," Heidegger writes in his 1929–1930 lecture course, "takes place in freedom" (*geschieht in Freiheit*),[21] an expression reformulated in the 1930 summer semester course in this way: "Human freedom now no longer means freedom as a property of man, but *man as a possibility of freedom*" (EHF, 94). To exist, to comport oneself toward being understandingly, as an opening to being as such, is possible only on the basis of freedom. This freedom has the sense of a *liberation of being* which, at the time of fundamental ontology, Heidegger called "transcendence": "Here, however, is the origin of 'possibility' as such. Only through freedom, only a free being can, as transcending, understand being—and it must do so in order to exist as such, i.e., to be "among" and "with" beings."[22] To exist means to exist on the basis of freedom, as freedom. Dasein is not a subject, but is released into itself from such a freeing throw.

As I noted, freedom is conceived of outside of the metaphysical constructs of free will, subjectivity, and causality. Heidegger, for instance in *The Essence of Human Freedom,* attempts to "free" freedom from the enframing of causality, arguing that causality only pertains to beings as present-at-hand. Reversing the relation between freedom and causality—

freedom is not a problem of causality, rather "causality is a problem of freedom" (EHF, 205)—Heidegger breaks with the predominance of subjectivity (freedom as a faculty), with the domination of will (freedom as a causal power), and also with an ontic interpretation of nature given over to rational calculation (so-called "cosmological freedom" in Kant). Let us think here of that passage, among many others, from *The Question Concerning Technology*, in which Heidegger asserts firmly that, "The essence of freedom is originally not connected with the will or even with the causality of human willing" (BW, 330). The metaphysical ways of enframing freedom in subjectivity, in the will, and in causality, prove inadequate to an ontological thought of freedom. Certainly, as Heidegger concedes in the *Beiträge*, one might state that it "is hardly possible in the end not to approach freedom as cause and faculty, hardly possible not to push the question of decision off into the 'moral-anthropological' dimension" (CP, 60). Yet the task is to do just that. In fact, freedom is never something merely human, since, as the 1930 course makes clear, it is rather the possibility of man. It is a matter of thinking the "free-ing" in freedom, what is freeing in our being, what makes us free, "sets us free," in what could be called "the free scope of freedom."[23] This scope of freedom is what Heidegger indicated when, already in *Being and Time*, he claimed that Dasein is characterized as "being-free [*Freisein*] *for* its ownmost potentiality-for-being," or that Dasein's "being toward a potentiality-for-being is itself determined by freedom" (SZ, 191). What sort of action is then freed when it is subtracted from those categories? It appears that the issue, in the end, is to think freedom as originary to Dasein's being and in a sense to being itself. The essence of freedom would then be the essence of being itself.

A Decision of Being

This de-subjectivizing of freedom and ethics is developed in Heidegger's rethinking of decision. We know that decision is traditionally assigned to a willful subject and an agent who decides, to the extent that decision in the end becomes only about such a subject. The stress is always on *who* decides, *who* has the *power* to decide, *who* leads and *who* the "deciders" are (in French, those who are in power are called *les décideurs*, literally "those who decide" or "the deciding ones"). In such a context, decision is identified with subjectivity and with the power of such a subject (subjectivity *as* power). One can see how decision participates in the metaphysical inflation of subjectivity, with all of its variations. In contrast, when in the *Contributions* Heidegger asks, "Who decides?" he immediately replies, "Everyone, even in not-deciding and not wanting to hear of it, in dodging the preparation" (CP, 69). Heidegger attempts to remove decision from the horizon of subjectivity. In §43 of the *Contributions,* he states clearly that ordinarily, when we speak "of de-cision (*Ent-scheidung*), we think of an activity of man, of an enactment, of a process." However, decision is not a power or a faculty of man: "But here neither the human character in an activity nor the process-dimension is essential" (CP, 60). This is why he clarifies that "Decision [is] related to the truth of being, not only related but *determined only from within it*" (CP, 69; my emphasis). Decision is no longer about the glorified subject, displaced from a subject-based thinking to a thinking which is concerned with what the decision is about, the "decisive."

Heidegger asks, what is decision about? The decision, he answers, is a "decision between either-or" (CP, 70). Radicalized, this either-or of decision is rethought in such a way that decision is then said to deal "originarily with deciding or not-deciding" (CP, 70). Decision thus deals with the *decisive.* Emphasizing the decisive, and the "decidedness" in decision, suggests that in the decision the matter is not already settled, not already decided. Rather, the matter is *to be decided.* This un-decidedness points toward the decidedness of any decision, and is its proper site. As Heidegger puts it, "Decision (*Entscheidung*) means already decidedness (*Entschiendenheit*)" (CP, 70). This is why decision is not a choice for Heidegger, which is always a choice between two pre-given established realities. Choosing always involves "only what is pregiven and can be taken or rejected" (CP, 69). Further, choice involves a subject of the choice (free will) and an understanding of being as what is already laid out available for manipulation. These are all inadequate representations for Heidegger. De-cision is not a choice between given ontic possibilities, but is "the essence of being itself," and in fact "*truth* itself is already *the very thing to be decided*" (CP, 70). Choice is the ontic representation of decision, whereas decidedness expresses the decision of and *for* be-ing: "*Entscheidung* für *das Seyn,*" writes Heidegger (CP, 63). The decisive is not the subject who decides, and Heidegger separates the freedom of decision—decision is "the necessary enactment of freedom"—from its subjectivist understanding in terms of causality of the will as a faculty of the subject—"this is how we think 'causally' and take freedom to be a faculty" (CP, 71). At the risk of tautology, one should say that what matters in decision is "the matter" of decision itself. This is why Heidegger says that decision is about decision itself, "about deciding or not-deciding" (CP, 70)!

Deciding *for* decision, the decidedness *of* decision, these expressions break with what Heidegger calls the greatest danger, the most certain sign of nihilistic machination—namely, the belief that matters are already decided. Hence the "lack of distress" that is the most distressful of all; the decided (lack of distress as utmost distress) has to be returned to the undecided (distress), so as to bring out decidedness as such. "Is not 'decision' also another very refined form of calculation? Or, because of this illusion, is decision not simply the extreme opposite, but also the *incomparable* (Unvergleichbare)?" (CP, 71). For Heidegger, decision is not to be taken in its "moral-anthropological" sense, but as pertaining to being itself in its decidedness. Decidedness is the site of being itself. As Richard Polt remarks, the hyphenated *Ent-scheidung* "indicates a division (*Scheidung*) that opens up a domain of unconcealment."[24] This domain, Heidegger writes, "must originarily and inceptually be opened up in a leap (*ersprungen werden*)" (CP, 323; translation modified)—the leap, precisely, of decision. Ultimately, decision is the dis-closure of being in a leap. In *Being and Time,* what was at issue for Dasein was the meaning of being itself. Here too being is what matters; being is what is at stake in the decision, and decision is about nothing but being. Being as the decisive, being as the matter of decision—away from the enclosure of subjectivity—this would be one of the main features of the ethicality of being.

Being is thus a matter of a decision, of what we might call a responsible decision. Yet, this responsibility is entirely de-subjectivized, is no longer the accountability of the subject, as Heidegger has stepped out of the horizon of subjectivity to engage a thinking for the sake of the truth of being itself. Heidegger's sense of responsibility stands in contrast to the accountability of the autonomous subject. We can even wonder whether such an originary responsibility can be characterized as at all *human,* following Heidegger's claim that "in the determination of the humanity of man as ek-sistence what is essential is not man but Being" (BW, 237). In fact, for Heidegger responsibility is not a human characteristic, but is instead a phenomenon that belongs to being itself (although, as we will see, humans are "enowned" and called by being). Just as in the case of decision, it is necessary to free responsibility from the anthropological or humanistic enclosure. In his thinking of responsibility, Heidegger breaks with a subject-based thinking, breaks from the tradition of autonomous subject, and with an anthropological way of thinking. The task is thus to think ethics, and responsibility, away from any subjectivist anthropological enclosure. One thinks here, for instance, of Heidegger's treatment of *evil*. Heidegger undertook a critique of the good/evil opposition in *Being and Time*, and characterized it as ontic (SZ, 286). Conscience, he explained, is "prior" to good and evil. However, later texts would elaborate a proper account of evil as pertaining to being itself; but one notes that his conception is neither anthropological nor moral-theological. Evil now names the "demonic" destructiveness of nihilism and technological thinking, that is, ultimately, the destructiveness of being. "With healing, evil appears all the more in the clearing of being, but rather in the malice of rage. The essence of evil does not consist in the mere baseness of human action, but rather in the malice of rage. Both of these, however, can essentially occur only in Being" (BW, 260). The entirety of ethics is to be recast in terms of being itself, and no longer based on the human subject. Responsibility will name the co-belonging of being and Dasein—a co-belonging which is not posited by man, but rather one in which man is thrown—and thinking "from *Ereignis*" will thus involve that "man [be] put back into the essential sway of be-ing and cut off from the fetters of 'anthropology'" (CP, 58).

The Ethicality of Being

In *God, Death, and Time*, Emmanuel Levinas brilliantly presents Heidegger's thought of being in the following way: "Heidegger opened the path of a rationality of disquietude or of nonquiet."[25] In what sense? In that being, in contrast with the Greek determination of the meaning of being as *ousia*, is understood as that which is "in question" or "at issue" in Dasein. Being in question, continues Levinas, attests to its being a "bottomless abyss," a "nonfoundation." In this sense, this determination of being represents for Levinas a fundamental break with the "Greek rationality of repose." Because being is no longer enframed in an ontology of substance, order, and *arkhē,* it becomes, as Levinas puts it, "a task of Being." This gives being an irreducible and originary practico-ethical sense: Being is to be, that is, "enacted" in an original freedom. We know that Levinas, when presenting Heidegger's thought, always begins by emphasizing that its major contribution is to have brought out the so-called "verbality" of being. Being is not a substance but an event, a "doing" or a "happening." One could say, in an impossible English, being *is* not but being be-*ings!*

One finds a strong indication of this non-substantiality of being—of its withdrawal—in Heidegger's rethinking of the *a priori* in the *Beiträge,* and in his thought of the simultaneity of be-ing and beings. Whereas in his early lecture courses, Heidegger had attempted to reappropriate the *a priori* away from the tradition of subjectivity in order to make it designate being itself (being as the true *a priori*), here he insists that the *a priori* is the "guiding-question" of metaphysics, and that the relation between be-ing and beings is "totally different" (CP, 155). Indeed, the truth of be-ing "and the essential swaying of be-ing is neither what is earlier nor what is later" (CP, 155). Heidegger rejects both the Platonic version of the *a priori* (priority of the *eidos,* as beingness over beings) and its modern subjectivist version (priority of the representing subject, as in Descartes's Second Meditation). In the preview, he explains that "be-ing is not something earlier—subsisting for and in itself" (CP, 10). Rather, *Ereignis* is the "temporal-spatial simultaneity of be-ing and beings" (CP, 10). Further on, he speaks of Dasein as the "simultaneity of time-space," the "between" and the "mid-point" in beings themselves (CP, 10). Being cannot be posited prior to beings; being is the between that can only be *enacted* in a leap. This is echoed in Nancy's *Being Singular Plural,* where we read: "Being absolutely does not preexist; nothing preexists; only what exists exists."[26] What is important for us in this discussion is that the simultaneity of be-ing and beings, this "leap in the between," can only be *enacted.* There is no grounding in an *a priori,* instead there is a *performativity of being.* This rethinking of being reveals its inescapable practicality, away from all representational thinking. This is why Nancy elsewhere explains that "*Dasein* is definitely not the name of a substance, but the sentence of an action" (HPP, 72). What Dasein is in so far as it has to act is not a specific aspect of its being—it is its very being itself. If Dasein—according to the opening formulations of *Being and Time*—is the being for which "in its very Being, that Being is *at issue* for it" (SZ, 12), it is because this 'being-at-issue' does not bring into play an interest which is merely theoretical or speculative. Rather, it destroys the supposed autonomy of such an interest. As we will see, there is no 'struggle for existence' in such an 'at-issue.' If, in Dasein, being is at issue, that is because being (as the being of Dasein) *is* what is at stake in its originary ethicality—and ethicality is the bringing into play of being. It is to this extent that we could say that this understanding of being consecrates how the end of a metaphysico-theological foundation to morality leads to *ethics as the ground of being.* In Nancy's terms, "*'Original ethics' is the more appropriate name for 'fundamental ontology.' Ethics properly is what is fundamental in fundamental ontology*" (HPP, 78).

In its very eventfulness, being withdraws, is the mystery; and such a withdrawal, as Heidegger stresses, *calls us.*[27] The event of being thus immediately engages an originary responsibility, a responsibility for being. Responsibility will have to be taken in terms of a responsiveness to this call of being, that is, from the withdrawal of being (for it is the withdrawal itself that calls us, "pulls" us toward it, as Heidegger explains in *What is Called Thinking?*). Original responsibility is a corresponding to this call, arising out of the withdrawal of being (and we recall that in Sartre, responsibility also arose out of a withdrawal, the withdrawal of essence). Let us investigate how responsibility is in play in such an ethicality of being.

SEVEN

Heidegger:
The Ontological Origins of Responsibility

Responsibility and Dasein

The first point to be borne in mind in any discussion of Heidegger and responsibility, is that if there is a notion of responsibility in his work it will not and cannot be that of *accountability* in the classical sense. Nor will it be, as in Levinas, its mere reversal. Rather, Heidegger will situate the question of responsibility outside of a problematic of the ego, outside of egology, and allow it to arise instead out of the very openness of being where the human being dwells as Dasein. The concept of responsibility has traditionally been associated, if not identified, with accountability, under the authority of a philosophy of free will and causality, which itself rested upon a subject-based metaphysics. Accountability—which has defined the traditional concept of responsibility, if not exhausted it—thus rests upon the notions of agency, causality, free will, and subjectivity. Responsibility *as* accountability thus designates the subject's capacity to be the cause of its acts, and ultimately to appropriate and "own" its acts and their meaning. In such an enframing, the phenomenological and ontological sources of what is called "responsibility" have remained obscure and neglected. The ambition of this chapter is to begin unfolding these ontological origins of responsibility. I will argue that Heidegger's thought provides key features which allow for a rethinking of what being-responsible as such could mean, namely, an ontological sense which is overlooked in the thought of accountability.

For Heidegger, responsibility cannot be accountability in the classical sense, for Heidegger's thinking of Dasein breaks decisively with the tradition of subjectivity.[1] Heidegger does not think the human being in terms of subject, and we also know that he does not think freedom in terms of free will or causality. This is the import of his thinking of Dasein: With the choice of this term, it was a matter for him of seizing the human being no longer as subject but in terms of the openness of being as such, and only in this respect. This is why the term, in later writings, is often hyphenated as Da-sein in order to stress the sheer relatedness to being, a relatedness that is not posited or initiated by us. Heidegger explained in a later text that with the term Dasein, it was a question for him of characterizing "with a *single* term both the relation [*Bezug*] of Being to the essence of man and the essential relation [*Wesenverhältnis*] of man to the openness ('there' [*Da*]) of Being [*Sein*] as such." To that end, "the name of 'Dasein' [there-being] was chosen for the essential realm [*Wesenbereich*] in which man stands as man."[2] That relation is not posited by human Dasein, but belongs to being itself. Responsibility will thus have to find another origin than that of the free autonomous subject. The basis for an identification of responsibility with accountability disappears in the thinking of being, which does not mean that it does not harbor another thought of responsibility. For responsibility does not disappear in the deconstruction of the *subjectum*. At the same time that Heidegger deconstructs the conceptual basis for any notion of accountability, he consistently maintains that Dasein—who is neither a subject nor an ego, nor a consciousness, person, or rational animal, nor even a man—is to be thought in terms of responsibility, in at least three respects: Responsibility defines the essence of Dasein as a concern for being; Dasein comes to itself in a responsiveness to a call; responsibility names man's relationship to being, that is, the co-belonging of being and man.

First, as I indicated above, the very concept of Dasein means to be a responsibility of and for oneself, as Dasein designates that entity in which being is at issue. Being is given in such a way that I have to take it over and be responsible for it. Dasein is delivered over to its being, it is "entrusted" with being or charged with the responsibility for its being (SZ, 41–42). Care, concern, solicitude, anxiety, authenticity, being-guilty, are all different names for such originary responsibility. Dasein is concerned about its own being, or about being as each time its own; this determination of Dasein from the outset defines it as a responsibility of being.

Second, responsibility is not thought as a consequence of a subject "owning" his or her actions, but is instead approached in terms of a response to an event that is also a call, thematized in *Being and Time* as the call of conscience and in later writings as the call or address (*Anspruch*) of being. Responsibility is not based on subjectness (accountability) but constitutes Dasein as the called one (responsiveness). Each time, Dasein is called to itself; this is a call that I have to answer. And therein lies the hidden source and resource of responsibility—to be responsible means, before anything else, to respond, *respondere*. In such a response, Dasein comes to itself. Dasein "has to be" the being that it is. Having to be oneself—such is the originary responsibility of Dasein, which can be heard in the "Become what you are!" evoked by Heidegger in *Being and Time* (SZ, 145). And this is not to be understood ontically as "Realize your potential!" but ontologically, as: What you are, you can only become it, because Dasein's being is "to-be," because "it *is* what it becomes or does not become" (SZ, 145). Dasein is defined by possibility, which as we know, "stands higher than actuality" (SZ, 38). In this "to-be" resides the ontological sense of responsibility as call to be, call of being. It is thus a responsibility that defines Dasein, insofar as it has to be its being in an originary "having-to-be." Dasein comes to itself from the call.

Third, after *Being and Time*, Dasein will be referred to more and more as "the called one" (*der Gerufene*), having to answer for the very openness and givenness of being and be its "guardian." To be responsible here means to have been struck, always already, by the event of being. Responsibility refers to that event by which being "enowns" humans, and represents human beings' very belonging to Being as well as their essence as humans. Let us look at each of these senses more closely.

1. One could go as far as to say that the very concept of Dasein *means* to be a responsibility. In the summer semester course in 1930, *The Essence of Human Freedom*, we read that self-responsibility (*Selbstverantwortlichkeit*) represents the very essence of the person: "*Self-responsibility* is the *fundamental kind of being* determining distinctively *human* action, i.e., *ethical praxis*" (GA 31, 263; EHF, 183). As we stressed, Dasein is that being for which and in which being is at issue. I am not myself as if I 'had' myself in the sense of a possession or a predicate; rather, I have being *to be* as my own, because such a being is addressed to me as a possible way of being, as a way to be, and not as a 'what.' I am not this being in the sense of a having, but I *have* this being *to be* (*Zu-sein*). Dasein is a being that never "is" what it is (as a present-at-hand being), because "The essence of this being lies in

its 'to be'" (SZ, 42). The being that I am is to be taken over. This determination of Dasein from the outset defines it as a responsibility. This is what the expression of "care" (*Sorge*) seeks to express, namely, the primordial responsibility of oneself that Dasein, as *Zu-sein,* is. Dasein does not "simply occur among other beings"; rather, Dasein "is concerned *about* its very being" (SZ, 12). This is why for the human being, the "ultimate demand," as Heidegger explains in the 1929–1930 lecture course on *The Fundamental Concepts of Metaphysics,* is that it "takes upon itself again, explicitly and expressly, its own Dasein and to be responsible for it" (GA 29/30, 254).

One recalls the well-known passage from *Sein und Zeit* where Heidegger writes that "The question of the meaning of Being is the most universal and the emptiest of questions, *but at the same time it is possible to individualize it very precisely for any particular Dasein*" (SZ, 39). On the one hand, this expression makes clear that the radical individuation of Dasein is no longer related to some subjective or individual ego-pole, but instead to being itself (Dasein is singularized only through being). It attests to the radical non-subjectivism of Heidegger's thinking of Dasein. On the other hand, and correlatively, it reveals that being itself, as Heidegger establishes in the very first paragraph of *Being and Time,* is not a generic universality but points toward its singularizing. Heidegger refers to this phenomenon as the "offensive" or "challenging" character of the question of being, its "strike-power," reaching to the singular being thus "touched" by being.[3] Being happens to Dasein. In its very givenness, being is singularized by "touching" or reaching Dasein, by engaging Dasein in its event. In this sense, being cannot be distinguished from the singular event of an existence that is each time delivered over to itself, and which is to that very extent responsible for itself. Being is thus nothing other than existence itself, which clarifies why fundamental ontology, though the existential analytic is subordinated to it, is located in an analysis of existence. Being engages a singular existence, thrown into its possibility-to-be, an existence that, *de facto,* can never relieve itself of its being—an existence that is encumbered with an original responsibility. Heidegger stresses that being is given to Dasein as its own alone. There lies the original responsibility of Dasein—no one can answer for this sending *in my place.* I must answer for being and can only do this in the first person. As Jean-Luc Marion explains, "the Dasein by itself can gain access to being only by properly putting itself at stake in the first person, by taking this risk as one exposes oneself to death."[4] Here, a generic conception of the universality of being is left behind. Existence is not a generic essence, but a responsibility "towards death," and being "in general" is declined only in this singular responsibility of factical existence. Existence then designates the phenomenon of being delivered over to oneself. "To be" immediately means "to be one's own," that is, to be oneself (the self is an existential phenomenon, not a substantial presence), for the essence of Dasein lies "in the fact that in each case it has its being to be, and has it as its own" (SZ, 12). This self-having does not imply that I have my being as a predicate, nor that it is posited by me. I belong to myself insofar as I am delivered over to the being that I am, and that I have to be as a possibility of being. Being is given to me in order that I be (ek-statically) its There, and be responsible for it. This self-having thus rests upon the givenness of existence, which *calls me* to be in an original responsibility.

2. We see from the outset that responsibility is not thought as a consequence of a subject whose actions can be imputed to it, but is instead approached in terms of a response to a call. I am *called* to be, and to make this being my own. This being-responsible originates, as we shall see, in an essential facticity of Dasein, that is, in its thrownness. Insofar as Dasein is not self-posited (like a transcendental subject), but is *thrown,* it has itself "announced" to itself, so to speak, by the call of existence. Indeed, I do not posit myself like a transcendental subject, but am called *to be* the being that I am. I am thrown in a having-to-be in its two senses of futurity and obligation. Dasein's delay with regard to itself, manifested in its being-called and its thrownness, obliges it to project its being in a having-to-be. I have to be the existence into which I am thrown (*being itself*) as my own. The I is thrown into its being in such a way that it comes out of this "throw" (*Wurf*) as *having to answer* for it. Dasein does not posit itself, but can only call itself, or better, be called to its own being. Ultimately, Dasein can only be as called. Further, the call is that which I *have to answer.* The call singularizes the existent and reveals the one called "as that which has been each time individuated [*jeweilig vereinzelte*] and which belongs to that particular Dasein" (SZ, 280; translation modified). And this not in some external or superficial way, but in the sense that "in the claim [*Forderung*], each Dasein must always conceive of this necessity for itself, from the ground of its essence" (GA 29/30, 255). Effectively, the call of conscience in its particular structure

as well as what it reveals manifests the essential constitution of Dasein. The I has to recognize itself as the called one, or as Jean-Luc Marion has written it, as "the summoned one" (*l'interloqué*). This having-to-be manifests an obligation which determines Dasein as a *responsibility for being*, one which the call of conscience will gives to hear as a being-guilty.

3. From the "interrogated" in the question of being in *Being and Time,* Dasein increasingly becomes described in the later works of Heidegger as the "called one" which as such has to answer for the very openness and givenness of being. The response to the call becomes rethought as belonging to the call, and ultimately as correspondence to being. In the lecture "What is Philosophy?" for example, Heidegger refers *antworten* ("to answer") to *ent-sprechen* ("to correspond"), so as to indicate that the response to the call (*Anspruch*) of being is an attuned listening, a responding as a corresponding that "listens [*hört*] to the voice" of being. "To answer" as "to correspond" means here a keeping of what being intones, a sheltering of the truth of being. In the *Zollikon Seminars,* Heidegger clarifies the sense of this correspondence, explaining that "The expression 'to correspond' means to answer the claim, to comport oneself in response to it. *Re*-spond [Ent-*sprechen*] → to answer *to* [Ant-*worten*]."[5] The response, we should stress, is not external to the call, but belongs intimately to it. This is why Heidegger stresses that the response does not follow the call, but is already given in the call, always already corresponding to the Saying (*Zusage*) of being, for this Saying has always already reached or touched man's being. In "The Turning," Heidegger evokes "the flashing [*Blitz*] of Being," and human beings are designated as "the ones who are struck" (*die Getroffenen*) in their essence by this "flashing" or "insight" (*Blick*) of being (Heidegger here plays on the proximity of *Blitz* and *Blick*).[6] Thought from the appropriation of humans to being, the Saying is an address that reaches us: Language's "vow is not empty. It has in fact already struck its target—whom else but man? For man is man only because he is granted the promise of language, because he is needful to language, that he may speak it."[7] Dasein cannot but answer the call, it has each time already answered, already said "yes" to this call of being, it has always already gained access to itself in such an answer, in a play of summons and response.

Responsibility would then designate humans' belonging to being, and the need that being has of us for its manifestation; in speaking of the "correspondence" of being and humans, Heidegger also speaks of being's "need" of humans for its givenness, and we will return to this. Humans are referred to as the guardians of the essence and truth of being, a task to which they are called. We are responsible insofar as we are claimed by being, which in turn needs us for its givenness. This is how Heidegger presents this circular (not a vicious circle, but the very opening of the open) phenomenon in the *Zollikon Seminars:*

> Being, the manifestness of being, is only given through the presence of beings. In order that beings can come to presence, and, therefore, that being, the manifestness of being, can be given at all, what is needed is the [ecstatic] standing-in [*Innestehen*] of the human being in the *Da* [there], in the clearing, in the clearedness [*Gelichtetheit*] of being as which the human being exists. Therefore, there cannot be the being of beings at *without* the human being.[8]

There cannot be the presence of being without the human receiving such presence. To this task, then, humans are called as always already appropriated by the event of being, in a correspondence that constitutes an original responsibility. In view of these considerations, we can say that the theme of the call of conscience in *Being and Time* anticipates Heidegger's later writings on the correspondence of Dasein to being in which such original responsibility (response, correspondence, attunement to being) represents the very essence of man.[9] To be responsible means here—to have been struck, always already, by the event and call of being. Responsibility designates such an event by which being "enowns" humans. It represents human beings' very belonging to being, as well as their essence as humans.

This thematic of the call, and the original responsibility it harbors, was elaborated in *Being and Time* as the call of conscience. In order to better understand the structure of the call of conscience in *Being and Time*, we need to return briefly to §9, where we find the following two propositions.

1) Dasein's "essence" is to exist: "The whatness (*essentia*) of this being must be understood in terms of its being (*existentia*) insofar as one can speak of it at all . . . *The 'essence' of Da-sein lies in its existence*" (SZ, 42).

2) The being of this being is each time *mine:* "That being which is an *issue* for this entity in its very being, is each time mine" (SZ,

42). Existence is each time *my* existence, that is, the existence of a being who relates to being as its own. Individuated existence is a way to be (*Weise zu sein*), a 'how' and not a 'what.' Indeed, existence is not the particularization of a universal essence, but the fact that being is put into play in the first person.

Heidegger thus conceives of the existence of this "I exist" as a "having-to-be," which itself is already manifesting the structure of a call.

One indeed notes a primordial responsibility in the very ontological constitution of Dasein. Dasein is first an opening, allowing for a relation to itself. Such self-relation is based on a concern, or a non-indifference to one's being. Heidegger presents Dasein as this being that *I am each time* in the sense that this being is not a matter of indifference to me and that, unlike present-at-hand entities, I have an interest in and am responsible for it. As the opening of all relations, existence first *opens* Dasein to the world that it is, to its being-with-others, and *to itself.* "It is peculiar to this entity that with and through its being, this being is disclosed to it" (SZ, 12). Self-relation arises out of the interest I have in that being that I have to be as a way of being. This opening to being (and to *our* own being) is what grounds the possibility of a self-relation. However, I do not constitute this opening but am thrown in it, called to exist in its throw. Here, existence is not to be understood as the immutable property of a being, but as a being that is addressed to me in such a way that I *have-to-be this being.* If existence is essentially determined as *Zu-sein,* having-to-be, then it is constituted in and by a certain obligation, a certain "call of being," if not a "law of Being" (*Gesetz des Seins*), according to a later expression. This is what Heidegger analyzes in *Being and Time* as the call of conscience, the site of an original, ontological responsibility.

The Call to Responsibility: An Authorless Call

The phenomenon of the call (*Ruf*) of conscience (*Gewissen*), which Heidegger analyzes in §§54–60 of *Sein und Zeit,* is generally interpreted as testifying to a turn from the improper mode of existence to the proper. Lost in the They, Dasein finds itself called (or called back) to its ownmost being, Heidegger presents this phenomenon within the framework of a problematic of "attestation" (*Bezeugung*), in which a proper *existential* possibility of Dasein is shown in an *existentiell* manner: "But because Dasein is *lost* in the 'they,' it must first *find* itself. In order to find *itself* at all, it must be 'shown' [*gezeigt*] to itself in its possible authenticity. In terms of its *possibility,* Dasein *is* already a potentiality-for-Being-its-Self, but it needs to have this potentiality attested" (SZ, 268). Surely the problematic of attestation is motivated by the fact that for Heidegger ontology must have an ontical basis. As Heidegger writes, "The roots of the existential analytic, on its part, are ultimately *existentiell,* that is, *ontical.* Only if the inquiry is itself seized upon in an existentiell manner as a possibility of the being of each existing Dasein, does it become at all possible to disclose the existentiality of existence and to undertake an adequately founded ontological problematic" (SZ, 13–14). Nonetheless, what is ultimately at stake in this attestation is the elucidation of an existential structure of Dasein, namely, the fundamental ontological constitution of Dasein in its own being-a-self as being-guilty. The call of conscience will reveal Dasein's originary responsibility as *Schuldigsein.* As Heidegger writes: "The call of conscience has the character of *summoning* Da-sein to its ownmost potentiality-of-being-a-self, by summoning it to its ownmost quality of being-guilty [*Schuldigsein*]" (SZ, 269).

It falls to the "voice of conscience," Heidegger writes, to attest to an authentic potentiality-of-being of Dasein. The fundamental character of conscience lies in the call, which, as such, *calls* Dasein to its ownmost potentiality-of-being-a-self. The call of conscience calls Dasein back to its own being. This is why Heidegger writes that "Conscience, in its basis and its essence, is *each time mine*" (SZ, 278), a statement that has led some commentators to speak of an autonomy or even solipsism of the call. The call is each time mine in two respects: On the one hand, because it is each time my ownmost being-a-self that is "called," and on the other hand, "because the call comes from that being which I am each time" (SZ, 278; translation modified). It would then seem that I am at once the origin and destination of the call, for Heidegger himself writes that "*Dasein calls itself in conscience*" (SZ, 275), and also that "Dasein is *at the same time* both the caller and the one summoned" (*Das Dasein ist der Rufer und der Angerufene* zumal) (SZ, 275).

Yet before we conclude that Dasein is closed upon itself in a solipsistic way, in a kind of soliloquy that would reproduce within some sphere of ownness of the self the Platonic 'dialogue of the soul with itself,'

or that the call of conscience manifests something like an 'auto-affection,' 'auto-interpellation,' or 'auto-nomy,' we ought to note that Heidegger does not say simply that the call comes 'from me.' Rather, the call
is said to come from the being "which I am each time." Now as we know,
I am this being only in the mode of a *zu-sein*, a having-to-be, that is, in
the manner of a possibility to be. I have to assume this being, whether
authentically or inauthentically. It does not therefore 'belong to me,' if
what is meant by this is projected by me. Nonetheless, I have to assume
it *as my own*. Therefore, when Heidegger writes that Dasein "calls itself,"
it does not mean that the 'I,' as author, is the origin of the call, and it does
not suppose a strict identity between the caller and the called one. In the
context of the passage, this statement intervenes when Heidegger is attempting to stress that the call does not come from an entity other than
Dasein, whether an ontical other or a theological other. Heidegger rejects
the theological notion of a call coming from God *and, in fact, from any
entity*. The theological representation of the call is also an ontical representation. Rather, to "call oneself" means that the call occurs in the dimension of the self, in which Dasein engages it, answers (for) it, takes it
on its shoulders, so to speak. What Heidegger seeks to claim is that there
is not an ontic origin of the call, and that there is not either a pre-given
subject or identity on the basis of which the call would be initiated. There
is no self at the basis of the call, because *the self itself arises out of the call*.
As conscience, Dasein calls from the bottom of its being; the one who
calls is neither a 'who' nor a 'what,' but Dasein itself in its bare 'that,' in
its sheer thrownness: "In its 'who,' the caller (*der Rufer*) is definable in a
worldly way by *nothing* at all. The caller is Dasein in its uncanniness:
primordial, thrown being-in-the-world as the 'not-at-home'—the bare
'that-it-is' in the 'nothing' of the world" (SZ, 276–277). The one summoned is Dasein lost in the They, called back to its ownmost being. The
call of conscience is thus above all a call *of* the self, in both senses of the
genitive. The self is not the author of the call, but is announced *in* and
as the call, since the caller disappears in the calling. Therefore what is at
issue in the call is nothing but the coming to oneself as such. This is
ultimately the meaning of the above-cited passage in which Heidegger
states that Dasein "calls itself." In the call, Dasein's being-a-self is at issue
and in play; the call is the space or the dimension of selfhood. Yet the
self is not the (ontical) origin of the call. The call makes itself heard in

the "space" or "dimension" of the self, as the "being from afar" of which Heidegger speaks. Dasein is not the author of the call, but comes to be in and *as* the call. I am called to myself, from afar. "The call is from afar unto afar. It reaches him who wants to be brought back" (SZ, 271). The call comes from afar, and "in passing" interrupts and constitutes—with shock and surprise, "the factor of a jolt, of an abrupt arousal" (SZ, 271)— the being who has always already been called to be itself.

This radical absence of a pre-given self-identity, the fact that the I is not self-posited but arises out of a non-subjective call, allows us to understand why the 'author' of the call, in a certain sense, escapes all attempts at identification (SZ, 274–275). The caller remains "in a striking indefiniteness," it "fails to answer questions about name, status, origin, and repute" (SZ, 274). The author of the call remains foreign, "absolutely distances any kind of becoming familiar" (SZ, 275). The 'caller' evades any attempt at identification simply because there is no 'author' of the call, no 'who' of the call—no God, no ego, no subject, no other person or other being whatsoever within the world. There is an origin to the call, but no agent. This agent is *other*, not as an anthropological or ontic other (for it does not let itself be identified as a 'who') but as *uncanny*. The 'caller' in fact merges with the calling itself, it is instead the very movement of the call which brings a self-to-come, it is the impersonal or pre-personal event of being that precedes and exceeds the one who will have to assume it as its own.

This is why Heidegger then clarifies that it is not sufficient to state that Dasein is *at the same time* the caller and the called one. For this "at the same time" is misleading; it is not synonymous with an identity of Dasein with itself. In fact, an asymmetry is becoming apparent: Heidegger asks, "When Dasein is summoned, *is* it not 'there' in another way from that in which it does the calling?" (SZ, 275). One needs to recognize a certain asymmetry in conscience allowing for the call to be heard. As Françoise Dastur remarks, this "interior knowledge [of conscience] thus supposes in some way that one makes oneself witness to oneself . . . But the witnessing of oneself demands that this Being-with-oneself be experienced in a rigorous dissymmetry, and this is brought forth by the call of the voice of conscience."[10] We should therefore qualify Heidegger's statements, "Dasein calls itself" or "the call comes from that being which I am each time" (SZ, 275, 278), as Heidegger himself invites us to do by noting the "formal character" of this "statement that Da-sein is at the same time the caller and the one summoned" (SZ, 277). Retrieved phenomenologically, these sentences say that the call comes from the being that I am (that is, *not* from another entity, an ontic other), but as something that *falls upon me*, thus in a sense, *as something that does not come from me*. This is why Heidegger clearly states that the "call is precisely something that *we ourselves* have neither planned nor prepared for nor willfully brought about" (SZ, 275). The call surprises me: "'It' calls, against our expectations and even against our will" (SZ, 275). Nonetheless, it calls *me*—"*es ruft micht*," we read (SZ, 277)—as if the self arose from the impersonal event of the call. It happens before me, without me, but nonetheless "it" happens only to me, because it calls me: *Es ruft micht*. The 'caller' is an "it," the event and advent of presence itself. Therein lies the verticality of the call, calling me from a height that is nonetheless not foreign to the self. These are the very terms that Heidegger uses: "The call comes *from* me and yet from *above and beyond* me": *Der Ruf kommt aus mir und doch über mich* (SZ, 275). In Jacques Derrida's words, "it falls *upon* the *Dasein* from *inside* itself" (GD, 46), an experience that is said to be the "basis" for autonomy in the Kantian sense. It is in this sense that conscience, as Françoise Dastur writes suggestively, is "the most intimate alterity," and autonomy is a heteronomy.

This alterity of the call is presented as a "phenomenal finding," from which there proceed the usual representations of the voice of conscience as an "alien power" arising "within Dasein." Autonomy is here founded upon a certain heteronomy, an alteration of the self, the self as what is other than the self, "oneself as another," a self that is constituted "right at" the other (*à même l'autre*). Thus it is correct to say that the caller and the called are "*at the same time* one's own Dasein *themselves*" (SZ, 279), if one recognizes that this sameness is not a simple identity, but that "thin wall" between the "authentic" self and the They (SZ, 278) of which Heidegger speaks. This difference is audible in the statement "*it* calls," or rather, the "*it* calls me" (*das es ruft micht*).

The Otherness of the Call

In that respect, the call of conscience manifests the heteronomy of the self. With respect to the alterity of the voice of conscience, Paul Ricoeur in *Oneself as Another* marks the dissymmetry of the call of conscience, a dissymmetry that will interrupt any autonomous self-relation, or introduce heteronomy in auto-nomy: "Unlike the dialogue of the soul with itself, of which Plato speaks, this affection by another voice presents a remarkable dissymmetry, one that can be called vertical, between the agency that calls and the self called upon."[11] This verticality, or asymmetry, prevents all autonomous closure of the self and in fact represents the irruption or the "breach" of transcendence within Dasein itself. This is what Françoise Dastur emphasizes, when she writes that "What is here essential for the verticality of the call (which constitutes the self as self)—that is, within the self-affection through which selfhood occurs, in the immanence of the self—is a breach of transcendence (i.e., the dimension of hetero-affection)" (HPP, 92). Auto-nomy is hetero-nomy, and the call of conscience is an auto-hetero-affection, manifesting the otherness at the heart of Dasein's selfhood. Because of this inscription of otherness in the coming to itself of the self, responsibility can no longer be for Heidegger a self-enclosed egological self-responsibility. As we know, Levinas opposes a responsibility for the other to self-responsibility. However, unlike Levinas, who situates the other outside of the ego (as exteriority), Heidegger inscribes otherness in the structure of the self as auto-hetero-affection, *rendering the opposition between a responsibility to the other and a responsibility-to-self moot.* This is what the determination of being-with as an existential of Dasein makes clear—the other is inscribed in the structure of selfhood. It is on the basis of this primordial openness of Dasein that a relation to others can occur. For as Heidegger puts it, hearing the call, the very capacity to hear the call "is Dasein's existential way of Being-open as Being-with for Others" (SZ, 163).

It is thus incorrect to claim that Heidegger privileged the 'pole' of the self over the openness to the other, or that he conceives of responsibility as being primarily for oneself, existence unfolding (an)ethically as an infamous 'struggle for existence.' Heidegger famously wrote that Dasein was essentially Being-with (SZ, 120), which means that being-with is co-extensive with Dasein's being-a-self. This situates the place and the necessity of the presence of the other in the existential analytic, and it can be situated properly only if one understands from the outset that it cannot be framed within an anthropological or egological enclosure. The other does not face an ego, as was the situation described by Levinas; rather the ego is instead a self, whose constitution is to be open, always already, to the other. The question of the other could only take the form of a question on the *being-*

with-others, outside of egology. No more than Dasein's selfhood can the other be reduced to egohood. This is why, one should note, the other cannot be approached in the context of egohood (as alter-ego), for instance in the schema of the "intersubjective" relation between the ego and the alter-ego. The other is not the alter-ego, it is not exterior to the ego. Heidegger explains this very clearly in the 1925–1926 winter semester lecture course titled *Logik: Die frage nach der Wahrheit*: "The other, the Thou, is not something like another ego to which my ego would be opposed."[12] In fact, Heidegger explicitly rejected social Darwinism as early as a 1921–1922 course, where he explains that "Caring is not a factually occurring *struggle for existence,* understood as elapsing and 'taking place' within so-called Objective unities of life" (PIA, 100). Care includes a care for others, because of the hetero-affection of Dasein and due to the fundamental constitution of Dasein as being-with. Heidegger consistently stressed the constitutive openness to the other of Dasein, from his early courses to his last seminars, as the following comment from the *Zollikon Seminars* reveals. Answering a question by Medard Boss as to the signification of the proposition from *Being and Time,* "Dasein is that being for which, in its being, that being is an issue," Heidegger replied: "Da-sein must always be seen as being-in-the-world, as concern for things, and as caring for other [Da-seins], as the being-with the human beings it encounters, and never as a self-contained subject."[13] To that extent, responsibility will always include a responsibility for others, because it is itself marked by otherness.

Such an otherness, which is inscribed in the dissymmetrical coming to itself of Dasein, or in the structure of self-affection which necessarily implies hetero-affection, is referred to in a 1928 lecture course, *The Metaphysical Foundations of Logic,* as a transcendental dispersion. This originary "dissemination" (*Zerstreutheit*) or "bestrewal" (*Streuung*) belongs to the essence of Dasein: "In its metaphysically neutral concept, Dasein's essence already contains a primordial bestrewal (*ursprüngliche Streuung*)" (GA 26, 173). The multiplicity that arises from such a dispersion affects primordial Dasein itself, and such a primordial dispersion represents a general, and of course, irreducible character of Dasein. Dasein can consequently never get hold of itself outside of this primordial dispersion, in some simple unity or identity. Even in the unity which is proper to it, Dasein cannot be thought outside of this (existential) stretching which primordially disseminates its being. This dissemination accounts for Dasein's being-with; there is not being-with because there are others, but on the contrary there are "others" only because being-with essentially belongs to Dasein. Further, there is no being-with except on the basis of this primordial dispersion and dissemination, to the extent that "being-with is a basic metaphysical feature of dissemination" (*das Mitsein eine metaphysische Grundbestimmung der Zerstreuung ist*) (GA 26, 175). It is this primordial dispersion that accounts for the essential openness and exposure of Dasein to the other.

Paradoxically, Heidegger's rejection of "empathy" (*Einfühlung*), understood as identification with the other, is based on this primordially open character of Dasein. Heidegger takes issue with empathy as a model for the relation to others precisely because that representation remains trapped within the egoistic understanding of selfhood. Thus, in *The Fundamental Concepts of Metaphysics,* he states that empathy, understood as the possibility to transpose oneself in another human being in the sense of identifying with an other, is a question "empty of content," "impossible," "meaningless," "absurd," and ultimately "superfluous" (GA 29/30, 301). Why? Simply because empathy is a possibility that *already* belongs to the being of Dasein as being-with—an existential structure that empathy inadequately designates. The question of knowing how the ego could come out of itself in order to then 'enter' into the other is an absurd question, for Dasein is always already 'in' others, that is, open to them. Empathy is thus derived from being-with, and presupposes it. Heidegger writes in *Being and Time:* "'Empathy' does not first constitute being-with; only on the basis of being-with does 'empathy' become possible" (SZ, 125). This being-with is so originary that it includes as deficient modes the difficulty in understanding others or genuinely accompanying them, loneliness and isolation, and conflictual relations in which one "walks away from one another" or two are "against one another" (GA 29/30, 302). In short, through this critique of *Einfühlung,* Heidegger violently challenges the "dogma that man would exist for himself as an individual, and that the individual ego would be, with its own sphere, precisely that which first and with most certainty is given to itself" (GA 29/30, 302). Starting with the correlation I-Thou solves nothing; the I-Thou correlation as the correlation of two egos would be a "solipsism for two." This is in fact what the notion of an 'existential solipsism' demonstrates, namely that it is not exclusive of a relation to the other. Responsibility for self will not be exclusive of a responsibility to others.

The notion of an existential solipsism appears paradoxically to be the basis for the possibility of being-with as such. On the one hand, Heidegger attributes actually experienced loneliness to the experience of a *lack* of the other, which thereby attests to the primacy of being-with. He thus explains that "Being-alone is a deficient mode of Being-with," that is, "the other can *be missing* only *in* and *for* a Being-with" (SZ, 120). On the other hand, and more radically, Being-with must be conceived of as co-extensive with metaphysical solitude, with Dasein's fundamental isolation. To understand this, we must begin by noting that each time Heidegger evokes the notion of solipsism, he does so in order to attack the Cartesian version of it, that is, the ego's *closure-upon-itself*. In fact, for Heidegger, the solipsist position of an isolated ego characterizes all of modern philosophy, from Descartes to Hegel[14] (and most likely Husserl as well), a tradition that he vigorously opposes. Thus, in *Basic Problems of Phenomenology* he rejects the "solipsism of the isolated I," and as we saw the "solipsism for two" represented by the I-Thou correlation, understood as the correlation of two egos. Heidegger's objective is not to derive being-with from the singular Dasein if one takes the latter to mean an isolated subject or ego. The singular Dasein is not an individual that exists in its own sphere. In *The Metaphysical Foundations of Logic,* Heidegger speaks of Dasein's "metaphysical isolation" (GA 26, 243/188), but this is to be distinguished from the individual self. Existential solipsism does not correspond to what it meant for Descartes, at the end of the Second Meditation, for example. Descartes's solipsism is that of an ego that is closed upon itself, a worldless ego without others; existential solipsism designates the solitude, isolation or individuation of the *existent.* As ex-istent, Dasein is essentially defined by its *openness* to beings. We thus have to think together Dasein's singularity and the opening to other beings and to others. Here, being-alone no longer means being closed upon oneself. The *solus ipse*—which is what Heidegger means by *existential* solipsism—far from signifying the closure of the ego upon itself that occurs with the reduction-destruction of the world, in fact opens Dasein to the totality of beings.[15]

Dasein is individuated as resolute being-toward-death. It is individuated in the sense that it is thrown back upon its ownmost possibility-of-being, which it is *alone* in being able to assume. Yet, as Heidegger insists, the responsibility that is resoluteness does not isolate Dasein in the sense of a free-floating 'I' separated from its world—and "how should it, when resoluteness as authentic disclosedness, is *authentically* nothing other than *Being-in-the-world*?" (SZ, 298). Anxiety isolates Dasein, but *as being-in-the-world and being-with-others*.[16] As an isolating mood, anxiety *opens* Dasein to its being, makes it free for beings. Heidegger explicitly makes the connection between Dasein's isolation and the opening to the world.

> Being-anxious discloses, primordially and directly, the world as world . . . the world as world is disclosed first and foremost by anxiety . . . Anxiety individualizes Dasein for its ownmost Being-in-the-world . . . Therefore . . . anxiety discloses Dasein as Being-possible, indeed as the only kind of thing which it can be of its own accord as something individualized in individualization. (SZ, 187–188)

As an openness to the world, resoluteness, understood in the sense of Dasein's proper selfhood, "pushes it into solicitous Being with Others" (SZ, 298), and this being-with-others is then *proper,* for resoluteness is what allows Dasein to let the others be others, that is, to leave them in their own, proper being. The proper existence that is chosen in resoluteness is therefore not a solipsism of the isolated I and could not be exclusive of others and the world, which, as *Mitsein* and *In-der-Welt-Sein,* are constitutive of Dasein. Consequently, "in choosing itself Dasein really chooses precisely its being-with-others and precisely its being among beings of a different character" (GA 26, 245/190).

This critique of egohood leads to the appropriation of the concept of Dasein as being-in-the-world, that is, precisely as a no-longer self-enclosed ego but an openness to beings as a whole. Dasein relates to itself, not as an isolated individual, but as openness to the whole of beings. Heidegger often specifies this openness in the following way: Dasein is opened to intraworldly entities, to the other Dasein, and to the entity that 'I am.' *The very concept of Dasein thus includes a responsibility to the other,* namely, to the other entity, to the other Dasein, and to itself as another. Heidegger often stresses that Dasein's being for the sake of itself should not be identified with an egoistic struggle for existence. In the *Beiträge* (for instance, §§48, 178, 179, and 197), he firmly rejects such a misunderstanding. Already at the time of *Sein und Zeit* and in the years immediately following its publication, Dasein's being-for-the-sake-of-itself—i.e., its self-responsibility—was said to be beyond or outside of the opposition of the ego and the alter-ego. It is rather to be thought, as Heidegger explains in a 1928 lecture course, in its "primordial metaphysical import," that is, as an ontological statement and not in its ontical or existentiell sense. Being-for-the-sake-of-oneself is the presupposition of ontic relations to oneself, and for this reason cannot be taken as a "solipsistic" or "egoistic" statement about Dasein's self-interest to the exclusion of others. Because of its ontological scope, *Dasein's self-responsibility in principle includes the possibility for Dasein to concern itself for others in their being.* Heidegger is then able to claim that being-for-the-sake-of-oneself is the "metaphysical ground of the possibility" that Dasein be "with others, for them and through them" (GA 26, 240). Being-responsible-for-oneself is a Being-responsible-for-others. Heidegger writes: "Being with Others belongs to the Being of Dasein, which is an issue for Dasein. Thus as Being-with, Dasein 'is' essentially for the sake of Others. This must be understood as an existential statement as to its essence" (SZ, 123).

One cannot oppose a 'care for others' to a 'care for oneself,' nor contrast examples of 'humane' sacrifices to Dasein's concern for itself, since "in choosing itself Dasein really chooses precisely its being-with-others and precisely its being among beings of a different character" (GA 26, 245). It should therefore come as no surprise if one of the forms of care (*Sorge*), as we know, is "care-for" others or solicitude (*Fürsorge*). This care or responsibility for others, which is an existential of Dasein, includes even those deficient modes that are "inconsiderateness" (*Rücksichtlosigkeit*) and "indifference" (*Naschsehen*). As deficient modes, these actually confirm Dasein's care for others. Heidegger distinguishes two fundamental modalities, or "extreme possibilities," of this caring-for-others: One kind of solicitude will consist in taking over the care of the other by substituting oneself for him or her; it consists in leaping in (*Einspringen*) for him or her, that is, in taking *away* his or her responsibility of being. This solicitude is clearly inauthentic, in at least three respects: First, because it treats the other Dasein as something ready-to-hand, as a *zuhandenes,* as Heidegger notes (SZ, 122); second, because it consists in taking the place of the other, taking "the other's 'care' away from him" (SZ, 122), such a substitution represents for Heidegger an inauthentic relation to others; and third, because it *disburdens* the other Dasein of his or her care and responsibility. Now the last is for Heidegger inauthenticity *par excellence,* if it is the case that inauthenticity consists in a fleeing of Dasein in the face of its own existence and of its weight, i.e., in being irresponsible. Inauthenticity thus means for Heidegger irresponsibility as a fleeing before one's ineluctable responsibility.

I can never be the other, I cannot take their responsibility away from them, though, in turn, I can never be without the other. Heidegger explains clearly in a 1929–1930 lecture course that to transpose oneself for another cannot mean taking the other Dasein's place, that is, by taking his or her responsibility. I can at most *accompany (mitgehen)* the other, and this is how Dasein is *with* others, this is how we are together. No identification, then, but accompaniment. In fact, everything takes place as if it was precisely the *disruption* of this commonality between the I and others, as Jean-Luc Nancy has emphasized, that provides the basis for the very emergence of the other *as other* and therefore for the very possibility of an ethics of responsibility. Heidegger mentions such an ethics of responsibility toward the other: This other kind of solicitude will not leap in for the other in order to unburden this other of his or her responsibility, but rather leaps *ahead of (vorausspringt)* the other so as to *free this other for* his or her own responsibility; "it helps the Other to become transparent to himself in his care and to become free for it" (SZ, 122). It frees the other for his or her own Being-toward-death and his or her own possibility-of-being; it therefore lets the other be *as other.* Authentic solicitude does not attempt to appropriate the other, but does justice to the infinite alterity of the other. Only in that sense can Dasein become, as Heidegger put it, the "conscience of others." It then appears that responsibility, once it is understood away from the tradition of egology, signifies an essential exposure to the other, and cannot simply be reduced to the responsibility of the "self-contained subject" of which the *Zollikon Seminars* spoke. Returning to the origins of responsibility thus allows one to reveal its otherness, which is in fact its very possibility. In addition to this inscription of otherness in responsibility, one notes as well that responsibility for Heidegger is tied to facticity, thrownness and finitude, to the extent that Heidegger will speak of a "facticity of responsibility" (*Faktizität der Überantwortung*) (SZ, 135). Far from any problematics of the accountability of a subject, responsibility will be understood as the assumption of our finitude, and as exposure to an inappropriable. This is what the analysis of the call of conscience reveals.

Responsibility to a Nullity

For what, in the end, does the call reveal? Heidegger tells us that it reveals Dasein's originary ontological constitution as "guilty." For Heidegger, the phenomenon of guilt, "which is not necessarily related to 'having debts' and law-breaking, can be clarified only if we first inquire in principle into Dasein's *being*-guilty—in other words, if we conceive the idea of 'Guilty!' in terms of Dasein's kind of being" (SZ, 283). The call of conscience will not reveal an ontical guilt (a moral guilt), but instead "discloses Dasein's most primordial potentiality-for-Being as Being-guilty (*Schuldigsein*)" (SZ, 288). The call or appeal (*Anruf*) calls Dasein out (*aufrufen*) to its being-guilty. Heidegger will attempt to grasp the *ontological* sense of guilt, distinguishing this sense from traditional representations of the phenomenon. The call of conscience has traditionally been interpreted as "bad conscience,"[17] as manifesting some type of fault, lack, debt or guilt. This is the common understanding of conscience: "All experiences and interpretations of the conscience are at one in that they make the 'voice' of conscience speak somehow of 'guilt'" (SZ, 280). But since what is at issue in Heidegger's analysis is not a religious or moral meditation on guilt or sin, but rather on the ontological constitution of Dasein, the first step will be to distinguish *being*-guilty from inadequate (ontical) characterizations thereof, such as moral fault or being indebted for something. Being-guilty refers to ontological constitution of Dasein. In fact, in being-guilty (*Schuldigsein*) the stress is on the "being" (*Schuldig*sein): It is as guilty that *I am*. In being-guilty it is being, the "I am," which is determinative. The complete statement of the "I am" is thus "I am guilty." This is why Heidegger writes: "But where do we get our criterion for the primordial, existential meaning of 'guilty'? From the fact that this 'guilty!' turns up as a predicate of the 'I am'" (SZ, 281). This being-guilty, as we will see, should instead be understood in the sense of an archi-ethical responsibility which is related to the very ontological constitution of Dasein. In being-guilty, the constitution of Dasein as delivered over to itself, as thrown into a responsibility, will appear. This is what the first lines of §9 of *Being and Time* already suggest: "We are ourselves the entities to be analyzed. The being of any such entity is each time mine. These entities, in their being, comport themselves towards their Being. As beings with such being, they are charged with the responsibility [*überantwortet*] for their own Being" (SZ, 41–42; translation modified).

The ontological or archi-ethical (rather than moral or ethical) scope of these statements cannot be missed here, as Paul Ricoeur rightly notes: "The introduction late in the discussion of the notion of *Schuld*," he writes, "by no means restores any ethical connotation to this uncanniness. The accent falls heavily on *sein* in *Schuldigsein* . . . If some failing is revealed here, it is not evil—war, Lévinas would say—but an ontological trait prior to any ethics" (OA, 349). In short conscience is, in Ricoeur's words, "beyond good and evil," or we might say, following Heidegger, "before" them.[18] In this ontological elucidation of guilt, we should follow the only possible trail, that of the "I am." This trail must nonetheless go through the common explanations of guilt, if it is the case that "whenever we see something wrongly, some injunction as to the primordial 'idea' of the phenomenon is revealed along with it" (SZ, 281). Heidegger identifies two main interpretations from the everyday understanding of guilt—guilt in the sense of debt, of owing something to someone; and guilt in the sense of being responsible for something ("he is guilty of . . ."), that is, being the cause or agent of something. Both senses, in any case, "will drop out" (SZ, 283) in an ontological analysis, or at least give way to more primordial motifs which give access to the existential sense of being-guilty.

These common senses of being-guilty can be combined into a single determination, namely, that of being at fault with regard to another person, of having harmed or wronged another. More formally, Heidegger states this determination as *being the basis for a lack of something in the Dasein of an other*. In both cases, guilt is seen "as a *lack* [*Mangel*]—when something which ought to be and which *can* be is missing [*Fehlen*]" (SZ, 283). Since the very concept of lack, however, does not apply to Dasein (lack is only of something that can be present-at-hand), this is an inadequate determination. "To be missing, however, means not-Being-present-at-hand. A lack, as the not-Being-present-at-hand of something which ought to be, is a definite sort of Being which goes with the present-at-hand."[19] This is why existence *lacks nothing*, not because it is finished or complete, but because in itself it escapes all problematics of lack and completion (and therefore of incompletion, as well). Even the not-yet of Dasein, such as death, is not be taken as missing: We *are* our own not-yet.

Being-*guilty* can be clarified only if one approaches it from the mode of being proper to Dasein, if one questions *being*-guilty as such while keeping one's distance from the realm of the everyday or the problematic of breaking the law. Heidegger does, however, retain two aspects of the common understanding of guilt that nonetheless reveal its ontological senses: In each characterization we find the idea of a negation, of a "not" (which remains to be determined ontologically), as well as the idea of responsibility—i.e., the fact of being the agent or cause of this "not." The "guilty!" can then be defined as "Being-the-basis of a nullity" (*Grundsein einer Nichtigkeit*) (SZ, 283). The existential concept of being-guilty can ultimately be understood only on the basis of the very structure of care, understood as the unity of thrownness and existentiality. "Care itself, in its very essence, is permeated with nullity through and through. Thus 'care'—Dasein's Being—means, as thrown projection, Being-the-basis of a nullity (and this Being-the-basis is itself null). This means that *Dasein as such is guilty.*"[20] The call of conscience summons a Dasein that is lost in the They back to its ownmost ontological constitution, which is to be guilty, that is, for Heidegger, *to be thrown:* The "nullity" lies in the fact of *not* being the basis of one's own being, of being *thrown* into existence; the "guilt" lies in the fact that I must make myself the origin or basis of this existence of which *I am not* the origin. How are we to understand this paradoxical structure? Dasein exists as thrown, that is to say, it did not bring *itself* into existence by first projecting itself on the basis of a pre-existing self. This thrownness constitutes the "nullity" of Dasein, as well as its paradox: Dasein at once belongs to itself and yet did not give itself to itself.

Dasein is thrown. Dasein is a not a self-posited ego but a thrown existence.[21] This means that it "has been brought into its 'there,' but *not* of its own accord" (SZ, 284). This also means that Dasein can never go back "behind its thrownness in such a way that it might first release this 'that-it-is-and-has-to-be' from *its Being*-its-self and lead it into its 'there'" (SZ, 284). There lies the fundamental and irreducible impotence or powerlessness of Dasein. *Dasein can never overcome the finitude of thrownness.* Heidegger would speak of such powerlessness in a course titled *Einleitung in die Philosophie,* claiming that the fact

> that by its own decision Dasein has nothing to search for in the direction
> of its origin, gives an essential prod to Dasein from the darkness of its
> origin into the relative brightness of its potentiality-for-Being. *Dasein*

exists always in an essential exposure to the darkness and impotence of its
origin, even if only in the prevailing form of a habitual deep forgetting in
the face of this essential determination of its facticity.[22]

There lies the powerlessness of Dasein, and there lies as well the "being-guilty" of which Heidegger speaks in *Being and Time*. Indeed, Dasein
is not thrown only once and for all; thrownness "does not lie behind it as
some event which has happened to Dasein, which has factually befallen
and fallen loose from Dasein again" (SZ, 284). Rather, "as long as Dasein
is, Dasein, as care, *is* constantly its 'that-it-is'" (SZ, 284). I am thrown into
existing, that is, into a possibility to be, a "having-to-be." Dasein exists only
in such a way that it projects itself toward possibilities in which it is thrown.
What it has to be, then, what it has to assume and be responsible for, is
precisely its being-thrown as such. Dasein is thrown in such a way that,
each time, it *has to be* this being-thrown, that is, *it has to be this not-being-
itself-the-basis-for its being.* Heidegger writes, "Although it has *not* laid that
basis *itself,* it reposes in the weight of it, which is made manifest to it as a
burden by Dasein's mood" (SZ, 284). I will return to this weight of responsibility in relation to moods shortly, but at this point we need to stress the
paradox of being-guilty, the paradox of being a "thrown basis." On the one
hand, there is in this thrownness the idea of a "not," of an impotence, and
on the other hand, being-a-basis refers to the ordinary sense of responsibility as being the cause or author of something. Hence the formal existential
definition of the idea of guilt as "Being-the-basis for a Being which has been
defined by a 'not'—that is to say, as *'Being-the-basis-of a nullity'*" (SZ, 283).
Being-guilty reveals the following paradox: It is this very thrownness that
I will have to appropriate, this very lack of authorship that I will have to
make myself the author of. The call of conscience calls me to make myself
the author of a being of which I am not the author. I am the paradoxical
unity of a thrown origin. This is the very weight of responsibility, as it
registers this incommensurability of being a thrown origin, of having to
make myself the basis of that of which I am not—and cannot be—the basis.
Let us develop this incommensurability: Being-a-basis means *"never* to
have power over one's ownmost Being from the ground up" (SZ, 284), and
making of that "never" the task of each time in existing. "The Self, which
as such has to lay the basis for itself, can *never* get that basis into its power;
and yet, as existing, it must take over Being-a-basis" (SZ, 284). Ultimately
for Heidegger, being-a-basis—that is, "never existing before its basis, but

only from it and as this basis" (SZ, 284), or existing (projecting) as thrown (projected)—presents the paradox or aporia of a responsibility-for having-to appropriate the inappropriable, in an experience of the impossible which Derrida will thematize as the very experience of responsibility.

To that extent, the expression "to be the basis of a nullity" is for Hei-degger a positive proposition, and *Nichtigkeit* a positive term. The "not" of being-guilty should be understood positively: As being-a-basis, I *am* my-self a nullity, which implies that this "not" has nothing in common with the negativity of a lack or privation. The "not," Heidegger insists, "is con-stitutive for this *Being* of Dasein—its thrownness" (SZ, 284). Being-the-basis does not have the same "not-character" of something that would be not-present-at-hand or not-subsisting. Being-a-basis in a positive sense means to exist, as we saw, "*from this basis* and *as this basis*" (SZ, 284). Da-sein did not lay this basis itself, but exists as this thrown basis, making that thrownness exist, so to speak: Thrownness is not a fact that has happened, but the throw into existence. This is why Heidegger concludes that Dasein "has been *released* [entlassen], not *through itself* [Nicht durch es selbst] but *to itself* [an selbst] so as to be *as this basis*" (SZ, 285). Responsibility as being-guilty signifies being-a-basis, that is, being and taking-on an inappropri-able, the very inappropriability of existence.

The call of conscience thus calls me back from the disburdened (de-responsibilized) existence in the everyday, back to my own being-guilty. The meaning of the call of conscience, once it is distinguished from its theological, moral or ontic interpretations, consists in the recognition that is has nothing to do with what I may have done or not done. Being-guilty is instead grasped in its ultimate ontological import.[23] Dasein is guilty from the ground up,[24] which means that guilt is not a fault that could be repaired or avoided, but the ontological constitution that I have to be authentically. Dasein must exist resolutely toward its own being-guilty: "Dasein need not first load a 'guilt' upon itself through its failures or omissions; it must only *be* 'guilty' *authentically*—'guilty' in the way in which it is" (SZ, 287). The summons to being-guilty "signifies a call-ing-forth to that potentiality-for-being which in each case I as Dasein am already" (SZ, 287). Existing authentically can mean only taking over or making oneself responsible for this "not." In short, taking-on one's finitude if it is the case, as Heidegger says in his 1929–1930 course, that finitude is characterized by "groundlessness" (*Grund-losigkeit*), or by the "concealment of the ground" (*Grund-verborgenheit*) (GA 29/30, 306). Heidegger states this quite clearly. By choosing itself, Dasein chooses its being-guilty and its finitude: "in so choosing, Dasein makes possible its ownmost being-guilty" (SZ, 288). Resoluteness, then, is the self-projection into one's ownmost being-guilty, the appropriation of this inappropriable. Heidegger writes:

> What one resolves upon in resoluteness has been prescribed ontologically in the existentiality of Dasein in general as a potentiality-for-Being in the manner of concernful solicitude. As care, however, Dasein has been determined by facticity and falling. Disclosed in its "there," it maintains itself both in truth and in untruth with equal primordiality. This "really" holds in particular for resoluteness as authentic truth. Resoluteness appropriates untruth authentically (*Sie eignet sich die Unwahrheit eigentlich zu*). (SZ, 298–299)

When I answer the call of conscience authentically, I do not make myself innocent; on the contrary, I project myself onto my *ownmost* "being-guilty," I free myself *for* being-guilty. To hear the call correctly

> is thus tantamount to having an understanding of oneself in one's ownmost potentiality-for-Being—that is, to projecting oneself upon one's *ownmost* authentic potentiality for becoming guilty. When Dasein lets itself be called forth to this possibility this includes its *becoming free* for the call—its readiness for the potentiality of getting appealed to. In understanding the call, Dasein is *in thrall to* [hörig] *its ownmost possibility of existence*. It has chosen itself. (SZ, 287)

My freedom is not limited by the inappropriability of my thrown existence, by this irremediable lagging behind my being: "Dasein constantly lags behind its possibilities" (SZ, 284). It is instead founded therein. The dispossession or expropriation that comes to light in my incapacity to make myself the author or master of my existence is precisely what opens this existence to itself, what frees it for itself. In this sense, by resolutely projecting being-guilty, Dasein appropriates the inappropriable *as* inappropriable. *I must be the improper (inauthentic) properly (authentically).*

Jacques Derrida follows Heidegger on this question; one need only think of the passage in the "Letter on Humanism" where we read, "What throws in projection is not man but Being itself, which sends man into the ek-sistence of Da-sein that is his essence." Derrida notes that this throw of thrownness is a "throw that Dasein cannot make its own in a project, in the sense of *throwing itself* as a subject that is the master of the throw."[25] Derrida thus stresses the inappropriability of thrownness, the impossibility of appropriating it. However, we should qualify this, for if indeed the throw does not occur on the part of Dasein, it is neither that which Dasein "cannot make its own" since this thrownness *is* its own! Thrownness is surely for Dasein the *inappropriable* itself, but Dasein is this inappropriable *itself*, as we saw in the analysis of being-guilty, which is taken on and projected by Dasein. As we recall, Heidegger stated that the "nullity" of Dasein is a positive phenomenon; this means that nullity is taken on in existence, in fact is the very motion of existence.[26] Death also is an inappropriable, but it is for Heidegger my ownmost possibility, even as possibility of the impossibility of existence. I can never get back behind or before the throw, and yet it is from it that I have to be the being that *I am*. Strictly speaking, then, responsibility as being-guilty signifies *the appropriation of the inappropriable, as inappropriable.* This is why, as I will attempt to show below through a discussion of passages from the *Contributions to Philosophy,* one cannot confuse authenticity, the proper, and property in the sense of reducing or taking what is other as a possession. To appropriate the inappropriable does not mean to maintain some sphere of ownness for Dasein, but to let that inappropriable be in and as one's existence.

The Facticity of Responsibility

Being-guilty, call of conscience, thrownness, taking-on the inappropriable—all of these motifs point to *facticity* as the site of ontological responsibility. Responsibility is to be thought in such facticity, as Heidegger stresses when he forges the expression *Faktizität der Überantwortung,* the "facticity of responsibility" (SZ, 135). The place and role of facticity cannot be underestimated in this rethinking of responsibility. As Merleau-Ponty famously stated, phenomenology as such can be defined as a return to facticity, away from idealistic constructions of metaphysical thought. Phenomenology is not about essences but rather is concerned with the facticity of existence: "Phenomenology," he writes, is "a philosophy which places essences back into existence, and does not expect to arrive at an understanding of man and the world from any starting point other than that of their 'facticity.'"[27] One knows the centrality of the notion of facticity, or "factical life" (*faktische Leben*), in the development of Heidegger's thought. Facticity (which is not to confused, as we saw, with Sartre's understanding of factuality or contingency) is an irreducible phenomenon for Heidegger, which cannot be "reduced" through some idealistic or transcendental intellectual operation. Nor can it be overcome by a transcendent freedom, as Sartre suggests in *Being and Nothingness,* when he explains that "it is impossible to grasp facticity in its brute nudity, since all that we find of it is already recovered and freely constructed" (BN, 132). Heidegger stressed that facticity is an *irreducible* phenomenon for philosophy, indeed the very horizon of philosophizing, philosophy itself being rooted in facticity and arising out of it as its self-interpretation: Philosophizing is factical life interpreting itself.[28] As early as his 1921–1922 lecture course on Aristotle, Heidegger wrote that the determinations of factical life

> are not merely trivial and arbitrary observations, such as the statement that "the thing there is red." Furthermore, it must be understood that they are alive *in facticity;* i.e., they include factical possibilities, from which they are (thank God) never to be freed. Therefore a philosophical interpretation which has seen the main issue in philosophy, namely, facticity, is (insofar as it is genuine) factical and specifically philosophical-factical. (PIA, 74)

The very element of philosophizing, then, is facticity. Facticity is also the element of the ethical and of responsibility.

This claim might seem at first paradoxical; the very motif of facticity, with its senses of opacity, finitude, and expropriation could indeed be seen as a challenge to the very possibility of responsible assumption. Indeed, facticity designates precisely not only what I am not responsible for, but also what I cannot in principle appropriate. However, although it represents for Heidegger an irreducible opacity and even expropriation for the human being, facticity should not be understood as an obstacle or an external limit to the possibility of responsibility and freedom, but rather as its very condition. There is a sense of responsibility which does *not* amount to accountability and which is *not* necessarily a simple appropriation and thus a reduction of facticity. In turn, facticity is not what opposes the position of a consciousness, but the "throw" of an existence that is called from such a throw to appropriate what will always remain inappropriable for it ("responsibility to a nullity"). Ultimately, one is responsible *from* out of the facticity of existence, and *for* it. Responsibility will then manifest the essential exposure of human beings to an inappropriable that always remains "other" for them. The sense of responsibility that will then emerge can no longer be confused with *accountability*, but will signify instead the very movement of a radically finite existence having to come to itself, and to itself as other, from an inappropriable (and thus always "other") ground. I will begin by identifying such inappropriability at the heart of existence in the phenomenon of moods.

Inappropriable Facticity

The first extensive engagement with facticity in *Being and Time* could be said to intervene in the discussion of moods or *Befindlichkeit*, at §§29–30.[29] We know the ontological import of these affective dispositions or moods, readily translated into the existential vocabulary of *Sein und Zeit*, as *Geworfenheit*: Facticity is given to be read in the phenomena of moods. Thrownness is *felt* in the mood, a mood that manifests an ontological truth of Dasein. What is most striking in those descriptions is how Heidegger describes moods (*Stimmungen*), in *Being and Time*, by emphasizing the element of opacity and withdrawal in them that seems to interrupt and foreclose any possibility of cognitive or practical appropriation. Heidegger explains that moods are beyond the reach of both will and cognition. In moods, which are a mode of disclosure, Dasein is said to be able to "burst forth as a naked 'that it is and has to be'" (SZ, 134). Moods disclose the being of the there in its "that it is." Heidegger writes: "A mood makes manifest 'how one is, and how one is faring.' In this 'how one is,' having a mood brings Dasein to its 'there'" (SZ, 134). Moods lead Dasein before the pure "that" of its There—which as such, Heidegger writes in a striking formulation, "stares at it [Dasein] with the inexorability of an enigma" (SZ, 136). Heidegger states that in being-in-a-mood, "Being has become manifest as a burden [*Last*]"; he then adds, "One does not *know why*" (SZ, 134). And he continues as to this "why," to say that Dasein "*cannot* know why" (SZ, 134; my emphasis). Cognition falls "far short," not because of some weakness of our cognitive powers, which could somehow be improved, but because of the peculiar phenomenon of moods as they exhibit the facticity of Dasein. And what is peculiar with this phenomenon is that the "that" of our being is given in such a way that "the whence and whither *remain obscure*" (SZ, 134; my emphasis). This is why cognition falls short: In the phenomenon of moods, there is a remaining withdrawn or obscurity that is irreducible. It is, Heidegger writes, a characteristic of Dasein's being (SZ, 135). Against this darkness or opacity any enlightenment is powerless, whether theoretical or practical. Facticity is "beyond the range of disclosure" of both cognition and volition, beyond their possibilities of mastery. This indicates that "against the phenomenal facts of the case," all the ideals of rational enlightenment "count for nothing" (SZ, 135). Moods thus reveal the opacity and inappropriability of our origins.

There is therefore a dimension in our being that resists appropriation. That dimension is nothing other than our very coming into being, and the sheer inappropriability of it. This, of course, mobilizes the question of birth. It is often said, following Hannah Arendt, that Heidegger neglected the phenomenon of birth and privileged being-toward-death. Notwithstanding the fact that thrownness *is* the ontological name for birth, and that in later seminars his writings on *physis* can be seen as a reflection on birth understood in a non-biological or naturalistic way,[30] it could be said that any discussion of thrownness and facticity already includes a reflection on birth. One might add that the question of birth is addressed explicitly in §72 of *Being and Time*. Dasein is said to exist *between* birth and death, not in the sense that Dasein would occupy an actual place between two external limits, but as stretching itself between birth and death, which means that Dasein *is* the between of birth and death. Being that between, Dasein exists toward each of them; it exists toward death, *and it exists toward birth*. This is why Heidegger explicitly writes of a "Being-toward-the-beginning," a *Sein zum Anfang* (SZ, 373).

Dasein exists "toward-the-end." But there are two ends, namely, birth and death. So principally, birth is an integral part of the existential analytic, and it is not accurate to say that Heidegger *ignored* or neglected the question of birth. Further, the charge that he *privileged* death over birth rests upon questionable philosophical assumptions—first, that birth and death are somehow opposed as phenomena, and second that one leaves birth "behind," so to speak, so as to only relate to death. Heidegger shows that in a sense birth and death should be thought as part of the *same* phenomenon, or that at least they should not be opposed. He for instance stresses that I am not born once in order to leave that event behind, so that I now only exist toward death (which is the basis of Hannah Arendt's critique of Heidegger in *The Human Condition*); rather, the event of birth is happening each time as I exist, stretching between birth and death, as being-toward birth and toward death. I am thus each time beginning, each time coming into being anew. Heidegger explains this very clearly: "Understood existentially, birth is not and never is something past in the sense of something no longer present-at-hand; and death is just as far from having the kind of Being of something still outstanding, not yet present-at-hand but coming along" (SZ, 374). As beginning, I am already dying. I exist as born, I exist as dying—the same event. I am born into death. "Factical Dasein exists as born; and as born it is already dying, in the sense of Being-towards-death" (SZ, 374). Dasein exists as born, that is, "in a natal manner," which immediately means, "always already dying." We thus exist both in a 'natal' way and in a 'mortal' way, in the sense that we relate to both of our ends. But are they really 'ours'? In fact, they remain for Heidegger inappropriable: I can no more go back behind my coming into being than I can appropriate death by making it somehow actual. Facticity, understood as thrownness, reveals that Dasein can never go back beyond this 'throw' to recapture its being from the ground up. Dasein can never become master of, can never appropriate its own ground and origins. I am thrown into existence on the basis of a completely opaque (non)ground which withdraws from all attempts at appropriation. It would then seem that in facticity I am expropriated from my own being, thereby rendering any meaningful sense of responsibility impossible. Facticity seems to represent a radical expropriation for the human being.

In "The Passion of Facticity,"[31] Giorgio Agamben underlines that facticity entails an element of non-originarity, and therefore of non-propriety, which is the very mark of finitude. "What is important here," Agamben writes, "is that for Heidegger, this experience of facticity, of a constitutive non-originarity, is precisely the original experience of philosophy, the only legitimate point of departure for thinking" (PF, 93). Drawing on an etymological analysis of the term, Agamben shows that "originally," facticity or *facticius* is opposed to *nativus,* and signifies "what is not natural, what did not come into Being by itself" (PF, 93) but was rather produced or made.[32] The factical means what is made (Descartes, in the Third Meditation, speaks of those ideas which are *factae,* are "produced" by me), and therefore means what is non-originary, if not non-true or false (as in the English "factitious," when one speaks of a "factitious illness or disorder" such as Munchausen syndrome). Agamben traces Heidegger's account of facticity to his reading of Augustine, who contrasted *facticius*—that which is made by humans and is unnatural and artificial—with *nativus* as that which is natural and created by God. This indicates that the term factical can be situated in "the semantic sphere of non-originarity and making" (PF, 93). For Agamben, the "originary facticity" of Dasein signifies that Dasein's opening is marked by an original *impropriety*. Such is the passion of facticity, a passion "in which man bears this nonbelonging and darkness" (PF, 107). This will allow Agamben to claim a "primacy of the improper" in Heidegger's thought of being. As he puts it, on Heidegger's account of facticity, "Dasein cannot ever appropriate the being it is, the being to which it is irreparably consigned" (PF, 100).

Does this indicate the failure and impossibility of responsibility, as that capacity to be properly one's own? And is it not precisely what Heidegger called Dasein's "being-guilty" (*Schuldigsein*) the essential "nullity" (*Nichtigkeit*) in Dasein's being? We should not be too quick to come to this conclusion, and Agamben's reading—granting a priority of the improper over the proper—may suffer from an overly oppositional (i.e., non-phenomenological) account of the proper and the improper, which conceals the possibility that the inappropriable (i.e., *Nichtigkeit*) may in fact be the secret resource of appropriation (i.e., responsibility as properly being one's own). To that extent, facticity might be the secret resource of responsibility. We recall how for Heidegger to be thrown is to be thrown into a responsibility, which means that one needs to understand facticity, as Heidegger invites us to do, as the facticity *of* responsibility;[33] this immediately means, in turn, that responsibility will be *for* that very thrownness. In *Einleitung in die Philosophie,* Heidegger thus explains that precisely that over which Dasein is not master must be "worked through" and "survived." He writes:

> Also that which does not arise of one's own express decision, as most things for Dasein, must be in such or such a way retrievingly appropriated, even if only in the modes of putting up with or shirking something; that which for us is entirely not under the control of freedom in the narrow sense . . . is something that is in such or such a manner taken up or rejected in the How of Dasein. (GA 27, 337)

If thrownness does not designate some fall from a higher realm, but the very facticity from which Dasein becomes a care and a responsibility for itself, then the weight of existence is from the outset an original responsibility.

The Weight of Responsibility

Let us thus dwell on this motif of weight, as it seems to harbor both the expropriation of facticity and the possibility of ethical responsibility. Ordinary language does speak of the connection between ethics, responsibility, and weight: One speaks of responsibility in the sense of carrying a weight, of "shouldering" a burden (and one notes here the etymological connection with the German *Schuld* and *schuldig*). Heidegger speaks of the human being as a being who is burdened or heavy with a weight, in a situation of care and concern, in contrast to the lightness or carelessness of irresponsible being. Heidegger thus evokes the fundamentally "burdensome character of Dasein, even while it alleviates the burden" (SZ, 134). So-called "moods of elation," which do lighten the burden, are said to be possible only on the basis of this burdensome character of Dasein's being. Dasein *is* a caring, and thus has being at issue for it. Being is a task, a weight I have to carry and be "responsible for." Dasein has to carry the weight of being, heavy with the responsibility for being and for its own being. In his early lecture courses, Heidegger stated that "factical life" (later renamed Dasein) is a fundamental caring, marked by the difficult weightiness of a task, and affected by an irreducible problematicity and questionableness. That weight, Heidegger claims in 1921–1922, "does not accrue to life from the outside, from something that lacks the character of life, but is instead present in and with life itself" (PIA, 75). Due to this burdensome character of factical life, Heidegger adds, "Factical life is always seeking the easy way" (PIA, 81). Responsibility as the carrying of the weight of existence is the originary phenomenon, and irresponsibility—that is, making things easy—is derivative. One sees this phenomenon in the so-called "difficulty of life." With respect to such difficulty, Heidegger stresses the following in his 1922 piece, "Phenomenological Interpretations in Connection with Aristotle" (not to be confused with his 1921–1922 lecture course on Aristotle):

> A characteristic of the being of factical life is that it finds itself hard to bear. The most unmistakable manifestation of this is the fact that factical life has the tendency to make itself easy for itself. In finding itself hard to bear, life *is* difficult in accord with the basic sense of its being, not in the sense of a contingent feature. If it is the case that factical life authentically

is what it is in this being-hard and being-difficult, then the genuinely fitting way of gaining access to it and truly safekeeping it can only consist in making itself hard for itself.[34]

The weight is here the weight of existence itself, an existence which is, as Heidegger puts it, "worrying about itself" (HS, 118). This weight designates the facticity of our experience, a facticity to which we are assigned and have to carry as our very finitude. What is the ethical import of such weight?

The inappropriable in existence (facticity), as we have seen in the phenomena of moods, is primarily felt as a weight or a burden. What weighs is the inappropriable. It is no accident that when he analyzes the disclosedness of existence into a There, that is, into an affective disposition, Heidegger speaks of a "burden" (*Last*). The being of the there, Heidegger writes, "become[s] manifest as a burden" (SZ, 134). But interestingly, the very concept of weight and burden reintroduces, as it were, the problematic of responsibility. In a marginal note added to this passage, Heidegger later clarified: "Burden: what weighs (*das Zu-tragende*); human being is charged with the responsibility (*überantwortet*) of Dasein, appropriated by it (*übereignet*). To carry: to take over one's belonging to being itself" (SZ, 134). The burden is described as "what weighs," as what has to be carried. The weight of facticity, i.e., the burden, is to be carried; Heidegger indicates that the taking-on of facticity is the carrying of the weight. The weight is facticity, and carrying is the taking-on of facticity—such is the "facticity of responsibility." The sentence continues thus: "man is charged with the responsibility (*überantwortet*) of Dasein, appropriated by it (*übereignet*)."

What Dasein has to be, and what it has to be responsible for, then, is precisely its very facticity, its being-thrown as such. What I have to make my own is thus what can never belong to me, what evades me, what will always have escaped me. As we saw, Heidegger underscored this incommensurability when he claimed that "The self, which as such has to lay the basis for itself, can never get that basis into its power; *and yet, as existing, it must take over being-a-basis*" (SZ, 284; my emphasis). For Heidegger, I am not thrown once to then exist freely, as Sartre believed; rather, I am delivered over to an existence that, because it has no ground, puts me in the situation of having to appropriate this absence of ground. As Agamben explains: "Everything is complicated, in Heidegger, by the fact that Dasein is not simply, as in Sartre, thrown into the 'there' of a given contingency; instead, Dasein must rather itself be its 'there,' be the 'there' (*Da*) of Being"

(PF, 92). This is what weighs—existence itself, as I have to assume it, here, now, each time. I am not responsible, as Kant claimed, because I am a subject who is the absolute origin of a series and therefore a subject to whom actions can be ascribed. I am responsible because I am thrown in an existence that I do not originate yet for which I have to answer. To be thrown (facticity) means to be called (responsibility), they are one and the same phenomenon; hence the "facticity of responsibility."

In his "Letter on Humanism," Heidegger explained that the phenomenon of thrownness and that of the call of being are one. For it is from the call (throw) of being that Dasein discovers itself to be thrown. He writes: Man is "called (*gerufen*) by being itself into the preservation of being's truth. The call (*Ruf*) comes as the throw (*Wurf*) from which the thrownness (*Geworfenheit*) of Da-sein derives" (BW, 245). Being withdraws in the very "throw" that brings Dasein into existence. But it is this withdrawal itself that *calls* Dasein, which summons it to be this being-thrown as its ownmost, if it is the case, as Heidegger explained in *What is called Thinking?* that "withdrawing is not nothing. Withdrawing is an event. In fact, what withdraws may even concern and claim man more essentially than anything present that strikes and touches him" (WCT, 9). This withdrawal calls us, and calls us to take it on as a weight to carry, insofar as we have to assume this withdrawal and thrownness in a "free throw." Hence, the primordial sense of responsibility is the appropriation of the inappropriable *as inappropriable.*

Ultimately, the motif of facticity indicates that I am responsible for finitude itself, that responsibility is in a sense identical to finitude. The call manifests the essential finitude of Dasein, thrown into *its* Being and having to "carry" it as its own. These motifs will be developed in Heidegger's later work from a thinking of *Ereignis,* as for instance in the *Contributions to Philosophy.* The call and the answer to it, the taking-on of thrownness, will be approached as belongingness to *Ereignis,* as the "counter-resonance" in *Ereignis* in which man and being co-belong. Responsibility will be approached in terms of this correspondence between being and man, and thought of more originarily from the truth of being itself. As Heidegger explains, "Thrownness will be experienced above all from within the truth of be-ing. In the first pre-liminary interpretation (*Being and Time*) thrownness still remains misunderstandable in the sense of man's accidentally appearing among other beings" (CP, 223). What senses of the call, of the response and of responsibility, could be thematized in a thinking that attempts to think "out of the truth of being itself"?

The Origins of Responsibility: The Call of *Ereignis*

In his later work, Heidegger rethinks thrownness and the call of conscience in terms of *Ereignis* and humans' belongingness to it. The projecting of the understanding of being that is thematized in *Being and Time* is not a spontaneous throw by a transcendentally free subject, but rather a *responding* to a call; it is already a responsibility as taking over of the call of *Ereignis*. Any projecting-open is thus thrown, and in the *Contributions to Philosophy*, thrownness is decidedly understood as belongingness to be-ing (that is, *not* as the project of the subject!), so that to be thrown now means to be en-owned. Thus in §134 of the *Contributions to Philosophy*, Heidegger shows that the "relation" (the term is here in quotation marks since Heidegger repeatedly underlines its limits, as it misleadingly implies a relationship between separate or mutually external domains) between Da-sein and be-ing was first grasped in *Being and Time* as "'understanding of being,' whereby understanding is grasped as projecting-open—and the opening-throwing as *thrown, and that means: belonging to en-ownment by be-ing itself*" (CP, 178; last emphasis mine). Thus, projecting-open (*Entwurf*) is thrown (*geworfen*), and thrownness (*Geworfenheit*) is belongingness to *Ereignis*. Dasein is not the projector of the throw, but is thrown in the throw and is thereby enowned by be-ing.

What is crucial here is that Da-sein is not a spontaneous subject who would be in the position of projecting from itself (as in Kant and 'transcendental freedom'), but rather originates *in and as an event*. One needs to think Dasein in its proper being-a-self as an event: *There is* self, self-being (*Selbstsein*). To originate first means, to come into being as coming into one's own; so Dasein is not already constituted, whether in the inappropriate form of egohood or as an extant "man." Instead, Dasein originates from a dimension (be-ing as enowning event or *Er-eignis*) in which it comes into its own. For "Da-sein as overcoming of all subjectivity arises from the essential swaying of be-ing" (CP, 214). This is why, in §197 of the *Contributions to Philosophy*, the analysis consists in retrieving the *origin* of selfhood, a non-subjective origin of coming-to-oneself that Heidegger designates as *Eigentum* or "ownhood": "As essential swaying of Da-sein, selfhood springs forth from the origin of Da-sein. And the origin of the self is *own-hood* [Eigen-tum], when this word is taken in the same way as the word *kingdom* [Fürsten-tum]" (CP, 224). Such originary ownhood, as we will see, occurs in the call of *Ereignis*.

Ownhood is an event, and Heidegger speaks indeed of the "occurrence" (*Geschehnis*) of ownhood, an event that eventuates us, enabling "man to come to 'himself' historically (*geschichtlich*) and to be with-himself" (CP, 224). In such an enowning event, there arises the original coming to oneself, ground of all modes of reflection onto self: "The retro-relation [*Rückbezug*] that is named in the 'itself,' to 'itself,' with 'itself,' for 'itself,' has what is ownmost in the owning (*Eignung*)" (CP, 225). It is by belonging to this enowning event that Dasein is properly *itself*: "Insofar as Da-sein is owned-to itself as belonging to enowning, it comes to itself" (CP, 225). Dasein does not come to itself as a separate self— "coming-to-oneself is never a prior, detached I-representation" (CP, 225)— since Dasein does not pre-exist the event from which it springs. What appears here, most importantly, is that Dasein can no longer be said to constitute a separate sphere, distinct from the event of be-ing that it would represent to itself as an object. On the contrary, Da-sein is *itself* and *its self* by standing in the truth of be-ing, by belonging to be-ing in answering its call. Heidegger parts with the motif of transcendence of Dasein, so prevalent in the writings surrounding *Being and Time*. Transcendence, as he explains in §199 of the *Contributions* (and already in §§7 and 110), is still too dependent on subjectivistic thinking (indeed, on Platonism!). Transcendence presupposes beings, which it surpasses, and the sphere of the subject, as that which surpasses. In both cases, the truth of be-ing itself, and the proper self that belongs to it, are missed. The abandonment of transcendence on the way to an originary thinking of Da-sein thus implies that its proper being-a-self not be understood as a proper subjective sphere. Da-sein comes to itself, but not "in such a manner as if the self were already an extant stock that has just not yet been reached" (CP, 224). Dasein is not already there, pre-given, and *then* returning to itself: Dasein *first* comes to itself from the enowning event, which indicates that it can only come to itself by first being exposed to the event of be-ing and by sustaining such an exposure. Conversely, being needs humans to happen, calling humans to its safeguarding. As Heidegger stresses: "Be-ing is nothing 'human,' and no human product;

and nevertheless the essential swaying of be-ing needs Da-sein and thus the inabiding of man" (CP, 187). There lies the origin of the call of which *Being and Time* spoke as the call of conscience; it is here thematized in terms of the belongingness to being and the need that being has of us. As Heidegger puts it, "Be-ing needs Da-sein and does not hold sway at all without this enownment" (CP, 179).

One could not emphasize enough the importance of such neediness for a redefinition of responsibility, as it now defines both the human being *and the essence of be-ing itself.* Heidegger goes so far as to state that "needing" (*Brauchen*) "makes up what is ownmost to be-ing" (CP, 177). "Needing" as the essence of be-ing reveals the co-belonging of man and be-ing. In a remarkably compact saying, Heidegger writes, "Be-ing needs man in order to hold sway; and man belongs to be-ing so that he can establish his utmost vocation (*Bestimmung*) as Da-sein" (CP, 177; translation modified). This is how the circular relation could be expressed: We are called by the sway of be-ing, because the essential sway of being "needs us." As such, this represents what Heidegger calls the "counter-resonance" (*Gegenschwung*) of needing and belonging—making up be-ing as enowning—or the "mirroring of call and belongingness" (CP, 219). Answering the call, the response is thus the indication of Dasein's belonging to the call, its in-abiding in *Ereignis.* This belongingness to being constitutes the "between" as the very dimension of Dasein's being, arising out of what the *Contributions* calls "ownhood" (*Eigentum*). Ownhood designates Da-sein's belongingness to being.

Be-ing needs us, Heidegger clarifies further, because "be-ing comes to truth only on the ground of Da-sein" (CP, 207). To that extent, "the essential swaying of be-ing needs the grounding of the *truth* of be-ing and this grounding must be enacted as *Da-sein*" (CP, 124). In fact, Dasein is no longer defined by Heidegger as that entity who has, and is, an understanding of being as "projecting," Dasein is no longer the "being-a-basis" of *Being and Time,* but is rather seen as being "the grounding of the truth of be-ing" (CP, 120). It is important to note that this grounding is not analogical to the projecting of a subject. Since "the origin of Dasein is in enowning and its turning," and consequently "Dasein has only to be *grounded* as and in the truth of be-ing," the grounding of the truth of be-ing by Dasein (from "the *human* side") can only mean: "grounding—*not creating*—is letting the ground be . . . so that man once again comes to himself and recovers self-being" (CP, 23; my emphasis). The grounding of the truth of being is a letting be of the ground, a thrown projecting, an originary responsibility of being in its truth.[35]

One notes such original responsibility in the taking-over (*übernahme*) by Dasein of its belongingness to the truth of be-ing in which it is *thrown* (that is to say, rethought from be-ing-historical thinking, *enowned*). In §198 of the *Contributions,* Heidegger would speak of the *über-nahme der Er-eignung*—a sort of original responsibility in *Ereignis,* the "taking-over of en-ownment"—as the way in which Dasein in its being-with-itself holds sway (CP, 226). That with-itself, far from indicating the enclosure or interiority of a subject, happens instead by standing-in (*Inständigkeit*) the open. Any 'intimacy' (and thereby any with-oneself), any responding and corresponding, can only happen in the open, that open dimension in which we are thrown and enowned, that is to say, always already called, struck, touched, by be-ing. Heidegger writes of the "taking over of the belongingness to the truth of being, leaping into the t/here": *Übernahme der Zugehörigkeit in die Wahrheit des Seins, Einsprung in das Da* (CP, 225). In fact, intimacy (*Innigkeit*) is rethought in such a way that "the more originarily we are ourselves, the further we are already removed into the essential swaying of be-ing, and vice-versa." Intimacy occurs when enowning "shines into selfhood" (CP, 187). Responsibility then means, enowned by the truth of be-ing and owning up to such enowning by inabiding it, enduring and taking-over the exposure to it. Heidegger captures this correspondence or co-belonging between belongingness and taking-over (being owned-to, owning up to) through the expressions of *Zueignung* and *übereignung,* owning-to and owning-over-to, which are said at the end of §197 to constitute the way in which what is ownmost to Dasein happens. Dasein becomes the "unfolding of the ownhoodship of the ownmost" (CP, 344).

It is in order to stress this original responsibility as correspondence or co-belonging that Heidegger insists that Da-sein is to be thought as the *between,* a "between" clearly marked in the new writing of Dasein with a hyphen, as Da-sein. "In the history of the truth of being Dasein is the essential *case of the between* (Zwischenfall), i.e., the case of falling-into that 'between' (*Zwischen*) into which man must be displaced (*ver-rückt*), in order above all to be *himself*" (CP, 223). That "between," which Heidegger in §7 explicitly contrasts with transcendence, is of course the play between the enowning throwing call of be-ing and the belongingness of Dasein as standing-in. It is what Heidegger calls the "counter-resonance" of *Ereignis*, because *Ereignis* itself is the resonance between the two: "En-ownment in its turning [*Kehre*] is made up neither solely of the call nor solely of the belongingness, is in neither of the two and yet resonates deeply in both" (CP, 240). This counter-resonance of needing and belonging, as we saw, defines be-ing as *Ereignis* (CP, 177). It is in that dimension that Dasein originates as response to the call of be-ing, and Heidegger speaks significantly of the "range in which the self resonates" (CP, 25) to stress the dimensionality of such a being-enowned by be-ing. Dasein is not some subject-point but "the turning-point in the turning of enowning, the self-opening midpoint of the mirroring of call and belongingness, the ownhood or own-dom" (CP, 219). What is that turning? The turning lies in that being only holds sway where and when there is Dasein, and that *in turn* Da-sein "is" only where and when there is be-ing. The turning speaks of the co-belonging of Da-sein and be-ing. The very term "relation" is explicitly excluded by Heidegger because it presupposes distinct spheres which enter *a posteriori* into relation. In §§134–135, Heidegger addresses the "relation" of Da-sein to be-ing, and notes that "strictly speaking, talk of a relation of Da-sein to be-ing is misleading, insofar as this suggests that be-ing holds sway 'for itself' and that Da-sein takes up the relating to be-ing" (CP, 179). There is no representation of be-ing, but there is an *intimation* (*Ahnung*) of be-ing, because be-ing enowns Da-sein to itself. Enowned by be-ing, Da-sein belongs to it by inabiding its "reign" (ownhood) and by responding to its call. Da-sein is itself by standing in be-ing and is exhausted in such a between. Who are we? We are the ones called by be-ing, needed by be-ing—the so-called *Zuruf der Notschaft*—to sustain its essential sway. Be-ing is my own, indeed my ownmost: Man "draws out of this belongingness—and precisely out of it—what is most originarily his ownmost" (CP, 351).

It is on the basis of belongingness to be-ing that the non-subjective, non-anthropocentric, non-individualist being of Da-sein would now be approached, i.e., in terms of the movement of coming to one's own, the movement and the event that delivers Da-sein to itself as it endures the between of call and belongingness. It is not "I" who is the subject of such enowning. On the contrary, I am thrown into it. Thrown, or enowned— by be-ing, in be-ing, and for the sake of be-ing, insofar as be-ing is my ownmost.[36] "When thought of from enowning, Da-sein—as the open midpoint of the selfhood that grounds truth—is thrown unto *itself* and becomes a self, then Dasein as the sheltered possibility of grounding the essential swaying of be-ing must in return belong to enowning" (CP, 286–287). Dasein now designates the *belonging-together of man and Being.* Being needs man to hold sway; man's own is be-ing. *Ereignis* is the name of such co-belonging, trans-propriation.

As we saw above, any projecting-open is a thrown projecting-open. That thrownness reveals that the origin of the I is *not* the I, and that therefore it must be dis-placed into that non-subjective event of throwing-enownment to first come to itself. Instead of securing the certainty of its position as *subjectum*, the I is dis-placed into be-ing, that "unentered domain," "in its utmost questionability, uniqueness, finitude, and strangeness" (CP, 144). The origin of Dasein is ownhood. Let us stress in closing, in order to prevent possible misunderstandings, that ownhood (*Eigentum*) is not a possessive appropriation but rather designates an "own" that is at play in the very event of be-ing, an event which has to be sustained as our very own. One's own is no simple possessive appropriation of otherness in an absolute "at-home," since one's ownmost is to stand in the uncanniness of be-ing, and indeed Heidegger stresses throughout the *Contributions,* the irreducible disowning (*Enteignis*) at the heart of enowning (*Ereignis*). Being is the withdrawal, and it calls us from this withdrawing. In this sense, expropriation (*Enteignis*) is the heart of appropriation (*Ereignis*). As the 1962 lecture "On Time and Being" states, expropriation (*die Enteignis*) belongs to appropriation to such an extent that in expropriation, *Ereignis* safe-keeps what is most proper to it. Corresponding to the event of *Ereignis* is hence an exposure to the expropriation that is its "heart" (*Innigkeit*), and responsibility, from the being-guilty of Dasein to the *Enteignis* of *Ereignis*, is the taking-over of an inappropriable.

EIGHT

Derrida:
The Impossible Origins of Responsibility

From the very heart of the im-possible one would hear the pulse or the beat of a "deconstruction."

PAPIER MACHINE

There is no responsibility without a dissident and inventive rupture with respect to tradition, authority, orthodoxy, rule, or doctrine.

THE GIFT OF DEATH

How could anything originate out of its opposite? For example, truth out of error? Or the will to truth out of the will to deception? Or selfless deeds out of selfishness? Or the pure and sunlike gaze of the sage out of lust? Such origins are impossible.

NIETZSCHE, BEYOND GOOD AND EVIL

The Aporias of Responsibility

What Heidegger's thinking with respect to responsibility has revealed is that to be responsible signifies the taking-on of an inappropriable: The call of conscience manifests an irreducible being-guilty; being properly one's own is projecting oneself resolutely toward such being-guilty; the call of *Ereignis* is from a withdrawal, indicating an expropriation or *Enteignis* at the heart of appropriation. In every instance, responsibility proves to be an experience of an inappropriable. For Heidegger, as for Derrida, responsibility cannot be conceived of as the imputation or ascription of an act to a subject-cause, but rather as the encounter and exposition to an event as inappropriable (which Derrida will seek to grasp as aporia). In *Being and Time,* these limits appeared in the notion of thrownness as it determines the phenomenon of moods and birth, in the finitude of Dasein as mortal being, and in Dasein's being-guilty. What is most striking in these phenomena is the fact that, far from preventing the possibility of ethical responsibility, they constitute what eminently obligates Dasein, and calls it to its ownmost being as finite (a finitude that Derrida would understand in terms of impropriety or impossibility). These limit-phenomena represent the origins of responsibility, and the site of the ethicality of ethics. The origin of responsibility is here a paradox. Jean-Luc Marion in fact claims that the call "always arises from a paradox," in his interpretation of the paradox of the "saturated phenomenon."[1] Our return to the origins of responsibility has revealed constitutive aporias in the very structure of responsibility, as if these origins were sites of aporia. Already with Nietzsche, we noted that it was out of the affirmation of an unaccountability of all things that another sense of responsibility, which was still to be fleshed out, emerged. In Sartre, one finds the aporia of having to decide without the possibility of relying on an *a priori* table of values, of having to choose without knowing how to choose, or the paradox of a responsibility for everything arising out of (the) nothing. In Levinas, the origin of ethics as responsibility for the other is at the same time the possibility of violence against the other. Furthermore, responsibility is the response to an infinite demand, a demand which necessarily and originarily exceeds the capacities of a finite responsible/responding subject. In Heidegger, as we saw, one finds the aporia of having to make oneself the basis of a nullity, i.e., of appropriating the inappropriable. Derrida will read these paradoxes as aporias, insisting that ethical responsibility ("if it exists," as he often adds) must be the experience, the undergoing or enduring, of an aporia, of a certain impossible.[2] And this formulation is all the more troubling as it is stated, precisely, in the perspective of a return to the conditions of *possibility* of ethics and responsibility.

A clarification is necessary at the outset, regarding Derrida's relation to ethics.[3] Although he underlines that ethical issues have never been absent from the work of deconstruction that he undertook from the early 1960s (albeit in an "oblique," non-thematic manner), Derrida concedes that his more explicit texts on ethics—whether those on justice, the right and the law, responsibility, ethical decision, forgiveness, hospitality, the gift, the secret, hospitality, etc.—do not propose a system of morality, a normative ethics in the received sense of the term. In an interview from January 2004, he explains: "In a way, ethical questions have always been present, but if by ethics one understands a system of rules, of moral norms, then no, I do not propose an ethics."[4] It would rather be an issue for him of problematizing (and in fact not just making it a problem but rendering aporetic!)[5] what he calls, following Levinas, the ethicality or ethicity of ethics (*l'éthicité de l'éthique*), that is, its very possibility. We recall that in his *Adieu à Emmanuel Levinas,* Derrida mentioned how Levinas had confided in a conversation that what interested him was not ethics but the holy. We will discover that Derrida's aporetic ethics is not very distant from this thinking of the holy, and that he would claim for himself the notion of an unconditional ethics as Levinas developed it, beyond ontology but also *beyond ethics.* As Derrida clarifies in the same text: "Yes, ethics before or beyond ontology, the state or politics, but ethics also beyond ethics" (*Adieu,* 15). Derrida will then speak of a "hyper-ethics"[6] or a hyperbolic ethics, following Levinas. At this juncture, let us simply note this similar movement in Levinas and Derrida, of an exceeding of ethics toward its ethicality, its possibility, which Derrida will understand as aporetic. The issue is to problematize the ethicality of ethics, as opposed to presupposing its senses.

It is indeed remarkable (and anomalous) that contemporary philosophical ethics, and in particular so-called "applied ethics," does not in general raise the preliminary question of the ethicality of ethics. The current and growing development of "applied ethics" in the curriculum is paradoxically accompanied by a peculiar blindness regarding the nature of ethics, and a neglect of a genuine philosophical questioning concerning the meaning of the ethical. Applied ethics becomes an ethics the meaning of which is ignored, not problematized, not reflected upon, and therefore presupposed. In this context, it would be crucial and indeed urgent to raise anew the question or questions on the meaning of ethical responsibility. Insisting on this necessity of the question in "Passions,"

Derrida asserts: "All this, therefore, still remains open, suspended, un-decided, questionable even beyond the question, indeed, to make use of another figure, absolutely aporetic. What is the ethicity of ethics? The morality of morality? What is responsibility? What is the 'What is?' in this case? Etc. These questions are always urgent."[7] These questions aim at reopening (or preventing the foreclosure of) a philosophical reflection on the ethicality of ethics. As such, they inaugurate Derrida's thinking of responsibility, a thinking that, without proposing an ethics, under-takes a return to its conditions of possibility.

However, returning to the possibilities of ethical responsibility at the same time implies undertaking a return to its limits, to its aporias, which are constitutive and incapacitating, possibilizing and impossibilizing, thus marking ethics with an irreducible impurity. One of the senses of decon-struction, as Derrida has conceived of and practiced it, has indeed been to reveal the aporias inherent in philosophical systems. Deconstruction as such, Derrida tells us, needs to be understood as aporetic thinking, and he still evoked in a late text "all the aporias or 'im-possibilities' that 'decon-struction' is concerned with" (*toutes les apories ou les 'im-possibles' qui occupent la 'déconstruction'*).[8] As early as *Positions,* Derrida already stressed that deconstruction consisted in accompanying "the internal, regulated play of philosophemes or epistememes by making them slide— without mistreating them—to the point of their nonpertinence, their ex-haustion, their closure,"[9] leading them, as it were, to the place where they no longer work. Deconstruction thus reveals the aporias within philo-sophical systems (a repressed outside of the system within the system), aporias that make those systems both impossible and . . . possible *as* im-possible. This is what Derrida clarifies in his later text on the secret, writing that "deconstruction, without being anti-systematic, is on the contrary, and nevertheless, not only a search for, but itself a consequence of, the fact that the system *is impossible.*"[10] In other words, in deconstruction, Derrida explains further, "it has been a question of showing that the system *does not work*" (TS, 4; my emphasis). Deconstruction reveals "a force of disloca-tion, a limit in the totalization, a limit in the movement of syllogistic syn-thesis," reveals a "certain dysfunction or 'disadjustment,' a certain incapac-ity to close the system . . . Basically, deconstruction as I see it is an attempt to train the beam of analysis onto this disjointing link" (TS, 4). In *Aporias,* Derrida returned to the long history of the aporetic in his own thinking:

"I recalled that, for many years now, the old, worn out Greek term *aporia,* this tired word of philosophy and of logic, *has often imposed itself upon me,* and recently it has done so even more often" (A, 13). A few lines further, Derrida gives a long list of the "numerous instances" where the theme of aporia has recurred in his own thinking, starting with *ousia* and *grammē* and the aporetics of time, the margins of undecidability, the "so-called undecidable quasi-concepts that are so many aporetic places of disloca- tion," the double-binds of *Glas,* the work of impossible mourning, the in- vention of the other as impossible, the gift as impossible, and all those phenomena that involve the impossible, beginning with ethics, decision, and responsibility.

For Derrida, the relation to aporia is the undergoing of an experi- ence, the experience of a limit that needs to be endured; as if an aporia, far from indicating a closure, instead represented a limit through which something announces itself in an affirmative fashion. This is why it is neither a matter of "stopping at it nor overcoming it" (A, 32). Rather, Derrida insists, it is a matter "of thinking according to the aporia" (A, 13). Aporias are constitutive of what they interrupt, and to that extent are positive phenomena. Hence the "positive" or "affirmative" sense that Derrida has always granted to deconstruction. He clarified this positive sense in the 2004 *Humanité* interview, in terms of an openness toward what comes: "A slogan, nonetheless, of deconstruction: being open to what comes, to the to-come, to the other." However, this "slogan" must always be associated with the privilege "constantly accorded to aporetic thinking" (V, 207 n. 3). The aporetic is affirmative, constitutive. It is in this sense that aporia becomes the very possibility of a way, a path. "The impossibility of finding one's way is the condition of ethics" (QE, 73).

The impossible becomes the possibility of the possible. Here we can glimpse the renewed thought of the possible and the impossible in Der- rida's thought, of the impossible as possible and the possible as impos- sible, of the possibility of the impossible. The impossible would no longer be the opposite of the possible, no longer the place where the possible ends, but on the contrary what "haunts the possible" (DE, 98), what truly "enables" or possibilizes the possible. The impossible, Derrida claims, *is* possible, not in the sense that it would become possible, but in a more radical sense in which the impossible, *as impossible,* is possible. In a parallel fashion, it would be a question of "converting the possible in the impossible," and of recognizing that if the impossible is possible (as impossible), the possible is in a certain way impossible, that is, arises out of an aporia. Such thinking will radically transform our understanding of the possible and the impossible. This is why, in *Voyous*, Derrida insists that "it is a question of an other thinking of the possible (of power, of the masterful and sovereign 'I can,' of selfhood itself) and of an im-possible that would not only be negative" (V, 197).[11] In the context of a discussion on the event, Derrida would suggest that the possible and the impossible, far from being opposite notions, are in a certain sense the same, that they belong to a same domain. He writes:

> I will say, I will try to show later in what sense impossibility, a certain impossibility of saying the event or a certain impossible possibility of saying the event, obliges us to think otherwise . . . what possible means in the history of philosophy. In other words, I will try to explain why and how I hear the word "possible" in the statement where this "possible" is not simply "different from" or the "contrary of impossible," why here "possible" and "impossible" say the same. (DE, 86; my emphasis)

The return to the conditions of possibility of ethics would thus be an aporetic gesture, a movement leading into an aporia, into an impossibility. However, the aporia will appear in such a way as to be described as the condition of possibility (or impossibility!)[12] of what it affects. This is why Derrida clarifies: "What interest me, in fact, are the aporias of ethics, its limits" (*Humanité* interview). It is in the aporia, in the impossible, that we should situate the ethicality of ethics:

> What I do is then just as much an-ethical as ethical. I question the impossible as possibility of ethics: unconditional hospitality is impossible, in the field of right or politics, even of ethics in the narrow sense. . . . To do the impossible cannot make an ethics, and yet it is the condition of ethics. I try to think the possibility of the impossible. (*Humanité* interview)

Ethics must do the impossible. To forgive can only happen where it is impossible to forgive; the gift, "if it is, if it is possible, must appear as impossible" (DE, 93). (Derrida even adds: "The gift is impossible, and can only be possible as impossible.") Hospitality must welcome unconditionally (which is impossible); responsible decision must judge without rules and without knowing how, etc. Each time, ethics can only happen as impossible. The impossible is the very possibility of ethics.

The Possibility of the Impossible

A twofold enigma will thus mark the Derridean thought of ethics and responsibility. On the one hand, ethical responsibility will be referred to an impossible to the extent that one may conclude that responsibility itself is impossible; but on the other hand, this very impossible will be presented as condition of possibility of responsibility. Let us enter further into this enigma.

First, it is necessary to return to the definition of ethical responsibility as an experience of the impossible. We know that Derrida, as we have just seen, attempts to reveal the possibility of the impossible as site of the ethicality of ethics. Now this expression, "possibility of the impossible," happens to be borrowed from Heidegger, and precisely from his thinking of death in *Being and Time,* which is defined there "as the possibility of the impossibility of existence in general" (SZ, 262). Heidegger also writes, "Death is the possibility of the pure and simple impossibility of Dasein" (SZ, 250; translation modified).[13] The very structure of the Derridean thought of responsibility is thus determined by this Heideggerian heritage. Derrida discusses this expression at length in *Aporias,* an expression he seeks to preserve—and complicate—in his thinking of the eventfulness of the event, of its arrival/happening (*l'arrivée*). For as Derrida clarifies, "this is indeed the possibility of a being-able-not-to or of a no-longer-being-able-to, but by no means the impossibility of a being-able-to" (A, 68). I *can* die, death is a possibility for Dasein. Indeed, in *Aporias,* Derrida identifies two senses of the possible in *Being and Time;* first, "the sense of the virtuality or of the imminence of the future," and second, the sense "of the possible as that of which I am capable, that for which I have the power, the ability, or the potentiality," concluding that "these two meanings of possibility co-exist in *die Möglichkeit*" (A, 62). I would here suggest a third sense, which is precisely the opposite of the second sense (possibility as power): The "I can" in "I can die" is more of a passibility, an exposure or a vulnerability, than a power. The possible here takes the sense of a being-exposed (passivity) to the possibility of death. I can die (i.e., am mortal) because I am exposed to death. It remains, whatever its senses, that death is for Heidegger a possibility. This is a crucial precision: Death is strictly approached as a possibility (of the impossibility of existence), and never as an impossibility (of existence as possibility). As Derrida explains, "The nuance is thin, but its very fragility is what seems to me both decisive and significant, and it probably is most essential in Heidegger's view" (A, 68). Heidegger claims that, "Death is a *possibility* of being that Dasein always has to take upon itself" (SZ, 250; my emphasis), in fact its ownmost and ultimate possibility. As I face my mortality, as I exist toward death, I am as it were returned to my most proper self. When Heidegger writes that death is not the impossibility of existence, but its most proper and ultimate possibility, Derrida echoes it by explaining that "death is consequently the event par excellence" (*Humanité* interview), even if he will eventually lend to this event the features of the impossible, something Heidegger does not do.

Seeking to collapse the proper into the improper, the possible into the impossible, Derrida writes that the Heideggerian thought of being as event, as *Ereignis,* involves a certain expropriation, an impossible. Going against the grain, one must admit, of many of his previous interpretations of Heidegger, where Derrida tended to stress an alleged privilege of the proper in Heidegger's work (still in *Aporias,* 56!), here on the contrary he states that "the thought of *Ereignis* in Heidegger would be turned not only toward the appropriation of the proper (*eigen*) but toward a certain expropriation that Heidegger himself names (*Enteignis*)."[14] In fact, in *Aporias* Derrida states that the expression "possibility of the impossible" should be read as the indication that an *Enteignis* "always inhabited *Eigentlichkeit*" (A, 77). He then adds, explicitly linking the Heideggerian thought of the event to the inappropriable and the impossible: "The undergoing [*l'épreuve*] of the event, that which in the undergoing or in the ordeal *at once opens itself up to and resists experience,* is, it seems to me, a certain inappropriability of what comes or happens [*ce qui arrive*]" (PTT, 90; translation modified). There is an irreducible inappropriable in the event. Even if Derrida recognizes that any event necessarily calls for a certain appropriative reception, in all of its various modes, he insists on the fact that "there is no event worthy of its name except insofar as this appropriation falters [*échoue,* literally: fails] at some border or frontier" (PTT, 90). Derrida here finds access to his own thinking of the impossible, in Heidegger's thought of the event (i.e., of *Ereignis* and of death), but also to his own reflection on ethics and responsibility.

One could indeed, within certain limits, discern in the Heideggerian text a thinking of responsibility, of being-responsible, which opens onto

Derrida's understanding of aporetic ethics. It is at this juncture, we recall, in this very "aporetic" moment, that Heidegger paradoxically situated the responsibility of Dasein, as arising out of the aporia. He called it Dasein's being-guilty (*Schuldigsein*), an original ontological responsibility arising from a negativity (*Nichtigkeit*), a paradoxical phenomenon that Derrida approaches with the neologism of "ex-appropriation." It is clear that what is to be 'carried' or shouldered is what remains inappropriable in existence, an inappropriable that calls human Dasein to be, to think, and to be responsible for it. The primordial sense of responsibility would hence be—the appropriation of the inappropriable, as inappropriable. It would be a matter of properly being the improper, according to the logic of ex-appropriation that is unveiled by Derrida. Derrida would conceive of these phenomena as aporias, and these aporias as the site of responsibility as an experience of the impossible.

Death as Aporia

Everything for Derrida is at stake in the expression, "the possibility of the impossible." How should it be understood? It is a matter, he tells us, "of knowing in which sense [*sens*] one reads the expression the possibility of impossibility" (A, 77), reminding the reader, following the polysemy of *sens* in French, that the term should also be heard as "direction." Hence if one reverses the direction, "the possibility of the impossible" becomes "the impossibility of the possible." How should it then be understood?

> Is this an aporia? Where do we situate it? In the impossibility or in the possibility of an impossibility (which is not necessarily the same thing)? What can the possibility of an impossibility be? How can we think that? How can we *say* it while respecting logic and meaning? How can we approach that, live, or exist it? How does one *testify* to it? (A, 68)

For Heidegger, as we know, death is *the most proper possibility* (*die eigenste Möglichkeit*) of Dasein; for Derrida, on the contrary, it will be an issue of emphasizing an aporetic structure or "logic," and placing the emphasis on the improper and expropriation. Indeed, as he explains in *Aporias,* if the most extreme and most proper possibility turns out to be the possibility of an impossibility, then we will have to say that expropriation always already inhabits the proper, and that to such an extent death becomes *the least proper possibility*:

> If death, the most proper possibility of Dasein, is the possibility of its impossibility, death becomes the most improper possibility and the most ex-propriating, the most inauthenticating one. From the most originary inside of its possibility, the proper of Dasein becomes from then on contaminated, parasited, and divided by *the most improper*. (A, 77; my emphasis)

This challenge to a "properly dying" (A, 30) involves a critique of Heidegger's distinctions between merely ending, perishing, and properly dying, between *verenden* and *sterben,* and also with demise, *ableben,* Derrida speaking of a contamination between these senses. At this stage, Derrida makes a crucial interpretative decision. When Heidegger speaks of the possibility of death "as that of the impossibility of existence in general" (*als die der Unmöglichkeit der Existenz überhaupt*), Derrida understands this "as" to mean that possibility is approached *as* impossibility, for as he explains, this is "not only the paradoxical possibility of a possibility of impossibility: it is possibility as impossibility" (A, 70). From this interpretation will follow radical consequences.

One word of caution is necessary here; to my knowledge, Heidegger never speaks of possibility *as* impossibility. Rather, he speaks of death *as* the possibility of the impossibility *of* existence in general. How does one slide from the possibility *of* an impossibility into possibility *as* impossibility? Clearly, through an interpretive violence in Derrida's part. Strangely, in a remarkable case of philosophical projection, Derrida accuses Heidegger of sliding, from possibility *as* impossibility to the expression possibility *of* the impossible! He writes: "For the moment, let us note that the *als* is translated or relayed by the genitive form of a complement of the noun. The text imperceptibly moves from the possibility *as possibility of* the impossibility to the simple possibility *of* impossibility" (A, 71). But Heidegger never spoke of possibility as impossibility! His phrase states, I am citing it in full, "The more unveiledly this possibility gets understood, the more purely does the understanding penetrate into it *as the possibility of the impossibility of existence in general*" (SZ, 262; cited by Derrida at A, 70). Doesn't the genitive itself, in Heidegger's expression "possibility of the impossibility," in fact prevent such an identification, such a collapse between possibility and impossibility? To be precise, the expression "possibility of the impossible" does indeed mean that the impossible is possible (and it is indeed Heidegger's entire effort in *Being and Time* to seize death as possibility, and not as actuality), but it does not mean the reverse, i.e., that the possible is impossible! Heidegger was always careful not to simply write that death is the impossibility of existence, but indeed the possibility of such impossibility. He even stressed, as if to prevent possible misunderstandings, that death is a possibility that "must not be weakened," that "it must be understood *as possibility*, cultivated *as possibility*, and endured *as possibility* in our relation to it" (SZ, 261). Yet Derrida still evokes "the impossibility of existing or of Dasein that Heidegger speaks of under the name of 'death'" (A, 75), when Heidegger only speaks of the possibility of such impossibility! Further, in our coming near death in its anticipation, one does not come near the actuality of death but its possibility, a "possibility of the possible [that] only becomes 'greater'" (SZ, 262). Finally, the not-yet of death as possibility is *not* the not-yet of an accomplishment which is to come. Death is rather to be seized solely as possibility, explains Heidegger. The being of Dasein is and lies in possibility only. Dasein *is* a possibility of being, never an actuality, and Derrida admits this: "The essence of Dasein as entity is precisely the possibility, the being-possible" (A, 63). We are capable of death, it is a possibility of our being. Yet Derrida will object to what he sees here as a transcendental mode of thinking: I die because I can die. In contrast, for Derrida the non-access to death, the aporia of "my death"—but death as *actuality* here, since there is indeed access to death as possibility, so that Derrida slides from possibility to actuality when speaking of death, just as he slides from possibility to impossibility (A, 75)—is what accounts for the fact that indeed, as Levinas wanted it, the death of the other is the first death! Derrida writes: "The death of the other in me is fundamentally the only death that is named in the syntagm 'my death'" (A, 76).

However, I do not know of any passage where Heidegger collapses the possible into the impossible, nor can I imagine how he would. And Derrida knows this full well, since on page 68 of *Aporias*, he writes that "this is indeed the possibility of a being-able-not-to or of a no-longer-being-able-to, but by no means the impossibility of a being-able-to." And yet on page 70, he speaks of the *disappearance* of the possible in the impossible, explaining that for Dasein, death "is both its *most proper* possibility and this same (most proper) possibility as impossibility," and is "hence, *the least proper,* I would say"—though Derrida immediately adds—"but Heidegger never says it like that" (A, 70). He continues by wondering "how a (most proper) possibility as impossibility can still appear as such without immediately disappearing, without the 'as such' already sinking beforehand" (A, 70). In fact, Heidegger maintains the "as such," and the mineness of death, principle of individuation, all gathered around the "on this side" of existence. Could it be that Heidegger's account of death as my ownmost possibility would be a defense against death as expropriation? The end of me—how should this expression be heard? As confirming myself, or as the undoing of my self? If not from the other side, then at least from the threshold or the secret of death as aporia, if it is the case that "Death is always the name of a secret" (A, 74)?

In short, and now against or at least outside Heidegger, it is matter for Derrida of understanding the expression "possibility of the impossible" as an aporia—and "There are several ways of thinking the possibility of impossibility *as aporia*" (A, 72)—even if he recognizes that Heidegger "would certainly not accept" this logic of aporia, since an aporetic logic would indeed lead to the collapse of the entire authenticity/inauthenticity opposition and *Being and Time*'s main conceptual demarcations (for instance, existentiell versus existential) and, in the end, to the collapse of the existential analytic itself! Derrida writes, "At stake for me would be approaching the place where such aporias risk paralyzing the ontological, hierarchical, and territorial apparatus to which Heidegger lends credit. These aporias risk interrupting the very possibility of its functioning and leading it to ruin" (A, 28). And death "would be the name of this threat," that is, aporia would be "what ruins the very possibility of the analysis from within" (A, 78), so that "one can turn what is thus at the very heart of the possibility of the existential analytic *against* the whole apparatus of *Being and Time*, against the very possibility of the existential analytic" (A, 76–77). Derrida sees in this motif of death, despite and in fact against Heidegger (as we have seen), the example of a logic of aporia—a figure of aporia that marks and determines "all that is only possible as impossible, if there is such a thing: love, the gift, the other, testimony, and so forth" (A, 79). And also, we could add here, responsibility itself.

The Aporia of the Law

Indeed, responsibility in Derrida is wed to the impossible, to the aporia. And we recall how what interested him in ethics, far from moralism or good conscience, far from any restoration of morality or even from a re-moralization of deconstruction (P, 15), are the aporias of ethics, its limits—that is, the an-ethical origins of ethics. Let us briefly reconstruct the four aporias that Derrida thematizes: These are the *epokhē* of the rule, the aporia of the undecidable, the aporia of responsible decision as heterogeneous to knowledge, and the aporia of a decision "of the other."

The first aporia marks the excess of ethical responsibility with respect to any norm or rule, indeed in relation to duty. It is in fact characteristic of the law, according to Derrida, that it is radically without ground, in the last analysis without foundation or justification; the law itself is without law! There is thus no law of the law, which explains why the *coup de force,* what the English language calls the "enforceability" of the law, is for Derrida inherent in the law itself. There is no law without such force, a force that is thus not external to the law, but rather the *coup de force of* the law, the self-institution of a law without foundation (and therefore deconstructible). Hence the law's originary performativity and violence: "Since the origin of authority, the foundation or ground, the position of the law can't by definition rest on anything but themselves, they are themselves a violence without ground."[15] Due to this abyssal violence of the law, Derrida clarifies that violence is never a physical or natural concept, but that "the concept of violence belongs to the symbolic order of law, politics and morals" (FL, 31). The act of positing the law—one says *faire la loi,* "to make law," as the establishing of a power—is a "law-making violence" (*die rechtsetzende Gewalt*) and an act of originary, ungrounded, and unjustifiable violence. Nothing is able to justify the justice and legality of this law, for at the moment of its foundation such a law is neither just nor unjust, neither legal nor illegal. There is no foundation of this performative foundation, which rests on nothing. No justifying discourse can play the role of a meta-language in relation to the performativity of the instituting language. The justification of a decision is hence *impossible* and, *a priori* and for structural reasons, a decision can never absolutely answer for itself. Therein lies the radical and irreducible irresponsibility of the law, the mark of its absence of ground. This is what Derrida understands as "the mystical foundation of authority," an element that he describes in the following terms: "Here a silence is walled up in the violent structure of the founding act" (FL, 14).

Therein also lies the *epokhē* of the rule: The "ought" of ethics and responsibility cannot and "must not even take the form of a rule" (P, 8), i.e., can never be the conformity to a duty, to an established or given norm. Merely applying a rule or following a norm would for Derrida amount to irresponsibility itself! There can be responsibility only when one does *not* have the rule. Not having the rule, and enduring this absence as an aporia—this would be the origin of responsibility. It would be a question of moving beyond the very language of duty, precisely out of faithfulness to the ethical command, a command that paradoxically always occurs beyond the rule: "In a word, ethics must be sacrificed in the name of duty. It is a duty not to respect, out of duty, ethical duty" (GD, 67). More precisely, the aporia of the rule is that the rule is both known and ignored or overcome. The aporia of the rule lies in the fact that "as in all normative concepts . . . it involves both rules and invention without rules" (P, 9), and here Derrida gives the example of politeness. In other words, in responsible decision "one knows the rule but is never bound by it" (P, 9). Ethical responsibility would here be a duty beyond duty, and Derrida breaks at this point with the Kantian formulation of duty: "Would there thus be a duty not to act *according to duty*: neither *in conformity to duty*, as Kant would say (*pflichtmässig*), nor even *out of duty* (*aus Pflicht*)?" (P, 7). A counter-duty, or rather a duty beyond duty, a hyperbolic duty or hyper-duty: We encounter again the Levinassian motif of an ethics beyond ethics, beyond the language of debt or duty. However, with Derrida we are better able to see how this hyperbolic ethics arises out of the aporetic structure of the law. It is because the ethical decision must judge without rules—it is a decision "that *cuts*, that divides" (FL, 24)—that it infinitely exceeds duty and norm, and thus is infinitized, i.e., opened onto the incalculable. Ethics would be rebellious to the rule, foreign to any normative concept, and responsibility or the experience of responsibility would not be reducible to duty. Rather, responsibility is an openness to the incalculable through the aporia of its lack of foundation.

The Undecidable

The aporia of the rule opens the responsible decision onto the undecidable. For Derrida, 'undecidable' does not mean the impossibility of decision, for on the contrary the undecidable is the condition for decision in the sense that for him there is no decision and no responsibility without a confrontation with the undecidable.[16] That is to say, with the impossible. A decision must decide without rules to follow, to apply or to conform to, and this is why it is each time (the singularity of an 'each time') a decision as an event. The undecidable designates the event-character of decision. A decision occurs as an event without rules, each time "the event of a decision without rules and without will in the course of a new experience of the undecidable" (P, 17; translation modified). The absence of rules throws decision into the undecidable. Ethical responsibility is thus a matter of invention, and not the application of a rule. A decision is a leap, happening outside of prior conditions of possibility (an event that Derrida will call, for that reason, im-possible), an absolute risk that can rely on nothing but its own absence of foundation: "There is no 'politics,' right, ethics, without the responsibility of a decision which, to be just, must not be content with simply applying existing norms or rules but take the absolute risk, in each singular situation, to justify itself again, alone, as if for the first time, even if it is inscribed in a tradition" (PM, 358).

"Undecidable" because not already decided, and in fact never decided and never decidable.[17] A decision made does not suppress the undecidable. Derrida is quite clear on this point: "The aporia I speak so much about is not a mere momentary paralysis before an impasse, but the experience of the undecidable through which alone a decision can take place. *But a decision does not end some aporetic phase.*"[18] The undecidable is thus not an objection to decision but its condition: "For me the undecidable is the condition of decision, of the event,"[19] a constitutive and permanent aporia for decision. The aporia itself (the impossible) is the condition of decision (its possibility) and the very locus of freedom: "Where I still have a space for choice, I am in the antinomy, the contradiction, and each time I want to keep the greatest possible freedom to negotiate between the two" (SP, 48).[20] This also why responsibility is never a 'good conscience,' for it always happens in the aporia, always in the experience of an impossible. The undecidable as impossible haunts any decision, including once a decision is made; decision *remains* confronted with the undecidable that makes it possible *as decision*.

Deciding without Knowing

A not-knowing is thus a condition of ethical decision, marking another appearance of the impossible. Derrida explains in his interview with *Humanité*:

> If I know what I must do, I do not make a decision, I apply a knowledge, I unfold a program. For there to be a decision, I must not know what to do . . . The moment of decision, the ethical moment, if you will, is independent from knowledge. It is when "I do not know the right rule" that the ethical question arises.

Of course, Derrida recognizes that "one must know as much as possible and as well as possible before deciding" (*De quoi demain*, 92), but there will always remain a gap between decision and knowledge. The moment of decision, the moment of responsibility, supposes a rupture with the order of knowledge, with calculative rationality, if it is the case that "a decision always takes place beyond calculation" (GD, 95). To that extent, there is what Derrida calls a "madness of the impossible" as opening to the incalculable.[21] A leap in the incalculable is necessary and it is a matter of deciding without knowing, as it were without seeing (*voir*) or foreseeing (*prévoir*), and thus from a certain invisible or unforeseeable, without being able to calculate all the consequences of the decision; a decision is made by entering, as Derrida says, into "the night of the unintelligible." Even the difference between good and evil does not depend on a knowledge; one does not *know* what the difference between good and evil is. Such a distinction can only be made in a moment of ethical decision, which always takes place in a leap beyond knowledge. Responsibility arises out of this aporia of the not-knowing of decision. Derrida thus speaks of a decision outside of knowledge, a responsible decision that is taken *without knowing*—to the extent that Derrida will even speak of an "unconscious decision" in *Politics of Friendship!*[22] He will also refer to such a decision, now tied and assigned to a "secret" that makes the I "tremble" (a secret of the self that is not *my* secret, that belongs to no one),[23] as a decision "of the other" because it exceeds the egological enclosure, a decision of the other in me that nonetheless does not absolve me of my responsibility. It is my responsibility, but "not in the sense of a (Kantian) autonomy by means of which I see myself acting in total liberty or according to a law that I make for myself, rather in the heteronomy . . . [of] whatever is commanding me to make decisions, decisions that will nevertheless be mine and which I alone will have to answer for" (GD, 91). I tremble "at what exceeds my seeing and my knowing [*mon voir et mon savoir*] although it concerns the innermost parts of me, right down to my soul, down to my bone, as we say" (GD, 54).

A Decision of the Other

If the decision takes place in a leap into the unknown, then it can never be 'my' decision. It takes place in the other. This is why for Derrida, I can never say, 'I made a decision.'

> One says too easily "I decide" or "I take the responsibility for something," "I am responsible for it." All these expressions seem unacceptable to me. To say "I decide," to say "you know that I decide, I know that I decide," would mean that I am capable of and master of my decision, that I possess a criterion that allows me to say that it is I who decide. (DE, 102)

Derrida here breaks in his thinking of responsible decision with the horizon of subjectivity and will (more precisely: he reverses it),[24] a horizon that dominates the traditional philosophy of responsibility as imputability of a free subject. Following Levinas, who precisely "always puts freedom after responsibility" (DE, 103), Derrida seeks to imagine an alterity of decision, a decision that would be *of the other,* and yet "would not absolve me of my responsibilities" (*De quoi demain,* 92), because just "as no one can die in my place, no one can make a decision, what we call 'a decision,' in my place" (GD, 60). It is a decision of the other in me, marking a hiatus within the subject. A decision worthy of this name should mark the splitting-open of the self in its identity or self-sameness, should mark a hiatus in the subject.

> A decision should split open or tear—this is what the term decision means—therefore should interrupt the thread of the possible [which is understood here as the "I can" of the ego, the power and will of the *selbst*].

Each time that I say "my decision" or "I decide," one can be sure that I am wrong . . . Decision should always be the decision of the other. My decision is in fact the decision of the other. My decision can never be mine, it is always the decision of the other in me and I am in a way passive in decision. (DE, 102)

With such a "passive decision,"[25] it is a matter of designating an alterity at the heart of responsible decision, an alterity or heteronomy from which and in which alone a decision can be made: "That is what I meant . . . by heteronomy, by a law come from the other, by a responsibility and decision of the other—of the other in me, an other greater and older than I am" (PTT, 134).[26]

The Future of Responsibility

In order to mark this heteronomy of responsibility, its heterogeneity with respect to the horizon of calculability of the subject, Derrida underlies what he calls the "im-possibility" of responsibility. Here im-possible does not mean "that which cannot be," but rather that which *happens* outside of the anticipating conditions of *possibility* of the egological subject, outside of the horizons of expectation proposed by the subject, outside of transcendental horizons of calculability. One can calculate up to a point, but "The incalculable happens" (TS, 61). Derrida speaks of the value of "unpredictable im-possibility" which he associates with that of "incalculable and exceptional singularity" (V, 203), writing "impossible" as "im-possible" in order to underline the excess with respect to the horizon of the conditions of possibility of the subject, and in so doing, to free (outside of these conditions of possibility) the possibility of the event. The im-possible is not what simply cannot be and is thus null and void, but rather the very opening of the event, which happens outside horizon. Derrida will oppose to the power of the subject as neutralization of the event, the im-possible as paradoxical possibility of the event. To the whole machination of the subject, to the establishment of the power of someone, some 'I can'—"to all this," Derrida writes, "I would oppose, in the first place, everything I placed earlier under the title of the im-possible, of what must remain (in a non-negative fashion) *foreign to the order of my possibilities,* to the order of the 'I can'" (PTT, 134). The issue is thus to free "the pure eventfulness of the event" (PTT, 134) by breaking the power of the ego and its attempts to neutralize it. As event, an event is said to be im-possible in the sense that it happens outside of the horizon of preparedness of the subject as 'I can.' Derrida writes, "An event or an invention is possible only as im-possible."[1] Furthermore, this impossible—and *"there is the impossible,"* we are told (PTT, 120)—marks the possibility of the event, according to the logic of the possibility of the impossible that we underlined above. "Un-predictable, an event worthy of this name . . . The event must announce itself as im-possible . . . An event or an invention are only possible as im-possible" (V, 198). For Derrida, for an event to be possible, it must arise from the im-possible (it must happen as the im-possible!), and not be made possible by conditions; it can only be an event by breaking the possible. "If only what is already possible, that is, expected and anticipated, happens, this is not an event. The event is possible only when come from the impossible. It happens (*arrive*) *as* the advent of the impossible" (PM, 285). It is indeed paradoxically the condition of possibility that impossibilizes the experience of which it claims to be the condition; and it is on the contrary the im-possible, as a leap outside of the horizon of expectations, which possibilizes the event, the eventfulness of the event, or what Derrida calls the happening/arrival of the *arrivant (l'arrivée de l'arrivant),*[2] and whose welcome is called, precisely, "ethics."

Derridean ethics indeed determines itself as an ethics of alterity, of the welcome of the other. We recall that hospitality is not a mere region of ethics but indeed is "ethicity itself, the whole and principle of ethics" (A, 94). Ethics would designate this openness to the other, an ethics of the other in the subjective sense of the genitive. The 'im-possible' names such an ethics, ethics becoming the experience of limits, of what remains inappropriable or 'impossible' in the event of alterity. In its aporetic structure, such ethics is the welcome of the event of the other and the obligation of hospitality. The im-possible is the site of this welcome, as the possibility of the event and of what arrives. When speaking of hospitality Derrida distinguishes a conditional hospitality, one that remains regulated by the pre-existing conditions of a welcoming power—and which is in fact no hospitality—from hospitality itself, which is unconditional. To be such, hospitality must not impose conditions, it must not 'choose' the guest (as French president Nicolas Sarkozy proposed, when he called for a "chosen immigration"). Tolerance, for instance—i.e., hospitality *up to a point*—is no hospitality but is in fact the "contrary" of hospitality, for the other is then "welcomed" on the basis of conditions laid out by the host, that is, by a welcoming *power.*[3]

As we have seen, one must radicalize hospitality to the point of a genuine welcome of the other, in the subjective genitive. The welcome of the other—of the *arrivant*—is not on the side of the host as master of the house, but on the side of the arriving guest. *Hospitality is on the side of the guest,* of who or what arrives. Hospitality comes from the other; for there to be hospitality, there must be the event of the arrival of the other. This arrival happens outside the subject. The other arrives when it arrives: "Whatever happens, happens, whoever comes, comes, and that, in the end, is the only event worthy of this name" (PTT, 129); hospitality registers such an arrival. In contrast to conditional hospitality—which is no hospitality, but an exercise of power by the host over the arriving other—Derrida proposes the notion of an un-conditional, absolute or pure hospitality, that is, a hospitality not relative to the *a priori* conditions of the subject, and therefore 'absolute' in this precise sense: "pure and unconditional hospitality, hospitality itself, opens or is in advance open to someone who is neither expected nor invited, to whomever arrives as an absolutely foreign *visitor,* as a new *arrival,* nonidentifiable and unforeseeable, in short wholly other" (PTT, 129). The term 'absolute' is the term for the *tout autre,* the "wholly other," and responsibility is the response to this arrival of the wholly other. Responsibility, as responsiveness to such arrival of the other, is incalculable, im-possible, and absolutely "of the other."

And this constitutes no theological turn, as we read sometimes. It is rather the inscription (or 'ex-scription'), at the heart and limit of the immanence of experience, of the transcendence of responsibility as responsiveness to the other. This transcendence happens *in* immanence, and does not constitute some theological beyond, nor even a teleological horizon. The im-possible does not await *at* the horizon, but pierces it in the urgency of its arrival, if it is the case that an event has no horizon or pierces the horizon—and in *Sur Parole,* Derrida states that "the absence of horizon is the condition of the event."[4] The im-possible is not an idea in the Kantian sense; it is not an idea but rather the most real. Derrida is quite clear on this point:

> This im-possible is not privative. It is not the inaccessible, and it is not what I can indefinitely defer: it is announced to me, sweeps down upon me, precedes me, and seizes me *here now,* in a nonvirtualizable way, in actuality and not potentiality . . . This im-possible is thus not a regulative *idea* or *ideal.* It is what is most undeniably real. Like the other. Like the irreducible and nonappropriable difference of the other. (PTT, 134)

The im-possible is thus not beyond, as it constitutes a here and now, a here that is marked by trauma and difference. The "im-possible" event is each time the interruption and constitution of a "threshold" (drawing its contours as it breaks it through dis-location and ex-appropriation), of a here as threshold (the threshold of the self . . .) and site of welcome. Aporia is about a certain threshold, and the event as the *arrivant* "affects the very experience of the threshold" (A, 33), the threshold of hospitality—a welcome of the arrivant.

Derrida recognized, in his interview with *Humanité,* the growing importance that this thinking of the event took for him. He insisted as well on the ethical scope of such thinking, explaining to his interlocutor:

> What you say about a privileged attention to the event is correct. It has become more and more insistent. The event, as that which happens (*arrive*) unpredictably, singularly. Not only what happens, but also who happens/arrives, the *arrivant.* The question "what is to be done with what/who arrives?" commands a thinking of hospitality, of the gift, of forgiveness, of the secret, of witnessing.

Ultimately for Derrida, the experience of responsibility is tied to the impossible, the aporetic, and to the event—that is, the event of who or what happens and arrives. Certainly, what unpredictably arrives "exceeds my responsibility," but from such an excess it calls for this responsibility. Responsibility thus becomes the response to such an absolute arrival. The event is "an arriving event (*une arrivance*) that surprises me absolutely and to which and to whom I cannot, I must not, *not answer and respond*—in a way that is as responsible as possible" (*De quoi demain,* 90–91).

The responsibility or responding-to who or what happens/arrives is a responsibility to the event as unpredictable. A predictable event is no longer an event. Hence Derrida continues by stressing: "What interests me in the event is its singularity. It happens once, each time once (*chaque fois une fois*). An event is thus unique, and unpredictable, that is to say, without horizon." An event has no horizon. There is no horizon either for the other or for death, writes Derrida (*De quoi demain,* 91). An event can never be included in a horizon of expectation, I cannot see it come: An event never arrives "horizontally," it does not appear or *present itself* on the horizon from where I may be able to fore-see it, anticipate it; rather, an event falls upon me, comes from above, vertically, from a (non-theological) height and is an absolute surprise. The surprise of an event that happens vertically, but also "by coming from behind me, or from underneath me, from the basement of my past, in such a way that I can never see it come, having to content myself at times to feel it or hear it, barely" (*De quoi demain,* 91). A surprise that suspends understanding, comprehension. Derrida would describe the surprise of the event in this way: "The event is what comes and, in coming, comes to surprise me, to surprise and to suspend comprehension: The event is first of all *that which* I do not first of all comprehend. Better, the event is first of all *that* I do not comprehend. The fact that I do not comprehend: my incomprehension" (PTT, 90). One will of course refer such incomprehension to the not-knowing of the moment of decision; but also to the invisibility of its vertical arrival. "The event, as the *arrivant,* is what falls upon me vertically without me being able to see it come: before arriving, the event can only appear to me as impossible" (DE, 97). And yet, it is to such impossible arrival that a responsibility is assigned. In *A Taste for the Secret,* Derrida speaks of the absolute weakness and disarmament which allows the incalculable to happen; he speaks of the event of "the occasion, chance, the aleatory," which means "exposing ourselves to what we cannot appropriate: it is there, before us, without us—*there is* someone, something, that happens, that happens to us, and that has no need of us to happen (to us)" (TS, 63).

Ultimately, responsibility is the responding-to this inappropriable event of the other, and will always arise from its unpredictable, futural arrival.

NOTES

Introduction

1. Friedrich Nietzsche, *On the Genealogy of Morals,* trans. Walter Kaufmann (New York: Vintage, 1967), 58; translation modified. Hereafter cited as GM, followed by page number. Nietzsche speaks of the "long history of the origins of responsibility" (*Geschichte der Herkunft der Verantworlichkeit*); in his preface, Nietzsche already mentioned his attempt at publishing hypotheses concerning "the origin of morality" (*Ursprung der Moral*) (GM, 16).

2. Maurice Merleau-Ponty, *The Primacy of Perception,* ed. James M. Edie, trans. William Cobb (Evanston, Ill.: Northwestern University Press, 1964), 30.

3. Jean-Luc Nancy, "Heidegger's 'Originary Ethics,'" in *Heidegger and Practical Philosophy,* ed. François Raffoul and David Pettigrew (Albany: SUNY Press, 2002), 66. Hereafter this volume is cited as HPP, followed by page number.

4. Jacques Derrida, "Jacques Derrida, penseur de l'évènement," interviewed by Jérôme-Alexandre Nielsberg for *l'Humanité,* 28 January 2004; accessed at http://www.humanite.fr/2004-01-28_Tribune-libre_-Jacques-Derrida-penseur-de-levenement. My translations.

5. "A slogan, nonetheless, of deconstruction: being open to what comes, to the to-come, to the other." Jacques Derrida, in the *Humanité* interview. On deconstruction as openness, see David Wood, *Thinking After Heidegger* (Cambridge: Polity Press, 2002); see also my review-article, "Openness and Thought: Review-Article of David Wood's *Thinking After Heidegger,*" *Research in Phenomenology* 34 (2004): 269–279.

6. Friedrich Nietzsche, *The Will to Power,* trans. Walter Kaufmann and R. J. Hollingdale (New York: Vintage / Random House, 1968), 148. Hereafter cited as WP, followed by page number.

7. G. W. F. Hegel, *Elements of the Philosophy of Right,* ed. Allen W. Wood, trans. H. B. Nisbet (New York: Cambridge University Press, 1991), 143, §115.

8. Later in his *Philosophy of Right,* Hegel states that "I can be made *accountable* for a deed only if *my will was responsible* for it" (ibid., 144, §117).

9. Kant writes: "The transcendental idea of freedom is far from constituting the whole content of the psychological concept of that name, which is for the most

part empirical, but constitutes only that of the absolute spontaneity of an action, as the real ground of its imputability; but this idea is nevertheless the real stumbling block for philosophy, which finds insuperable difficulties in admitting this kind of unconditioned causality." Immanuel Kant, *The Critique of Pure Reason,* trans. Paul Guyer and Allen W. Wood (Cambridge: Cambridge University Press, 1998), 486, A 448/B 476. Hereafter cited as CPR, followed by A and B edition pages.

10. Jacques Derrida, *The Gift of Death,* trans. David Wills (Chicago and London: University of Chicago Press, 1996), 25. Hereafter cited as GD, followed by page number. In fact: "We must continually remind ourselves that some part of irresponsibility insinuates itself wherever one demands responsibility without sufficiently conceptualizing and thematizing what 'responsibility' means; *that is to say everywhere*" (GD, 25).

11. As Larry Hatab explains, "The search for a decisive ground in ethics can be understood as an attempt to escape the existential demands of contention and commitment. Moral 'decisions' and the sense of 'responsibility' for decisions may in fact be constituted by the global *undecidability* of ethical questions." Lawrence J. Hatab, *Nietzsche's* On the Genealogy of Morality: *An Introduction* (Cambridge: Cambridge University Press, 2008), 241.

12. Friedrich Nietzsche, *Beyond Good and Evil,* trans. Walter Kaufmann (New York: Vintage, 1989), 98. Hereafter cited as BGE, followed by page number.

13. Friedrich Nietzsche, *The Gay Science,* trans. Walter Kaufmann (New York: Vintage, 1974), 285. Hereafter cited as GS, followed by page number.

14. Jacques Derrida, "Passions," in *On the Name,* ed. Thomas Dutoit (Stanford, Calif.: Stanford University Press, 1995), 16. Hereafter cited as P, followed by the page number.

15. Jean-Luc Marion, "The Saturated Phenomenon," in *Phenomenology and the "Theological Turn": The French Debate,* ed. Dominique Janicaud (New York: Fordham University Press, 2000), 204; translation modified.

16. Jacques Derrida, with Elisabeth Roudinesco, *De quoi demain . . .* (Paris: Fayard / Galilée, 2001), 87.

17. Hans Jonas, *The Imperative of Responsibility: In Search of an Ethics for the Technological Age* (Chicago: University of Chicago Press, 1985). Hereafter cited as IR, followed by page number.

18. Jonas claims that the very model or paradigm for conceiving of ethics is that of the solicitude of the parent toward his or her children. It is, he writes, "the archetype of all responsible actions" (IR, 39). The parent-child relation becomes the archetype of all responsibility of humans toward other humans, toward the world, and toward the future of the earth.

19. For instance, Hegel considers the question of our responsibility for the consequences of our acts by attempting to circumscribe what belongs to our responsibility—to our will—and what does not in the "external translation" into the world of our actions (what Kant had already distinguished as a causality of freedom operating within natural causality). He writes, "Furthermore, action has multiple *consequences* in so far as it is translated into external existence [*Dasein*]; for the latter, by virtue of its context in external necessity, develops in all directions. These consequences, as the [outward] *shape* whose *soul* is the *end* to which the action is directed, belong to the action as an integral part of it. But the action, as the end translated into the *external world,* is at the same time exposed to external forces which attach to it things quite different from what it is for itself, and impel it on into remote and alien consequences.

The will thus has the right to *accept responsibility* only for the first set of consequences, since they alone were part of its *purpose*" (Hegel, *Philosophy of Right,* 145, §118).

20. Emmanuel Levinas, *Ethics and Infinity,* trans. Richard A. Cohen (Pittsburgh: Duquesne University Press, 1985), 96. Hereafter cited as EI, followed by page number.

21. Jean-Paul Sartre, *Being and Nothingness: A Phenomenological Essay on Ontology,* trans. Hazel E. Barnes (New York: Washington Square Press, 1992), 707. Hereafter cited as BN, followed by page number.

22. Jean-Luc Nancy, "Responding to Existence," in *Studies in Practical Philosophy* 1, no. 1 (Spring 1999): 1. Another translation, by Sara Guyer, is provided in *A Finite Thinking,* ed. Simon Sparks (Stanford, Calif.: Stanford University Press, 2003), 287–299.

23. Jean-Luc Nancy, *Being Singular Plural,* trans. Robert Richardson and Anne O'Byrne (Stanford, Calif.: Stanford University Press, 2000), 3. Hereafter cited as BSP, followed by page number.

24. *Sein und Zeit* (Tübingen: Max Niemeyer Verlag, 1953), 134. Hereafter cited as SZ for the German pagination; all citations of the work are from *Being and Time,* trans. Joan Stambaugh (Albany: SUNY Press, 1996).

25. See for instance P, 15, where Derrida uses the term "responsiveness" in English in the original; and see GD, 3.

26. Jacques Derrida. *The Politics of Friendship* (London and New York: Verso, 2005), 250; translation modified.

27. In his book, *Ethics and Finitude,* Larry Hatab seeks to advance a notion of responsibility "that can be characterized as 'answerability' (cf. the German *verantwortlich*), rather than what I would call moralistic 'accountability.' With these formulations I mean to distinguish responsibility from autonomous agency and a related sense of accountability." Lawrence J. Hatab, *Ethics and Finitude* (Lanham, Md.: Rowman & Littlefield, 2000), 185.

28. Martin Heidegger. *The Zollikon Seminars,* trans. Franz Mayr and Richard Askay (Evanston, Ill.: Northwestern University Press, 2001), 217; translation modified. Hereafter cited as ZS, followed by page number.

29. Jean-Luc Marion, *Being Given: Toward a Phenomenology of Givenness,* trans. Jeffrey L. Kosky (Stanford, Calif.: Stanford University Press, 2002), 293; translation modified.

30. Friedrich Nietzsche, *Human, All Too Human: A Book for Free Spirits,* ed. Richard Schacht, trans. R. J. Hollingdale (New York: Cambridge University Press, 1996), 16. Hereafter cited as HH, followed by page number.

31. In the *Genealogy of Morals,* Nietzsche states: "My desire, at any rate, was to point out to so sharp and disinterested an eye . . . in the direction of an actual *history of morality* [*wirklichen* Historie der Moral]" (GM, 21).

32. For an interesting reconstruction of the history of the *term* 'responsibility,' see Robert Bernasconi, "Before Whom and for What? Accountability and the Invention of Ministerial, Hyperbolic, and Infinite Responsibility," in *Difficulties of Ethical Life,* ed. Shannon Sullivan and Dennis J. Schmidt (New York: Fordham University Press, 2008).

33. Jean-Luc Nancy, *Dis-enclosure: The Deconstruction of Christianity,* trans. Bettina Bergo, Gabriel Malenfant, and Michael B. Smith (New York: Fordham University Press, 2008), 48.

34. On this "double aspect of subjection," see Judith Butler, *The Psychic Life of Power: Theories in Subjection* (Stanford, Calif.: Stanford University Press, 1997), 12.

35. Immanuel Kant, *The Metaphysics of Morals,* in *Practical Philosophy,* ed. Mary J. Gregor (New York: Cambridge University Press, 1999), 378.

36. Immanuel Kant, "What is Enlightenment?" in *Selections,* ed. Lewis White Beck (Englewood Cliffs, N.J.: Prentice Hall, 1988), 462.

37. Jean-Paul Sartre, "The Humanism of Existentialism," in *Essays in Existentialism,* trans. Bernard Frechtman (New York: Citadel Press, 1995), 40. Hereafter cited as HE, followed by the page number. At the end of the essay, Sartre reiterates this perspective and concludes with these words: "From these few reflections it is evident that nothing is more unjust than the objections that have been raised against us. *Existentialism is nothing else than an attempt to draw all the consequences of a coherent atheistic position*" (HE, 62; my emphasis).

38. Emmanuel Levinas, *Entre Nous,* trans. Michael B. Smith and Barbara Harshav (New York: Columbia University Press, 1998), 35.

39. Martin Heidegger, *Basic Writings,* rev. edition, ed. David Farrell Krell (San Francisco: HarperSanFrancisco, 1993), 235.

40. Jacques Derrida, with Gad Soussana and Alexis Nouss, *Dire l'événement, est-ce possible?* (Paris: L'Harmattan, 2001), 103; my translation.

41. Giovanna Borradori, *Philosophy in a Time of Terror: Dialogues with Jürgen Habermas and Jacques Derrida* (Chicago: University of Chicago Press, 2003), 134.

1. Aristotle: Responsibility as Voluntariness

1. In particular in contrast with fortune (*tuchē*), as he explicitly states at 1099b 25–27. Virtue and happiness are *up to us,* not dependent on fortune.

2. As Sarah Broadie emphasizes, the term voluntary applies only to the person itself as cause and origin of the act; *Ethics with Aristotle* (New York: Oxford University Press, 1991), 124.

3. Aristotle, *Nicomachean Ethics,* trans. with intro. and notes Terence Irwin (Indianapolis: Hackett, 1999). All citations of the *Nicomachean Ethics* are from Irwin's translation.

4. I wish to thank Robert Gibbs from the University of Toronto for suggesting that term to describe Aristotle's "account."

5. Aristotle, *Eudemian Ethics,* trans. Michael Woods (New York: Oxford University Press, 1992), 1223b 24–27. All citations of the *Eudemian Ethics* are from Woods's translation.

6. As William Hardie notes, when he clarifies that "Aristotle is formulating the criteria of imputability"; "The Distinction between the Voluntary and the Involuntary," in *Aristotle's Ethical Theory* (New York: Oxford University Press, 1980), 153. Those criteria will include the voluntary and an account of decision and deliberation, i.e., rational agency.

7. I already alluded to the etymological connection between being the "cause of" and being "responsible for": the word for "cause" is *aitia* or *aition,* and the "responsible agent" is the *aitios.*

8. At 1135a 27–28, Aristotle provides the further example of a man who seizes the arm of another in order to use it to strike another person, to also conclude that the person was not responsible as the act was not "up to him."

9. In book VI of the *Nicomachean Ethics,* Aristotle stresses that *phronēsis* or

practical wisdom does not apply itself to necessity, as "it is impossible to deliberate about what exists by necessity" (1139a 36). *Phronēsis* is not a pure science; it does not pertain to universals but to particulars—"since it is concerned with action and action is about particulars" (1141b 16–17)—and it "deals with things that can be other than they are" (1140b 28–29).

10. Indeed, for Aristotle, decision pertains to character and virtue, and allows one to praise or blame, not simply the action, but the character of the agent itself: Decision seems to be most proper to virtue, that is, it allow us "to distinguish characters from one another better than actions do" (1111b 6–7). We will see the same extension from action to character in his subsequent definition of responsibility: one will not only be responsible for one's actions, but also for one's character. Character is *up to us* as well. Therefore virtue is said to be "up to us," as is vice, since "vice is voluntary" (1113b 17).

11. In contrast, Derrida will claim that decision is always of the impossible, an encounter with the impossible, and never simply the unfolding of a possible project. If decision were restricted to the possible, one could not speak of a responsible decision worthy of that name. For Derrida, there is no responsible decision except as an engagement with the impossible; we will return to this in chapter 8.

12. We will see how the area of what is "up to us" has grown in the history of philosophy to encompass the whole of reality, to the extent that reason becomes both practical and absolutized. For Sartre, for instance, *everything* is *up to us* (including what is clearly not, *stricto sensu,* up to us!), and no area escapes our responsibility.

13. Here again, we note the radical break from this conception in Sartre's philosophy: For Sartre, we are responsible for all humans, and it would bad faith to limit one's responsibilities to the particular groups or sub-groups to which one belongs. As for the very notion of an "up to us," it will be entirely destroyed in Levinas's thought, as my responsibility is for the other, and not dependent on my agency or freedom.

14. In *The Gift of Death,* Derrida will pursue this thought of a decision "beyond knowledge," stating that "the concept of responsibility has, in the most reliable continuity of its history, always implied involvement in action, doing, a *praxis,* a *decision* that exceeds simple conscience or simple theoretical understanding" (GD, 25). Consequently, one should state that responsibility, the "activating of responsibility (decision, act, *praxis*) will always take place before and beyond any theoretical or thematic determination" (GD, 26).

2. Kant: Responsibility as Spontaneity of the Subject

1. Immanuel Kant, *The Metaphysics of Morals,* in *Practical Philosophy,* ed. Mary J. Gregor (New York: Cambridge University Press, 1999), 378.

2. Immanuel Kant, *The Critique of Practical Reason,* 3d edn., trans. Lewis White Beck (New York: MacMillan, 1993), 99, 100, 101. Hereafter cited in the text as CPrR, followed by page number.

3. Kant, *Metaphysics of Morals,* 378.

4. Kant, *Critique of Practical Reason,* 3.

5. Henry Allison, *Kant's Theory of Freedom* (New York: Cambridge University Press, 1990), 11. On a discussion of the Third Antinomy in terms of a reflection on

responsibility, one may also consult Paul Ricoeur, *Le Juste* (Paris: Editions Esprit, 1995), 41–70, esp. 47–50.

6. Immanuel Kant, *The Critique of Pure Reason,* trans. Paul Guyer and Allen W. Wood (Cambridge: Cambridge University Press, 1998), 533, A 533/B 561. Hereafter cited as CPR, followed by page number and A and B edition pages.

7. On the limits of situating the question of freedom in the context of causality, see Jean-Luc Nancy, *The Experience of Freedom,* trans. Bridget McDonald (Stanford, Calif.: Stanford University Press, 1994), 25–26, where Nancy comments upon a passage from Heidegger's *The Essence of Human Freedom* in which Heidegger states that, "Causality, in the sense of the traditional comprehension of the being of beings, in ordinary as well as in traditional metaphysics, is precisely the fundamental category of being as presence-at-hand" (GA 31, 300; cit. Nancy, *Experience of Freedom,* 26), and that therefore the question of freedom must be approached in a more originary sense than in relation to causality. I will return to this critique of causality, whether in Nietzsche's genealogy, in Sartre's radicalization of freedom as original freedom, or in Heidegger's critique of causality as improper access to being.

8. For instance, one reads in the first lines of the preface of the *Foundations of the Metaphysics of Morals,* "Material philosophy, however, which has to do with definite objects and the laws to which they are subject, is divided into two parts. This is because these laws are either laws of nature or laws of freedom. The science of the former is physics, and that of the latter ethics; the former is also called theory of nature and the latter theory of morals." Immanuel Kant, *Foundations of the Metaphysics of Morals,* trans. Lewis White Beck, in *Selections* (Englewood Cliffs, N.J.: Prentice Hall, 1988), 244. Hereafter cited as FMM, followed by page number.

9. Including *our own* nature, as Sartre recognized when he wrote that we do not have a human nature because we are free.

10. Also, in the "Clarification of the cosmological idea of a freedom in combination with the universal natural necessity," one reads: "The law of nature that everything that happens has a cause, that since the causality of this cause, i.e., the *action,* precedes in time and in respect of an effect that has *arisen* cannot have been always but must have *happened,* and so must also have had its cause among appearances, through which it is determined, and consequently that all occurrences are empirically determined in a natural order—this law, through which alone appearances can first constitute one *nature* and furnish objects of one experience, is a law of the understanding, from which under no pretext can any departure be allowed or any appearance be exempted; because otherwise one would put this appearance outside of all possible experience, thereby distinguishing it from objects of possible experience and making it into a mere thought-entity and a figment of the brain" (CPR, 538, A 542/B 570).

11. Further, Kant writes that "among the causes in appearance there can surely be nothing that could begin a series absolutely and from itself. Every action, as appearance, insofar as it produces an occurrence, is itself an occurrence, or event, which presupposes another state in which its cause is found; and thus everything that happens is only a continuation of the series, and no beginning that would take place from itself is possible in it. Thus in the temporal succession all actions of natural causes are themselves in turn effects, which likewise presuppose their causes in the time-series. An *original* action, through which something happens that pre-

viously was not, is not to be expected from the causal connection of appearances" (CPR, 538, A 543/B 571).

12. Still in the "Clarification of the cosmological idea of a freedom," Kant explains that such a free causality would be considered as "an original action of a cause in regard to appearances, which to that extent is not appearance but in accordance with this faculty intelligible," although it must, at the same time, as a link in the chain of nature, be regarded as "belonging to the world of senses" (CPR, 539, A 544/B 572).

13. Indeed, it *cannot be* part of the phenomenal world, as it contradicts the fundamental law of causality which structures the unity of the world as nature. In fact, such freedom is "contrary to the law of nature," "to all possible experience" (CPR, 676, A 803/B 831). Henry Allison clarifies that "transcendental freedom is opposed to the conditions of the unity of experience (as specified in the 'law of causality') and therefore can never be met within any possible experience" (*Kant's Theory of Freedom*, 20).

14. As Nancy comments in his own thinking of free decision, it is a question of a decision for "what is in no way given in advance, but which constitutes the irruption of the new, unpredictable because without face, and thus the 'beginning of a series of phenomena' by which the Kantian freedom is defined in its relation to the world." Jean-Luc Nancy, *The Creation of The World or Globalization*, trans. François Raffoul and David Pettigrew (Albany: SUNY Press, 2007), 59.

15. Heidegger would stress Kant's debt toward this ontology of the *subjectum*, an indebtedness that constitutes for Heidegger the insufficiency of Kant's determination of subjectivity, the fact that it turns out to be incapable of developing an authentic ontology of Dasein. Heidegger's reproach can be summarized as follows: By characterizing the ego as a *subject*, that is, as the ultimate *subjectum* of its predicates (and of its actions in the practical sense), Kant maintains the traditional ontology of the substantial, and thereby continues to conceive of the I inadequately as the "supporting ground (as substance or subject)"; see *Sein und Zeit* (Tübingen: Max Niemeyer Verlag, 1953), 317. As Heidegger explains, to define the ego as a subject is to approach it in a mode that is not appropriate to the being that we are.

16. Henry Allison clarifies the distinction between autonomy and heteronomy in these terms: "either the will gives the law to itself, in which case we have autonomy, or the law is somehow given to the will from without, in which case we have heteronomy" (*Kant's Theory of Freedom*, 99).

17. With respect to the Kantian determination of the moral person as end-in-itself, Heidegger argues that it is not sufficient to merely add finality as a predicate to a being whose mode of being is still grasped in the sense of presence-at-hand, and the task is to conceive of it ontologically, as a *way to be*. At the same time, one could state that Heidegger's analysis is also indebted to Kant's theory of the moral person, for instance, when Heidegger writes (no longer distinguishing between person and Dasein): "The person is a thing, *res*, something, that exists as its own end. To this being belongs purposiveness. Its way of being is to *be* the end or purpose of its own self. *This determination, to be the end of its own self, belongs indisputably to the ontological constitution of the human Dasein.*" Martin Heidegger, *Die Grundprobleme der Phänomenologie*, GA 24 (Frankfurt am Main: Vittorio Klostermann, 1975), 199; my emphasis. Hereafter cited as GA 24, followed by page number. See the English translation by Albert Hofstadter, as *The Basic Problems of Phenomenology* (Bloomington and Indianapolis: Indiana University Press, 1982).

18. Kant, *Critique of Practical Reason,* 76.

19. Friedrich Nietzsche, *The Twilight of the Idols,* trans. Richard Polt (Indianapolis and Cambridge: Hackett, 1997), 74; translation modified. Hereafter cited as TI, followed by page number.

20. Immanuel Kant, "What is Enlightenment?" in *Selections,* ed. Lewis White Beck (Englewood Cliffs, N.J.: Prentice Hall, 1988). Hereafter cited as E, followed by page number.

21. Michel Foucault, "What is Enlightenment?" in *The Foucault Reader,* ed. P. Rabinow (New York: Pantheon, 1984), 34.

22. One thinks here of Étienne de La Boétie's *The Politics of Obedience: The Discourse of Voluntary Servitude* (New York: Free Life, 1975), the relinquishing of one's freedom and responsibility for the sake of a ruler, such that it is the one oppressed under the ruler that gives that ruler the power. The relevance here is that in giving the power to another, one is attempting to relinquish one's responsibility, something that will ultimately prove impossible.

23. Foucault, "What is Enlightenment?" 34–35.

24. We will return to this thematic of a weight of responsibility, of the difficulty of existence and the role of responsibility in such a task, in our chapters on Sartre and Heidegger.

25. Foucault, "What is Enlightenment?" 34. Further on in this essay, Foucault develops this proximity between Kant's text on enlightenment and his three *Critiques.* He writes: "Nevertheless, notwithstanding its circumstantial nature, and without intending to give it an exaggerated place in Kant's work, I believe that it is necessary to stress the connection that exists between this brief article and the three *Critiques.* Kant in fact describes Enlightenment as the moment when humanity is going to put its own reason to use, without subjecting itself to any authority; now it is precisely at this moment that the critique is necessary, since its role is that of defining the conditions under which the use of reason is legitimate in order to determine what can be known [*connaître*], what must be done, and what may be hoped. Illegitimate uses of reason are what give rise to dogmatism and heteronomy, along with illusion; on the other hand, it is when the legitimate use of reason has been clearly defined in its principles that its autonomy can be assured. The critique is, in a sense, the handbook of reason that has grown up in Enlightenment; and, conversely, the Enlightenment is the age of the critique."

3. Nietzsche's Deconstruction of Accountability

Nietzsche, *Human, All Too Human,* 34.

1. Maurice Merleau-Ponty, *The Primacy of Perception,* ed. James M. Edie, trans. William Cobb (Evanston, Ill.: Northwestern University Press, 1964), 30.

2. For instance in *Daybreak,* where Nietzsche remarks that the "fundamental insights into the origin of morality are so difficult for us latecomers, and even when we have acquired them we find it impossible to enunciate them, because they sound so uncouth or because they seem to slander morality"; in *The Nietzsche Reader,* ed. Keith Ansell Pearson and Duncan Large (Malden, Mass.: Blackwell, 2006), 191.

3. Friedrich Nietzsche, *The Gay Science,* trans. Walter Kaufmann (New York: Vintage, 1974), 285. Hereafter cited as GS, followed by page number.

4. Friedrich Nietzsche, *The Will to Power,* trans. Walter Kaufmann and R. J.

Hollingdale (New York: Vintage / Random House, 1968), 148. Hereafter cited as WP, followed by page number.

5. Friedrich Nietzsche, *On the Genealogy of Morals,* trans. Walter Kaufmann (New York: Vintage, 1967), 58; translation modified. Hereafter cited as GM, followed by page number.

6. David B. Allison, *Reading the New Nietzsche* (Lanham, Md.: Rowman & Littlefield, 2001), 78.

7. Friedrich Nietzsche, *Human, All Too Human: A Book for Free Spirits,* ed. Richard Schacht, trans. R. J. Hollingdale (New York: Cambridge University Press, 1996), 16. Hereafter cited as HH, followed by page number.

8. Friedrich Nietzsche, *On Truth and Lies in a Nonmoral Sense,* trans. Daniel Brazeale (Atlantic Highlands, N.J.: Humanities Press, 1979), 79. (Hereafter cited as TL, followed by page number.) The original title reads *Über Wahrheit und Lüge im aussermoralischen Sinne,* and as Brazeale recognizes, a more accurate or literal translation would be "On Truth and Lie in an Extramoral Sense." As Nietzsche states in the preface to *Human, All Too Human,* he is "speaking unmorally (*unmoralisch*), extra-morally (*aussermoralisch*), 'beyond good and evil'" (HH, 6). On the sense of this notion of "extramoral," one should understand it in the precise way articulated by Nietzsche in *The Gay Science,* when he wrote: "'Thoughts about moral prejudices,' is they are not meant to be prejudices about prejudices, presuppose a position *outside* morality, some point beyond good and evil" (GS, 380). Also see Nietzsche, *Beyond Good and Evil,* trans. Walter Kaufmann (New York: Vintage, 1989), 44.

9. Nietzsche states that "here one may certainly admire man as a mighty genius of construction, who succeeds in piling an infinitely complicated dome of concepts upon an unstable foundation, and, as it were, on running water" (TL, 85).

10. "We call a person 'honest' and then we ask 'why has he behaved so honestly today?' Our usual answer is, 'on account of his honesty.' Honesty! This in turn means that the leaf is the cause of the leaves. We know nothing whatsoever about an essential quality called 'honesty'; but we do know of countless individualized and consequently unequal actions which we equate by omitting the aspects in which they are unequal and which we now designate as 'honest' actions. Finally we formulate from them a *qualitas occulta* which has the name 'honesty.' In place of such imaginary notion, there is an X 'which remains inaccessible and undefinable for us'" (TL, 83).

11. One recalls here how David Hume, in his *Treatise of Human Nature,* had to have recourse to the distinction between simple and complex impressions (impressions "of sensation" and impressions "of reflection"), in order to produce some connection between impressions and ideas when such a connection was tenuous at best. See David Hume, *A Treatise of Human Nature,* ed. David Fate Norton and Mary J. Norton (New York: Oxford University Press, 2000), 11.

12. Friedrich Nietzsche, *On the Genealogy of Morals and Ecce Homo,* trans. Walter Kaufmann (New York: Vintage, 1967), 326. Hereafter cited as EH, followed by page number.

13. Compare with §258 of *The Will to Power* where Nietzsche, after stating his main claim—"*My chief proposition: there are no moral phenomena, there is only a moral interpretation of these phenomena*"—adds, "*This interpretation itself is of extra-moral origin*" (WP, 149). Morality as an allegedly 'pure domain' is here deconstructed, revealing its impure, extramoral origins.

14. In *The Anti-Christ*, Nietzsche analyzes other Kantian moral concepts in that light: "'Virtue,' 'duty,' 'good in itself,' impersonal and universal—phantoms, expressions of decline, of the final exhaustion of life, of Königsbergian Chinadom." Respect for virtue, Nietzsche adds, "harms life." See Friedrich Nietzsche, *Twilight of the Idols and The Anti-Christ*, ed. Michael Tanner, trans. R. J. Hollingdale (New York: Penguin, 1990), 133–134. This edition of *The Anti-Christ* is hereafter cited as AC, followed by page number.

15. As we cited above, for Nietzsche, "There are *no eternal facts*, just as there are no absolute truths. Consequently what is needed from now on is *historical philosophizing*, and with it the virtue of modesty" (HH, 13).

16. "What defines me, what sets me apart from the whole rest of humanity is that I *uncovered* Christian morality" (EH, 332).

17. Levinas would speak of "a defeat of the originary intentionality in every act," in his *God, Death, and Time*, trans. Bettina Bergo (Stanford, Calif.: Stanford University Press, 2000), 172.

18. "Everybody knows the book by the famous Cornaro where he promotes his skimpy diet as a prescription for a long, happy—and virtuous—life. I have no doubt that hardly any book (with the exception of the Bible, as is only fair) has done as much damage, has *shortened* as many lives as this curiosity which was so well-meaning. The reason: confusing the effect with the cause" (TI, 30). Cornaro believed his diet was the *cause* of his long life, when it was his slow metabolism that was the cause of his diet. His frugality was *not* a matter of free will, he simply became sick when he ate more.

19. Judith Butler, *Giving an Account of Oneself* (New York: Fordham University Press, 2005), 14.

20. Everyone knows the experience in a dream when the dreamer hears a sound which then becomes included in the narrative in a causal way. What was first a sheer event, perceived outside any causal network, is then integrated in the dream and reconstructed as causal origin in the narration.

21. Lawrence J. Hatab, *Nietzsche's* On the Genealogy of Morality: *An Introduction* (Cambridge: Cambridge University Press, 2008), 62.

22. On this point see Hatab, ibid., 134.

23. This taking-over of existence is also apparent in this passage where Nietzsche writes that, "'You shall become master over yourself, master also over your virtues. Formerly *they* were your masters; but they must be only your instruments beside other instruments" (HH, 9).

24. "One may conjecture that a spirit in whom the type 'free spirit' will one day become a ripe and sweet to the point of perfection has had its decisive experience in a *great liberation* [*einer* grossen Loslösung] and that previously it was all the more a fettered spirit and seemed to be chained for ever to its pillar and corner" (HH, 6).

4. Sartre: Hyperbolic Responsibility

1. In an article on the French reception (and non-reception!) of Heidegger, Françoise Dastur stresses how Sartre remains indebted to the Cartesian tradition and thereby misses some of the insights he was trying to exploit in Heidegger's thought of being: "Did Sartre manage to truly open himself to the Heideggerian problematic and

thus to 'free himself from the context of Cartesian philosophy' within which he had been trained? That is the question. We know that modern philosophy since Descartes understood the being of the human as 'consciousness' or as 'subject.' Sartre situated himself in this same perspective, whereas Heidegger decisively broke with it." See Françoise Dastur, "The Reception and Nonreception of Heidegger in France," in *French Interpretations of Heidegger*, ed. David Pettigrew and François Raffoul (Albany: SUNY Press, 2008), 268. Hereafter cited as HF, followed by page number. On Sartre's relationship to Heidegger's thought, also see Dominique Janicaud's account in *Heidegger en France* (Paris: Albin Michel, 2001), 55–79.

2. Jacques Derrida, *Sur Parole* (Paris: Éditions de l'Aube, 1999), 83–84.

3. Jean-Paul Sartre, *Being and Nothingness: A Phenomenological Essay on Ontology*, trans. Hazel E. Barnes (New York: Washington Square Press, 1992), 707. Hereafter cited as BN, followed by page number.

4. Robert Bernasconi notes a "transformation" of the notion of responsibility in Sartre's work, as his "sense of responsibility is clearly very different from the ordinary sense of responsibility according to which I am accountable only for those acts of which I am indisputably the author," and later clarifies that the "Sartrean conception . . . arises from his conviction that in choosing myself in the sense of my project, I determine the way that the world appears to me and to that extent can be said to choose the world." See Robert Bernasconi, "Before Whom and for What? Accountability and the Invention of Ministerial, Hyperbolic, and Infinite Responsibility," in *Difficulties of Ethical Life*, ed. Shannon Sullivan and Dennis Schmidt (New York: Fordham University Press, 2008), 139. One point remains to be made here, namely, that "transformation" of the classical notion of responsibility is in fact a hyperbolic paroxysm of the sense of authorship: Sartre extends authorship to embrace the whole world, as I now become responsible not only for what I have done but also for what I have not done. I become the *author* of all there is, the *author* of the meaning of being. The transformation of responsibility is more a confirmation or infinitization than a change in its concept. We nonetheless continue to note that this paroxystic extension of responsibility as authorship is accompanied by a radical lack of foundation, as my responsibility for the whole world is based on my being nothing. This is why the paroxysm is paradoxical: The extension of responsibility as accountability is made possible *and undermined* by its lack of foundation.

5. Jean-Paul Sartre, "The Humanism of Existentialism," in *Essays in Existentialism* (New York: Citadel Press, 1995), 40. Hereafter cited as HE, followed by the page number.

6. This primacy of the subject in Sartre's philosophy is constitutive. For instance, in "The Humanism of Existentialism," he writes: "It is also what is called subjectivity, the name we are labeled with when charges are brought against us. But what do we mean by this, if not that man has a greater dignity than a stone or table? For we mean that man first exists, that is, that man first of all is the being who hurls himself toward a future and who is conscious of imagining himself as being in the future. Man is at the start a plan who is conscious of itself, rather than a patch of moss, a piece of garbage, or a cauliflower" (HE, 36). Or: "Subjectivism means, on the one hand, that an individual chooses and makes himself; and, on the other, that it is impossible for man to transcend human subjectivity. The second of these is the essential meaning of existentialism" (HE, 37). Or: "Subjectivity of the individual is

indeed our point of departure, and this for strictly philosophic reasons" (HE, 50). Or moreover: "There is no other universe except the human universe, the universe of human subjectivity." And finally, this remarkable statement: "There can no other truth to start from than this: *I think; therefore, I exist*" (HE, 51)!

7. As for instance Risieri Frondizi, "Sartre's Early Ethics: A Critique," in *The Philosophy of Jean-Paul Sartre*, ed. Paul Arthur Schilpp (La Salle, Ill.: Open Court, 1981).

8. Sartre would speak of the "long and difficult task" of "becoming-an-atheist," in his essay "The Singular Universal" (1964), in *Kierkegaard: A Collection of Critical Essays*, ed. Josiah Thompson (Garden City, N.Y.: Anchor, 1972).

9. Jean-Luc Nancy, "Responding to Existence," in *Studies in Practical Philosophy* 1, no. 1 (Spring 1999): 7. Hereafter cited as RE, followed by the page number. (The original title is *Répondre de l'existence*, which could perhaps be rendered more accurately as "Answering for Existence.")

10. As Nancy pursues, "such is our responsibility, which is not added to us like a task, but which makes up our being" (RE, 8).

11. On this boundlessness of responsibility, beyond measure and calculation, see the remarks by Jean-Luc Nancy in "Responsabilité—Du sens à venir," a dialogue with Jacques Derrida, in *Sens en tous sens. Autour des travaux de Jean-Luc Nancy* (Paris: Galilée, 2004), 173–174.

12. One finds a further element on the status of ethics in Sartre's work in his interviews with Benny Levy, in which Levy asks him first whether his subsequent and "exhausting" debate with Marxism was not an attempt to escape from the dialectics of bad faith in *Being and Nothingness*. To this, Sartre replies: "Unquestionably." Levy follows up and asks: "At the end of *Being and Nothingness* you thought you were opening up a new perspective on ethics, and then what we get is not a book on ethics but this debate with Marxism. The two things must be intimately connected." Sartre replies to this, "Yes, intimately"—and adds that what he sought in Hegel and Marx was "the true social ends of ethics." Jean-Paul Sartre and Benny Levy, *Hope Now: The 1980 Interviews* (Chicago: Chicago University Press, 1996), 60. Hereafter cited as HN, followed by page number.

13. As Françoise Dastur explains: "Indeed, Sartre developed in *Being and Nothingness*, a philosophy of consciousness even though he was not unaware that Heidegger had precisely introduced the task of abandoning the notion of consciousness in favor of that of existence" (HF, 268).

14. On the belonging of atheism to Christianity, see Jean-Luc Nancy's reflections in *Dis-Enclosure: The Deconstruction of Christianity* (New York: Fordham University Press, 2008), esp. 32–35, and 143–144, which I discuss in my "The Self-Deconstruction of Christianity," in *Retreating Religion: Deconstructing Christianity with Jean-Luc Nancy*, ed. Ignaas Devisch, under contract with Fordham University Press.

15. "We can avoid confusion by always using the interpretive expression *objective presence [Vorhandenheit]* for the term *existentia*, and by attributing existence as a determination of being only to Da-sein" (SZ, 42).

16. That is to say, in terms of the principle of sufficient reason, of the rendering of reasons. Sartre thus still maintains a dependency with the classical thought of causality, when in fact, as Jean-Luc Nancy remarked, it is possible to free the thought of facticity of the world from the necessity-contingency conceptual couple by considering this fact of the world "without referring it to a cause (neither efficient nor final)" (CW, 45).

17. The nothing constitutes the transcendence of the for-itself, as Sartre clarified in *Being and Nothingness* (in the chapter titled "The Origin of Negation"), stating that nothingness is the "heart of transcendence" (BN, 52).

18. In his words of the late years, "First, as you know, for me there is no a priori essence; and so what a human being is has not yet been established. We are not complete human beings. We are beings who are struggling to establish human relations and arrive at a definition of what is human" (HN, 66).

19. Thomas Flynn thus characterizes the "root concept of freedom in Sartrean existentialism," that is, original freedom, as "nihilating freedom," explaining that for Sartre nihilation is "the most basic form of ontological freedom." Thomas Flynn, *Sartre and Marxist Existentialism* (Chicago: University of Chicago Press, 1984), 7.

20. Jean-Paul Sartre, *War Diaries: Notebooks from a Phony War* (New York: Verso, 1999), 133.

21. This is why it is incorrect to state, as Risieri Frondizi does, that "since there are no pre-established moral rules or principles, Sartre maintains that man has neither obligation nor commitment until he freely chooses them" (art. cit., 387). Man *is* obligated for Sartre, by and to his freedom, having to choose because of *having to* be free. Sartre clearly states that "freedom . . . is characterized by a constantly renewed *obligation* to remake the *Self* which designates the free being" (BN, 72; my emphasis). The situation of choice indicates that to exist means to be in a constant state of obligation.

22. For instance in Jacques Derrida, "Passions," in *On the Name*, ed. Thomas Dutoit (Stanford, Calif.: Stanford University Press, 1995), 7-9.

23. For instance Risieri Frondizi, who states that "I am only maintaining that if I can make anything right by the mere act of freely choosing it, I am destroying the very notion of 'right' and 'wrong'" (art. cit., 375).

24. Jacques Derrida, interview with *l'Humanité*, 28 January 2004.

25. On this notion of a creation that occurs against the background of a radical absence of the given, see Jean-Luc Nancy, *The Creation of The World or Globalization*, trans. François Raffoul and David Pettigrew (Albany: SUNY Press, 2007), 51.

26. Sartre, "The Singular Universal" (1964). One could here draw a relation with what Jean-Luc Nancy calls the "Singular Plural," how each singularity communicates with *all* other singularities. Yet the difference lies in the fact that Nancy does not rely on a concept of universality, insisting instead on the *plurality* of singularities. But in both cases, the singular engages the others. On this, see my "Nancy and The Logic of the With," in *Studies in Practical Philosophy* 1, no. 1 (1999).

27. In all fairness, in the later years Sartre did recognize the limits of his early egological perspective, conceding that his early philosophy was overly individualistic. For instance, in *Hope Now* he explains that in *"Being and Nothingness* my theory of others left the individual too independent. I did raise some questions that showed the relationship to others in a new light . . . It had to do with a relationship of each to each . . . Nonetheless I did consider that each consciousness in itself, and each individual in himself, was relatively independent of the other. I hadn't determined what I am trying to determine today: *the dependence of each individual on all other individuals"* (HN, 71-72; my emphasis).

28. In a 1960 interview with *Le Monde*, Sartre explained that "first, all men must be able to become men by the improvement of their conditions of existence, so that a universal morality can be created" (cit. Frondizi, in art. cit., 14).

29. As Thomas Flynn comments, "freedom and responsibility are correlative terms in the strict sense that they imply each other. If and inasmuch as the for-itself is free, it must be responsible; the extent of its responsibility is precisely that of its freedom" (*Sartre and Marxist Existentialism*, 16). Similarly, David Wood notes that with Sartre, "The hyperbole of freedom leads to a hyperbole of responsibility"; *The Step Back: Ethics and Politics after Deconstruction* (Albany: SUNY Press, 2005), 143.

30. An excess that might be proper to the experience of responsibility as such, if it is the case, as Jacques Derrida writes, that "responsibility is excessive or it is not a responsibility"; in "'Eating Well,' or the Calculation of the Subject: An Interview with Jacques Derrida," in *Who Comes After the Subject*, ed. Eduardo Cadava et al. (New York and London: Routledge, 1991).

31. I will return to this point; Levinas makes a similar claim on responsibility as carrying the weight of the world on our shoulders. However, we will see that it is for opposite reasons: Whereas for Sartre, responsibility is overwhelming because of my absolute freedom, for Levinas I carry the world on my shoulders not because I am free, but because I am infinitely subjected to the other.

32. Provoking this reaction from Thomas Flynn: "Consequently, the range of imputability is simply staggering: it extends to all that I am or do, to the meaning (*sens*) of what others do, and indeed to the very fact that 'there is' a world at all" (*Sartre and Marxist Existentialism*, 14).

33. Derrida, *Sens en tous sens*, 168–169; my emphasis.

34. Flynn, *Sartre and Marxist Existentialism*, 13.

35. Jean-Luc Nancy, *Being Singular Plural* (Stanford, Calif.: Stanford University Press, 2000), 15; my emphasis. Hereafter cited as BSP, followed by page number.

36. On these questions, see my "The Creation of the World," in *Jean-Luc Nancy and Plural Thinking: Expositions of World, Politics, Art and Sense*, ed. Marie-Eve Morin and Peter Gratton, under contract with SUNY Press.

37. In a 1970 interview, Sartre would return to this extreme position with some skepticism and exclaim: "When I read that, I said to myself: It is incredible: I have really thought so!" *Situations* IX (Paris: Gallimard, 1972), 100.

38. Significantly, Sartre would clarify that thought a few lines below, as "here again I encounter only myself and my projects," which clearly betrays how his thinking of responsibility is tied to an egology. We will return to this.

39. Marion analyzes birth in strikingly similar terms, writing that "I have never seen [my birth] with my own eyes" and that "I must rely on eyewitnesses or a birth certificate," that is, to indirectly have access to it; see Jean-Luc Marion, *In Excess: Studies of Saturated Phenomena*, trans. Robyn Horner and Vincent Berraud (New York: Fordham University Press, 2002), 41. He continues by emphasizing that elusiveness of birth, noting that birth "is accomplished without me and even, strictly speaking, before me." Now, whereas Sartre will argue from this elusiveness of birth to emphasize our responsibility toward it (birth is only accessible through my responsibility), Marion will argue that birth constitutes an authentic phenomenon, to be precise, a saturated phenomenon which "affects me more radically than any other, since it alone determines me, defines my ego, even produces it" (ibid., 42). Birth becomes an event *par excellence*, "from the fact that it *gives me to myself* when it gives *itself*" (ibid., 43). Birth is that phenomenon that shows itself by . . . not showing itself! Or, there is self-giving, but there is no self-showing (ibid., 43). In the end,

the positions are not so far apart, as the excess of the saturated phenomenon is what calls for my responsibility in Marion's work. This is why, as Marion puts it in Sartrean terms, "My whole life is solely occupied, for an essential part, with reconstituting [birth], attributing to it a meaning and responding to its silent appeal" (ibid., 42). For another interesting phenomenological approach to birth, see Claude Romano, *Event and World* (New York: Fordham University Press, 2009), 69–82.

40. Martin Heidegger, *Four Seminars*, trans. Andrew Mitchell and François Raffoul (Bloomington and Indianapolis: Indiana University Press, 2003), 41.

41. We know that for Husserl, the most fundamental Being-distinction is that which separates immanence from transcendence, that is, consciousness as an absolute, immanent sphere, from the transcendent thing appearing in consciousness. For instance, Husserl wrote in *Ideas I*, §49: "Consciousness, considered in its 'purity,' must be reckoned as a *self-contained system of Being*, as a system of *Absolute Being*, into which nothing can penetrate, and from which nothing can escape; which has no spatio-temporal exterior, and can be inside no spatio-temporal system; which cannot experience causality from anything nor exert causality upon anything." See Edmund Husserl, *Ideas Pertaining to a Pure Phenomenology and to a Phenomenological Philosophy—First Book: General Introduction to a Pure Phenomenology*, trans. F. Kersten (The Hague: Martinus Nijhoff, 1982).

5. Levinas's Reversal of Responsibility

1. Emmanuel Levinas, *Ethics and Infinity* (Pittsburgh: Duquesne University Press, 1985), 96. Hereafter cited as EI, followed by page number.

2. Emmanuel Levinas, *Autrement qu'être ou au-delà de l'essence* (Dordrecht: Kluwer Academic, 1996), 46. Hereafter cited as AE, followed by page number; all translations of this work are mine.

3. Emmanuel Levinas, *Entre Nous*, trans. Michael B. Smith and Barbara Harshav (New York: Columbia University Press, 1998), 105. Hereafter cited as EN, followed by page number.

4. For instance in Jacques Derrida, with Elisabeth Roudinesco, *De quoi demain . . .* (Paris: Fayard / Galilée, 2001), 92.

5. Jacques Derrida, *The Gift of Death*, trans. David Wills (Chicago and London: University of Chicago Press, 1992), 46. Hereafter cited as GD, followed by page number.

6. Levinas, "Useless Suffering," in EN, 101.

7. As Judith Butler explains: "For Levinas, who separates the claim of responsibility from the possibility of agency, responsibility emerges as a consequence of being subject to the unwilled address of the other." See her *Giving an Account of Oneself* (New York: Fordham University Press, 2005), 85.

8. Levinas cites a Lithuanian rabbi of the eighteenth century, Rabbi Haim of Volozhin, who stated that "each one of them—a unique person in the world—is responsible for the entire universe!" (EN, 206).

9. See for instance Levinas, EI, 37–38; and Emmanuel Levinas, *Is It Righteous to Be?* ed. Jill Robbins (Stanford, Calif.: Stanford University Press, 2001), 31–37. The latter text will be cited hereafter as RB, followed by page number.

10. On this early reception, see Dominique Janicaud, *Heidegger en France* (Paris: Albin Michel, 2000), esp. 31–36, concerning Levinas's role in it.

11. Also, in "Philosophy, Justice, and Love," Levinas states that "the relation to the other is the beginning of the intelligible" (EN, 109).

12. Emmanuel Levinas, *Totalité et Infini; Essai sur l'extériorité* (Paris: Le Livre de Poche, 1994), 32. Hereafter cited as EE, followed by page number; all translations of this work are mine.

13. Emmanuel Levinas, *Le Temps et l'autre* (Paris: Presses Universitaires de France, 1983), 88. Hereafter cited as T, followed by page number.

14. Emmanuel Levinas, *Humanisme de l'autre homme* (Montpellier: Fata Morgana, 1972); this is now published in an English translation by Nidra Poller, as *Humanism of the Other* (Urbana and Chicago: University of Illinois Press, 2005).

15. Emmanuel Levinas, *On Escape*, trans. Bettina Bergo (Stanford, Calif.: Stanford University Press, 2003). Hereafter cited as OE, followed by page number.

16. See also Emmanuel Levinas, *Existence and Existents*, trans. Alphonso Lingis (Pittsburgh: Duquesne University Press, 2001).

17. On this point, see also RB, 45.

18. The following analyses draw from my earlier essay, "Being and the Other: Ethics and Ontology in Heidegger and Levinas," in *Addressing Levinas*, ed. Eric Sean Nelson, Antje Kapust, and Kent Still (Evanston, Ill.: Northwestern University Press, 2006).

19. On this point, see my *Heidegger and the Subject* (Amherst, N.Y.: Prometheus, 1999).

20. In *Ethics and Infinity,* Levinas wonders: "Does 'existing with' represent a veritable sharing of existence?" (EI, 58). A few pages later, he responds that "true togetherness" is not a togetherness of synthesis, but a "togetherness of face to face" (EI, 77), a face to face that cannot be synthesized.

21. Jacques Derrida, *Adieu à Emmanuel Lévinas* (Paris: Galilée, 1997). Hereafter cited as *Adieu,* followed by page number.

22. At the beginning of his *Adieu à Emmanuel Lévinas,* Derrida narrates an anecdote in which (we are told that) Levinas confided to him one day during a walk through the streets of Paris that what interested him most was not ethics—not, for instance, a prescriptive system of rules—but "the holy, the holiness of the holy" (*Adieu,* 15).

23. For a more developed account, see my "The Subject of the Welcome," in *Symposium: Journal of the Canadian Society of Hermeneutics* 2, no. 2 (Fall 1998).

24. Jacques Derrida, *Sur Parole* (Paris: Éditions de l'Aube, 1999), 65.

25. "In human existence, there is, as it were, interrupting or surpassing the vocation of being, another vocation: that of the other, his existing, his destiny" (RB, 228).

26. The French word *visage* immediately gives a human character to the face as it is thematized by Levinas, since *visage* refers exclusively to the human face, whereas for animals one speaks of a *gueule.* Thus the humanism of Levinas's thought is already inscribed linguistically, in the French language.

27. For instance in Hans Jonas, *The Imperative of Responsibility: In Search of an Ethics for the Technological Age* (Chicago: University of Chicago Press, 1985), 6–7.

28. Jean-Luc Marion, *In Excess: Studies of Saturated Phenomena,* trans. Robyn Horner and Vincent Berraud (New York: Fordham University Press, 2002), 51.

29. In Martin Heidegger, *Four Seminars,* trans. Andrew Mitchell and François Raffoul (Bloomington and Indianapolis: Indiana University Press, 2002).

30. Jean-Luc Marion, "The Saturated Phenomenon," in *Phenomenology and the "Theological Turn": The French Debate,* ed. Dominique Janicaud (New York: Fordham University Press, 2000), 176–216.

31. Derrida thus explained how he has attempted to "show the way in which Levinas meant to remain faithful to phenomenology at the very same time that he questioned the results or claims of a Husserlian phenomenology" (*Sur parole,* 89).

32. On the relation between violence and ethics in Levinas's thought in relation to the trauma of the other, see Judith Butler's *Giving an Account of Oneself,* 90–96, 100–101.

33. Marion, *In Excess,* 78.

34. Emmanuel Levinas, *God, Death, and Time,* trans. Bettina Bergo (Stanford, Calif.: Stanford University Press, 2000), 158. Hereafter cited as GDT, followed by page number.

35. See IR, 26–28, 202. On the role of fear in Jonas's account of responsibility, see Jean Greisch, "L'amour du monde et le principe responsabilité," in *La responsabilité. La condition de notre humanité,* ed. Monette Vacquin (Paris: Editions Autrement, 1995), 72–93.

36. In a striking passage from *Otherwise than Being or Beyond Essence,* Levinas writes: "The Good has chosen me before I have chosen it. No one is good willfully" (AE, 25).

37. Derrida, *De quoi demain,* 16.

38. Françoise Dastur, "The Call of Conscience: The Most Intimate Alterity," in *Heidegger and Practical Philosophy,* ed. François Raffoul and David Pettigrew (Albany: SUNY Press, 2002), 88.

39. In Françoise Dastur, *La phénoménologie en questions, langage, altérité, temporalité, finitude* (Paris: Vrin, 2004), 101.

40. Ibid., 87.

41. Ibid., 87.

42. Ibid., 88.

43. Ibid., 88.

44. Ibid., 89.

45. Françoise Dastur, *Heidegger et la question anthropologique* (Louvain: Editions Peeters, 2003), 21. Hereafter cited as HQA, followed by page number.

46. It is in this perspective that Dastur evokes the analytic of *Gemüt:* The entire Heideggerian enterprise focuses on a task that was already Kant's, according to Ricoeur (as cited by Dastur), namely the elaboration of an analytic of *Gemüt,* that is to say, of "the self determined as a 'receptive structure' . . . for the other than oneself" (Dastur, "The Call of Conscience," 89). Because the self is a finite structure of receptivity, it must be considered as an openness to the other. The hermeneutics of the self then escapes egology and avoids the pitfall of a mere reversal of egology, even in its most paroxystic formulations.

47. Jean-Luc Nancy, "The Being-With of the Being-There," in *Rethinking Facticity,* ed. François Raffoul and Eric Sean Nelson (Albany: SUNY Press, 2008), 113–128, here 123.

48. On this point, see my *Heidegger and the Subject,* esp. 208–254.

49. Martin Heidegger, *The Fundamental Concepts of Metaphysics,* trans. William McNeill and Nicholas Walker (Bloomington and Indianapolis: Indiana University Press, 1995), 301.

50. For further elaborations on this point, see Nancy, "The Being-With of the Being-There."

51. Note the reflexive used by Françoise Dastur—*s'émouvoir* literally means "to move oneself," indicating the presence of the self.

52. See here Claude Romano, *Event and World* (New York: Fordham University Press, 2009), 115.

53. Jean-Luc Nancy, *The Inoperative Community*, ed. Peter Connor (Minneapolis: University of Minnesota Press, 1991). Hereafter cited as IC, followed by page number.

54. Emmanuel Levinas, *De Dieu qui vient à l'idée* (Paris: Vrin, 2000), 135.

55. Françoise Dastur, "The Reception and Nonreception of Heidegger in France," in *French Interpretations of Heidegger*, ed. David Pettigrew and François Raffoul (Albany: SUNY Press, 2008), 271.

56. For instance, in Paul Ricoeur, *Autrement. Lecture d'Autrement qu'être ou au-delà de l'essence d'Emmanuel Levinas* (Paris: Presses Universitaires de France, 1997).

57. Dominique Janicaud, ed., *Phenomenology and the "Theological Turn,"* esp. 35–49.

6. Heidegger's Originary Ethics

Heidegger, *The Zollikon Seminars*, 217.

1. Martin Heidegger, *Basic Writings*, rev. and exp. edition, ed. David Farrell Krell (San Francisco: HarperSanFrancisco, 1993), 258.

2. Heidegger says, "I know nothing about how this thought has an 'effect.' It may be, too, that the way of thought today may lead one to remain silent in order to protect this thought from becoming cheapened within a year. It may also be that it needs 300 years in order to have an 'effect.'" See the *Spiegel* interview (1966), "Only a God can Save us," in *Heidegger: The Man, The Thinker*, ed. Thomas Sheehan (Chicago: Precedent, 1981), 60.

3. Heidegger, *Basic Writings*, 256.

4. Jean-Luc Nancy, "Heidegger's 'Originary Ethics,'" in *Heidegger and Practical Philosophy*, ed. François Raffoul and David Pettigrew (Albany: SUNY Press, 2002), 65. Hereafter cited as HPP, followed by page number.

5. Martin Heidegger, *Phenomenological Interpretations of Aristotle: Initiation into Phenomenological Research*, trans. Richard Rojcewicz (Bloomington and Indianapolis: Indiana University Press, 2001), 124. Hereafter cited as PIA, followed by page number.

6. Nancy also writes, "*ethos* is nothing external to or superimposed on Being; it is not added to it and does not occur to it, nor does it give it any rules that come from elsewhere" (HPP, 79).

7. Martin Heidegger, *Supplements*, ed. John Van Buren (Albany: SUNY Press, 2002), 168.

8. Martin Heidegger, *Die Grundbegriffe der Metaphysik: Welt, Endlichkeit, Einsamkeit*, GA 29/30 (Frankfurt am Main: Vittorio Klostermann, 1992), 246. English translation by William McNeill and Nicholas Walker, *The Fundamental Concepts of Metaphysics: World, Finitude, Solitude* (Bloomington and Indianapolis: Indiana University Press, 1995).

9. Martin Heidegger, *Phänomenologische Interpretation von Kants Kritik der reinen Vernunft*, GA 25 (Frankfurt am Main: Vittorio Klostermann, 1995), 20. English translation by Parvis Emad and Kenneth Maly, *Phenomenological Interpretation of Kant's* Critique of Pure Reason (Bloomington and Indianapolis: Indiana University Press, 1997), 15. Existence is thus always a matter of decision, of choice and of freedom. On this point, see Jean-Luc Nancy's essay "The Decision of Existence," in *The Birth to Presence*, trans. Brian Holmes et al. (Stanford, Calif.: Stanford University Press, 1993), 82–109.

10. On this history, see the classic study by Theodore Kisiel, *The Genesis of Heidegger's* Being and Time (Berkeley and London: University of California Press, 1993).

11. Martin Heidegger, *Zur Bestimmung der Philosophie*, GA 56/57 (Frankfurt am Main: Vittorio Klostermann, 1987), 59. English translation by Ted Sadler, *Towards the Definition of Philosophy* (London: Continuum, 2002).

12. Martin Heidegger, *Plato's* Sophist (Bloomington and Indianapolis: Indiana University Press, 1997), for instance §§19–20.

13. Martin Heidegger, *Vom Wesen der menschlichen Freiheit. Einleitung in die Philosophie*, GA 31 (Frankfurt am Main: Vittorio Klostermann, 1982). English translation by Ted Sadler, *The Essence of Human Freedom* (London: Continuum, 2002). Hereafter cited as EHF, followed by page number.

14. On this point, see Frank Schalow, "Freedom, Finitude, and the Practical Self: The Other Side of Heidegger's Appropriation of Kant," in *Heidegger and Practical Philosophy*, ed. François Raffoul and David Pettigrew (Albany: SUNY Press, 2002), 29–41.

15. Martin Heidegger, *Introduction to Metaphysics*, trans. Gregory Fried and Richard Polt (New Haven, Conn.: Yale University Press, 2000), 9. Hereafter cited as IM, followed by page number.

16. Martin Heidegger, *Beiträge zur Philosophie (Vom Ereignis) (1936–38)*, GA 65 (Frankfurt am Main: Vittorio Klostermann, 1989). English translation by Parvis Emad and Kenneth Maly, *Contributions to Philosophy (From Enowning)* (Bloomington and Indianapolis: Indiana University Press, 1999), 33. Hereafter cited as CP, followed by page number of translation.

17. John Sallis, *The Verge of Philosophy* (Chicago: University of Chicago Press, 2008), 147; my emphasis. Hereafter cited as VP, followed by page number.

18. Martin Heidegger, *Four Seminars*, trans. Andrew Mitchell and François Raffoul (Bloomington and Indianapolis: Indiana University Press, 2003), 41, 47. Hereafter cited as FS, followed by page number.

19. Friedrich-Wilhelm von Herrmann, "Contributions to Philosophy and Enowning-Historical Thinking," in *Companion to Heidegger's* Contributions to Philosophy, ed. Charles E. Scott, Susan M. Schoenbohm, Daniela Vallega-Neu, and Alejandro Vallega (Bloomington and Indianapolis: Indiana University Press, 2001), 105.

20. Martin Heidegger, *Nietzsche*, ed. David Farrell Krell (San Francisco: Harper & Row, 1991), vol. 4, 141.

21. Heidegger, *Fundamental Concepts of Metaphysics*, 28. Hereafter cited as GA 29/30 (see note 8, above), followed by page number.

22. Martin Heidegger, *Metaphysische Anfangsgründe der Logik im Ausgang von Leibniz*, GA 26 (Frankfurt am Main: Vittorio Klostermann, 1976), 244. English translation by Michael Heim, *The Metaphysical Foundations of Logic* (Bloomington and Indianapolis: Indiana University Press, 1984), 189.

23. On this discussion, see John Sallis's "Free Thinking," in HPP, 3–12.

24. Richard Polt, "The Event of Enthinking the Event," in *Companion to Heidegger's* Contributions to Philosophy, 91.

25. Emmanuel Levinas, *God, Death, and Time* (Stanford, Calif.: Stanford University Press, 2000), 136.

26. Jean-Luc Nancy, *Being Singular Plural* (Stanford, Calif.: Stanford University Press, 2000), 29. Hereafter cited as BSP, followed by page number.

27. Martin Heidegger, *What is Called Thinking?* trans. J. Glenn Gray (New York: Harper & Row, 1968), 7–10, 17–18. Hereafter cited as WCT, followed by page number.

7. Heidegger: The Ontological Origins of Responsibility

1. On this point, I take the liberty of referring the reader to my *Heidegger and the Subject* (Amherst, N.Y.: Prometheus, 1999).

2. Martin Heidegger, "The Way Back into the Ground of Metaphysics," introduction to *What is Metaphysics?* (1949) in *Pathmarks,* ed. William McNeill (New York: Cambridge University Press, 1998), 283.

3. Martin Heidegger, *The Essence of Human Freedom,* trans. Ted Sadler (London: Continuum, 2002), 10. A few pages later, Heidegger explains that the question on the totality of beings is a "going-to-the-root," which in turn "must take aim *at us*" (EHF, 24), and represents a challenge to us.

4. Jean-Luc Marion, "Le sujet en dernier appel," *Revue de métaphysique et de morale* 96, no. 1 (1991): 77–95, here 79.

5. Martin Heidegger, *The Zollikon Seminars,* trans. Franz Mayr and Richard Askay (Evanston, Ill.: Northwestern University Press, 2001), 161.

6. Martin Heidegger, "The Turning," in *The Question Concerning Technology and Other Essays,* trans. William Lovitt (New York: Harper & Row, 1977), 47.

7. Martin Heidegger, *On the Way to Language,* trans. Peter D. Hertz (New York: Harper & Row, 1971), 90.

8. Heidegger, *Zollikon Seminars,* 176.

9. Levinas recognized this belonging of Dasein to the call of being. He explains in *Of God Who Comes to Mind* that "Dasein is so much given over to being that being is its own. It is on the basis of my incapacity to refuse taking part in this adventure that it becomes my adventure, that it becomes *eigen,* that *Sein* is *Ereignis*." Emmanuel Levinas, *De Dieu qui vient à l'idée* (Paris: Vrin, 2000), 146–147.

10. Françoise Dastur, "The Call of Conscience: The Most Intimate Alterity," in *Heidegger and Practical Philosophy,* ed. François Raffoul and David Pettigrew (Albany: SUNY Press, 2002), 92.

11. Paul Ricoeur, *Oneself as Another,* trans. Kathleen Blamey (Chicago: University of Chicago Press, 1995), 342. Hereafter cited as OA, followed by page number.

12. Martin Heidegger, *Logik: Die frage nach der Wahrheit,* GA 21 (Frankfurt am Main: Vittorio Klostermann, 1976), 236. An English translation by Thomas Sheehan titled *Logic: The Question of Truth,* is forthcoming from Indiana University Press (2010).

13. Heidegger, *Zollikon Seminars,* 159.

14. In the 1929–1930 course, Heidegger refers solipsism back to its starting point

in the subject or in consciousness, *a starting point which Hegel embraces.* He writes: "This theory according to which man, who is initially subject and consciousness, is so given to himself first of all and most certainly, is a theory which is born within the context of the foundation of metaphysics in Descartes ... From there, it has extended across all of modern philosophy, and in Kant underwent a peculiar, though inessential, transformation. This transformation then led, in Hegel's philosophy, to the absolutization of an attitude that takes the isolated ego-subject as its starting point" (GA 29/30, 305).

15. In his *Experience of Freedom,* Nancy emphasizes this paradoxical logic of singularity. If the singular being, in conformity with its definition, must be thought of as totally alone, cut off from everything, it is nonetheless in this very separation that there opens the relation to others, or better, that the existent is opened as an indissociably singular *and* plural being. In Nancy's terms, "One could say: the singular of 'mine' is by itself a plural"; see Jean-Luc Nancy, *The Experience of Freedom,* trans. Bridget McDonald (Stanford, Calif.: Stanford University Press), 67. He continues by stating that, "in solitude and even in solipsism—at least understood as a *sola ipsa* of singularity—ipseity is itself constituted by and as sharing" (ibid., 70). Existential solipsism designates the indissociably singular and common character of the existent, that is, Dasein's singularity-with-others.

16. As Françoise Dastur rightly notes, it is not the relation to others and to the world as such which is interrupted in proper (authentic) existence, only their improper (inauthentic) modes. For example, she writes: "Heidegger goes as far here as speaking of Dasein in terms of '*solus ipse*;' yet, he immediately adds that this is an *existential* 'solipsism.' Anxiety indeed isolates in the sense that it individualizes Dasein, that it accomplishes that existentiell modification by which the self as the They becomes an 'authentic' self. It isolates Dasein, thus, in the sense that it tears Dasein away from its absorption in the world of concern to throw it towards its ownmost being-in-the-world; *it therefore does not cut Dasein off from the world but rather makes Dasein realize that it is bound to it. In anxiety, Dasein does not break with the world, but with the familiarity that characterizes everyday being-in-the-world.*" Françoise Dastur, *Heidegger and the Question of Time,* trans. François Raffoul and David Pettigrew (Atlantic Highlands, N.J.: Humanities Press, 1998); my emphasis.

17. Heidegger writes: "In all interpretations of conscience, the 'evil' or 'bad' conscience gets the priority: conscience is primarily 'bad'" (SZ, 290). This is why having a "good" conscience can be reduced to "not having a bad conscience." Later, Heidegger will criticize this characterization, after having distinguished the phenomenon of conscience from any moral problematic, and in fact announced that "our interpretation takes no account of the basic forms of the phenomenon—'bad' conscience and 'good,' that which 'reproves' and that which 'warns'" (SZ, 290).

18. Being-guilty precedes good and evil, precedes morality, and makes them possible: "This essential being guilty is, equiprimordially, the existential condition of the possibility of the 'morally' good and evil, that is, for morality in general and its possible factical forms." Heidegger then concludes: "primordial being-guilty cannot be defined by morality because morality already presupposed it for itself" (SZ, 286).

19. SZ, 283. We encounter the same charges laid against the ontical determinations of debt and lack in the analyses of being-toward-death, particularly in §48 of *Being and Time* (SZ, 242–243).

20. SZ, 285. Also, further: "The call is the call of care. Being-guilty constitutes the Being to which we give the name of 'care'" (SZ, 286).

21. In a marginal note added to his personal copy of *Sein und Zeit*, Heidegger explains that Dasein does not exist as substantial ego, "not egotistically, but on the contrary *as thrown, it is to be taken over*": *Nicht egoistisch, sondern als zu übernehmend geworfen* (SZ, 191). Also, in §44b of *Sein und Zeit*, one reads that, "To Dasein's state of Being belongs *thrownness;* indeed it is constitutive for Dasein's disclosedness. In thrownness is revealed that in each case Dasein, as my Dasein and this Dasein, is already in a definite world" (SZ, 221). In §60, he reiterates this point: "Thrown into its 'there,' every Dasein has been factically submitted (*angewiesen*) to a definite 'world'—its world" (SZ, 297). Dasein is delivered over to itself (it is thrown) in order that it may take over that thrown existence. Taking-over one's thrownness will constitute the meaning of being-guilty.

22. Martin Heidegger, *Einleitung in die Philosophie (WS 1928/29)*, GA 27 (Frankfurt am Main: Vittorio Klostermann, 1996), 340; my emphasis. Hereafter cited as GA 27, followed by page number.

23. This primordial, ontological Being-guilty finds an echo in an ontical or existentiell guilt—thrown toward its possibilities, Dasein must choose between them: "it always stands in one possibility or another" (SZ, 285). Some possibility is thus in each case neglected or abandoned. By choosing one possibility, Dasein does *not* choose another.

24. "Beings whose being is care can not only burden themselves with factical guilt, but they *are* guilty in the ground of their being" (SZ, 286).

25. Jacques Derrida, "*Geschlecht,* différence sexuelle, différence ontologique," in *Heidegger, Cahiers de l'Herne,* ed. Michel Haar (Paris: Editions de Poche, 1983), 589.

26. Heidegger called that nullity in early writings, "ruinance" (*Ruinanz*), and makes the point that such ruinance constitutes life's own motion and possibility. Life's movedness (which Heidegger calls "collapse," *der Sturtz*), is a movement which "by itself forms itself—and yet not by itself but by the emptiness in which it moves; its emptiness is its possibility of movement" (PIA, 98). *Life comes out of a "not,"* if it is the case that "this 'not' resides in the very structure of facticity" (PIA, 120). He proposes to call this phenomenon "ruinance (*ruina*—collapse)" (PIA, 98). Further, he explains that ruinance can be characterized as "the movedness of factical life which 'actualizes itself' and 'is' factical life *in* itself, *as* itself, *for* itself, *out of* itself, and, in all this, *against* itself" (PIA, 98).

27. Maurice Merleau-Ponty, *Phenomenology of Perception,* trans. Colin Smith (London and New York: Routledge, 2002), vii. Dominique Janicaud also emphasized that, "From a philosophical point of view, facticity designates above all the actual anchoring point (*le point d'ancrage effectif*) of existential thought when it no longer speculates about pure essences but is committed to articulating our being-in-the-world as it is given in a situation as thrown." Dominique Janicaud, *Heidegger en France* (Paris: Albin Michel, 2001), 67.

28. On this, see my "Factical Life and the Need for Philosophy" in *Rethinking Facticity,* ed. François Raffoul and Eric Sean Nelson (Albany: SUNY Press, 2008), 69–85.

29. Jean Greisch has rightly noted the essential connection between *Befindlichkeit* and *Faktizität* in *Being and Time;* see "Heidegger et Lévinas interprètes de la

facticité," in *Emmanuel Levinas. Positivité et Transcendance*, ed. Jean-Luc Marion (Paris: Presses Universitaires de France, 2000), 189.

30. For instance in *The Zollikon Seminars*, Heidegger analyzes the Latin term *natura* to claim that it "derives from *nasci*, 'to be born,'" and then *physis* is interpreted as such a birth, that is, as emerging "in the sense of coming from concealment [*Verborgenheit*] to unconcealment" (ZS, 158).

31. Giorgio Agamben, "The Passion of Facticity," in *Rethinking Facticity*, ed. François Raffoul and Eric Sean Nelson (Albany: SUNY Press, 2008), 89–112. Hereafter cited as PF, followed by page numbers.

32. The word "fact" has a long lineage, originating with the Roman *factum*, which is not an assertion about nature but is primarily associated with human activity and production. The early modern Italian philosopher Giambattista Vico continued to use the word in this sense in his principle, *verum factum* ("the true is the made"). This sense of fact as human doing and making is still at work in German Idealism—especially in Fichte, for whom *factum* is still to be understood in relation to action (*Tat*)—and then in Marxism.

33. As Françoise Dastur explains, responsibility needs to be understood "as a constitutive structure of a being that understands itself only by responding for itself, assuming responsibility for itself, since its facticity, far from being assimilable to the *factum brutum* of a natural being, must on the contrary be understood as that which constrains Dasein to assume responsibility for its own Being" (HPP, 91).

34. Martin Heidegger, "Phenomenological Interpretations in Connection with Aristotle: An Indication of the Hermeneutical Situation," in *Supplements*, ed. John Van Buren (Albany: SUNY Press, 2002), 113. Hereafter cited as HS, followed by page numbers.

35. For a careful analysis of the various senses of such grounding, see John Sallis's essay, "Grounders of the Abyss," in *Companion to Heidegger's Contributions to Philosophy*, ed. Charles E. Scott, Susan M. Schoenbohm, Daniela Vallega-Neu, and Alejandro Vallega (Bloomington and Indianapolis: Indiana University Press, 2001), 181–197.

36. Heidegger insists that care "is always a care *for the sake of be-ing*—not the be-ing of man, but the be-ing of beings in the whole" (CP, 12).

8. Derrida: The Impossible Origins of Responsibility

Derrida, *Papier Machine*, 308; Derrida, *Gift of Death*, 27; Nietzsche, *Beyond Good and Evil*, 9–10.

1. Jean-Luc Marion, *Being Given: Toward a Phenomenology of Givenness*, trans. Jeffrey L. Kosky (Stanford, Calif.: Stanford University Press, 2002), 293; translation modified.

2. For instance, "Responsibility, if there is such a thing [*s'il y en a*], will only have emerged [*commencé*] with the experience of the aporia." Jacques Derrida, *L'autre cap* (Paris, Minuit, 1991), 43; my translation.

3. An earlier version of the following pages appeared as "Derrida and the Ethics of the Im-possible," *Research in Phenomenology* 38, no. 2 (Spring 2008): 270–290.

4. Jacques Derrida, "Jacques Derrida, penseur de l'évènement," interviewed by Jérôme-Alexandre Nielsberg for *l'Humanité*, 28 January 2004; accessed at http://

www.humanite.fr/2004-01-28_Tribune-libre_-Jacques-Derrida-penseur-de-levenement. My translations.

5. Here following the contrast made by Derrida between problem (*problēma*) and aporia in *Aporias*, trans. Thomas Dutoit (Stanford, Calif.: Stanford University Press, 1993), 11–13. Hereafter cited as A, followed by the page number.

6. For instance in Jacques Derrida, *Voyous* (Paris: Galilée, 2003), 210. Hereafter cited as V, followed by the page number. My translations.

7. Jacques Derrida, "Passions," in *On the Name,* ed. Thomas Dutoit (Stanford, Calif.: Stanford University Press, 1995), 16. Hereafter cited as P, followed by the page number.

8. Jacques Derrida, with Elisabeth Roudinesco, *De quoi demain . . .* (Paris: Fayard / Galilée, 2001), 85.

9. Jacques Derrida, *Positions* (Chicago: University of Chicago Press, 1981), 6.

10. Jacques Derrida and Maurizio Ferraris, *A Taste for the Secret,* ed. G. Donis and D. Webb (Malden, Mass.: Polity Press, 2001), 4; my emphasis. Hereafter cited as TS, followed by page number.

11. Also see Jacques Derrida, *Papier Machine* (Paris: Galilée, 2001), 291. Hereafter cited as PM, followed by page number; my translations.

12. An expression one finds for instance at PM, 292, 307.

13. In Derrida's words, "Death is the possibility of the absolute impossibility of Dasein" (A, 69).

14. Jacques Derrida, "Autoimmunity: Real and Symbolic Suicides," in Giovanna Borradori, *Philosophy in a Time of Terror: Dialogues with Jürgen Habermas and Jacques Derrida* (Chicago: University of Chicago Press, 2003), 85–136, here 90. Hereafter cited as PTT, followed by the page number.

15. Jacques Derrida, "Force of Law: The 'Mystical Foundation of Authority,'" in *Deconstruction and the Possibility of Justice,* ed. D. G. Carlson, D. Cornell, and M. Rosenfeld (New York: Routledge, 1992), 14. Hereafter cited as FL, followed by the page number.

16. Among many examples, see PM, 358.

17. One will compare here Derrida's undecidable with Heidegger's decidedness (*Entschiendenheit*), and generally with Heidegger's treatment of decision in the *Beiträge,* where it is said that the greatest danger, the most certain sign of nihilistic machination, is to believe that matters are decided; hence the "lack of distress" that is the most distressful of all. The issue is that Derrida remains, if to exceed it toward the other, in the egological tradition of decision, whereas Heidegger thinks decision outside of egology altogether, arising out of the truth of be-ing itself.

18. Jacques Derrida, "Autrui est secret parce qu'il est autre," interviewed by Antoine Spire for *Le Monde de l'Education* (July–August 2001); accessed at www.lemonde.fr/mde/ete2001/derrida.html.

19. Jacques Derrida, *Sur Parole* (Paris: Éditions de l'Aube, 1999), 52. The undecidable is also the condition of the future and of desire, Derrida continues to argue in this passage.

20. When Derrida evokes the question of freedom, and the necessity to articulate a "post-deconstructive account of freedom," it is to associate its senses with those of the unpredictable coming of the other and the undecidable. Freedom would belong to such a semantic sphere, with the following list: "The 'free,' the in-

calculable, the unpredictable, the undecidable, the event, the arriving one, the other," all terms he uses when evoking "what comes" (*De quoi demain*, 90).

21. In *A Taste for the Secret,* Derrida maintained that "the moment of decision, and thus the moment of responsibility, supposes a rupture with knowledge, and therefore an opening to the incalculable" (TS, 61).

22. "A decision is in sum unconscious, as senseless as it seems, it always includes the unconscious and yet it remains responsible." Jacques Derrida, *Politiques de l'amitié* (Paris: Galilée, 1994), 88.

23. Jacques Derrida, *The Gift of Death,* trans. David Wills (Chicago and London: University of Chicago Press, 1996), 92.

24. Let us note here that Derrida's thinking of decision follows Levinas's reversal of the traditional concept of responsibility, with the limits that this reversal implies, and which we already identified. This is confirmed by the fact that when Derrida treats of ethics, of responsibility, he always does so within a problematics of decision, taken as decision of the subject, even if he then attempts, following Levinas, to reverse the deciding I into a decision "of the other in me."

25. An expression one finds for instance at V, 210.

26. One also finds this expression of a decision "of the other in me," in "Hospitality, Justice and Responsibility: A Dialogue with Jacques Derrida," in *Questioning Ethics,* ed. R. Kearney and M. Dooley (New York: Routledge, 1999), 67. Hereafter cited as QE, followed by the page number.

Conclusion

1. Jacques Derrida, "The 'World' of the Enlightenment to Come," *Research in Phenomenology* 33, no. 1 (2003): 9–52, here 35.

2. This term, *l'arrivant,* literally "the arriving one," echoes a term that one finds in Heidegger's "Letter on Humanism," namely the *avenant* (BW, 264). The *avenant* plays on adventure but mostly on the one who is coming, the to-come. David Farrell Krell notes, "*L'avenant* (cf. the English *advenient*) is most often used as an adverbial phrase, *à l'avenant,* to be in accord, conformity, or relation to something. It is related to *l'aventure,* the arrival of some unforeseen challenge, and *l'avenir,* the future, literally, what is to come" (BW, 264). Being "arrives" or "presences." I am grateful to David Krell for reminding me that the term *l'avenant* originally appeared in Jean Beaufret's letter to Heidegger. In a footnote in *Aporias,* Derrida mentions that "after the fact," he had recalled a 1977 play by Hélène Cixous called, precisely, "*l'arrivante*"; the arriving one was there a feminine. See Jacques Derrida, *Aporias,* trans. Thomas Dutoit (Stanford, Calif.: Stanford University Press, 1993), 86 n. 14.

3. On Derrida's reservations with respect to the notion of tolerance, its dogmatism and relativism, see Jacques Derrida and Maurizio Ferraris, *A Taste for the Secret,* ed. G. Donis and D. Webb (Malden, Mass.: Polity Press, 2001), 62–64.

4. Jacques Derrida, *Sur Parole* (Paris: Éditions de l'Aube, 1999), 50. A few lines further on, we read: "The absence of horizon is frightening, but it is perhaps the condition for something unprecedented to happen. That thing can be death, as always."

INDEX

a priori, 138, 140–142, 147, 206, 240,
317n18; Good, 7, 134; morality, 134,
142; table of values, 30, 123, 125,
134–135, 137, 139, 145, 283
accountability, 1, 4–8, 12, 18, 21, 23–25,
35, 54, 60, 94–95, 100, 112–114, 117–
120, 122–124, 153, 180, 183, 196, 242–
244, 260, 315n4; as basis for punishment, 6, 21, 23, 42, 55, 100,
112–114, 117; in a constant state of
self-deconstruction, 21; deconstruction of, 4, 27; as distinct from
responsibility, 4–10, 12, 18–19, 21,
24–25, 32, 35, 268–269; error of, 80,
92–94, 115–116; Nietzsche's historical genealogy of, 79; as only *one*
sense of responsibility, 19; of the
subject, 1, 10, 12, 18–19, 32, 57, 68,
96, 100, 105, 108, 151, 238, 260–261
Adieu à Emmanuel Levinas, 175–176,
179, 181–183, 218, 284, 320n22
address, 189, 247; of being, 18, 244; of
the other, 165, 319n7
Agamben, Giorgio, 271–272, 274, 327n31
agency, 4, 6, 8–9, 21, 25–26, 28, 31, 34,
39–40, 42–43, 45, 47–51, 54, 57, 69,
83, 93–94, 105, 119–120, 178, 184,
218, 220, 229, 242, 254, 307n27,
309n13, 319n7; as fiction, 28, 81, 107;
free, 67, 107, 114; lack of, 117–118; ra-

tional, 9, 25, 39, 47, 58, 120, 308n6;
subjective, 229; willful, 26, 178, 184
agent, the, 5, 8, 22–23, 25, 31, 39, 41–48, 53,
55–57, 60, 63, 67, 69, 97, 100, 107–109,
112–114, 116, 118–119, 123–124, 163–
164, 177, 183, 236, 252, 262–263,
309n10; free, 6, 116, 163; as "master"
(*kurios*) of one's effects, 26; as principle (*arkhē*) of the act, 26; rational, 42,
49, 79; responsible, 9, 26, 71, 308n7
Allison, David, 83, 88, 90
Allison, Henry, 60, 61, 311nn13,16
alterity, 9, 13, 17, 23, 28, 32, 38, 81, 164–
165, 168–171, 173–174, 180, 183–184,
206–208; absolute, 186, 216, 218,
253, 260, 298–299, 301; as opposed
to exteriority, 208–209, 215, 254; of
the self, 208. *See also* otherness
aporia, 13–14, 23, 36–37, 138, 140, 146–
147, 151, 159, 188–189, 265, 283, 286–
287, 290, 292–293, 293–297, 303,
328n5; of natural causality, 64, 66;
of responsibility, 282, 327n2; as the
very locus of freedom, 296. *See also*
Im-possible, the
Aporias, 285, 288, 289, 290, 292, 329n2
application, 6–7, 30, 35, 86, 227–230; of
rules, 30, 37, 140, 224, 295
appropriation, 11, 17, 27, 30, 36, 84–85,
104, 180, 218, 226, 232, 247, 258,

François Raffoul is Professor of Philosophy at Louisiana State University. He is author of *Heidegger and the Subject* and editor of several works on Lacan and Heidegger. He is translator (with Andrew Mitchell) of Martin Heidegger, *Four Seminars* (Indiana University Press, 2003).

Printed and bound by CPI Group (UK) Ltd, Croydon, CR0 4YY

13/04/2025